Math on Call

A Mathematics Handbook

GReaT SouRCe
EDUCATION GROUP
A Houghton Mifflin Company

Acknowledgments

We gratefully acknowledge the following teachers and mathematics supervisors who helped make Math on Call a reality.

Philip Breen
K–12 Math Coordinator
Billerica School District
Billerica, MA

Diane Gillespie
Mathematics Department
Chairperson
Hamilton Middle School
Houston, TX

Mary Anne Green
Math/Science Teacher
Kyrene Middle School
Tempe, AZ

Joanna D. Krainski
Mathematics Curriculum
Coordinator
John W. Wynn Middle School
Tewksbury, MA

Mary Anne Koch Ledford
Teacher
Garces Memorial High
School
Bakersfield, CA

Dr. Marsha W. Lilly
Secondary Mathematics
Coordinator
Alief ISD
Alief, TX

Donna J. Long
Mathematics, Title I, and
Assessment Coordinator
MSD Wayne Township
Indianapolis, IN

Denise M. Walston
Senior Coordinator,
Mathematics
Norfolk Public Schools
Norfolk, VA

Brenda D. Wright
Math Specialist
Newport News Public
Schools
Newport News, VA

Writing: Andrew Kaplan
Editorial: Carol DeBold, Susan Rogalski; Pat Boudreau, Kane Publishing Services
Design and Production: Bill SMITH STUDIO
Production Management: Betsy Donaghey
Marketing: Lisa Bingen
Illustration credits: pg 609

Printed in the United States of America

International Standard Book Number -13: 978-0-669-50818-5 (hardcover)
International Standard Book Number -10: 0-669-50818-7 (hardcover)

5 6 7 8 9 0   RRDC   09 08 07 06

International Standard Book Number -13: 978-0-669-50819-2 (softcover)
International Standard Book Number -10: 0-669-50819-5 (softcover)

6 7 8 9 0   RRDC   09 08 07 06

Table of Contents

Graphs and Statistics 262

Geometry 314

Ratio, Proportion, and Percent 423

Probability and Odds 456

Almanac 473

How This Book Is Organized

Math on Call is a resource book. That means you are not expected to read it from cover to cover. Instead, you will want to keep it handy for those times when you are not clear about a math topic and need a place to look up definitions, procedures, explanations, and rules.

Because this is a resource book and because there may be more than one topic on a page, we have given each topic an item number 237. So, when you are looking up a specific topic, look for its item number.

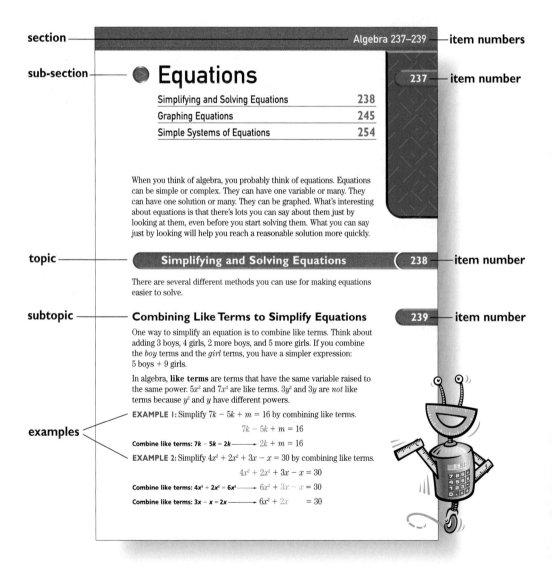

section ———————— Algebra 237–239 —— item numbers

sub-section ———— ● **Equations** 237 —— item number

Simplifying and Solving Equations	238
Graphing Equations	245
Simple Systems of Equations	254

When you think of algebra, you probably think of equations. Equations can be simple or complex. They can have one variable or many. They can have one solution or many. They can be graphed. What's interesting about equations is that there's lots you can say about them just by looking at them, even before you start solving them. What you can say just by looking will help you reach a reasonable solution more quickly.

topic ———— **Simplifying and Solving Equations** 238 —— item number

There are several different methods you can use for making equations easier to solve.

subtopic ———— **Combining Like Terms to Simplify Equations** 239 —— item number

One way to simplify an equation is to combine like terms. Think about adding 3 boys, 4 girls, 2 more boys, and 5 more girls. If you combine the *boy* terms and the *girl* terms, you have a simpler expression: 5 boys + 9 girls.

In algebra, **like terms** are terms that have the same variable raised to the same power. $5x^2$ and $7x^2$ are like terms. $3y^2$ and $3y$ are *not* like terms because y^2 and y have different powers.

examples —— **EXAMPLE 1:** Simplify $7k - 5k + m = 16$ by combining like terms.

$$7k - 5k + m = 16$$

Combine like terms: $7k - 5k = 2k$ ⟶ $2k + m = 16$

EXAMPLE 2: Simplify $4x^2 + 2x^2 + 3x - x = 30$ by combining like terms.

$$4x^2 + 2x^2 + 3x - x = 30$$

Combine like terms: $4x^2 + 2x^2 = 6x^2$ ⟶ $6x^2 + 3x - x = 30$

Combine like terms: $3x - x = 2x$ ⟶ $6x^2 + 2x = 30$

A good way to get started in this book is to thumb through the pages. Find these parts:

■ **Table of Contents**
This lists the major sections and sub-sections of the book.

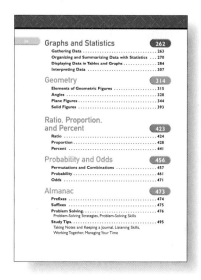

■ **Sections and Sub-Sections**
Each section of the handbook has a short table of contents so you know what is in the section. Sections have several sub-sections and each of these also has its own short table of contents. Notice the color bars across the top of the pages. Each section has a different color to make it easy to find.

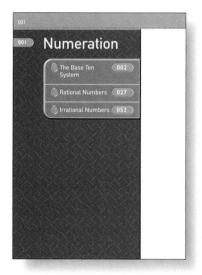

001

001 Numeration

The Base Ten System — 002
Rational Numbers — 027
Irrational Numbers — 052

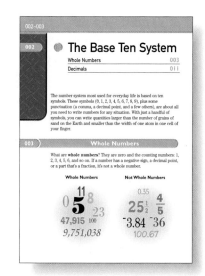

002–003

002 **The Base Ten System**

Whole Numbers — 003
Decimals — 011

The number system most used for everyday life is based on ten symbols. These symbols (0, 1, 2, 3, 4, 5, 6, 7, 8, 9), plus some punctuation (a comma, a decimal point, and a few others), are about all you need to write numbers for any situation. With just a handful of symbols, you can write quantities larger than the number of grains of sand on the Earth and smaller than the width of one atom in one cell of your finger.

003 **Whole Numbers**

What are **whole numbers**? They are zero and the counting numbers: 1, 2, 3, 4, 5, 6, and so on. If a number has a negative sign, a decimal point, or a part that's a fraction, it's not a whole number.

Whole Numbers	Not Whole Numbers
$0 \overset{11}{\mathbf{5}} {}^{8}$ $_{-23}$	0.35 $25\frac{1}{2}$ $\frac{4}{5}$
$47{,}915 \ {}_{100}$	$^{-}3.84 \ ^{-}36$
$9{,}751{,}038$	100.67

■ **Almanac**

This includes some very
helpful tables and lists.
It also has hints on how
to study, take a test, and
solve problems. Check out
all the Almanac entries —
you will want to refer to
them often.

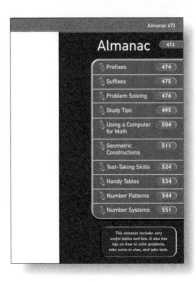

■ **Yellow Pages**

This part of the handbook
has two glossaries. The
Glossary of Mathematical
Formulas is the place
to look if you forget a
formula. In the Glossary
of Mathematical Terms,
you will find math terms
that your teacher and textbook use, and terms your
parents use.

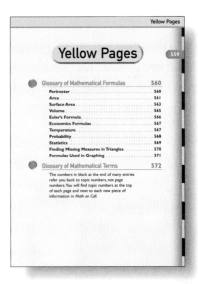

■ **Index**

This is at the very end of the book.

■ **Inside back cover**

Here you will find a useful map of North America that includes time
zones.

How to Use This Book

There are three ways to find information about the topic in which you are interested:

1 Look in the Index

We listed topics in the Index using any word we thought you might use to describe the topic. For example, you will find "volume of cones" under both "Volume" and "Cones."

Remember that you are being directed to item numbers, not page numbers. Use the item numbers located at the top of each page to help you find the topic you are looking for.

2 Look in the Glossary

The Glossary of Mathematical Terms in this handbook is one of the most extensive mathematics glossaries around. Mathematics has a language all its own. Once you learn the language, the rest is much easier. Think of this Glossary as your personal interpreter and turn to this part of the book whenever you see an unfamiliar word.

congruent (≅): Having exactly the same size and shape. **(381)**

Most Glossary entries will give you an item number to refer to if you want more information about the topic.

3 Look in the Table of Contents

All the major topics covered in this book are listed in the Table of Contents. If you are looking for a general topic — like Plane Figures — rather than a very specific one — like Right Triangles — the Table of Contents is a quick way to find it. Notice that the color of each section's item number in the Table of Contents matches the color of the bar across the top of the pages for that section. This makes it easy to locate a section.

001

Numeration

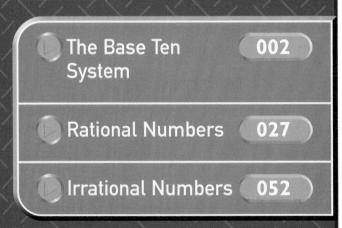

Before numbers were invented,
math homework was REALLY easy.

Do you ever think about how you use numbers each day? What are all the different ways that numbers are expressed around you?

WE USE NUMBERS FOR:	EXAMPLE
counting	101 medals won by the U.S. in the 1996 Olympic Games
measuring	1675 miles from New York City to Houston, Texas
comparing	1045 square miles is less than 145,556 square miles (area of Rhode Island) (area of Montana)
recording amounts below zero	¯70° F, the lowest temperature ever recorded in the U.S.
recording huge amounts	95,900,000 homes in the U.S. have a TV.
recording small amounts	0.03 mph, the speed of a garden snail

(Source: Information Please Almanac)

Numbers like these and how they work together are in this section.

The number system most used for everyday life is based on ten symbols. These symbols (0, 1, 2, 3, 4, 5, 6, 7, 8, 9), plus some punctuation (a comma, a decimal point, and a few others), are about all you need to write numbers for any situation. With just a handful of symbols, you can write quantities larger than the number of grains of sand on the Earth and smaller than the width of one atom in one cell of your finger.

003   Whole Numbers

What are **whole numbers**? They are zero and the counting numbers: 1, 2, 3, 4, 5, 6, and so on. If a number has a negative sign, a decimal point, or a part that's a fraction, it's not a whole number.

Whole Numbers	Not Whole Numbers

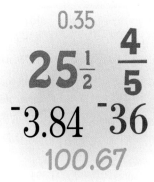

Whole Numbers

0   11   **5**   8   23   **47,915**   100   *9,751,038*

Not Whole Numbers

0.35   **25½** $\frac{4}{5}$ ⁻3.84   ⁻36   100.67

Whole Numbers: Place Value

You probably use place value all the time without even knowing it. Place value tells you the value of each digit in a number. In our numeration system, each place has ten times the value of the place to its right. The pattern makes it easier to use our number system.

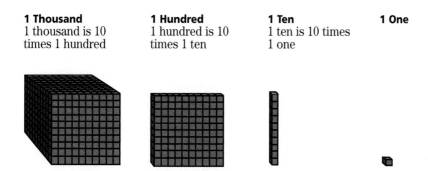

| **1 Thousand** | **1 Hundred** | **1 Ten** | **1 One** |
| 1 thousand is 10 times 1 hundred | 1 hundred is 10 times 1 ten | 1 ten is 10 times 1 one | |

We also arrange numbers into groups of three places called **periods**. Note that the places within periods repeat (hundreds, tens, ones; hundreds, tens, ones; and so on). In America, we usually use commas to separate the periods. Knowing the place *and* period of a number will help you find values of digits in any number as well as read and write numbers.

EXAMPLE: What is the value of the digit **9** in 71,**9**05,346,521?

BILLIONS PERIOD			MILLIONS PERIOD			THOUSANDS PERIOD			ONES PERIOD		
HUNDREDS	TENS	ONES	HUNDREDS	TENS	ONES	HUNDREDS	TENS	ONES	HUNDREDS	TENS	ONES
	7	1,	9	0	5,	3	4	6,	5	2	1

The digit 9 is in the *hundred millions* place.

Its value is 9 hundred million, or 900,000,000.

A stack of 900,000,000 dollar bills would reach 61 miles into space!

Ways of Writing Whole Numbers

There are many ways to write the same whole number.

MORE HELP
See 071

Form	Example
Standard form	832,964
Word form	eight hundred thirty-two thousand, nine hundred sixty-four
Short word form	832 thousand, 964
Expanded form	(8 x 100,000) + (3 x 10,000) + (2 x 1000) + (9 x 100) + (6 x 10) + (4 x 1)
Exponential form	$(8 \times 10^5) + (3 \times 10^4) + (2 \times 10^3) + (9 \times 10^2) + (6 \times 10^1) + (4 \times 10^0)$

Whole Numbers: Powers of 10

When you multiply 10s together, the product is called a **power of 10**. You can use an **exponent** to show a power of 10. The exponent gives the number of times that 10 is a factor.

MORE HELP
See 015, 071

EXAMPLE: There are more than 100,000,000,000 stars in the Milky Way galaxy. How can you rewrite this number in a shorter way?

(Source: World Book Encyclopedia)

 Here are some ways to express a large number.

FORM	EXAMPLE
Standard form	100,000,000,000
Factor form	$10 \times 10 \times 10 \times 10 \times 10 \times 10 \times 10 \times 10 \times 10 \times 10 \times 10$
Exponential form	Write: 10^{11} **The 10 is called the base and the 11 is an exponent.** Say: *ten to the eleventh power*, or just *ten to the eleventh*

That's more than 10^{11} stars!

 You can also express a very large number by writing it as a product of a power of 10 and another number. For example, $3,000,000 = 3 \times 10^6$. This form is called **scientific notation**.

Comparing Whole Numbers

How can you compare two whole numbers?

 You can compare two numbers by using a number line.

EXAMPLE I: Compare 78 and 87.

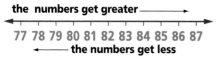

the numbers get greater ———→

77 78 79 80 81 82 83 84 85 86 87

←——— the numbers get less

Remember, the wider side of the symbol is beside the greater number.

Write: Say:
78 < 87   *78 is less than 87.*
87 > 78   *87 is greater than 78.*

 You can also use what you know about place value.

EXAMPLE 2: In a video game, you score 32,565 points. Your friend scores 32,609 points. Who wins?

❶ LINE UP THE PLACE VALUES BY LINING UP THE ONES.	❷ BEGIN AT THE LEFT. FIND THE FIRST PLACE WHERE THE DIGITS ARE DIFFERENT.	❸ COMPARE THE VALUES OF THE DIGITS.
32,565	32,565	600 > 500
32,609	32,609	So, 32,609 > 32,565.

same ——⌐⌐⌐—— different

You can write 32,609 > 32,565 or 32,565 < 32,609. Either way, your friend wins.

MATH ALERT Lining Up by Place Value

Be sure to line up digits with the same place value.

EXAMPLE: You score 108,464 points. Your friend scores 97,996 points. Who wins?

When one whole number has more digits than another, it is greater.

Lined up incorrectly   **Lined up correctly**
108,464   108,464
97,996   97,996

You can write 108,464 > 97,996 or 97,996 < 108,464. Either way, you win.

009 Ordering Whole Numbers

If you know how to compare two whole numbers, you also know how to put a group of whole numbers in order.

EXAMPLE: Order these salaries from 2000, from greatest to least.

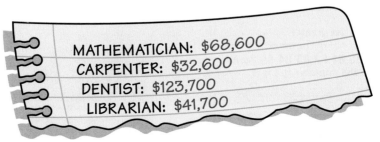

MATHEMATICIAN: $68,600
CARPENTER: $32,600
DENTIST: $123,700
LIBRARIAN: $41,700

(Source: Bureau of Labor Statistics)

MORE HELP
See 007

❶ LINE UP THE NUMBERS AT THE ONES PLACE.	❷ BEGIN TO COMPARE AT THE LEFT.	❸ COMPARE THE REMAINING NUMBERS. FIND THE FIRST PLACE WHERE THE DIGITS ARE DIFFERENT.
41,700 68,600 32,600 123,700	41,700 68,600 32,600 123,700 ←**123,700 has the greatest number of hundred thousands. It is the greatest.**	41,700 68,600 **60,000 > 40,000 and** 32,600 **40,000 > 30,000** So, 68,600 > 41,700 and 41,700 > 32,600.

From greatest to least, the salaries are $123,700; $68,600; $41,700; $32,600.

010 Rounding Whole Numbers

You can round numbers to give a rough idea of an amount.

 ONE WAY You can round numbers by using a number line.

361

| | | | | | | | | | | |
|300|310|320|330|340|**350**|360|370|380|390|**400**|

EXAMPLE 1: Round 361 to the nearest hundred.

361 is closer to 400 than to 300. So, 361 rounds to 400.

You can also round numbers by using place value.

EXAMPLE 2: The population of Greene County, New York, was 48,348 in 2000. To the nearest thousand, about how many people lived in Greene County in 2000? *(Source: 2000 U.S. Census)*

- Find the thousands place.   48,348
- Look at the digit one place to its right.   48,348
  If the digit is 5 or greater, round up.
  If the digit is less than 5, don't change. $3 < 5$ **Don't change.**

So, to the nearest thousand, about 48,000 people lived in Greene County in 2000.

EXAMPLE 3: To the nearest ten thousand, about how many people lived in Greene County in 2000?

- Find the ten thousands place.   48,348
- Look at the digit one place to its right.   48,348
  If the digit is 5 or greater, round up.
  If the digit is less than 5, don't change. $8 > 5$ **Round up.**

So, to the nearest ten thousand, about 50,000 people lived in Greene County in 2000.

Decimals   011

Decimals are numbers that are expressed using a **decimal point**.

A whole number is also a decimal. For example, 235 can also be written as 235.0, 235.00, and so on.

MORE HELP
See 043

4.75

↑
decimal point

Decimals   **Not Decimals**

10,100.2

$1.\overline{3}$ ⁻0.68

27.3684   ⁻5.6

4.0

$-\dfrac{13}{10}$ $\dfrac{37}{100}$

$\dfrac{35}{97}$ $-\dfrac{4}{5}$ $25\frac{1}{2}$

Decimals: Place Value

 ONE WAY You can think of money to help you understand decimals and their place values.

MORE HELP
See 005

1 dollar $\frac{1}{10}$ **dollar or 0.1 dollar** $\frac{1}{100}$ **dollar or 0.01 dollar**

 ANOTHER WAY You can also understand decimals by using the place value pattern. Place value tells you the value of each digit in a number. In our decimal system, each place has ten times the value of the place to its right.

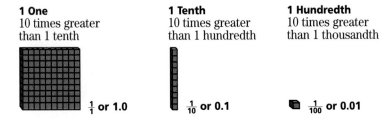

1 One
10 times greater than 1 tenth

$\frac{1}{1}$ **or 1.0**

1 Tenth
10 times greater than 1 hundredth

$\frac{1}{10}$ **or 0.1**

1 Hundredth
10 times greater than 1 thousandth

$\frac{1}{100}$ **or 0.01**

You can use place value to read a decimal or find the value of a digit in a decimal.

EXAMPLE 1: Read 13.578.

TENS	ONES		TENTHS	HUNDREDTHS	THOUSANDTHS
1	3	.	5	7	8

To read a decimal:

- Read the whole number part, if there is one.
- Read the decimal point as *and*.
- Read the number to the right of the decimal point as you would a whole number.
- Read the place value of the last digit.

Say: *thirteen and five hundred seventy-eight thousandths*

EXAMPLE 2: Read 38.346. What is the value of the digit **4** in 38.346?

TENS	ONES			TENTHS	HUNDREDTHS	THOUSANDTHS
3	8	.		3	4	6

The digit 4 is in the hundredths place. It has a value of 0.04, or
4 hundredths.

MATH ALERT Interpreting *and* in Decimal Numbers

013

When you read a number, do NOT say *and* in any old place. If
you do, you'll have trouble when you need to read the decimal
point as "and." Sometimes, pretty funny misunderstandings can
happen.

EXAMPLE: Which is more likely to weigh two hundred and
twenty-five thousandths pounds: a baby elephant or a baby
hamster?

If you mean 0.225, say
two hundred twenty-five
thousandths.

Two hundred and twenty-five thousandths

IS:	IS NOT:
200.025	0.225

A baby elephant could weigh two hundred and twenty-five
thousandths pounds.

014

Writing Decimals

There are many ways to write the same decimal.

The moon revolves around Earth once every twenty-seven and three thousand, two hundred seventeen ten-thousandths days.

Form	Example
Standard form	27.3217
Word form	twenty-seven and three thousand two hundred seventeen ten-thousandths
Short word form	27 and 3217 ten-thousandths
Expanded form	$(2 \times 10) + (7 \times 1) + (3 \times 0.1) + (2 \times 0.01) + (1 \times 0.001) + (7 \times 0.0001)$
Exponential form	$(2 \times 10^1) + (7 \times 10^0) + (3 \times 10^{-1}) + (2 \times 10^{-2}) + (1 \times 10^{-3}) + (7 \times 10^{-4})$

015

Decimals: Powers of 10

MORE HELP
See 006, 047

In the decimal system, the value of each place is a different **power of 10**. Powers of 10 can also be less than 1: they can have negative exponents.

THOUSANDS	HUNDREDS	TENS	ONES	TENTHS	HUNDREDTHS	THOUSANDTHS
1000	100	10	1	0.1	0.01	0.001
10^3	10^2	10^1	10^0	10^{-1}	10^{-2}	10^{-3}

016

Scientific Notation

MORE HELP
See 006, 014,
047, 073

Sometimes you need to write decimals that are very small or very large. You can use **scientific notation** to write these decimals. With scientific notation, you don't need to count lots of zeros every time you read the number. To write a number in scientific notation, write it as a product of two factors: (a decimal greater than or equal to 1 but less than 10) × (a power of 10)

EXAMPLE 1: Light travels at a speed of about 18,000,000,000 meters per minute. Write this number in scientific notation.

(Source: Encyclopedia Britannica)

$$18,000,000,000 = 1.8 \times 10,000,000,000 = 1.8 \times 10^{10} \longleftarrow \textbf{power of 10}$$

a decimal $\geq$ 1 and $<$ 10

Shortcut

Here's a shortcut for writing a number in scientific notation.

- Count how many places you move the decimal point to the left.

- For the exponent, use the number of places that the decimal point moved.

$$18,000,000,000 = 1.8 \times 10^{10}$$

Move the decimal 10 places left.

1.8 is greater than 1 and less than 10.

Use 10 as the exponent.

EXAMPLE 2: Light travels 1 meter in 0.0000000033 second. Write 0.0000000033 in scientific notation.

To write numbers between 0 and 1 in scientific notation, you use negative exponents.

$$0.0000000033 = 3.3 \times 0.000000001 = 3.3 \times 10^{-9} \longleftarrow \textbf{power of 10 with a negative exponent}$$

a decimal $\geq$ 1 and $<$ 10

Shortcut

Here's a shortcut for writing a number between 0 and 1 in scientific notation.

- Count how many places you move the decimal point to the right.

- For the exponent, use a negative sign and the number of places that the decimal point moved.

$$0.0000000033 = 3.3 \times 10^{-9}$$

Move the decimal 9 places right.

3.3 is greater than 1 and less than 10.

Use $^{-}$9 as the exponent.

Equivalent Decimals

Decimals that name the same amount are **equivalent decimals**.

MORE HELP
See 018, 102, 131

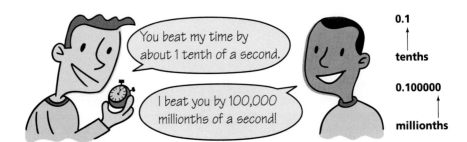

You beat my time by about 1 tenth of a second.

I beat you by 100,000 millionths of a second!

0.1
↑
tenths

0.100000
↑
millionths

0.3 (three tenths) of the square is blue.

0.30 (thirty hundredths) of the square is blue.

equivalent decimals
↓   ↓
$$0.3 = 0.30$$
three tenths = thirty hundredths
$$\frac{3}{10} = \frac{30}{100}$$

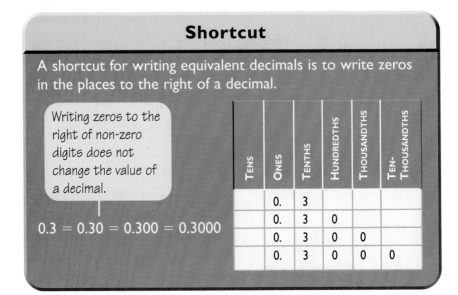

Shortcut

A shortcut for writing equivalent decimals is to write zeros in the places to the right of a decimal.

Writing zeros to the right of non-zero digits does not change the value of a decimal.

$$0.3 = 0.30 = 0.300 = 0.3000$$

TENS	ONES	TENTHS	HUNDREDTHS	THOUSANDTHS	TEN-THOUSANDTHS
	0.	3			
	0.	3	0		
	0.	3	0	0	
	0.	3	0	0	0

Comparing Decimals

Comparing decimals is much like comparing whole numbers.

EXAMPLE: In the Olympic long-jump competition, Heike Drechsler of Germany jumped 22.9375 feet in 2000. In 1996 Chioma Ajunwa of Nigeria jumped 23.375 feet. Who jumped farther? *(Source: World Almanac)*

❶ LINE UP THE DECIMAL POINTS.	❷ BEGIN AT THE LEFT. FIND THE FIRST PLACE WHERE THE DIGITS ARE DIFFERENT.	❸ COMPARE THE VALUES OF THE DIGITS.
22.9375 23.375	22.9375 23.375	3 is greater than 2 So, 23.375 > 22.9375

Chioma Ajunwa jumped farther.

MATH ALERT Sometimes Greater Isn't Better!

Be very careful when comparing times and scores. Sometimes the lower score wins (as in golf), and usually the *lower* time wins.

EXAMPLE: In the Olympic 100-meter butterfly swimming race, Denis Pankratov of Russia won in 1996 with a time of 52.27 seconds. In 2000 Lars Froelander of Sweden won with a time of 52.0 seconds. Who had the faster time? *(Source: World Almanac)*

❶ LINE UP THE DECIMAL POINTS.	❷ BEGIN AT THE LEFT. FIND THE FIRST PLACE WHERE THE DIGITS ARE DIFFERENT.	❸ COMPARE THE VALUES OF THE DIGITS.
52.27 52.0	52.27 52.0 **52.0 = 52.00** **You can write equivalent decimals to help you compare.**	0.00 is less than 0.27 So, 52.0 < 52.27.

Lars Froelander had the faster time.

020

Ordering Decimals

If you know how to compare two decimals, you also know how to put a group of decimals in order.

EXAMPLE: During the softball season, Tara's batting average was 0.322, Kelley's average was 0.212, and Keesha's average was 0.300. Order the averages from greatest to least.

MORE HELP
See 018

❶ LINE UP THE DECIMAL POINTS.	❷ BEGIN AT THE LEFT. FIND THE FIRST PLACE WHERE THE DIGITS ARE DIFFERENT.	❸ COMPARE THE REMAINING DECIMALS.
0.322	0.322 **0.3 > 0.2**	0.322
0.212	0.212 **So, 0.322 > 0.212, and 0.300 > 0.212.**	0.300 **0.02 > 0.00 So, 0.322 > 0.300.**
0.300	0.300 **0.212 is the least.**	

From greatest to least, the batting averages are 0.322, 0.300, 0.212.

021

Rounding Decimals

You can round decimals just as you round whole numbers.

MORE HELP
See 010

EXAMPLE 1: To the nearest hundredth of a mile per hour, how fast did the girl run?

I RAN A MARATHON IN 3.5 HOURS.
26.5 MILES ÷ 3.5 HOURS ≈
7.5714286 MILES PER HOUR

- Find the hundredths place.   7.5714286
- Look at the digit one place to its right.   7.5714286
  If the digit is 5 or greater, round up.
  If the digit is less than 5, don't change.   1 < 5 **Don't change.**

To the nearest hundredth, the girl ran about 7.57 miles per hour.

EXAMPLE 2: A calculator shows that a marathoner averages 6.9736842 miles per hour. To the nearest mile per hour, how fast does the runner run?

- Find the ones place.   6.9736842
- Look at the digit one place to its right.   6.9736842
  If the digit is 5 or greater, round up.
  If the digit is less than 5, don't change. $9 > 5$ **Round up.**

The marathoner runs about 7 miles per hour.

Reading Decimals as Fractions

022

How are decimals like fractions? Try saying the decimal aloud. When you do, you'll see that it sounds like a fraction. After you've written the decimal as a fraction, you can simplify it like any other fraction.

MORE HELP
See 037

EXAMPLE: $0.50 =$ fifty hundredths $= \frac{50}{100} = \frac{5}{10} = \frac{1}{2}$

023

MATH ALERT Repeating Decimals

Sometimes when you divide, you can keep going forever!

A **repeating decimal** has 1 or more digits that repeat.

EXAMPLE: What's the average weight of three trout Ty caught? He caught a 6-pounder, a 5-pounder, and a *huge* 9-pounder.

MORE HELP
See 274

Add: $6 + 5 + 9 = 20$

Divide: $20 \div 3$

The decimal 6.66 . . . is a repeating decimal. You can use a bar to show the digits that repeat.

6.66 . . . $= 6.\overline{6}$

The average weight is $6.\overline{6}$ pounds. That's between 6.66 and 6.67 pounds.

$$
\begin{array}{r}
6.66 \ldots \\
3\overline{)20.000} \\
\underline{18} \\
20 \\
\underline{18} \\
20 \\
\underline{18} \\
2
\end{array}
$$

←The digit 6 repeats forever

Write the decimal point and zeros.

The same remainder repeats forever.

Writing a Repeating Decimal as a Fraction

At first, repeating decimals may seem hard to work with, but you can write them as compact, tidy fractions.

EXAMPLE: Suppose your total bowling score for 9 games is 875. To find your average score, you divide 875 by 9. The quotient, $97.\overline{2}$, has a repeating decimal.

> **97.222222**

You can write $97.\overline{2}$ as a fraction.

After dividing 875 by 9 and finding the quotient 97 and remainder 2, use the remainder to write the fraction $\frac{2}{9}$. The answer in fraction form is $97\frac{2}{9}$.

$$
\begin{array}{r}
97 \quad \longleftarrow \textbf{quotient} \\
9\overline{)875} \\
\underline{810} \\
65 \\
\underline{63} \\
2 \quad \longleftarrow \textbf{remainder}
\end{array}
$$

$875 \div 9 = 97\frac{2}{9}$

So, your average score would be $97\frac{2}{9}$.

025

MATH ALERT Non-Repeating, Non-Terminating Decimals

Some decimals continue without end, but do not have a repeating pattern. These decimals are known as **non-repeating, non-terminating** decimals.

MORE HELP
See 052

- The ratio between the circumference of a circle and its diameter is $\pi \approx 3.1415926\ldots$

  "…" means the decimal continues without end.

- The diagonal of a square with a side of 1 is $\sqrt{2} = 1.4142135\ldots$

These are impossible to measure precisely. We usually compute with rounded approximations of these numbers.

Can you create a non-repeating, non-terminating decimal such as 3.121121112…?

Relating Decimals and Percents

026

A **percent (%)** is a **ratio** that compares a number to 100. The word *percent* means "per hundred." You can use hundredths or percents to express the same number.

MORE HELP
See 425–426, 441–442

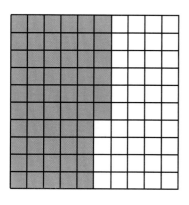

56 of 100 squares are blue.
0.56 of the squares are blue.
56% of the squares are blue.
$\frac{56}{100} = 0.56 = 56\%$

 # Rational Numbers

Your English teacher will tell you that *rational* means "makes sense." And it's true that rational numbers make a lot of sense. But in mathematics, *rational* means "written as a ratio." A **ratio** is the comparison of two quantities by division. Any number that can be written with an integer numerator and denominator is rational. Therefore, simple fractions are rational. But do you know that whole numbers and most decimal numbers can be expressed as rational numbers? For example, 7 can be written as $\frac{7}{1}$ and 0.23 can be written as $\frac{23}{100}$. There ARE some numbers that are not rational (like $\sqrt{2}$ and π).

028) Fractions

A **fraction** is a number that represents part of something. The **denominator** tells how many equal parts are in a whole. The **numerator** tells how many of those parts we're talking about.

$\frac{3}{8}$ ←— numerator (parts you are talking about)
   ←— denominator (equal parts in a whole)

Why would you need to use a fraction? There are two main reasons.

CASE I You can use a fraction to name a part of one thing.

$\frac{3}{8}$ ←— slices of pie that are gone
   ←— slices of pie in all

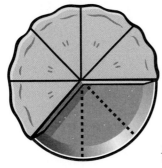

$\frac{3}{8}$ of the pie is gone.

CASE 2 You can use a fraction to name part of a collection of things.

$\dfrac{3}{8}$ ◄——**boys in the group**
◄——**students in the group**

$\frac{3}{8}$ of the students are boys.

MATH ALERT Using Fractions to Show Ratios

029

You can use a fraction to show a ratio. In a ratio, the numerator shows the part of a group you're interested in, and the denominator shows *either* the rest of the group *or* the whole group.

EXAMPLE: In the picture below, what is the ratio of boys to girls? Of boys to the total number of kids?

MORE HELP
See 425–426

The ratio of boys to girls is 5 to 8, or $\frac{5}{8}$.

$\dfrac{5}{8}$ ◄——**number of boys**
◄——**number of girls**

The ratio of boys to the total number of students is 5 to 13, or $\frac{5}{13}$.

$\dfrac{5}{13}$ ◄——**number of boys**
◄——**total number of students**

MATH ALERT Using Fractions to Show Division

A fraction can mean division.

EXAMPLE: $\frac{3}{8}$ means $3 \div 8$.

You can use this meaning of fractions to write a decimal equivalent for a fraction:

$\frac{3}{8} = 3 \div 8 = 0.375$

$$
\begin{array}{r}
0.375 \\
8{\overline{)3.000}} \\
2\,400 \\
\hline
600 \\
560 \\
\hline
40 \\
40 \\
\hline
0
\end{array}
$$

Reading Fractions

Reading a fraction is different than reading a whole number. The numerator is easy, just say the number. To read the denominator, use words to describe the total number of parts. (thirds, fourths, twenty-seconds, etc.)

Benchmark Fractions

Some fractions are used *a lot* and are helpful in picturing other fractions. These fractions are known as **benchmark fractions**.

Knowing benchmark fractions can help you:

- compare and order fractions and mixed numbers; $\frac{3}{4} > \frac{1}{2}$

- round fractions and mixed numbers; $\frac{1}{4}$ rounds down to 0 because $\frac{1}{4}$ is closer to 0 than to 1.

- estimate sums and differences of fractions and mixed numbers. $\frac{3}{4} + \frac{1}{3}$ is greater than 1 because $\frac{1}{3}$ is greater than $\frac{1}{4}$.

Fractions Greater than One

You can use fractions for numbers that are greater than 1.

$$\tfrac{9}{4} \text{ cups of milk} = 2\tfrac{1}{4} \text{ cups of milk}$$

A fraction with a numerator that is greater than or equal to its denominator is greater than or equal to 1.

A mixed number has a part that is a whole number and a part that is a fraction.

You can rewrite a fraction greater than 1 as a mixed number or as a whole number.

EXAMPLE 1: Write $\tfrac{9}{4}$ as a mixed number.

① DIVIDE THE NUMERATOR BY THE DENOMINATOR.	② USE THE REMAINDER TO WRITE THE FRACTION PART OF THE QUOTIENT.
$\begin{array}{r} 2 \\ 4\overline{)9} \\ \underline{8} \\ 1 \end{array}$	$\begin{array}{r} 2\tfrac{1}{4} \\ 4\overline{)9} \\ \underline{8} \\ 1 \end{array}$

So, $\tfrac{9}{4}$ can be rewritten as $2\tfrac{1}{4}$.

You can rewrite a mixed number or whole number as a fraction.

EXAMPLE 2: Write $2\tfrac{1}{4}$ as a fraction.

① WRITE THE WHOLE NUMBER PART AS A FRACTION.	② ADD THE FRACTIONS.	OR, MULTIPLY THE DENOMINATOR AND WHOLE NUMBER AND ADD THE NUMERATOR.
$2 \times 4 = 8$ So, $2 = \tfrac{8}{4}$.	$\tfrac{8}{4} + \tfrac{1}{4} = \tfrac{9}{4}$	$2\tfrac{1}{4} = \dfrac{(2 \times 4) + 1}{4} = \tfrac{9}{4}$

So, $2\tfrac{1}{4}$ can be rewritten as $\tfrac{9}{4}$.

MATH ALERT Improper Fractions

A fraction with a numerator greater than (or equal to) its denominator is sometimes called an improper fraction. Since a number like this has done nothing wrong, it's OK to write a fraction this way. The term *improper fraction* isn't used very much any more.

Rounding Fractions

You can round fractions or mixed numbers to give an approximate amount.

EXAMPLE 1: The shoelace for a sneaker is $31\frac{3}{8}$ inches long. To the nearest inch, about how long is the shoelace?

ONE WAY Round $31\frac{3}{8}$ to the nearest whole number by looking at the fraction part of the number ($\frac{3}{8}$) and deciding if it is closer to 0 or to 1. Think of 0 and 1 as fractions and compare the numerators.

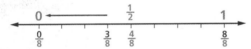

Since 3 is closer to 0 than to 8, $\frac{3}{8}$ is closer to 0 than to 1.

ANOTHER WAY Round $31\frac{3}{8}$ to the nearest whole number by looking at the numerator of the fraction part. $\frac{3}{8}$ is less than $\frac{1}{2}$ because 3 is less than half of 8.

To the nearest inch, the shoelace is about 31 inches long.

EXAMPLE 2: To the nearest $\frac{1}{2}$ inch, about how long is the shoelace? To round $31\frac{3}{8}$ to the nearest half inch, look at the fraction part of the number ($\frac{3}{8}$) and decide if it is closer to 0 or to $\frac{1}{2}$. Think of 0, $\frac{3}{8}$, and $\frac{1}{2}$ as fractions with common denominators and compare numerators.

Since 3 is closer to 4 than to 0, $\frac{3}{8}$ is closer to $\frac{1}{2}$ than to 0.

To the nearest half inch, the shoelace is about $31\frac{1}{2}$ inches long.

Equivalent Fractions

Equivalent fractions are fractions that name the same amount. Use equivalent fractions to add, subtract, and compare fractions.

$$\frac{1}{2} = \frac{2}{4} = \frac{4}{8} = \frac{8}{16}$$

To find equivalent fractions, you can multiply or divide the numerator and denominator by the same non-zero number. This does not change the value of the fraction because you're really just multiplying by a different name for 1.

EXAMPLE 1:

$$\frac{1}{2} = \frac{1 \times 4}{2 \times 4} = \frac{4}{8}$$

Same amount shaded, but 4 times as many parts, so 4 times as many parts shaded.

EXAMPLE 2:

$$\frac{2}{4} = \frac{2 \div 2}{4 \div 2} = \frac{1}{2}$$

Same amount shaded, but half as many parts shaded.

MORE HELP
See 039–041, 104–107, 132–135, 241

Sometimes, you may need to find missing numerators or denominators in equivalent fractions.

EXAMPLE 3: Find b.

$$\frac{5}{8} = \frac{b}{32}$$ **Since 8 × 4 = 32, multiply 5 × 4 to find b.**

$$\frac{5}{8} = \frac{5 \times 4}{8 \times 4} = \frac{20}{32}$$

So, $b = 20$.

EXAMPLE 4: Find a.

$$\frac{2}{7} = \frac{10}{a}$$ **Cross multiply to find a.**

$$2a = 7 \times 10$$
$$a = 70 \div 2$$

So, $a = 35$

037 Simplest Form

A fraction is in simplest form when its numerator and denominator have no common factor other than 1.

MORE HELP
See 065–066

EXAMPLE: Find the simplest form of $\frac{12}{18}$.

 ONE WAY You can divide the numerator and denominator by common factors until the only common factor is 1.

$$\frac{12}{18} = \frac{12 \div 2}{18 \div 2} = \frac{6}{9} \qquad \frac{6 \div 3}{9 \div 3} = \frac{2}{3}$$

2 and 3 have no common factor greater than 1.

↑
2 is a common factor of 12 and 18.

↑
3 is a common factor of 6 and 9.

 ANOTHER WAY You can also divide the numerator and denominator by the **greatest common factor (GCF)**.

Factors of 12: 1, 2, 3, 4, 6, 12

Factors of 18: 1, 2, 3, 6, 9, 18

2, 3, and 6 are common factors of 12 and 18.

$$\frac{12}{18} = \frac{12 \div 6}{18 \div 6} = \frac{2}{3}$$

↑
6 is the GCF of 12 and 18.

Either way, $\frac{12}{18}$ in simplest form is $\frac{2}{3}$.

038 Least Common Denominator

MORE HELP
See 067–068

When fractions have the same denominator, you can say they have a **common denominator**. To find the **least common denominator**, **LCD**, of two or more fractions, find the **least common multiple (LCM)** of the denominators of the fractions.

EXAMPLE: Find the LCD for $\frac{3}{8}$ and $\frac{5}{12}$.

❶ FIND THE LEAST COMMON MULTIPLE FOR THE MULTIPLES OF THE DENOMINATORS.	❷ MULTIPLY THE NUMERATORS AND DENOMINATORS BY THE FACTOR THAT TURNS THE DENOMINATOR INTO THE LCM.
multiples of 8 ⟶ 8, 16, 24	$\frac{3}{8} = \frac{3 \times 3}{8 \times 3} = \frac{9}{24}$
multiples of 12 ⟶ 12, 24	$\frac{5}{12} = \frac{5 \times 2}{12 \times 2} = \frac{10}{24}$

The LCD for $\frac{3}{8}$ and $\frac{5}{12}$ is 24.

Comparing Fractions with Common Denominators

How can you compare two fractions? It depends on whether the fractions have a common denominator.

EXAMPLE: Roland walks $\frac{5}{8}$ mile. Sarah walks $\frac{7}{8}$ mile. Who walks a greater distance?

When fractions have a common denominator, compare the numerators.

$7 > 5$, so $\frac{7}{8} > \frac{5}{8}$.

Sarah walks a greater distance.

> This makes sense because 7 of something is more than 5 of something.
> 7 hours > 5 hours
> 7 eighths > 5 eighths

Comparing Fractions Without Common Denominators

When fractions have different denominators, you may use different methods to compare them.

 ONE WAY You can compare them to your favorite benchmarks.

EXAMPLE 1: Roland walks $\frac{3}{8}$ mile and Sarah walks $\frac{3}{4}$ mile. Who walks a greater distance?

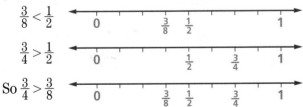

$\frac{3}{8} < \frac{1}{2}$

$\frac{3}{4} > \frac{1}{2}$

So $\frac{3}{4} > \frac{3}{8}$

Sarah walks a greater distance.

MORE ▶

You can find equivalent fractions with a common denominator.

MORE HELP
See 036

EXAMPLE 2: Ben walks $\frac{5}{6}$ mile. Sari walks $\frac{3}{4}$ mile. Who walks a greater distance?

❶ FIND EQUIVALENT FRACTIONS WITH THE SAME DENOMINATOR.	❷ COMPARE THE NUMERATORS.
$\frac{5}{6} = \frac{5 \times 2}{6 \times 2} = \frac{10}{12}$ $\qquad$ $\frac{3}{4} = \frac{3 \times 3}{4 \times 3} = \frac{9}{12}$	$10 > 9$ Since $\frac{10}{12} > \frac{9}{12}$, then $\frac{5}{6} > \frac{3}{4}$.

Ben walks a greater distance.

041 Ordering Fractions and Mixed Numbers

CASE 1 If you know how to compare two fractions, you also know how to order a group of fractions.

MORE HELP
See 038, 067

EXAMPLE 1: Sam measured his science-project plants on three Fridays in a row and recorded the data. Which week had the least growth?

PLANT GROWTH
First Week $\frac{11}{16}$ inch
Second Week $\frac{5}{8}$ inch
Third Week $\frac{3}{4}$ inch

❶ REWRITE THE FRACTIONS WITH COMMON DENOMINATORS.	❷ COMPARE THE NUMERATORS.
Multiples of 4 ⟶ 4, 8, 12, 16, . . . **Multiples of 8 ⟶ 8, 16, . . .** **Multiples of 16 ⟶ 16, 32, . . .** **The least common denominator is 16.** $\frac{11}{16} = \frac{11}{16}$ $\quad$ $\frac{5}{8} = \frac{10}{16}$ $\quad$ $\frac{3}{4} = \frac{12}{16}$	$12 > 11 > 10$ Since $\frac{12}{16} > \frac{11}{16} > \frac{10}{16}$, then $\frac{3}{4} > \frac{11}{16} > \frac{5}{8}$.

So, the least growth was in week two.

CASE 2 To order mixed numbers, first compare and order the whole-number parts. Then, if the whole-number parts are the same, compare and order the fraction parts.

EXAMPLE 2: Order from least to greatest: $3\frac{11}{16}, 2\frac{5}{8}, 2\frac{3}{4}$

❶ Look at the whole-number parts.	❷ Compare the fraction parts of the remaining numbers.
$3\frac{11}{16}, 2\frac{5}{8}, 2\frac{3}{4}$ $3 > 2$, so $3\frac{11}{16}$ is greatest.	$\frac{5}{8} = \frac{5}{8}$ $\qquad$ $\frac{3}{4} = \frac{6}{8}$ Since $\frac{5}{8} < \frac{6}{8}$, then $2\frac{5}{8} < 2\frac{3}{4}$.

So, $2\frac{5}{8} < 2\frac{3}{4} < 3\frac{11}{16}$.

Complex Fractions

042

You might think that most fractions seem pretty complex, at least compared to whole numbers. However, the term **complex fraction** describes a special kind of fraction in which the numerator, denominator, or both, are fractions.

MORE HELP
See 030

Complex Fractions   **Simple Fractions**

$$\frac{\frac{2}{3}}{4} \qquad \frac{\frac{1}{2}}{\frac{3}{8}} \qquad \frac{7}{\frac{3}{5}} \qquad\qquad \frac{4}{9} \qquad \frac{1}{3} \qquad \frac{3}{11}$$

MORE ▶

MORE HELP
See 223

For any complex fraction, you can write a simple fraction.

EXAMPLE: Luke is biking to Mark's house, which is $\frac{2}{3}$ mile away. After going $\frac{1}{4}$ of the way, he stops at the gas station to put air in his tires. How far has he gone? What is $\frac{1}{4}$ of $\frac{2}{3}$, or $\frac{\frac{2}{3}}{4}$?

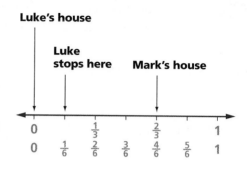

❶ WRITE THE FRACTION AS A DIVISION EXPRESSION.	❷ MULTIPLY BY THE RECIPROCAL.	❸ WRITE THE FRACTION IN SIMPLEST FORM.
$\frac{\frac{2}{3}}{4} = \frac{2}{3} \div \frac{4}{1}$	$\frac{2}{3} \times \frac{1}{4} = \frac{2}{12}$	$\frac{2}{12} = \frac{1}{6}$

Luke has gone $\frac{1}{6}$ mile.

043 Writing Decimals as Fractions

Decimals are fractions with a special set of denominators (tenths, hundredths, etc.) and a special written form. Writing fractions for decimals with denominators like 10, 100, and 1000 is easy. All you need to do is say the fraction aloud.

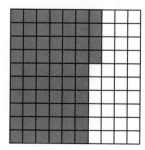

Decimal: 0.9

Word name: nine tenths

Fraction: $\frac{9}{10}$

Decimal: 0.64

Word name: sixty-four hundredths

Fraction: $\frac{64}{100}$

Writing Fractions as Decimals

To write a decimal for any fraction, even a fraction with a denominator that is not a power of 10, divide the numerator by the denominator. This works because a fraction is a way of showing division.

EXAMPLE: Write $\frac{3}{8}$ as a decimal.

Think: $\frac{3}{8} = 3 \div 8$

 ONE WAY You can use pencil and paper.

 ANOTHER WAY You can use a calculator.

MORE HELP
See 030

$$
\begin{array}{r}
0.375 \\
8\overline{)3.000} \\
\underline{24} \\
60 \\
\underline{56} \\
40
\end{array}
$$

3 ÷ 8 = 0.375

MATH ALERT Very Long Decimals on the Calculator

Be on the alert when you are using a calculator to divide or to help you write a fraction as a decimal. A calculator can't show every digit of a very long decimal (especially when you have a repeating decimal), and there are two ways it can show the last digit in its display. To check what your calculator shows, press:

2 ÷ 3

If your display ends with a 6, your calculator **truncates** (cuts off) the quotient.

0.6666666

If your display ends with a 7, your calculator rounds the quotient.

0.6666667

Positive and Negative Numbers

Positive numbers are numbers that are greater than zero. **Negative numbers** are numbers that are less than zero. Zero is neither positive nor negative. You can show positive and negative numbers on a number line.

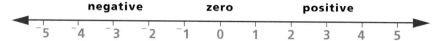

Opposite numbers are the same distance from zero in an opposite direction. Every whole number, fraction, or decimal has an opposite.

3 and ⁻3 are opposites.   2.6 and ⁻2.6 are opposites.

$4\frac{1}{5}$ and ⁻$4\frac{1}{5}$ are opposites.   Zero is its own opposite.

Integers

Integers are the set of whole numbers and their opposites:

... ⁻5, ⁻4, ⁻3, ⁻2, ⁻1, 0, 1, 2, 3, 4, 5 ...

Whole number	4	8	25	183	500	1062	10,000
Opposite	⁻4	⁻8	⁻25	⁻183	⁻500	⁻1062	⁻10,000

Comparing Rational Numbers

There are two ways to compare any two rational numbers.

 ONE WAY You can use a number line.

EXAMPLE 1: Compare: ⁻$2\frac{3}{8}$ and 1.5.

A negative number is less than a positive number.

MORE HELP
See 018, 020, 040, 041

So, ⁻$2\frac{3}{8}$ < 1.5.

EXAMPLE 2: Compare: ⁻1.8 and ⁻3 ¼.

The negative number closer to 0 is greater.

So, ⁻1.8 > ⁻3 ¼.

 You can write both numbers as fractions or both as decimals.

EXAMPLE 3: Compare: ⁻0.5 and $-\frac{7}{16}$.

Show both numbers in the same form and then compare:

MORE HELP
See 017

■ as decimals

$$⁻0.5 = ⁻0.5000$$

$$-\frac{7}{16} = ⁻7 \div 16 = ⁻0.4375$$

$$⁻0.5000 < ⁻0.4375$$

■ as fractions

$$⁻0.5 = \frac{-1}{2} = \frac{-8}{16}$$

$$-\frac{7}{16} = \frac{-7}{16}$$

$$\frac{-8}{16} < \frac{-7}{16}$$

So, ⁻0.5 < $-\frac{7}{16}$

Ordering Rational Numbers

049

If you know how to compare two rational numbers, you also know how to order a group of rational numbers.

MORE HELP
See 018, 020

EXAMPLE 1: For a science project, you record your dog's change in weight after each month as you vary its diet and exercise program. In which month did your dog lose the most weight?

To solve this problem, order the numbers from least to greatest.

Month 1:
Lose ⅜ of a pound.

Month 2:
Gain 1 pound.

Month 3:
Use another scale,
lose 0.8 pound.

 You can use a number line.

Numbers increase as you go from left to right on the number line.

From left to right on the number line, the numbers are: ⁻0.8, $-\frac{3}{8}$, 1.

MORE ▶

You can also write all the numbers in the same form and then compare.

■ Find decimal equivalents, then compare.

$$\frac{-3}{8} = {}^-0.375$$

$$1 = 1.000$$

$${}^-0.8 = {}^-0.800$$

$${}^-0.800 < {}^-0.375 < 1$$

■ Find fraction equivalents, then compare.

$$\frac{-3}{8} = \frac{-15}{40}$$

$$1 = \frac{40}{40}$$

$${}^-0.8 = \frac{-8}{10} = \frac{-32}{40}$$

$$\frac{-32}{40} < \frac{-15}{40} < \frac{40}{40}$$

From least to greatest, the numbers are $^-0.8$, $\frac{-3}{8}$, 1. So, your dog lost a little weight in Month 1 ($\frac{3}{8}$ pound) and lost the most weight in Month 3 (0.8 pound).

050 Absolute Value

The **absolute value** of a number is its distance from zero on the number line. You can use the symbol | | to show absolute value.

$^-4\frac{1}{2}$ is $4\frac{1}{2}$ units to the left of zero.

Write:

$|{}^-4\frac{1}{2}| = 4\frac{1}{2}$

$|1.72| = 1.72$

Say:

The absolute value of $^-4\frac{1}{2}$ is $4\frac{1}{2}$.

The absolute value of 1.72 is 1.72.

051 MATH ALERT Absolute Values Are Always Positive

The absolute value of a number is *always positive*. This is because absolute value tells the *distance* from zero, not the direction from zero. You can think about absolute value like this:

■ The absolute value of a positive number is itself. $|4| = 4$
■ The absolute value of a negative number is its opposite. $|{}^-3| = 3$
■ But, the negative of the absolute value of a number is negative. $^-|6| = {}^-6$

Irrational Numbers

A rational number is a number that can be represented by a ratio of two integers.

An **irrational number** is a number that cannot be represented by a ratio of two integers.

Irrational numbers can be represented by decimals that do not end and are not repeating. For example, 0.343343334… is an irrational number.

Irrational Numbers	Rational Numbers
$\sqrt{2}$	7
0.343343334…	$^{-}23.9$ $^{-}16$
π	$\dfrac{4}{5}$ $\dfrac{16}{2}$

MORE HELP
See 027, 047, 424

Pi (π) and the square root of two ($\sqrt{2}$) are also examples of irrational numbers. We never find exact values for these numbers in fraction or decimal form, just approximations.

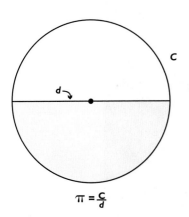

$\pi = \dfrac{c}{d}$

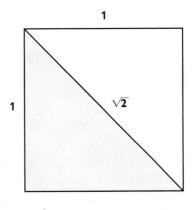

Number Theory

Earnest P. Whitherstone was certain that if he could come up with just one good number theory, they'd give him his mathematician's license.

Number theory is a part of mathematics where you look for properties of numbers and relationships between numbers. Number theory may sound like it's for mathematicians only. But, some of the things you'll learn can help you save time and effort when you have to make calculations. For example, in this section, you'll find shortcuts for telling whether:

- 23 is prime or composite;
- 12 is abundant, defective, or perfect;
- 324 is divisible by 2, 3, 4, 5, 6, 9, or 10.

Understanding the properties of numbers will help you understand and use mathematical relationships.

▶ Factors and Multiples

Factors and multiples are powerful tools for working with fractions, exponents, and roots. They help you break down numbers to make multiplication and division easier. They also play a major role in modern codes, like the ones used to keep computer files secure.

055) Even and Odd Numbers

All **even numbers** are divisible by 2. This means any even number can be divided into two equal-size groups or divided into pairs, with *no* leftovers. Every even number has 0, 2, 4, 6, or 8 in its ones place.

The 12 socks are all in pairs. There is an even number of socks.

Odd numbers are *not* divisible by 2. When an odd number is divided into two equal-size groups or divided into pairs, there is always 1 left over. Every odd number has 1, 3, 5, 7, or 9 in its ones place.

No matter what you do, there's an extra sock when you try to put 11 in pairs.

You can use even and odd number patterns to check your computation. Test these patterns using your own numbers.

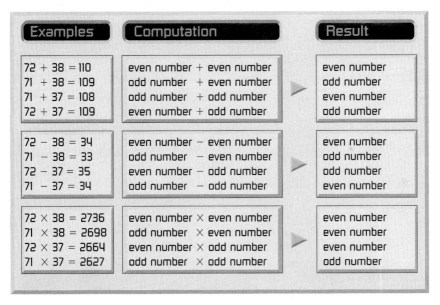

Examples	Computation	Result
72 + 38 = 110	even number + even number	even number
71 + 38 = 109	odd number + even number	odd number
71 + 37 = 108	odd number + odd number	even number
72 + 37 = 109	even number + odd number	odd number
72 − 38 = 34	even number − even number	even number
71 − 38 = 33	odd number − even number	odd number
72 − 37 = 35	even number − odd number	odd number
71 − 37 = 34	odd number − odd number	even number
72 × 38 = 2736	even number × even number	even number
71 × 38 = 2698	odd number × even number	even number
72 × 37 = 2664	even number × odd number	even number
71 × 37 = 2627	odd number × odd number	odd number

Note that we didn't show patterns for division. This is because adding, subtracting, and multiplying whole numbers always give integer answers. But dividing whole numbers may or may not give integer answers (for example, $6 \div 4 = \frac{6}{4} = 1\frac{1}{2}$).

056) Factors

Pick a whole number (15). Now find two whole numbers whose product is your number ($3 \times 5 = 15$). You've found two **factors** of your number.

EXAMPLE: Find all the factors of the product 36.

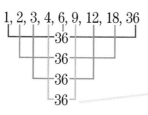

$3 \times 5 = 15$, so 3 and 5 are factors of 15.

The factors of 36 are:

$36 = 1 \times 36$
$36 = 2 \times 18$
$36 = 3 \times 12$
$36 = 4 \times 9$
$36 = 6 \times 6$

1, 2, 3, 4, 6, 9, 12, 18, 36
36
36
36
36

When the factors are the same or close together, you're done.

MORE HELP
See 037, 066, 069

Being able to find factors of a number can help you find the greatest common factor of two numbers, write fractions in simplest form, and tell whether one number is divisible by another.

057 Factorials

MORE HELP
See 460

Take any whole number, we'll call it n. Multiply all of the counting numbers from 1 through n. The product is called **n factorial ($n!$)**.

EXAMPLE: Find the number of ways you can arrange 5 people in a line. To find the number of possible arrangements for a number of items, you find the factorial of the number of items.

$$5! = 5 \times 4 \times 3 \times 2 \times 1 = 120$$

So, 5 people can be arranged in 120 different lines.

058) Prime Numbers

CASE 1 If you're talking about whole numbers, a **prime number** has exactly two different factors, 1 and itself.

EXAMPLE 1: $13 = 1 \times 13$. Since there are no other whole-number factors of 13, 13 is a prime number.

CASE 2 If you're talking about integers, a **prime number** has no factors other than 1, ⁻1, itself, and its opposite.

EXAMPLE 2: ⁻5 = ⁻1 × 5 and ⁻5 = 1 × ⁻5. Since there are no other factors of ⁻5, it is prime.

All the prime numbers from 1 to 100 are in color.

1	2	3	4	5	6	7	8	9	10
11	12	13	14	15	16	17	18	19	20
21	22	23	24	25	26	27	28	29	30
31	32	33	34	35	36	37	38	39	40
41	42	43	44	45	46	47	48	49	50
51	52	53	54	55	56	57	58	59	60
61	62	63	64	65	66	67	68	69	70
71	72	73	74	75	76	77	78	79	80
81	82	83	84	85	86	87	88	89	90
91	92	93	94	95	96	97	98	99	100

If you don't believe they are prime numbers, just try to find more than two whole-number factors for them. Bet you can't!

MATH ALERT One Is Not Prime

059

The number 1 is not prime. Neither is ⁻1. A common assumption is that 1 is a prime number. It is really a lonely number because it is neither prime nor composite! It's not prime because it does not have exactly two factors, and it's not composite because it does not have more than two factors.

Composite Numbers

060

Every whole number except 1 is either a composite number or a prime number. In the table above, the numbers in black from 4 to 100 are composite numbers.

MORE HELP
See 058

EXAMPLE: Tell whether each number is composite or prime: 14, 98, 89.

$14 = 1 \times 14$
$14 = 2 \times 7$ } 4 factors   composite

$98 = 1 \times 98$
$98 = 2 \times 49$ } 6 factors   composite
$98 = 7 \times 14$

$89 = 1 \times 89$ } exactly 2 factors   prime

Composite numbers are like composite materials. They're made of more than two different factors!

Prime Factoring

Breaking up a composite number into its prime factors can help you understand the number and compute with it.

A composite number written as the product of prime numbers is called the **prime factorization** of the number.

 You can find the prime factorization by making a **factor tree**. First, express the number as a product of two numbers. Continue to express each number as a product of two numbers until you can't do it anymore.

EXAMPLE 1: Find the prime factorization of 132.

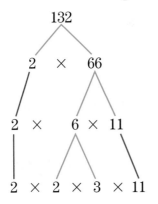

Write the number you are factoring at the top of the tree.

Choose any pair of factors as branches. If either of these factors is not prime, you need to factor again.

Choose a pair of factors for each composite number. Continue the branches for the prime factor(s).

Keep factoring until you have a row of prime factors.

The prime factorization of 132 is $2 \times 2 \times 3 \times 11$, or $2^2 \times 3 \times 11$.

EXAMPLE 2: Find the prime factorization of 72.

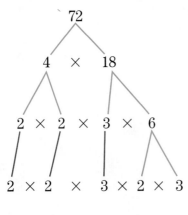

Write the number you are factoring at the top of the tree.

Here, both factors are composite numbers.

Choose a pair of factors for each composite number. One of these factors is composite.

Continue the prime-number branches and factor the composite number. The last row shows only prime factors.

The prime factorization of 72 is $2 \times 2 \times 2 \times 3 \times 3$, or $2^3 \times 3^2$.

You can find the prime factorization by using division.

To find the prime factorization of 105, begin by dividing 105 by a prime number. Then continue to divide each quotient you get by a prime number until the quotient is 1.

$$\frac{21}{5)105} \quad \frac{7}{3)21} \quad \frac{1}{7)7}$$

If you try a prime number and you get a remainder, try a different prime number.

The prime factorization of 105 is the product of the divisors: $5 \times 3 \times 7$, or $3 \times 5 \times 7$, or $7 \times 5 \times 3$.

Perfect Numbers

062

To Olympic divers and gymnasts, 10 is a perfect number.

In mathematics, a **perfect number** is equal to the sum of all its whole-number factors, except itself.

EXAMPLE: Tell whether 28 and 10 are perfect numbers.

Factors of 28, except for 28 itself:
1, 2, 4, 7, 14
$1 + 2 + 4 + 7 + 14 = 28$

Factors of 10, except for 10 itself:
1, 2, 5
$1 + 2 + 5 \neq 10$.

Abundant Numbers

063

Suppose you add all the whole-number factors of a number, except the number itself. If the sum is greater than the number, then the number is an **abundant number**.

EXAMPLE: Tell whether 12 and 15 are abundant numbers.

Factors of 12, except for 12 itself:
1, 2, 3, 4, 6
$1 + 2 + 3 + 4 + 6 = 16 \quad 16 > 12$

Factors of 15, except for 15 itself:
1, 3, 5
$1 + 3 + 5 = 9 \qquad 9 < 15$

064 **Defective Numbers**

Is there any hope of fixing this defective number?

Sorry.

Suppose you add all the whole-number factors of a number, except the number itself. If the sum is less than the number itself, then the number is a **defective number**, sometimes called a **deficient number**.

EXAMPLE: Tell whether 39 and 20 are defective numbers.

Factors of 39, except for 39 itself:
1, 3, 13
$1 + 3 + 13 = 17$ $\qquad$ $17 < 39$

Factors of 20, except for 20 itself:
1, 2, 4, 5, 10
$1 + 2 + 4 + 5 + 10 = 22$ $\quad$ $22 > 20$

If a number is not defective or abundant, then it is perfect.

065 **Common Factors**

A group of two or more whole numbers may have some factors that are the same. These factors are called **common factors**.

EXAMPLE 1: Find the common factors of 16, 24, and 32.

Factors of 16: 1, 2, 4, 8, 16

Factors of 24: 1, 2, 3, 4, 6, 8, 12, 24

Factors of 32: 1, 2, 4, 8, 16, 32

The common factors of 16, 24, and 32 are 1, 2, 4, and 8.

EXAMPLE 2: Find the common factors of 9, 18, and 81.

Factors of 9: 1, 3, 9

Factors of 18: 1, 2, 3, 6, 9, 18

Factors of 81: 1, 3, 9, 27, 81

The common factors of 9, 18, and 81 are 1, 3, and 9.

Greatest Common Factor

The greatest number that is a factor of two or more whole numbers is the **greatest common factor (GCF)** of the numbers.

 Find the GCF of numbers by listing the factors of the numbers. Then look for the greatest number common to both lists.

EXAMPLE 1: Find the GCF of 18 and 30.

Factors of 18: 1, 2, 3, ⑥ 9, 18
Factors of 30: 1, 2, 3, 5, ⑥ 10, 15, 30

The common factors of 18 and 30 are 1, 2, 3, and 6.

The greatest common factor (GCF) of 18 and 30 is 6.

 Find the GCF of numbers by using prime factorization.

MORE HELP
See 037, 061

EXAMPLE 2: Find the GCF of 96 and 144.

1. First find the prime factorizations of each number.

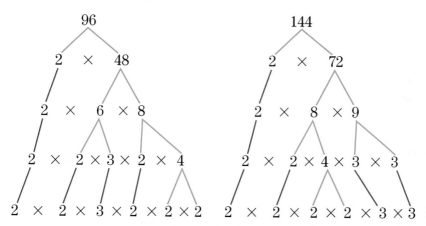

2. Then find the prime factors that are common and multiply them.

$$96 = 2 \times 2 \times 2 \times 2 \times 2 \times 3$$
$$144 = 2 \times 2 \times 2 \times 2 \times 3 \times 3$$

Each factor that has a match is used to find the GCF.

The GCF of 96 and 144 is $2 \times 2 \times 2 \times 2 \times 3 = 48$.

Multiples

Multiples of a number are the products of the number and other factors.

Multiply to find multiples:

$$\left.\begin{array}{rcl} 1 \times 5 &=& 5 \\ 2 \times 5 &=& 10 \\ 3 \times 5 &=& 15 \\ 4 \times 5 &=& 20 \\ 5 \times 5 &=& 25 \\ 6 \times 5 &=& 30 \\ 7 \times 5 &=& 35 \\ 8 \times 5 &=& 40 \\ 9 \times 5 &=& 45 \end{array}\right\}\text{multiples of 5} \qquad \left.\begin{array}{rcl} 1 \times 12 &=& 12 \\ 2 \times 12 &=& 24 \\ 3 \times 12 &=& 36 \\ 4 \times 12 &=& 48 \\ 5 \times 12 &=& 60 \\ 6 \times 12 &=& 72 \\ 7 \times 12 &=& 84 \\ 8 \times 12 &=& 96 \\ 9 \times 12 &=& 108 \end{array}\right\}\text{multiples of 12}$$

068

Least Common Multiple

The smallest number (other than zero) that is a multiple of two or more whole numbers is the **least common multiple (LCM)** of the numbers.

 ONE WAY Find the LCM of numbers by listing their non-zero multiples until you find a match.

MORE HELP
See 038, 061

EXAMPLE 1: Find the LCM of 8, 9, and 12.

Multiples of 8: 8, 16, 24, 32, 40, 48, 56, 64, 72, . . .
Multiples of 9: 9, 18, 27, 36, 45, 54, 63, 72, . . .
Multiples of 12: 12, 24, 36, 48, 60, 72, . . .

The least common multiple (LCM) of 8, 9, and 12 is 72.

 ANOTHER WAY Find the LCM of numbers by using prime factorization.

EXAMPLE 2: Find the LCM of 18 and 30.

❶ FIND THE PRIME FACTORIZATION OF EACH NUMBER.	❷ FIND THE COMMON FACTORS.	❸ MULTIPLY THE COMMON FACTORS AND THE EXTRA FACTORS.
18 = 2 × 3 × 3 30 = 2 × 3 × 5	18 = ②×③× 3 30 = ②×③× 5 **Both numbers have one 2 and one 3 in their lists. The 18 has an extra 3 and the 30 has an extra 5.**	2 × 3 × 3 × 5 = 90 ↖↗ ↖↑ **common extra** **factors factors**

The LCM of 18 and 30 is 90.

Divisibility

One whole number is divisible by another whole number if the remainder is zero when you divide. Mathematicians have discovered patterns that make it easier to tell if one number is divisible by another. Try this with your own numbers.

A number is divisible by:	If:	Test with 324
2	the ones digit is 0, 2, 4, 6, or 8 (or, it is an even number)	324: 4, an even number, is in the ones place. So, 324 is divisible by 2.
3	the sum of the digits is divisible by 3	324: 3 + 2 + 4 = 9 9 is divisible by 3. So, 324 is too.
4	the number formed by the last two digits is divisible by 4	324: 24 is divisible by 4. So, 324 is too.
5	the last digit is 0 or 5	324: 4, the last digit, is not 0 or 5. So, 324 is not divisible by 5.
6	the number is divisible by 2 and by 3	324: 324 is divisible by 2. 324 is divisible by 3. So, 324 is divisible by 6.
9	the sum of the digits is divisible by 9	324: 3 + 2 + 4 = 9 9 is divisible by 9. So, 324 is too.
10	the final digit is 0	324: 4, the final digit, is not 0. So, 324 is not divisible by 10.

Divisibility tests for 7 and 8 are not as simple as the tests for the other numbers from 1 through 10. Just go ahead and do the division.

MORE

How can divisibility rules help you? Here are two ways:

1. They can help you determine the factors of numbers.

   The number 360 ends in 0, the sum of its digits is 9, and the number formed by its last two digits is 60. The divisibility rules tell you that 2, 3, 4, 5, 6, 9, and 10 are some of the factors of 360.

   Aha! If 360 is divisible by 4, then 4 is a factor of 360!

FACTORS OF 360

   The number 175 ends in 5, the sum of its digits is 13 and the number formed by its last two digits is 75. The divisibility rules tell you that 5 is a factor of 175 and 2, 3, 4, 6, 9, and 10 are not.

   So, if you're looking for common factors of 360 and 175, you know 5 works and you can rule out 2, 3, 4, 6, 9, and 10 and their multiples.

2. They can help you decide whether a bunch of things can be put into equal groups.

   There will be 138 people at a party. Can the host fill tables of 5? No, 138 is not divisible by 5. Can the host fill tables of 6? Yes, 138 is divisible by 6.

Powers and Roots

Powers, roots, and logarithms sound like topics from history, physics, biology, and music rather than mathematics. In this section, you'll see that powers offer a shorter way to write factors, that roots are special factors of a number, and that logarithms are a way to think about factors that helps you deal with very large and very small numbers.

Positive Exponents

071

Suppose you multiply by the same factor more than once. You can show the repeated factors using exponential form, where the base is the repeated factor, and the exponent tells the number of repetitions.

$3 \times 3 \times 3 \times 3 \times 3 = $ $3^5 \leftarrow$ **exponent**

 **base**

MORE ◢

This table shows how to write and read positive exponents. Note that there are special ways to read numbers when the exponent is 2 or 3.

Repeated Factors	Write	Say	Standard Form
3 × 3	3^2	*three to the second power* or *three squared*	9
3 × 3 × 3	3^3	*three to the third power* or *three cubed*	27
3 × 3 × 3 × 3	3^4	*three to the fourth power*	81
2 × 2 × 3 × 3 × 3	$2^2 × 3^3$	*two squared times three cubed*	108

You can use positive exponents to describe growth patterns.

EXAMPLE: Would you rather have $100 a day for 30 days or 2¢ on Day 1, 4¢ on Day 2, 8¢ on Day 3, and so on?

MORE HELP
See 006, 016, 075

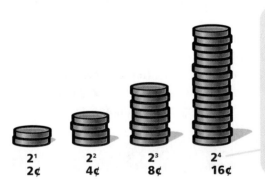

2^1
2¢

2^2
4¢

2^3
8¢

2^4
16¢

Since the amount in the pattern starts at 2¢ and doubles each day, you can use a base of 2 and an exponent to show the day. This may not seem like much money, but the amount grows fast. Try figuring it out day by day for a month and you'll see.

072

MATH ALERT Zero as an Exponent

There is an agreement among mathematicians that any number to the zero power is one. So, $4^0 = 1$ and $62^0 = 1$.

Negative Exponents

Look at the pattern on the right. As you can see, when the base is 4 each time you decrease the exponent by 1, the value is $\frac{1}{4}$ as large.

If the base were 25, each time you decreased the exponent by 1, the value would be $\frac{1}{25}$ as large. So, **negative exponents** turn whole numbers into fractions.

$$4^3 = 64 \atop 4^2 = 16 \Bigg\} \text{ 16 is } \tfrac{1}{4} \text{ of 64.}$$

$$4^1 = 4 \atop 4^0 = 1 \Bigg\} \text{ 1 is } \tfrac{1}{4} \text{ of 4.}$$

$$4^{-1} = \tfrac{1}{4^1} = \tfrac{1}{4} \atop 4^{-2} = \tfrac{1}{4^2} = \tfrac{1}{16} \Bigg\} \tfrac{1}{16} \text{ is } \tfrac{1}{4} \text{ of } \tfrac{1}{4}.$$

$$4^{-3} = \tfrac{1}{4^3} = \tfrac{1}{64}$$

MORE HELP
See 160–164

Shortcut

You can follow this shortcut rule to interpret any number with a negative exponent: For any non-zero number b and integer n, $b^{-n} = \frac{1}{b^n}$.

For example, $3^{-4} = \frac{1}{3^4} = \frac{1}{81}$ and $10^{-5} = \frac{1}{10^5} = 0.00001$

EXAMPLE: A radioactive substance such as Phosphorus-32 does not stay radioactive forever. The time it takes for half of the element to decay is called a **half-life**. The half-life for Phosphorus-32 is 14 days.

(*Source: CRC Handbook of Chemistry and Physics*)

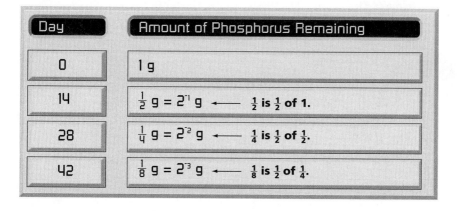

Day	Amount of Phosphorus Remaining
0	1 g
14	$\frac{1}{2}$ g $= 2^{-1}$ g ← $\frac{1}{2}$ is $\frac{1}{2}$ of 1.
28	$\frac{1}{4}$ g $= 2^{-2}$ g ← $\frac{1}{4}$ is $\frac{1}{2}$ of $\frac{1}{2}$.
42	$\frac{1}{8}$ g $= 2^{-3}$ g ← $\frac{1}{8}$ is $\frac{1}{2}$ of $\frac{1}{4}$.

Fractional Exponents

What do fractional exponents, such as $8^{\frac{1}{3}}$, mean?

To understand **fractional exponents**, think of the base as a product. The denominator of the exponent gives the number of times a factor is repeated to make the base. Find that factor and raise it to the power in the numerator of the exponent.

$8^{\frac{1}{3}}$ ←——exponent

base —↑

EXAMPLE 1: Evaluate $8^{\frac{1}{3}}$

❶ LOOK AT THE DENOMINATOR OF THE EXPONENT.	❷ NOW LOOK AT THE NUMERATOR OF THE EXPONENT AND RAISE THE FACTOR YOU FOUND IN STEP 1 TO THAT POWER.
The denominator of the exponent is 3. **So, a factor is repeated 3 times to make 8.** That factor is 2: $2 \times 2 \times 2 = 8$	The numerator of the exponent is 1: $2^1 = 2$ So, $8^{\frac{1}{3}} = 2$.

EXAMPLE 2: Evaluate $81^{\frac{3}{4}}$

❶ LOOK AT THE DENOMINATOR OF THE EXPONENT.	❷ NOW LOOK AT THE NUMERATOR OF THE EXPONENT AND RAISE THE FACTOR YOU FOUND IN STEP 1 TO THAT POWER.
The denominator of the exponent is 4. **So, a factor is repeated 4 times to make 81.** That factor is 3: $3 \times 3 \times 3 \times 3 = 81$	The numerator of the exponent is 3: $3^3 = 27$ So, $81^{\frac{3}{4}} = 27$.

Using a Calculator with Exponents

You can use a calculator to evaluate numbers with exponents.

EXAMPLE 1: Evaluate 5^4. | 5 | y^x | 4 | = | | 625. |

—— power key

EXAMPLE 2: Evaluate 2^{-3}. | 2 | y^x | 3 | +/− | = | | 0.125 |

—— change sign key

EXAMPLE 3: Evaluate $27^{\frac{2}{3}}$.

| 2 | 7 | y^x | (| 2 | ÷ | 3 |) | = | | 9. |

Squares and Square Roots

A square rug with sides of 6 feet has an area of 6 ft × 6 ft, or 36 ft^2.

When a number is multiplied by itself, the product is the **square** of the number.

Factor form: $6 \times 6 = 36$
Write: $6^2 = 36$
Say: *6 squared is equal to 36 or 36 is the square of 6.*

When the product of two identical factors is a second number, the factor is the **square root** of the number.

Write: $\sqrt{36} = 6$
Say: *The square root of 36 is equal to 6.*

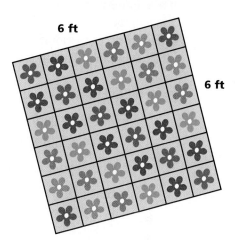

6 ft

6 ft

MORE HELP
See 078–079, 082

My number is the square of yours.

Then mine must be the square root of yours.

MATH ALERT Square Roots Can Be Negative

077

You know that if you multiply two positive numbers, you get a positive product. Two negative factors also have a positive product.

$$6 \times 6 = 36$$
$$^-6 \times {}^-6 = 36$$

That means $^-6$ is also a square root of 36. However, $\sqrt{}$ means the **principal square root**, which is the positive root. For example, $\sqrt{25} = 5$ and $\sqrt{100} = 10$.

078 Estimating Square Roots

If a number is not a perfect square, its square root is not an integer. You can use a calculator or a square root table to find this kind of square root. But even if you don't have a calculator or a square root table, you can still estimate.

MORE HELP
See 082, 083, 540

EXAMPLE: Find $\sqrt{14}$ to the nearest hundredth.

1. Find two perfect squares that 14 lies between.

$\sqrt{9} = 3$ and $\sqrt{16} = 4$, so $\sqrt{14}$ must be between 3 and 4.

A good estimate comes from continually estimating!

2. Refine your estimate.

Since 14 is closer to 16 than 9, $\sqrt{14}$ must be closer to 4 than 3. Try squaring values that are close to 4, such as 3.7 and 3.8, to see which square is closer to 14.

$(3.7)^2 = 13.69; (3.8)^2 = 14.44$

3. If you need to, refine your estimate further.

Since 14 is about halfway between $(3.7)^2$ and $(3.8)^2$, try squaring decimals halfway between 3.7 and 3.8, such as 3.74 and 3.75.

$(3.74)^2 = 13.9876; (3.75)^2 = 14.0625.$

14 is closer to $(3.74)^2$ than to $(3.75)^2$, so $\sqrt{14}$ is closer to 3.74 than to 3.75. So, $\sqrt{14} \approx 3.74$. (Use $\approx$ instead of $=$ when the numbers are approximate.)

079 Using a Table of Powers and Roots

MORE HELP
See 540

The table shows squares and square roots for the numbers 1 through 10.

To use the table to find the square root of a number, first look for the number in the column labeled n. Then move right along the row to find the number in the column labeled $\sqrt{n}$. For non-perfect squares, the roots are approximate. $\sqrt{7} \approx 2.646$, for example.

n	n^2	$\sqrt{n}$
1	1	1.000
2	4	1.414
3	9	1.732
4	16	2.000
5	25	2.236
6	36	2.449
7	49	2.646
8	64	2.828
9	81	3.000
10	100	3.162

Cubes and Cube Roots 080

A cube with sides of 2 meters has a volume of 2 m × 2 m × 2 m, or 8 m³.

The product of 3 equal factors is the **cube** of the factor.

Factor form: $2 \times 2 \times 2 = 8$
Write: $2^3 = 8$
Say: *2 cubed is equal to 8 or 8 is the cube of 2.*

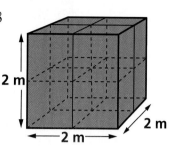
2 m
2 m
2 m

The **cube root** of a number n is the number (x) whose cube (x^3) equals the number n.

Write: $\sqrt[3]{8} = 2$
Say: *The cube root of 8 is equal to 2.*

MATH ALERT A Cube Root of a Positive Number Is Always Positive 081

When a cube root is one of three factors of a positive number, it must be positive. If it were negative, the cube itself would be negative. If you multiply a negative number by a negative number, you get a positive number. BUT if you multiply that positive number by *another* negative number, you get a negative number. When you start taking roots of negative numbers, you get into imaginary numbers, which aren't discussed in this book.

Using a Calculator to Find Roots 082

There are several ways you can use a calculator to find square roots and cube roots.

EXAMPLE 1: Find $\sqrt{25}$.

 ONE WAY You can use the square root key: $\boxed{\sqrt{}}$
Press: $\boxed{2}$ $\boxed{5}$ $\boxed{\sqrt{}}$

 ANOTHER WAY Since $\sqrt{25} = 25^{\frac{1}{2}}$, you can press:

$\boxed{2}$ $\boxed{5}$ $\boxed{y^x}$ $\boxed{(}$ $\boxed{1}$ $\boxed{\div}$ $\boxed{2}$ $\boxed{)}$ $\boxed{=}$

The square root of 25 is 5.

MORE ◢

EXAMPLE 2: Find $\sqrt[3]{64}$.

Here are two ways to find $\sqrt[3]{64}$.

ONE WAY You can use the $\boxed{\sqrt[x]{y}}$ key. Press:

$$\boxed{6}\ \boxed{4}\ \boxed{\sqrt[x]{y}}\ \boxed{3}\ \boxed{=}$$

MORE HELP
See 080

If your calculator does not have the $\boxed{\sqrt[x]{y}}$ key, look for another key (or

key combination) that does the same thing: $\boxed{\sqrt[y]{x}}$, $\boxed{\text{inv}}$ $\boxed{y^x}$,

or $\boxed{\text{2ndF}}$ $\boxed{y^x}$.

ANOTHER WAY Since $\sqrt[3]{64} = 64^{\frac{1}{3}}$, you can press:

$$\boxed{6}\ \boxed{4}\ \boxed{y^x}\ \boxed{(}\ \boxed{1}\ \boxed{\div}\ \boxed{3}\ \boxed{)}\ \boxed{=}$$

---

083 **Perfect Powers**

The cube root of 64 is 4.

Any number that is the product of repeated whole-number factors is a **perfect power**.

MORE HELP
See 080

PERFECT POWERS	NOT PERFECT POWERS
$36 = 6^2$ So, 36 is a **perfect square**.	$20 = 4.472^2$ So, 20 is not a perfect square.
$27 = 3^3$ So, 27 is a **perfect cube**.	$5 = 2.466^3$ So, 5 is not a perfect cube.
$32 = 2^5$ So, 32 is a perfect power.	30 has no whole-number roots. So, 30 is not a perfect power.

EXAMPLES:

Use a calculator for nonperfect squares and nonperfect cubes.

Irrational Roots

If a whole number is not a perfect square, its square root is **irrational**. This means it cannot be represented as a ratio of integers. It is represented by a non-repeating decimal that does not end.

$$\sqrt{2} = 1.4142135\ldots \qquad \sqrt{11} = 3.3166247\ldots$$

MORE HELP
See 024–025, 082

A square root table or a calculator will give you an approximate root. So, when you calculate with a root that is not perfect, your answer will not be exact.

"..." means the decimal does not end.

Logarithms

Scientists use logarithms to measure the magnitude of earthquakes. A logarithm is an exponent. A common **logarithm** (or **log**) is just an exponent of 10. So, if someone asks for the log of 1000, they're asking for the exponent that would go with 10 to have a value of 1000. In other words, 10 raised to what power is equal to 1000? The answer is 3.

$$\log 1000 = 3$$ ◄——**The log of 1000 is 3 because 10^3 is 1000.**

Sometimes we use logs to indicate exponents of other numbers (called **bases**). So if someone asks for the log to the base 2 of 16, they're asking for the exponent that would go with 2 to have a value of 16. In other words, 2 raised to what power is equal to 16? The answer is 4.

$$\log_2 16 = 4$$ ◄——**The log to the base 2 of 16 is 4 because $2^4 = 16$.**

Any equation in exponential form can also be written with logarithms.

Exponential Form	Logarithmic Form
$3^2 = 9$	$\log_3 9 = 2$
$10^5 = 100{,}000$	$\log 100{,}000 = 5$
$2^{-5} = \frac{1}{32}$	$\log_2 \frac{1}{32} = {}^-5$

Write: $\log 1000 = 3$

Say: *The log of 1000 is 3* (because $10^3 = 1000$).

Write: $\log_2 16 = 4$

Say: *The log to the base 2 of 16 is 4* (because $2^4 = 16$).

Computation

Many people think computing is all there is to mathematics. It's not, but it's a big part of the mathematics you learn in elementary school, and it's a big part of the mathematics you'll use every day as you begin to take care of business. This section of the book reviews basic computing—addition, subtraction, multiplication, and division—with all the number types you have encountered so far in your educational career.

Addition

Addition may be the most important mathematical operation.

- Subtraction is the opposite of addition, so you can't subtract unless you can add.
- Multiplication is adding the same thing over and over again, so you can't multiply unless you understand addition.
- Division is the opposite of multiplication, so even division is related to addition!

Terms you may hear used in addition are **addend** and **sum**.

$$
\begin{array}{r}
14 \leftarrow \textbf{addend} \\
+42 \leftarrow \textbf{addend} \\
\hline
56 \leftarrow \textbf{sum}
\end{array}
$$

Mental Addition

Every day, you probably add using mental math. Sometimes, it's because the numbers are easy; at other times, paper or a calculator might not be helpful.

> $999 + 1 = ?$
> Why would it be faster to add this mentally than to use a calculator?

Making Tens to Add

 ONE WAY You can add using mental math by making groups of 10.

EXAMPLE 1: Five classes are going on a field trip. There are 16, 23, 17, 25, and 24 students in these classes. If all the students go, how many will be on the trip?

To solve the problem, you can add.

There are 8 tens.

$$
\begin{array}{r}
16 \\
23 \\
17 \\
25 \\
+24 \\
\hline
\end{array}
$$

6 + 4 = 10

7 + 3 = 10

There are 10 + 10 + 5 = 25 ones.

MORE HELP
See 217

8 tens plus 25 ones is 80 + 25, or 105.

So, 105 students will be on the trip.

With decimals, when adding to make tens, you can also make ones.

EXAMPLE 2: How much money did you earn doing odd jobs this week?

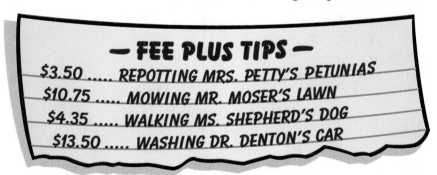

— FEE PLUS TIPS —
$3.50 ..... REPOTTING MRS. PETTY'S PETUNIAS
$10.75 ..... MOWING MR. MOSER'S LAWN
$4.35 ..... WALKING MS. SHEPHERD'S DOG
$13.50 ..... WASHING DR. DENTON'S CAR

To solve the problem, you can add.

Make tens.

4 + 3 + 3 = 10

$$
\begin{array}{r}
3.50 \\
10.75 \\
4.35 \\
+13.50 \\
\hline
\end{array}
$$

Make ones.

0.50 + 0.50 = 1

0.75 + 0.35 = 1 + 0.10

10 + 10 + 10 = 30

1 + 1 + 0.10 = **2.10**

30 + 2.10 = 32.10

So, you earned $32.10 this week.

Breaking Apart and Putting Together Numbers to Add

Sometimes you can take from one number and give the same amount to another to make it easier to add.

EXAMPLE 1: Rob buys speakers and a CD player. How much money does he spend for both items?

MORE HELP
See 213, 217

To solve the problem, you can add $189 + 95$.

STEREO DEPOT
1227 Main Street, Middleton
SALE!
2 STEREO SPEAKERS
$189⁰⁰
CD PLAYER
$95⁰⁰

It's easier to add 100 than 95. Take 5 from 189 and use it to make 95 into 100.

$$189 \ + \ 95$$
$$- \ 5 \qquad + \ 5$$
$$184 \ + \ 100 \ = \ 284$$

Since $189 + 95 = 184 + 100$, then $189 + 95 = 284$. Rob spends \$284.

EXAMPLE 2: Use mental math to add $7.7 + 9.4$.

$$7.7 \ + \ 9.4$$

It's easier to add 8 than 7.7. Take 0.3 from 9.4 and use it to make 7.7 into 8.

$$+ \ 0.3 \qquad - \ 0.3$$
$$8.0 \ + \ 9.1 \ = \ 17.1$$

Since $7.7 + 9.4 = 8.0 + 9.1$, then $7.7 + 9.4 = 17.1$.

EXAMPLE 3: Use mental math to add $25\frac{1}{2} + 14\frac{3}{4}$.

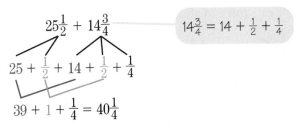

$$25\frac{1}{2} \ + \ 14\frac{3}{4}$$

$$14\frac{3}{4} = 14 + \frac{1}{2} + \frac{1}{4}$$

$$25 + \frac{1}{2} + 14 + \frac{1}{2} + \frac{1}{4}$$

$$39 + 1 + \frac{1}{4} = 40\frac{1}{4}$$

So, $25\frac{1}{2} + 14\frac{3}{4} = 40\frac{1}{4}$.

Grouping in Column Addition

Suppose you want to add a few numbers in your head. You can group them in the way that makes it easiest for you to add.

EXAMPLE 1: You're traveling through Arizona. It's 26 miles on Route 66 from Interstate 40 to Grand Canyon Caverns. It's 36 miles from the caverns on to Hackberry and 24 miles farther to where you can pick up I-40 again. If you want to take this scenic route along Route 66, how many miles will you travel? *(Source: AAA)*

Group the numbers in the way that makes adding easiest.

MORE HELP
See 093, 217

$$
\begin{array}{r} 26 \\ 36 \\ +24 \\ \hline \end{array}
\qquad
\begin{array}{r} 36 \\ 26 \\ +24 \\ \hline \end{array}
\qquad
\begin{array}{r} 36 \\ +50 \\ \hline 86 \end{array}
$$

> Just because 36 and 26 are the first two numbers, you don't need to start with them. If you think 26 and 24 are easier to add, do that first!

So, you will travel 86 miles on Route 66.

EXAMPLE 2: Use mental math to add $1.5 + 7.3 + 2.7 + 8.0$.

$$
\begin{array}{r} 1.5 \\ 7.3 \\ 2.7 \\ +8.0 \\ \hline \end{array}
\qquad
\begin{array}{r} 1.5 \\ 10.0 \\ +\ 8.0 \\ \hline 19.5 \end{array}
$$

> $7.3 + 2.7 = 10$, and tens are easy to add.

So, $1.5 + 7.3 + 2.7 + 8.0 = 19.5$.

EXAMPLE 3: Use mental math to add $8\frac{1}{4} + 1\frac{3}{4} + 42 + 4\frac{1}{2}$.

$$
\begin{array}{l} 8\frac{1}{4} \\ 1\frac{3}{4} \\ 42 \\ +\ 4\frac{1}{2} \end{array}
\qquad
8\frac{1}{4} + 1\frac{3}{4} = 10
$$

$$
10 + 42 = 52
$$
$$
52 + 4\frac{1}{2} = 56\frac{1}{2}
$$

So, $8\frac{1}{4} + 1\frac{3}{4} + 42 + 4\frac{1}{2} = 56\frac{1}{2}$.

A **sum** is the result of adding two or more numbers. Sometimes, you don't need an exact sum. In these cases you can estimate. You can also use estimates to check computation.

EXAMPLE 1: Is $2000 enough money to buy a computer and a printer? Do you need an exact sum or an estimate?

MORGAN'S COMPUTER CENTER SALE!

COMPUTERS!
COMPACT-3000
$1595⁰⁰

PRINTERS!
KWIKPRINT 750
$819⁰⁰

Since you only need to know whether 1595 + 819 is less than or equal to 2000, you do not need an exact sum. An estimate is enough.

$1595 + 819 \approx 1600 + 800$, and $1600 + 800 = 2400$.

$2000 is not enough money.

EXAMPLE 2: A grand piano weighs 610 pounds. An upright piano weighs 480 pounds. Could you put both pianos in an elevator with a weight limit of 1000 pounds?

Since the question only asks if 610 + 480 is greater than 1000, you don't need an exact sum. An estimate is enough.

$610 + 480 \approx 600 + 500$, and $600 + 500 = 1100$. That's over the weight limit.

EXAMPLE 3: You add 457,804 + 369,750 on your calculator. The display shows `627554`. To check this answer, you can estimate the sum and compare. If the number on the display is not close to your estimate, you should re-compute the sum.

Using Compatible Numbers to Estimate Sums

Compatible people are people who get along. **Compatible numbers** are numbers that get along, too. Number pairs that are easy to add are compatible.

Fives are compatible:

$75 + 25 = 100$ $15 + 35 = 50$

Tens and any numbers that make tens are compatible:

$30 + 40 = 70$ $33 + 47 = 80$

When estimating sums, you can replace a pair of addends with compatible numbers before adding.

EXAMPLE 1: A double-decker train car has 77 people on the top and 27 people on the bottom. About how many people are in the train car?

To solve the problem, you can estimate.

77 + 27

↓   ↓

75 + 25 = 100

> Use compatible numbers 75 and 25, which are easy to add and close to 77 and 27.

Since $75 + 25 = 100$, $77 + 27$ is a bit more than 100. There are about 100 people in the train car.

EXAMPLE 2: Use compatible numbers to estimate $14.18 + 4.83$.

14.18 + 4.83

↓   ↓

14   +   5 = 19

> Another pair of compatible numbers is 14.2 and 4.8. Can you think of others?

Since $14 + 5 = 19$, $14.18 + 4.83$ is about 19.

EXAMPLE 3: Use compatible numbers to estimate $92\frac{1}{8} + 34\frac{1}{5}$.

$92\frac{1}{8}$ + $34\frac{1}{5}$

↓   ↓

90   +   35 = 125

Since $90 + 35 = 125$, $92\frac{1}{8} + 34\frac{1}{5}$ is about 125.

Front-End Estimation of Sums

CASE 1 Another way to estimate sums is to add the front digits.

EXAMPLE 1: Paul's father takes a lot of trips for business. He flew 8450 miles during April, 9816 miles during May, and 8640 miles during June. As a Frequent Flyer member, he earns a free airplane ticket every 25,000 miles. Did these trips earn him a free ticket?

To solve the problem, you can estimate. Using front-end estimation, add the values of the digits in the front place (thousands).

> Front-end estimation always gives a sum *less* than the actual sum.

$$
\begin{array}{ccc}
8450 & \longrightarrow & 8000 \\
9816 & \longrightarrow & 9000 \\
+8640 & \longrightarrow & +8000 \\
\hline
& & 25{,}000
\end{array}
$$

Front-end estimation shows that Paul's father flew at least 25,000 miles. He earned a free ticket.

CASE 2 You can still use front-end estimation when the addends have a different number of digits.

EXAMPLE 2: Estimate $2106 + 742 + 895 + 309$.

One of the front digits is in the thousands place. The others are in the hundreds place. To estimate the sum, you can use the thousands and hundreds digits. Add the values of the digits in those two places.

$$
\begin{array}{ccc}
2106 & \longrightarrow & 2100 \\
742 & \longrightarrow & 700 \\
895 & \longrightarrow & 800 \\
+\,309 & \longrightarrow & +\,300 \\
\hline
& & 3900
\end{array}
$$

The sum is greater than 3900.

Adjusting Front-End Estimation of Sums

You can adjust front-end estimates so they are closer to the actual sum.

EXAMPLE 1: The theater sells 1721, 1278, 1549, and 1454 tickets to magic shows. About how many tickets are sold?

❶ ADD THE VALUES OF THE FRONT DIGITS.	❷ ESTIMATE THE SUM OF THE REMAINING DIGITS. YOU CAN MAKE THOUSANDS OR USE COMPATIBLE NUMBERS.	❸ COMBINE YOUR RESULTS.
1721 ⟶ 1000 1278 ⟶ 1000 1549 ⟶ 1000 +1454 ⟶ +1000 ———— 4000	1721 ⟩ about 1000 1278 1549 ⟩ about 1000 +1454 ———— about 2000	4000 ←front-end estimate +2000 ←adjustment ———— 6000 ←adjusted estimate

About 6000 tickets were sold.

EXAMPLE 2: Estimate $4.53 + 6.49 + 8.02 + 3.15$.

❶ ADD THE VALUES OF THE FRONT DIGITS.	❷ ESTIMATE THE SUM OF THE REMAINING DIGITS.	❸ COMBINE YOUR RESULTS.
4.53 ⟶ 4 6.49 ⟶ 6 8.02 ⟶ 8 +3.15 ⟶ +3 ———— 21	4.53 ⟩ about 1 6.49 8.02 ⟩ about 0 +3.15 ———— about 1	21 ←front-end estimate + 1 ←adjustment ———— 22 ←adjusted estimate

So, $4.53 + 6.49 + 8.02 + 3.15$ is about 22.

EXAMPLE 3: Estimate $3\frac{3}{4} + 7\frac{1}{8} + 4\frac{15}{16} + 6\frac{7}{8}$.

❶ ADD THE VALUES OF THE FRONT DIGITS.	❷ ESTIMATE THE SUM OF THE FRACTIONS.	❸ COMBINE YOUR RESULTS.
$3\frac{3}{4}$ ⟶ 3 $7\frac{1}{8}$ ⟶ 7 $4\frac{15}{16}$ ⟶ 4 $+6\frac{7}{8}$ ⟶ +6 ———— 20	$3\frac{3}{4}$ ⟩ about 1 $7\frac{1}{8}$ $4\frac{15}{16}$ ⟩ about 2 $+6\frac{7}{8}$ ———— about 3	20 ←front-end estimate + 3 ←adjustment ———— 23 ←adjusted estimate

So, $3\frac{3}{4} + 7\frac{1}{8} + 4\frac{15}{16} + 6\frac{7}{8}$ is about 23.

096 Adding with Whole Numbers

The great thing about adding whole numbers is that no matter how big they get, you don't have to learn anything new to add them. If you know how to add ones and tens, you also know how to add hundreds, thousands, hundred thousands, and even billions. That's because of **place value**. When you line numbers up and add them place by place, what you do in each place is the same. It's just as easy to add two digits in the millions place as it is to add two digits in the ones place.

097 Adding Without Regrouping

EXAMPLE: Cindy gets 1136 people to sign a petition. Robert gets 853 people to sign the same petition. How many people do they get to sign?

MORE HELP
See 005

To solve the problem, add 1136 + 853.

 ONE WAY You can add this way.

You can use graph paper to keep places lined up nicely.

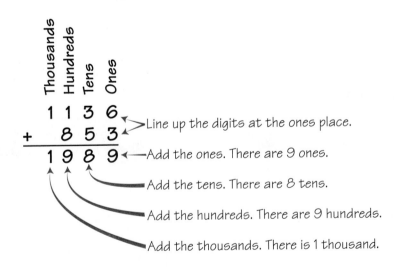

Thousands	Hundreds	Tens	Ones

```
  1 1 3 6
+   8 5 3
  1 9 8 9
```

> Line up the digits at the ones place.

Add the ones. There are 9 ones.

Add the tens. There are 8 tens.

Add the hundreds. There are 9 hundreds.

Add the thousands. There is 1 thousand.

You can also write the addends in expanded form and add them.

$$\begin{array}{r} 1136 \\ + \ 853 \\ \hline \end{array} \longrightarrow \begin{array}{r} 1100 + 30 + 6 \\ + \ 800 + 50 + 3 \\ \hline 1900 + 80 + 9 = 1989 \end{array}$$

Either way, Cindy and Robert got 1989 people to sign the petition.

MATH ALERT Regrouping to Add

098

Sometimes you have too many digits to squeeze into the one-digit space for each place value. Adding 8 tens to 7 tens gives you 15 tens, but the tens place only has room for one digit. There are some creative ways to think about numbers that will help you compute in these situations.

EXAMPLE 1: How can you show 15 tens so that there is just one digit in each place?

You started with 15 tens.   15 tens is the same as 1 hundred + 5 tens.

You now have 1 hundred 5 tens, or 150.

EXAMPLE 2: How can you show 11 tens 14 ones so that there is just one digit in each place?

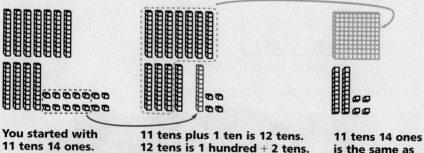

You started with 11 tens 14 ones.   11 tens plus 1 ten is 12 tens. 12 tens is 1 hundred + 2 tens.   11 tens 14 ones is the same as 1 hundred + 2 tens + 4 ones.

You now have 1 hundred 2 tens 4 ones, or 124.

Adding with Regrouping

Sometimes when you add, the sum in a place has 2 digits or more. You can use place value to regroup the sum so that there is just one digit in each place.

EXAMPLE: A caravan of buses brings 564 people to see Elvis Presley's home, Graceland. There are already 392 people waiting for the gates to open. How many people are there?

To solve the problem, add 564 + 392.

 You can add this way.

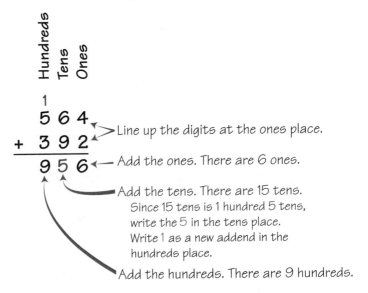

Hundreds Tens Ones

```
        1
      5 6 4
    + 3 9 2
      9 5 6
```

Line up the digits at the ones place.

Add the ones. There are 6 ones.

Add the tens. There are 15 tens. Since 15 tens is 1 hundred 5 tens, write the 5 in the tens place. Write 1 as a new addend in the hundreds place.

Add the hundreds. There are 9 hundreds.

You can also add by using the expanded form and then adding.

$$
\begin{aligned}
564 &\longrightarrow\ \ 500 + 60 + 4 \\
+392 &\longrightarrow +300 + 90 + 2 \\
&\qquad\ \ 800 + 150 + 6 = 956
\end{aligned}
$$

Either way, there are 956 people waiting to get into Graceland.

Checking Addition

No matter how good you are at addition, it never hurts to check your answer. Checking your computation is a good way to be sure that your mind didn't wander as you wrote the numbers, or that your fingers didn't hit the wrong calculator keys.

 Check your addition by using subtraction. This is because subtraction is the inverse of addition. If you start with a sum and subtract one of the numbers you added, the answer should be the other number you added. If it isn't, you should try doing the addition again.

EXAMPLE 1: Does 8692 + 7435 = 16,127? Use subtraction to check.

MORE HELP
See 125–130

Since completing the subtraction gives the other addend, the addition is correct.

You can also check your addition by adding again in a different order.

EXAMPLE 2: Does 3964 + 872 = 4736? Add in a different order to check.

$$
\begin{array}{r}
3964 \\
+\ 872 \\
\hline
4736
\end{array}
\quad \text{Add down.}
\qquad
\begin{array}{r}
3964 \\
+\ 872 \\
\hline
4836
\end{array}
\quad \text{Add up.}
$$

$\neq$

When adding in a different order gives you a different sum, you should do the addition again.

Column Addition

Sometimes you need to add more than two numbers. You can still add place by place and regroup when necessary just as you do when you have only two addends.

The list at the right shows the number of tornadoes that occurred in these states between 1950 and 1995. *(Source: NCDC, NOAA)*

How many tornadoes occurred in these six Western states between 1950 and 1995?

To solve the problem, add
$159 + 221 + 123 + 49 + 48 + 55$.

STATE	NUMBER OF TORNADOES
Arizona	159
California	221
Idaho	123
Nevada	49
Oregon	48
Washington	55

MORE HELP
See 089, 090, 093

```
        Hundreds
         Tens
          Ones

      2 3
    1 5 9
    2 2 1
    1 2 3
      4 9
      4 8
  +   5 5
    6 5 5
```

Line up the digits at the ones place.
Add the ones. There are 35 ones.
    Since 35 ones is 3 tens 5 ones, write the 5 in the ones place.
    Write the 3 as a new addend in the tens place.

Add the tens. There are 25 tens.
    Since 25 tens is 2 hundreds 5 tens, write the 5 in the tens place.
    Write the 2 as a new addend in the hundreds place.

Add the hundreds. There are 6 hundreds.

There were 655 tornadoes in these six states between 1950 and 1995.

Over 600 tornadoes sounds like a lot, but Texas alone had over 5000 tornadoes in the same years!

Adding with Decimals

If you know how to add whole numbers, you also know how to add decimals. With both decimals and whole numbers, there are a few important things to remember. Pay attention to place value, add in each place, and regroup when needed. You still need to line up the ones digits. This means the decimal points line up, too.

EXAMPLE: Add $7.983 + 3.450 + 9.816 + 7.000$.

MORE HELP
See 012–014, 096–101

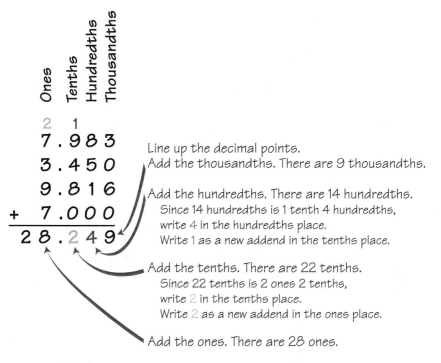

Line up the decimal points.
Add the thousandths. There are 9 thousandths.

Add the hundredths. There are 14 hundredths.
Since 14 hundredths is 1 tenth 4 hundredths, write 4 in the hundredths place.
Write 1 as a new addend in the tenths place.

Add the tenths. There are 22 tenths.
Since 22 tenths is 2 ones 2 tenths, write 2 in the tenths place.
Write 2 as a new addend in the ones place.

Add the ones. There are 28 ones.

So, $7.983 + 3.450 + 9.816 + 7.000 = 28.249$.

It is also helpful to estimate the sum when adding decimals to make sure your answer is reasonable.

$$
\begin{array}{rcr}
7.983 & \approx & 8 \\
3.450 & \approx & 3 \\
9.816 & \approx & 10 \\
+7.000 & \approx & +\ 7 \\
\hline
28.249 & & 28
\end{array}
$$

$\approx$ means "is approximately equal to."

So, 28.249 is a reasonable answer.

MATH ALERT What to Do with a Ragged Right Side

Sometimes you line up the ones and decimal points and the right side of your problem looks ragged. To make it easier to keep track while you compute, you can give all your decimals the same number of places by filling in zeros.

MORE HELP
See 017

EXAMPLE: Write equivalent decimals for 4, 3.5, 8.02, and 1.333 so all four numbers have the same number of places.

The number in this group with the greatest number of decimal places is one and three hundred thirty-three thousandths. You need to write 4, 3.5, and 8.02 as decimals in thousandths.

4	is 4 *and* 0 tenths, 0 hundredths, 0 thousandths	4.000
3.5	is 3 *and* 5 tenths, 0 hundredths, 0 thousandths	3.500
8.02	is 8 *and* 2 hundredths, 0 thousandths	8.020
<u>1.333</u>	is one and three hundred thirty-three thousandths	<u>+1.333</u>
		16.853

Adding with Fractions

You can't add fractions the way you add whole numbers. That makes sense because digits in fractions have different meanings than they do in whole numbers.

MORE HELP
See 028–031

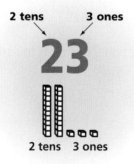

2 tens   3 ones

23

2 tens   3 ones

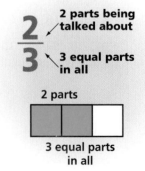

$\dfrac{2}{3}$

2 parts being talked about

3 equal parts in all

2 parts

3 equal parts in all

MATH ALERT Add ONLY the Numerators

Adding fractions is a lot like adding oranges or paper cups. When you add 4 oranges to 3 oranges you have 7 oranges—the *number* of things changes $(3 + 4 = 7)$, but the *kind* of thing (oranges) doesn't.

This works when you add fractions, too. When you add 3 eighths and 4 eighths, you have 7 eighths—the *number* of things changes $(3 + 4 = 7)$, but the *kind* of thing (eighths) doesn't. One nice thing about fractions is that if the kind of thing doesn't start out the same (say, fourths and sixths), you can change them to things (twelfths) that *are* the same.

Adding Fractions with Common Denominators

How can you add two fractions? If the fractions have the same denominator, just add the numerators and use the same denominator.

EXAMPLE 1: The Art Club is painting 8 equal-size panels of a very large mural. So far, the 3 left-most panels and the right-most panel are on the wall. How much of the mural is on the wall?

Since there are 8 equal-size panels, each panel is one eighth ($\frac{1}{8}$) of the mural. To solve the problem, you can add $\frac{3}{8} + \frac{1}{8}$.

 ONE WAY You can understand the addition by drawing a picture.

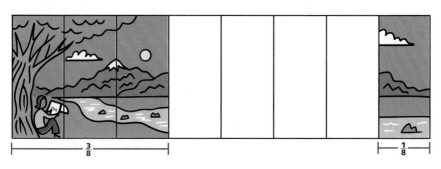

$\frac{3}{8}$ $\frac{1}{8}$

$\frac{3}{8} + \frac{1}{8} = \frac{4}{8}$, or $\frac{1}{2}$

MORE ▷

MORE HELP
See 037

 Here's how to add $\frac{3}{8} + \frac{1}{8}$ without drawing a picture.

❶ THE FRACTIONS HAVE THE SAME DENOMINATOR. WRITE THAT COMMON DENOMINATOR.	❷ ADD THE NUMERATORS.	❸ WRITE THE SUM IN SIMPLEST FORM.
$\frac{3}{8} + \frac{1}{8} = \frac{}{8}$	$\frac{3}{8} + \frac{1}{8} = \frac{4}{8}$	$\frac{4}{8} = \frac{4 \div 4}{8 \div 4} = \frac{1}{2}$

Either way, $\frac{4}{8}$, or $\frac{1}{2}$, of the painting is on the wall.

EXAMPLE 2: Patricia bakes pies to sell at her pie stand. She cuts each into 6 equal pieces. Patricia sells 5 pieces to a family. She sells 2 pieces to a truck driver. How many pies has she sold so far?

❶ THE FRACTIONS HAVE THE SAME DENOMINATOR. WRITE THAT COMMON DENOMINATOR.	❷ ADD THE NUMERATORS.	❸ WRITE THE SUM IN SIMPLEST FORM, AS A MIXED NUMBER IF YOU CAN.
$\frac{5}{6} + \frac{2}{6} = \frac{}{6}$	$\frac{5}{6} + \frac{2}{6} = \frac{7}{6}$	$\frac{7}{6} = \frac{6}{6} + \frac{1}{6} = 1\frac{1}{6}$

Patricia has sold $\frac{7}{6}$, or $1\frac{1}{6}$, pies so far.

Adding Fractions with Unlike Denominators

To add fractions that have unlike denominators, such as $\frac{5}{8}$ and $\frac{1}{2}$, rewrite them as fractions with a common denominator.

MORE HELP
See 038–040

EXAMPLE: Maria needs $\frac{5}{8}$ yard of ribbon for the pocket trim on the dress she's making. She needs $\frac{1}{2}$ yard of the same ribbon for the cuffs. How much ribbon does she need?

To solve this problem, you can add $\frac{5}{8} + \frac{1}{2}$.

❶ FIND EQUIVALENT FRACTIONS WITH A COMMON DENOMINATOR.	❷ ADD THE FRACTIONS.	❸ WRITE THE SUM IN SIMPLEST FORM, AS A MIXED NUMBER IF YOU CAN.
$\frac{5}{8} + \frac{1}{2}$ ↓ ↓ $\frac{5}{8} + \frac{4}{8}$	$\frac{5}{8} + \frac{4}{8} = \frac{9}{8}$	$\frac{9}{8} = 1\frac{1}{8}$

Maria needs $1\frac{1}{8}$ yards of ribbon.

Adding with Negative Numbers

What gets smaller when you add more to it? A hole.

MORE HELP
See 050

A number can get smaller when you add a negative number to it. It's usually best to think about signs (⁺ and ⁻) on a number as direction symbols for a number line: ⁺ means right, or positive, and ⁻ means left, or negative. Just keep in mind that the direction symbol is part of the number itself.

One way to think about adding is with a number line.

EXAMPLE 1: Show 1 + 4 on a number line.

1. Place the first addend above the number line. This is your starting point.

2. The second addend is positive. Draw an arrow as long as the second addend in the positive direction.

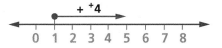

Your arrow ends at the sum. So, 1 + 4 = 5.

MORE ▷

EXAMPLE 2: Show ⁻3 + ⁻6 on a number line.

1. Place the first addend above the number line. This is your starting point.

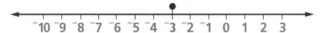

2. The second addend is negative. Draw an arrow as long as the second addend in the negative direction.

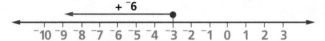

Your arrow ends at the sum. So, ⁻3 + ⁻6 = ⁻9.

EXAMPLE 3: Show ⁻1.2 + 3.8 on a number line.

1. Place the first addend above the number line. This is your starting point.

2. The second addend is positive. Draw an arrow as long as the second addend in the positive direction.

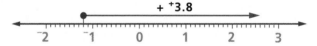

Your arrow ends at the sum. So, ⁻1.2 + 3.8 = 2.6.

EXAMPLE 4: Show $4\frac{1}{2}$ + ⁻$2\frac{1}{4}$ on a number line.

1. Place the first addend above the number line. This is your starting point.

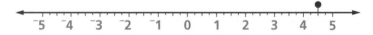

2. The second addend is negative. Draw an arrow as long as the second addend in the negative direction.

Your arrow ends at the sum. So, $4\frac{1}{2}$ + ⁻$2\frac{1}{4}$ = $2\frac{1}{4}$.

Shortcut

You can also use absolute value and follow some simple rules to add with signed numbers.

Signs on Addends	Rule	Examples
To add positive + positive	Add absolute values. The sum is positive.	$\|^+64\| + \|^+72\|$ $\downarrow$ $64 + 72 = 136$ $\downarrow$ $^+64 + {}^+72 = {}^+136$
To add negative + positive or positive + negative	Subtract the smaller absolute value from the greater. The sum has the sign of the number with the greater absolute value.	$\|^+64\| + \|^-72\|$ $\downarrow$ $72 - 64 = 8$ $\downarrow$ $^+64 + {}^-72 = {}^-8$
To add negative + negative	Add absolute values. The sum is negative.	$\|^-64\| + \|^-72\|$ $\downarrow$ $64 + 72 = 136$ $\downarrow$ $^-64 + {}^-72 = {}^-136$

$|72| = 72$
$|^-72| = 72$

You can use a calculator to add signed numbers or decimals.

Locate these keys on your calculator:

- +
- ▪ =
- ▪ .
- ▪ +/−

EXAMPLE 1: Use a calculator to add 5987 + 6545.

| 5 | 9 | 8 | 7 | + | 6 | 5 | 4 | 5 | = | *12532.* |

EXAMPLE 2: Use a calculator to add 3.73 + 46.298.

| 3 | . | 7 | 3 | + | 4 | 6 | . | 2 | 9 | 8 | = | *50.028* |

EXAMPLE 3: Use a calculator to add 437 + ⁻1764.

| 4 | 3 | 7 | + | 1 | 7 | 6 | 4 | +/− | = | *-1327.* |

Special Keys

Some calculators have special keys that you can use to work with fractions. For example:

■ [/] makes fractions.

  To show $\frac{6}{8}$, press [6] [/] [8]   6/8 .

■ [Simp] simplifies fractions.

  To simplify $\frac{6}{8}$, press [6] [/] [8] [Simp] [=]   3/4 .

■ [Ab/c] shows a fraction as a mixed number.

  To show $\frac{9}{7}$ as a mixed number, press [9] [/] [7] [Ab/c]   1 u 2/7 .

■ [Unit] is used to enter a mixed number.

  To show $1\frac{3}{8}$, press [1] [Unit] [3] [/] [8]   1 u 3/8 .

MORE HELP
See 207–209

■ [( ] [ )] Grouping symbols are used to be sure of order of operations.

MATH ALERT Your Calculator May Be Different

Your calculator may have different keys that do the same thing as the keys above. Check the directions for your calculator.

Adding Fractions with Fraction Keys

EXAMPLE 1: Add $\frac{1}{4} + \frac{1}{12}$.

[Simp] [=]   2/6

[Simp] [=]   1/3

If you are not sure whether the answer is in simplest form, press [Simp] and [=]. If the fraction does not change, it is in simplest form.

EXAMPLE 2: Add $1\frac{5}{8} + \frac{3}{4}$.

[Ab/c]   2 u 3/8

Use [Ab/c] when the fraction part of the answer is greater than 1.

113   **Adding Fractions Without Fraction Keys**

When you divide the numerator by the denominator, you're finding a decimal equivalent for the fraction.

Even if your calculator doesn't have special keys for fractions, you can still use it to add fractions. Just enter each fraction as the numerator divided by the denominator and then add. Your answer will be a decimal. If your answer needs to be in fraction form, you may be better off not using your calculator this way.

EXAMPLE 1: Add $\frac{1}{4} + \frac{3}{8}$.

$$(\quad 1 \quad \div \quad 4 \quad) \quad + \quad (\quad 3 \quad \div \quad 8 \quad) \quad = \quad \boxed{0.625}$$

MORE HELP
See 023

EXAMPLE 2: Add $\frac{4}{5} + \frac{1}{3}$.

$$(\quad 4 \quad \div \quad 5 \quad) \quad + \quad (\quad 1 \quad \div \quad 3 \quad) \quad = \quad \boxed{1.1333333}$$

Since the decimal is a repeating decimal, write the number as $1.1\overline{3}$.

114   **MATH ALERT Do Your Calculator Answers Make Sense?**

Always check the answer on your calculator display to see that it makes sense. It's easy to accidentally press a wrong key. If you estimate first, you can tell when the answer is not reasonable.

Subtraction

You use subtraction for several different reasons:

- If you want to take away one quantity from another, you subtract.

  You have $25. You spend $13. Subtract to find what you have left.

- If you want to compare one quantity to another, you subtract.

  Your book bag weighs $14\frac{1}{2}$ pounds. Roy's weighs $9\frac{3}{4}$ pounds. Subtract to see how much more weight you carry around all day.

- If you know part of a quantity and the whole quantity but need to know the other part, you subtract.

  Your little brother can find 16 of his marbles. The set you bought him contained 50 marbles. Subtract to find out how many are rolling around under the furniture, waiting to sneak out and trip you when you least expect it.

Three terms you may hear used in subtraction are **minuend**, **subtrahend**, and **difference**.

$$
\begin{array}{r}
53 \quad \longleftarrow \textbf{minuend} \\
-48 \quad \longleftarrow \textbf{subtrahend} \\
\hline
56 \quad \longleftarrow \textbf{difference}
\end{array}
$$

You subtract using mental math all the time. For instance, when you think about how much money you will have left, when you try to figure out how many pages you have left to read, or when you want to know how many runs your team needs to score, you use mental math.

117

Subtracting in Parts

One way to subtract in your head is to subtract a number in parts.

EXAMPLE 1: You have 64¢. You want to buy a banana for 26¢. How much money will you have left?

To solve the problem, you can subtract $64 - 26$.

$$64 - 20 = 44 \quad \textbf{Think of 26 as 20 + 6.}$$

$$44 - 4 = 40 \quad \textbf{Think of 6 as 4 + 2.}$$

$$40 - 2 = 38$$

You will have 38¢ left.

EXAMPLE 2: Use mental math to subtract $36.5 - 28.3$.

$$36.5 - 20 = 16.5 \quad \textbf{Think of 28.3 as 20 + 8 + 0.3.}$$

$$16.5 - 8 = 8.5$$

$$8.5 - 0.3 = 8.2$$

So, $36.5 - 28.3 = 8.2$.

EXAMPLE 3: Use mental math to subtract $125\frac{3}{4} - 83\frac{1}{2}$.

You can subtract in parts.

$125\frac{3}{4} - 80 = 45\frac{3}{4}$ **Think of $83\frac{1}{2}$ as 80 + 3 + $\frac{1}{2}$.**

$\quad\quad 45\frac{3}{4} - 3 = 42\frac{3}{4}$

$\quad\quad\quad\quad 42\frac{3}{4} - \frac{1}{2} = 42\frac{1}{4}$

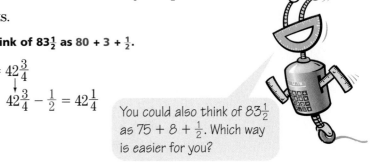

You could also think of $83\frac{1}{2}$ as 75 + 8 + $\frac{1}{2}$. Which way is easier for you?

So, $125\frac{3}{4} - 83\frac{1}{2} = 42\frac{1}{4}$.

Counting Up to Subtract

Sometimes it's easier to work backward from the number you're subtracting to the number you started with.

EXAMPLE 1: Your dental appointment is the 21st of this month. Today is the 9th. How many days before you need to put on your best smile?
Start at 9:

$9 + 1 = 10$ **1 day until the 10th**

$\quad\quad 10 + 10 = 20$ **another 10 days until the 20th**

$\quad\quad\quad\quad 20 + 1 = 21$ **1 more day until the 21st**

$$\text{+1} \quad\quad\quad\quad \text{+ 10} \quad\quad\quad\quad \text{+1}$$

9 10 11 12 13 14 15 16 17 18 19 20 21

$1 + 10 + 1 = 12$

Your dental appointment is in 12 days.

EXAMPLE 2: Count up to subtract $138.02 - 87.45$.

Start at 87.45:

$87.45 + 0.55 = 88$

$\quad\quad 88 + 50 = 138$

$\quad\quad\quad\quad 138 + 0.02 = 138.02$

$0.55 + 50 + 0.02 = 50.57$

So, $138.02 - 87.45 = 50.57$.

MORE ▶

EXAMPLE 3: Count up to subtract $44\frac{3}{8} - 26\frac{5}{8}$.

Start at $26\frac{5}{8}$:

$$26\frac{5}{8} + \frac{3}{8} = 27$$
$$\downarrow$$
$$27 + 3 = 30$$
$$\downarrow$$
$$30 + 14 = 44$$
$$\downarrow$$
$$44 + \frac{3}{8} = 44\frac{3}{8}$$

$$\frac{3}{8} + 3 + 14 + \frac{3}{8} = 17\frac{6}{8}$$

So, $44\frac{3}{8} - 26\frac{5}{8} = 17\frac{6}{8}$, or $17\frac{3}{4}$.

Finding Easier Numbers to Subtract

The pattern below shows a great way to make mental subtraction easy.

14 – 10 = 4

13 – 9 = 4

12 – 8 = 4

8 9 10 11 12 13 14 15 16 17 18 19 20 21

That makes sense! If you move the left and right endpoints of the bar the same distance to the right or left, the bar will stay the same length!

EXAMPLE: Cereal companies donate computers to schools in exchange for box tops. Your school has collected 98 box tops. You need 150 box tops to get the computer you want. How many box tops do you still need to collect?

MORE HELP
See 238

To solve this problem, you need to subtract 150 – 98.

$$150 \quad - \quad 98$$
$$\downarrow \qquad\qquad \downarrow$$
$$+\,2 \qquad\quad +\,2$$
$$\downarrow \qquad\qquad \downarrow$$
$$152 \quad - \quad 100 = 52$$

98 is hard to subtract. If you add 2 to each side, you can subtract 100.

You still need to collect 52 box tops.

Estimating Differences   120

When subtracting, if you do not need an exact answer, you can estimate the difference. You can also use estimates to check computation.

EXAMPLE 1: You have $7.00 with you. If you buy a burger meal for $5.19, can you pay the $2.50 subway fare to get home? Since you only need to know whether $7.00 − $5.19 is greater than or equal to $2.50, you don't need to find the exact difference. An estimate is enough.

$7.00 − $5.00 = $2.00   You don't have enough money.

EXAMPLE 2: You want to find 73,532 – 26,096. Your calculator display shows ⎢ 57436. ⎥. You can estimate to check the reasonableness of your answer. If the number in the display is not close to your estimate, you should re-compute the difference.

Using Compatible Numbers to   121
Estimate Differences

Compatible numbers are numbers that work well together. Numbers with the same final digit or digits are compatible.

73 − 33 = 40   365 − 165 = 200

When estimating differences, you can use compatible numbers that are close to the original numbers. Tens and hundreds are easy to subtract.

100 − 70 = 30   400 − 200 = 200

EXAMPLE 1: 105 kids enter the softball tournament. By the end of 3 hours, 47 kids are out. About how many kids are still in?

To solve the problem, you can estimate 105 − 47
To estimate, find compatible numbers close to 105 and 47.

105 − 47
 ↓   ↓
105 − 45

> 45 is close to 47 and is easy to subtract from 105.
> 105 − 47 is close to 105 − 45.

Since 105 − 45 = 60, about 60 kids are still playing softball.

MORE ▷

EXAMPLE 2: Use compatible numbers to estimate 89.45 − 42.006.

89.45 − 42.006
↓ ↓
90 − 40

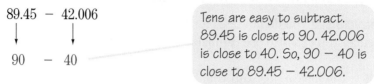

Tens are easy to subtract. 89.45 is close to 90. 42.006 is close to 40. So, 90 − 40 is close to 89.45 − 42.006.

Since 90 − 40 = 50, 89.45 − 42.006 is about 50.

MORE HELP
See 032

EXAMPLE 3: Use compatible numbers to estimate $1\frac{4}{5} - \frac{16}{19}$.

$1\frac{4}{5} - \frac{16}{19}$
↓ ↓
2 − 1

To estimate with fractions, use your benchmarks: 0, $\frac{1}{2}$, and 1.

Since 2 − 1 = 1, $1\frac{4}{5} - \frac{16}{19}$ is close to 1.

122 Front-End Estimation of Differences

One way to estimate differences is to subtract the front digits.

EXAMPLE: Your high score on a computer game is 14,661. Your mom's high score is 12,843. About how much does her score need to improve so she can be as good as you are?

To solve the problem, you can estimate 14,661 − 12,843

To use front-end estimation, you can subtract the values of the digits in the front place (ten thousands), but that won't tell you much.

$$
\begin{array}{r}
14{,}661 \longrightarrow 10{,}000 \\
-12{,}843 \longrightarrow -10{,}000 \\
\hline
0
\end{array}
$$

If you need a little closer estimate, you can subtract the values of the digits in the front two places.

$$
\begin{array}{r}
14{,}661 \longrightarrow 14{,}000 \\
-12{,}843 \longrightarrow -12{,}000 \\
\hline
2{,}000
\end{array}
$$

Your mother needs to improve her score by about 2000 points to be as good as you are.

MATH ALERT Different Numbers of Digits

Sometimes you might have numbers with different numbers of digits. You can still use front-end estimation.

EXAMPLE: Estimate 36,515 − 8,274.

One of the front digits is in the ten-thousands place. The other is in the thousands place. To estimate the difference, you can use the front *two* digits, the ten thousands and the thousands. Subtract the values of the digits in those two places.

$$\begin{array}{r} 36{,}515 \longrightarrow \quad 36{,}000 \\ -\ 8{,}274 \longrightarrow -\ 8{,}000 \\ \hline 28{,}000 \end{array}$$

So, 36,515 − 8,274 is about 28,000.

Adjusting Front-End Estimation of Differences

You can adjust front-end estimates to be closer to the exact answer.

EXAMPLE 1: About how many more residents lived in Todd County than in Tripp County in 1999? *(Source: U.S. Bureau of the Census)*

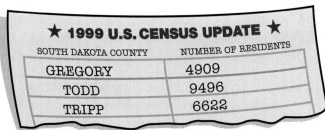

★ **1999 U.S. CENSUS UPDATE** ★

SOUTH DAKOTA COUNTY	NUMBER OF RESIDENTS
GREGORY	4909
TODD	9496
TRIPP	6622

To answer the question, you can estimate 9496 − 6622.

❶ SUBTRACT THE VALUES OF THE FRONT DIGITS.	❷ ADJUST YOUR ESTIMATE BY COMPARING THE SECOND DIGITS.
$\begin{array}{r} 9496 \longrightarrow 9000 \\ -6622 \longrightarrow -6000 \\ \hline 3000 \end{array}$	$\begin{array}{r} 9496 \\ -6622 \quad 4 < 6 \end{array}$ **The exact answer is less than 3000 because you'd need to regroup to subtract 6 hundreds.**

In 1999, Tripp County had about 3000 fewer residents than Todd County.

MORE ▷

EXAMPLE 2: Adjust front-end estimation to estimate $5.87 – $2.29.

❶ SUBTRACT THE VALUES OF THE FRONT DIGITS.	❷ ADJUST YOUR ESTIMATE BY COMPARING THE SECOND DIGITS.
$\begin{array}{r} 5.87 \longrightarrow 5 \\ -2.29 \longrightarrow -2 \\ \hline 3 \end{array}$	$\begin{array}{r} 5.87 \\ -2.29 \quad 8 > 2 \\ \hline \end{array}$ **The actual answer is greater than $3.00.**

So, $5.87 – $2.29 is greater than $3.00.

EXAMPLE 3: Adjust front-end estimation to estimate $8\frac{3}{32} - 6\frac{1}{2}$.

❶ SUBTRACT THE VALUES OF THE FRONT DIGITS.	❷ ADJUST YOUR ESTIMATE BY COMPARING THE FRACTIONS.
$\begin{array}{r} 8\frac{3}{32} \longrightarrow 8 \\ -6\frac{1}{2} \longrightarrow -6 \\ \hline 2 \end{array}$	$\begin{array}{r} 8\frac{3}{32} \\ -6\frac{1}{2} \quad \frac{3}{32} < \frac{1}{2} \\ \hline \end{array}$ **The actual answer is less than 2 because you'd have to regroup if you subtracted the fractions.**

So, $8\frac{3}{32} - 6\frac{1}{2}$ is less than 2.

125) Subtracting with Whole Numbers

If you know how to subtract tens and ones you also know how to subtract hundreds, thousands, and even billions. That's because of **place value**. When you line numbers up and subtract them place by place, what you do in each place is the same. It's just as easy to subtract two digits in the millions place as it is to subtract two digits in the ones place.

$5 - 2 = 3$

$50 - 20 = 30$

$500 - 200 = 300$

$5000 - 2000 = 3000$

$50,000 - 20,000 = 30,000$

Subtracting Without Regrouping

To subtract two whole numbers, all you have to do is begin at the ones place and subtract them one place at a time. If you are writing the two numbers yourself, remember to line them up at the ones place.

EXAMPLE: A group called "Friends of the Park" raised $2984. The group spent $612 on new plants. How much money does the group have left?

To solve the problem, subtract 2984 − 612

ONE WAY You can subtract this way.

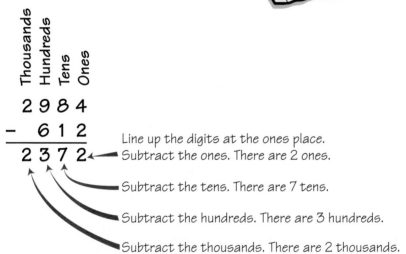

```
Thousands
   Hundreds
      Tens
         Ones

   2 9 8 4
 −   6 1 2
   2 3 7 2
```

Line up the digits at the ones place.
Subtract the ones. There are 2 ones.

Subtract the tens. There are 7 tens.

Subtract the hundreds. There are 3 hundreds.

Subtract the thousands. There are 2 thousands.

ANOTHER WAY Sometimes it's easier to use expanded form, find the differences, then add them.

MORE HELP
See 219

```
 2984 ⟶     2000 + 900 + 80  + 4
− 612 ⟶   − (0 + 600 + 10  + 2)
            2000 + 300 + 70  + 2  = 2372
```

Either way, the group has $2372 left.

MATH ALERT Regrouping to Subtract

Sometimes the digit you're subtracting is too big. Think about subtracting 4 tens from 3 tens. If the entire number is big enough, you can think about it in creative ways to help you subtract.

EXAMPLE 1: How can you regroup 434 so you can subtract 4 tens from it?

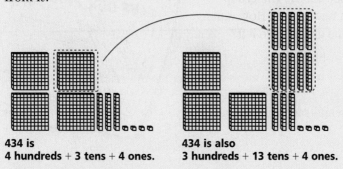

**434 is
4 hundreds + 3 tens + 4 ones.**

**434 is also
3 hundreds + 13 tens + 4 ones.**

Your problem would be set up like this:

$$
\begin{array}{r}
434 \longrightarrow 3^{1}34 \\
-\ 40 \longrightarrow -\ 40
\end{array}
$$

EXAMPLE 2: How can you regroup 675 so that you can subtract 289 from it?

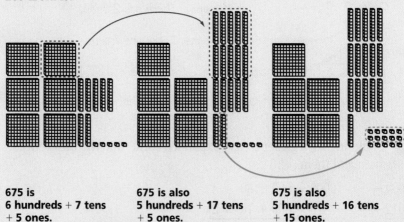

**675 is
6 hundreds + 7 tens
+ 5 ones.**

**675 is also
5 hundreds + 17 tens
+ 5 ones.**

**675 is also
5 hundreds + 16 tens
+ 15 ones.**

Your problem would be set up like this:

$$
\begin{array}{r}
675 \longrightarrow 5^{1}6^{1}5 \\
-289 \longrightarrow -2\ 8\ 9
\end{array}
$$

Subtracting with Regrouping

Sometimes when you subtract place by place, it looks like you need to subtract a number that's too big. When that happens, you need to regroup from a greater place.

EXAMPLE: How much more rain does Ookala, Hawaii, get in an average year than Seattle Tacoma Airport? *(Source: Western Regional Climate Center)*

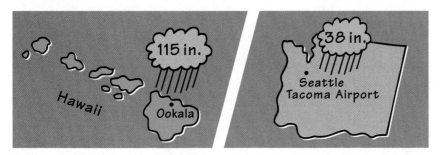

To solve the problem, subtract 115 – 38.

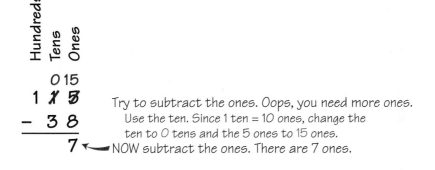

Try to subtract the ones. Oops, you need more ones. Use the ten. Since 1 ten = 10 ones, change the ten to 0 tens and the 5 ones to 15 ones. NOW subtract the ones. There are 7 ones.

Try to subtract the tens. You need more tens. Use the hundred. Since 1 hundred = 10 tens, change the 1 hundred to 0 hundreds and 0 tens to 10 tens. NOW subtract the tens. There are 7 tens.

Subtract the hundreds. There are no hundreds.

Ookala, Hawaii, gets about 77 more inches of rain per year than Seattle Tacoma Airport.

MATH ALERT Tricky Regrouping

EXAMPLE: There are 6002 light bulbs in your electronic sign. A power surge blows out all of the bulbs. You have 1648 bulbs in stock. How many more bulbs do you need?

To solve the problem, subtract 6002 − 1648.

1000 = 10 hundreds

10 hundreds = 9 hundreds + 10 tens

9 hundreds + 10 tens = 9 hundreds + 9 tens + 10 ones

Thousands	Hundreds	Tens	Ones
5	9	9	12
6̶	0̶	0̶	2̶

− 1 6 4 8

Try to subtract the ones. Oops, you need more ones to subtract from.

There aren't any tens or hundreds to use, so use one of the thousands. Change the number of thousands from 6 to 5. Then raise the number of hundreds from 0 to 9, the number of tens from 0 to 9, and the number of ones from 2 to 12.

4 ← NOW you can subtract the ones. There are 4 ones.

Thousands	Hundreds	Tens	Ones
5	9	9	12
6̶	0̶	0̶	2̶

− 1 6 4 8

4 3 5 4

Subtract the tens. There are 5 tens.

Subtract the hundreds. There are 3 hundreds.

Subtract the thousands. There are 4 thousands.

You need 4354 more light bulbs.

Checking Subtraction

Even if subtraction is easy for you, it's a good idea to check your answers.

One way to check your subtraction is to use addition. This is because addition is the inverse of subtraction. If you add the difference and the number you subtracted, the answer should be the original number you subtracted from.

MORE HELP
See 096–101

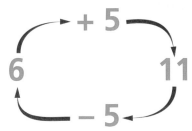

If it isn't, you should try doing the subtraction again.

EXAMPLE 1: Does $46,528 - 16,371 = 30,157$? Use addition to check.

To check the subtraction, add the difference to the number you subtracted.

$$\begin{array}{r} 46,528 \\ -\,16,371 \\ \hline 30,157 \end{array} \qquad \begin{array}{r} 30,157 \\ +\,16,371 \\ \hline 46,528 \end{array}$$

$46,528 = 46,528$ So, the subtraction is correct.

EXAMPLE 2: Does $25,005 - 7,348 = 18,657$? Use addition to check.

To check the subtraction, add the difference to the number you subtracted.

$$\begin{array}{r} 25,005 \\ -\,7,348 \\ \hline 18,657 \end{array} \qquad \begin{array}{r} 18,657 \\ +\,7,348 \\ \hline 26,005 \end{array}$$

$25,005 \neq 26,005$
$25,005$ does not equal $26,005$.

So, you should do the subtraction again.

Hey, I just add from the bottom up!

$$\begin{array}{r} 26,005 \\ 25,005 \\ -7,348 \\ \hline 18,657 \end{array}$$

131 — Subtracting with Decimals

MORE HELP
See 012, 014, 103, 125–130

If you know how to subtract whole numbers, you also know how to subtract decimals. With both decimals and whole numbers, there are a few things to remember. Pay attention to place value, subtract in each place, and regroup when you have to. Be sure to line up the ones (or the decimal points).

EXAMPLE: Subtract $5.04 - 3.681$.

Line up the decimal points.
Write both numbers as three-place decimals.

Try to subtract the thousandths. You need more thousandths.
　Use one of the hundredths.
　Since 1 hundredth = 10 thousandths, change the number of the hundredths from 4 to 3 and the number of thousandths from 0 to 10.
NOW subtract the thousandths.
There are 9 thousandths.

$1 = 10$ tenths, and
$1 = 9$ tenths $+ 10$ hundredths

Ones | Tenths | Hundredths | Thousandths

$$
\begin{array}{r}
3\ 10 \\
5.0\,\cancel{4}\,\cancel{0} \\
-\,3.6\,8\,1 \\
\hline
9
\end{array}
$$

Try to subtract the hundredths.
You need more hundredths.
　There are no tenths to use, so use a one. Change the number of ones from 5 to 4. Raise the number of tenths from 0 to 9 and the number of hundredths from 3 to 13.
NOW subtract the hundredths.
There are 5 hundredths.

Subtract the tenths. There are 3 tenths.

Subtract the ones. There is 1 one.

$$
\begin{array}{r}
4\quad 9\ 13 \\
10\ \cancel{3}\ 10 \\
\cancel{5}.\cancel{0}\ \cancel{4}\ \cancel{0} \\
-\,3.6\,8\,1 \\
\hline
1.3\,5\,9
\end{array}
$$

So, $5.04 - 3.681 = 1.359$.

132 — Subtracting with Fractions

MORE HELP
See 029–031, 104–107

You can't subtract fractions the way you do whole numbers because digits in fractions have different meanings than they do in whole numbers.

2 tens　　3 ones

23

2 parts being talked about

$\dfrac{2}{3}$

3 equal parts in all

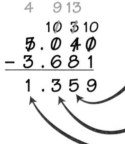

MATH ALERT Subtract ONLY the Numerators

Subtracting fractions is a lot like subtracting apples or wing nuts. When you subtract 4 apples from 11 apples you have 7 apples— the *number* of things changes (11 − 4 = 7), but the *kind* of thing (apples) doesn't!

This works when you subtract fractions, too. When you subtract 4 eighths from 11 eighths, you have 7 eighths—the *number* of things changes (11 − 4 = 7), but the *kind* of thing (eighths) doesn't. One nice thing about fractions is that if the kind of thing doesn't start out the same you can change them to things that are the same.

Subtracting Fractions with Common Denominators

134

CASE 1 Suppose you want to subtract fractions. If the fractions have the same denominator, subtract the numerators and use the same denominator.

EXAMPLE 1: The distance from Ted's home to school is $\frac{5}{8}$ of a mile. He has biked $\frac{3}{8}$ of a mile. How much farther does he have to bike?

To solve the problem, you can subtract $\frac{5}{8} - \frac{3}{8}$.

 You can understand the subtraction by drawing a picture.

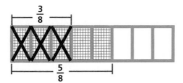

$\frac{5}{8} - \frac{3}{8} = \frac{2}{8}$, or $\frac{1}{4}$

 Here's how you can subtract $\frac{5}{8} - \frac{3}{8}$ without drawing a picture.

MORE HELP
See 037

① THE FRACTIONS HAVE THE SAME DENOMINATOR. WRITE THAT COMMON DENOMINATOR.	② SUBTRACT THE NUMERATORS.	③ WRITE THE SUM IN SIMPLEST FORM. TO DO THIS, DIVIDE NUMERATOR AND DENOMINATOR BY THE GCF.
$\frac{5}{8} - \frac{3}{8} = \frac{}{8}$	$\frac{5}{8} - \frac{3}{8} = \frac{2}{8}$	$\frac{2}{8} = \frac{2 \div 2}{8 \div 2} = \frac{1}{4}$

Ted had $\frac{2}{8}$ mile, or $\frac{1}{4}$ mile, left to bike.

MORE ▷

CASE 2 Sometimes when you subtract from a mixed number, you need to regroup.

EXAMPLE 2: A cake recipe calls for $3\frac{1}{4}$ cups of flour. You have already put in $1\frac{3}{4}$ cups. How much more should you add?

❶ COMPARE THE FRACTIONS. $\frac{3}{4} > \frac{1}{4}$ REGROUP A ONE AS $\frac{4}{4}$.	❷ SUBTRACT THE FRACTIONS. SUBTRACT THE WHOLE NUMBERS.	❸ WRITE THE SUM IN SIMPLEST FORM.
$3\frac{1}{4} \rightarrow 2 + \frac{4}{4} + \frac{1}{4} \rightarrow 2\frac{5}{4}$	$\begin{array}{r} 2\frac{5}{4} \\ -1\frac{3}{4} \\ \hline 1\frac{2}{4} \end{array}$	$1\frac{2}{4} = 1\frac{1}{2}$

You should add $1\frac{1}{2}$ more cups of flour.

Subtracting Fractions with Unlike Denominators

Sometimes you subtract fractions like $\frac{15}{16}$ and $\frac{3}{8}$. In those cases, you can rewrite them as fractions with a common denominator.

EXAMPLE 1: In 2002, one share of cheap stock sold for $0.9375, or $\frac{15}{16}$ of a dollar. In 2003, the stock dropped $\frac{3}{8}$ of a dollar. How much was the share of stock worth then?

To solve the problem, you can subtract $\frac{15}{16} - \frac{3}{8}$.

 You can understand the subtraction by drawing a picture.

Here's how to subtract $\frac{15}{16} - \frac{3}{8}$ without drawing a picture.

❶ FIND EQUIVALENT FRACTIONS WITH A COMMON DENOMINATOR.	❷ SUBTRACT THE FRACTIONS.	❸ WRITE THE DIFFERENCE IN SIMPLEST FORM.
$\frac{15}{16} - \frac{3}{8}$ $\downarrow$ $\frac{15}{16} - \frac{3 \times 2}{8 \times 2}$ $\downarrow$ $\frac{15}{16} - \frac{6}{16}$	$\frac{15}{16} - \frac{6}{16} = \frac{9}{16}$	$\frac{9}{16}$ is in simplest form.

Either way, the share of stock was worth $\frac{9}{16}$ of a dollar.

EXAMPLE 2: Subtract $\frac{3}{4} - \frac{5}{10}$.

❶ FIND EQUIVALENT FRACTIONS WITH A COMMON DENOMINATOR.	❷ SUBTRACT THE FRACTIONS.	❸ WRITE THE DIFFERENCE IN SIMPLEST FORM.
$\frac{3}{4} \quad - \quad \frac{5}{10}$ $\downarrow \qquad \downarrow$ $\frac{3 \times 5}{4 \times 5} - \frac{5 \times 2}{10 \times 2}$ $\downarrow \qquad \downarrow$ $\frac{15}{20} - \frac{10}{20}$	$\frac{15}{20} - \frac{10}{20} = \frac{5}{20}$	$\frac{5}{20} = \frac{1}{4}$

MORE HELP
See 036, 037

Other equivalent fractions you could use include $\frac{3}{4} - \frac{2}{4}$ ($\frac{5}{10} = \frac{1}{2}$, and $\frac{1}{2} = \frac{2}{4}$).

So, $\frac{3}{4} - \frac{5}{10} = \frac{1}{4}$.

Subtracting with Negative Numbers

When you think about it, subtracting a negative number sounds strange. It's just like a double negative in English.

Subtracting a negative number is just like adding a positive number. The easiest way to keep subtraction with negative numbers straight is to rewrite subtraction as addition.

One way to think about subtracting is with a number line.

EXAMPLE 1: Use a number line to show $^-1.2 - 3.8$.

1. Rewrite subtraction as addition.
   $^-1.2 - 3.8 = ^-1.2 + ^-3.8$

2. Place the first addend above the number line.

3. Start at the first addend. Draw an arrow as long as the second addend in the negative direction.

Your arrow ends at the difference. So, $^-1.2 - 3.8 = ^-5$.

EXAMPLE 2: Use a number line to show $^-2 - ^-5$.

1. Rewrite subtraction as addition.
   $^-2 - ^-5 = ^-2 + ^+5$

2. Place the first addend above the number line.

3. Start at the first addend. Draw an arrow as long as the second addend in the positive direction.

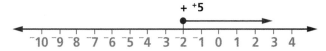

Your arrow ends at the difference. So, $^-2 - ^-5 = 3$.

Shortcut

You can also use absolute value and follow some simple rules to subtract with signed numbers.

MORE HELP
See 050

Signs on Addends	Rule	Examples
To subtract positive – positive	Subtract the smaller absolute value from the greater. The difference is positive if the first number is greater; otherwise, it is negative.	$\|{}^+64\| - \|{}^+72\|$ ↓ $72 - 64 = 8$ ↓ ${}^+64 - {}^+72 = {}^-8$
To subtract negative – positive	Add the absolute values. The difference is negative.	$\|{}^-72\| - \|{}^+64\|$ ↓ $72 + 64 = 136$ ↓ ${}^-72 - {}^+64 = {}^-136$
To subtract positive – negative	Add the absolute values. The difference is positive.	$\|{}^+72\| - \|{}^-64\|$ ↓ $72 + 64 = 136$ ↓ ${}^+72 - {}^-64 = {}^+136$
To subtract negative – negative	Subtract the smaller absolute value from the greater. The difference is negative if the first absolute value is greater; otherwise, it is positive.	$\|{}^-72\| - \|{}^-64\|$ ↓ $72 - 64 = 8$ ↓ ${}^-72 - {}^-64 = {}^-8$

$|64| = 64$
$|{}^-64| = 64$

To use a calculator to subtract signed
numbers or decimals, you need to
be able to locate these keys on
your calculator:

- $-$
- $=$
- $.$
- $+/-$

EXAMPLE 1: Use a calculator to subtract $34,009 - 9784$.

| 3 | 4 | 0 | 0 | 9 | – | 9 | 7 | 8 | 4 | = | 24225. |

EXAMPLE 2: Use a calculator to subtract $12.06 - 3.754$.

| 1 | 2 | . | 0 | 6 | – | 3 | . | 7 | 5 | 4 | = | 8.306 |

EXAMPLE 3: Use a calculator to subtract $^-5 - {}^-4$.

| 5 | +/– | – | 4 | +/– | = | -1. |

The sign change key changes the sign of the number entered before it.

EXAMPLE 4: Use a calculator to subtract $^-2 - 3$.

| 2 | +/– | – | 3 | = | -5. |

Special Keys

138

Some calculators have special keys that you can use to work with fractions. For example:

- $\boxed{/}$ makes fractions.
  To show $\frac{6}{8}$, press $\boxed{6}$ $\boxed{/}$ $\boxed{8}$ $\boxed{\textit{6/8}}$.

- $\boxed{\text{Simp}}$ simplifies fractions.
  To simplify $\frac{6}{8}$, press $\boxed{6}$ $\boxed{/}$ $\boxed{8}$ $\boxed{\text{Simp}}$ $\boxed{=}$ $\boxed{\textit{3/4}}$.

- $\boxed{\text{Ab/c}}$ shows a fraction as a mixed number.
  To show $\frac{9}{7}$ as a mixed number, press $\boxed{9}$ $\boxed{/}$ $\boxed{7}$ $\boxed{\text{Ab/c}}$ $\boxed{\textit{1 u 2/7}}$.

- $\boxed{\text{Unit}}$ is used to enter a mixed number.
  To show $1\frac{3}{8}$, press $\boxed{1}$ $\boxed{\text{Unit}}$ $\boxed{3}$ $\boxed{/}$ $\boxed{8}$ $\boxed{\textit{1 u 3/8}}$.

MORE HELP
See 207

- $\boxed{(}$ $\boxed{)}$ Grouping symbols are used to be sure of order of operations.

MATH ALERT Your Calculator May Be Different

139

Your calculator may have different keys that do the same thing as the keys above. Check the directions for your calculator.

Subtracting Fractions with Fraction Keys

140

EXAMPLE 1: Subtract $\frac{19}{24} - \frac{1}{8}$.

$\boxed{1}$ $\boxed{9}$ $\boxed{/}$ $\boxed{2}$ $\boxed{4}$ $\boxed{-}$ $\boxed{1}$ $\boxed{/}$ $\boxed{8}$ $\boxed{=}$ $\boxed{\textit{16/24}}$

$\boxed{\text{Simp}}$ $\boxed{=}$ $\boxed{\textit{8/12}}$

$\boxed{\text{Simp}}$ $\boxed{=}$ $\boxed{\textit{4/6}}$ If you are not sure whether the answer is in simplest form, press $\boxed{\text{Simp}}$ and $\boxed{=}$. If the fraction does not change, it is in simplest form.

$\boxed{\text{Simp}}$ $\boxed{=}$ $\boxed{\textit{2/3}}$

EXAMPLE 2: Subtract $3\frac{1}{5} - 1\frac{1}{2}$.

$\boxed{3}$ $\boxed{\text{Unit}}$ $\boxed{1}$ $\boxed{/}$ $\boxed{5}$ $\boxed{-}$ $\boxed{1}$ $\boxed{\text{Unit}}$ $\boxed{1}$ $\boxed{/}$ $\boxed{2}$ $\boxed{=}$ $\boxed{\textit{1 u 7/10}}$

Subtracting Fractions Without Fraction Keys

Even if your calculator doesn't have special keys for fractions, you can still use it to subtract fractions. Just enter each fraction as the numerator divided by the denominator and then subtract. Your answer will be a decimal. If your answer needs to be a fraction, you may not want to use your calculator in this way.

EXAMPLE 1: Subtract $\frac{7}{16} - \frac{1}{8}$.

| (| 7 | ÷ | 1 | 6 |) | – | (| 1 | ÷ | 8 |) | = | 0.3125 |

EXAMPLE 2: Subtract $\frac{5}{6} - \frac{1}{2}$.

| (| 5 | ÷ | 6 |) | – | (| 1 | ÷ | 2 |) | = | 0.3333333 |

Since the decimal is a repeating decimal, write the number as $0.\overline{3}$.

Multiplication

Multiplication is a shortcut for addition. Imagine that the class can-collection drive has been hugely successful. There are 1275 cans waiting to be redeemed for 5¢ apiece. You are class treasurer and you certainly don't want to add 5¢ 1275 times, so you're really glad you know how to multiply.

Two terms you may hear used in multiplication are **factor** and **product**.

$$\begin{array}{r} 1275 \\ \times \quad 5 \\ \hline 6375 \end{array}$$ ◄——— factor
◄——— factor
◄——— product

Mental Multiplication
143

10 hours of work at $6.50 per hour is $65.

One bottle serves 6 people. 5 bottles are enough for 30 people.

Any time you have groups of equal size, and you want to find the total number in all the groups without using paper and pencil or a calculator, you might multiply in your head.

Multiplying by Powers of 10

Shortcut

Thanks to the patterns in our number system, there's a great shortcut for multiplying by a **power of 10**, such as 10, 100, and 1000. All you need to do is count the number of zeros in the power of 10 and then write that number of zeros after the other factor.

EXAMPLE: What is the face value of 6 of these bills?

To find the value, you can multiply 6 × 10,000 in your head.

There are 4 zeros in 10,000. So, 6 × 10,000 = 60,000.

The face value of 6 of these bills is $60,000. But if you had these bills, you might not want to spend them or put them in the bank. These bills are so rare they are worth more than twice their face value! *(Source: Stack's Coin Company)*

Multiplying by Multiples of 10

When one or both factors are **multiples of 10** (say 40, 400, or 4000), you can multiply in your head. Look at these patterns to find out how:

6 × 4 = 24	5 × 8 = 40
6 × 40 = 240	5 × 80 = 400
6 × 400 = 2400	5 × 800 = 4000
6 × 4000 = 24,000	5 × 8000 = 40,000
60 × 400 = 24,000	50 × 800 = 40,000
600 × 400 = 240,000	500 × 800 = 400,000

That makes sense, because 6 × 4 tens = 24 tens and 6 × 4 hundreds = 24 hundreds.

To multiply by multiples of 10, first find the **product** of the front non-zero digits. Then tack on the sum of the zeros in both **factors**.

EXAMPLE: Souvenir pens are packed 500 to a box. The stadium orders 60 boxes. How many pens are in 60 boxes?

You need to multiply 60×500. You can do this in your head.

$$60 \times 500$$

Think: 6×5 3 zeros

$$30 \quad 000 = 30,000$$

There are 30,000 pens in 60 boxes.

Using Repeated Doubling to Multiply

Sometimes you can find a product in your head by **doubling**.

EXAMPLE: A typical Boeing 747-400 jet designed for domestic flights carries 560 passengers. How many passengers can 2 jets carry? How many can 4 jets carry? How many can 8 jets carry?

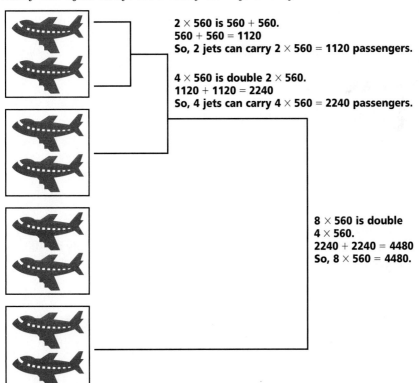

2×560 is $560 + 560$.
$560 + 560 = 1120$
So, 2 jets can carry $2 \times 560 = 1120$ passengers.

4×560 is double 2×560.
$1120 + 1120 = 2240$
So, 4 jets can carry $4 \times 560 = 2240$ passengers.

8×560 is double 4×560.
$2240 + 2240 = 4480$
So, $8 \times 560 = 4480$.

So, 8 of the Boeing 747-400 jets can carry 4480 passengers.

Multiplying with Easy Numbers

You may find that some numbers are easy to multiply in your head.

Multiplying by 2
To multiply by 2, find the answer by adding a number to itself.

EXAMPLE 1: $2 \times 480 = ?$

$$480 + 480 = 960 \qquad \text{So, } 2 \times 480 = 960.$$

MORE HELP
See 220–221

Multiplying by 5
To multiply by 5, think of 5 as $10 \div 2$. Multiply by 10, then divide by 2.

EXAMPLE 2: $5 \times 120 = ?$

120	120	120	120	120
120	120	120	120	120

$10 \times 120 = 1200$

5×120 is half of 10×120. So, $5 \times 120 = 1200 \div 2 = 600$.

Multiplying by 9
When you multiply by 9, think of 9 as $10 - 1$. You can first multiply by 10, then subtract the original factor.

EXAMPLE 3: $9 \times 86 = ?$

86	86	86	86	86	86	86	86	86	86

$$9 \times 86 = 10 \times 86 - 86$$
$$= 860 - 86$$
$$= 774 \qquad \text{So, } 9 \times 86 = 774.$$

Multiplying by 25
There are four 25s in 100. To multiply by 25, you can multiply by 100, then divide by 4.

EXAMPLE 4: $12 \times 25 = ?$

$$12 \times 100 = 1200$$
$$1200 \div 4 = 300 \qquad \text{So, } 12 \times 25 = 300.$$

Multiplying by 50

To multiply by 50 in your head, think of 50 as 100 ÷ 2. Multiply by 100, then divide by 2.

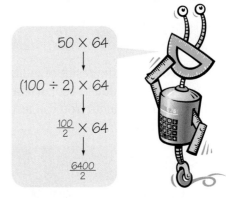

$$50 \times 64$$
$$\downarrow$$
$$(100 \div 2) \times 64$$
$$\downarrow$$
$$\frac{100}{2} \times 64$$
$$\downarrow$$
$$\frac{6400}{2}$$

EXAMPLE 5: $50 \times 64 = ?$

$$100 \times 64 = 6400$$
$$6400 \div 2 = 3200$$

So, $50 \times 64 = 3200$.

Breaking Apart and Putting Together Numbers to Multiply

148

One way to multiply in your head is to break the factors into parts and multiply the parts.

EXAMPLE: The Disc Dive has a new CD by Salamander Sam. There are 84 CDs in each box. During the first month, the store sold 15 boxes of CDs. How many CDs did the store sell?

To solve the problem, you can multiply 15×84. Think of 15 as $10 + 5$.

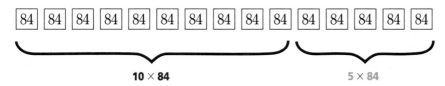

| 84 | 84 | 84 | 84 | 84 | 84 | 84 | 84 | 84 | 84 | 84 | 84 | 84 | 84 | 84 |

10 × 84   **5 × 84**

840 + **420** = **1260**

$$15 \times 84 = (10 + 5) \times 84$$
$$= (10 \times 84) + (5 \times 84)$$
$$= 840 + 420$$
$$= 1260$$

The store sold 1260 CDs.

Estimating Products

A **product** is the result of multiplication. Sometimes when you multiply, you don't need an exact product. In these cases you can *estimate* products. You can also use estimates to check exact answers you've found.

EXAMPLE 1: You can rent a car for $69 per day, with no extra charge for the number of miles driven. Is $300 enough to rent the car for 5 days? Since you only need to find out whether 5 × 69 is less than or is equal to 300, you can use an estimate to answer this question.

$$5 \times 70 = 350 \quad \text{You don't have enough money.}$$

EXAMPLE 2: You want to find 43 × 621. Your calculator displays ▢ 26703. as the product. You can estimate to check whether your exact answer is reasonable. If your estimate isn't even close, you should compute again.

$$40 \times 600 = 24,000 \quad \text{Your answer is reasonable.}$$

Front-End Estimation of Products

To estimate products, you can multiply the front digits.

EXAMPLE 1: The air mileage between Chicago and New York is 714 miles. Suppose you made the trip 52 times (26 round trips) in one year, and you earned 1 point for each mile flown. Did you earn enough for a bonus that requires 30,000 points? *(Source: World Almanac and Book of Facts)*

Since you only need to know whether you've flown more than or less than 30,000 miles, you can estimate 52 × 714.

$$\begin{array}{r} 714 \longrightarrow 700 \\ \times\,52 \longrightarrow \times\,50 \\ \hline 35,000 \end{array}$$

The exact product is greater than 35,000, so you can be sure you earned enough points.

EXAMPLE 2: You're heading for the checkout stand with 5 cans of orange juice priced at $1.35 apiece when you see a magazine you really want to read. You have $10 in your pocket. Can you buy the orange juice and the $3 magazine?

To solve the problem, you can estimate the cost of the orange juice to see whether paying for the juice will leave you with at least an extra $3.

Front-end estimation would be $5 \times 1 = 5$. $5 + $3 is only $8, so if you trusted your estimate, you'd pick up the magazine. But, you know that a front-end estimate is less than the exact product.

To be a little more certain, you might adjust your estimate:
$5 \times 0.30 = 1.5$, another $1.50 for the orange juice.
This is getting awfully close to $10, all you have in your pocket, so an estimate might not really be enough to help you make your decision.

Using Compatible Numbers to Estimate Products

Compatible numbers are numbers that work well together. In multiplication, they are number pairs that are easy to multiply.

To estimate products, replace one or both factors with compatible numbers.

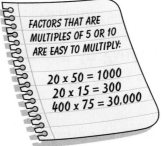

FACTORS THAT ARE MULTIPLES OF 5 OR 10 ARE EASY TO MULTIPLY:

$20 \times 50 = 1000$
$20 \times 15 = 300$
$400 \times 75 = 30,000$

EXAMPLE 1: There are 18 weeks in the school semester. You need to plan snacks for 18 eighth-grade weekly meetings. About how many snacks need to be ordered for 618 eighth-graders?

Find compatible numbers for 18 and 618 and use them to estimate the product. Try 20×600.

$$
\begin{array}{r}
618 \longrightarrow 600 \\
\times\, 18 \longrightarrow \times\, 20 \\
\hline
12{,}000
\end{array}
$$

618 is close to 600. 18 is close to 20. So, 18×618 is close to 20×600. So, you'll need to order about 12,000 snacks!

MORE ▷

EXAMPLE 2: Use compatible numbers to estimate 986×431.

$$
\begin{array}{r}
431 \longrightarrow \quad 431 \\
\times 986 \longrightarrow \times 1000 \\
\hline
431{,}000
\end{array}
$$

> Use powers of 10 to multiply.

986 is close to 1000.
So, 986×431 is close to 1000×431.

$1000 \times 431 = 431{,}000$
So, 986×431 is about $431{,}000$.

Multiplying with Whole Numbers

If you know how to multiply 1-digit numbers such as 7×5, you can also multiply larger numbers such as 7×555. That's because multiplying multi-digit numbers is done one digit at a time. Each product is called a **partial product**. First, multiply the value of each digit from one factor by the value of each digit from the other factor. Then add up the partial products.

Multiplying by a 1-Digit Number

To multiply a multi-digit factor by a 1-digit factor, multiply the values of the places one at a time.

EXAMPLE: The fire department in a large city responded to 555 calls per day for a week. How many calls did they answer in that week?

To solve the problem, multiply 7×555.

 ONE WAY You can multiply by listing all the partial products.

$$
\begin{array}{r}
555 \\
\times \quad 7 \\
\hline
35 \\
350 \\
3500 \\
\hline
3885
\end{array}
$$

    35 ◀——Multiply the ones.   **7×5 ones = 35 ones**

  350 ◀——Multiply the tens.   **7×5 tens = 35 tens = 350**

3500 ◀——Multiply the hundreds. **7×5 hundreds = 35 hundreds = 3500**

3885 ◀——Add the partial products.

You can also multiply without listing the partial products.

Hundreds	Tens	Ones
3	3	
5	5	5
×		7
3	8 8	5

Multiply the ones.
Since 35 ones is 3 tens and 5 ones, write 5 in the ones place. Write 3 above the tens so you don't forget it.

Multiply the tens.
Since 35 tens is 3 hundreds and 5 tens, add the 5 tens to the 3 tens you already have. Write 8 in the tens place. Write 3 above the hundreds so you don't forget it.

Multiply the hundreds.
Since 35 hundreds is 3 thousands and 5 hundreds, add the 5 hundreds to the 3 hundreds you already have. Write 8 in the hundreds place. Write 3 in the thousands place.

Using either method, the fire department answered 3885 calls in that one week.

Two Ways to Multiply Whole Numbers

EXAMPLE: You're making decorations for the middle-school dance. Each person attending will be given a small memento made with 24 cm of ribbon. You expect 674 people at the dance. How much ribbon should you buy?

MORE HELP
See 005

To solve the problem, multiply 24× 674.

 You can multiply the value of each digit in one factor by the value of each digit in the other factor, record each product, and then add these partial products.

```
      Hundreds
       Tens
        Ones

      6 7 4
    ×   2 4
    ─────────
        1 6       Multiply by the ones.
      2 8 0         4 × 4 = 16
    2 4 0 0         4 × 70 = 280
                    4 × 600 = 2400

        8 0       Multiply by the tens.
    1 4 0 0         20 × 4 = 80
  1 2 0 0 0         20 × 70 = 1400
  ─────────         20 × 600 = 12,000

  1 6,1 7 6       Add the partial products.
```

You can also find the same product without listing every partial product.

Hundreds
Tens
Ones

```
  2 1
  6 7 4
×   2 4
─────────
2 6 9 6
```

Multiply by the ones: 4 × 674 = ?
4 × 4 = 16 ─────────→ 6 ones with 1 ten
                      to regroup
4 × 70 = 280 ───────→ 8 tens + 1 ten with
                      2 hundreds to regroup
4 × 600 = 2400 ─────→ 24 hundreds +
                      2 hundreds

```
    1
  2 1
  6 7 4
×   2 4
─────────
  2 6 9 6
1 3 4 8 0
─────────
1 6,1 7 6
```

Multiply by the tens: 20 × 674 = ?
20 × 4 = 80 ────────→ 8 tens and 0 ones
20 × 70 = 1400 ─────→ 4 hundreds with
                      1 thousand to regroup
20 × 600 = 12,000 ─→ 12 thousands +
                      1 thousand

Add the partial products.

Did you notice that when you multiply numbers like 24 × 674, you are finding 6 products and several sums? That's why it's important to record every step.

Either way, you should buy at least 16,176 cm of ribbon.

MATH ALERT Zeros in Factors and Products

When a factor like 902 has one or more zeros, don't forget to multiply the zero.

EXAMPLE: You're positive your mother tells you 902 times a week to clean up your room. If this is true, how many times a year do you get this reminder? (Hint: There are 52 weeks in a year.)

To find the answer, you need to multiply 52 × 902.

```
   Hundreds
   │ Tens
   │ │ Ones
   9 0 2
 ×   5 2
 1 8 0 4
```

Estimate: 50 × 900 = 45,000

Multiply by the ones: 2 × 902 = ?
2 × 2 = 4 ⟶ 4 ones
2 × 0 = 0 ⟶ 0 tens
2 × 900 = 1800 ⟶ 18 hundreds

```
       1
   9 0 2
 ×   5 2
 1 8 0 4
 4 5 1 0 0
 4 6,9 0 4
```

Multiply by the tens: 50 × 902 = ?
50 × 2 = 100 ⟶ 1 hundred and 0 tens
50 × 0 = 0
0 + 100 = 100 ⟶ 1 hundred
50 × 900 = 45,000 ⟶ 45 thousands

Add the partial products.

You think your mother reminds you 46,904 times a year to clean up your room.

Checking Multiplication by Dividing

156

You should always check your answer. Checking helps you make sure that you correctly recorded each step in the multiplication and that you hit the right calculator keys.

One way to check multiplication is to use division. If you divide the product by one of the factors, the answer should be the other factor.

MORE HELP
See 179–181

EXAMPLE 1: Does $27 \times 78 = 2106$? Use division to check.

$2106 \div 78 = 27$ $2106 \div 27 = 78$

Either way, since dividing the product by one factor gives the other factor, the multiplication is correct.

EXAMPLE 2: Does $59 \times 204 = 13{,}076$? Use division to check.

$13{,}076 \div 59 \neq 204$ $13{,}076 \div 204 \neq 59$

Either way, since dividing the product by one factor does not give the other factor, you should try the multiplication again.

Checking Multiplication by Reversing the Factors

157

Another way to check your multiplication is to reverse the factors. Since multiplication is **commutative**, reversing the factors should produce the same product.

MORE HELP
See 214

EXAMPLE 1: Does $17 \times 25 = 425$? Reverse the factors.

$$
\begin{array}{r} 25 \\ \times 17 \\ \hline 425 \end{array}
\qquad
\begin{array}{r} 17 \\ \times 25 \\ \hline 425 \end{array}
$$

If reversing the factors gives the same product, the multiplication is correct.

EXAMPLE 2: Does $13 \times 126 = 1738$? Reverse the factors.

$$
\begin{array}{r} 126 \\ \times\ 13 \\ \hline 1738 \end{array}
\qquad
\begin{array}{r} 13 \\ \times 126 \\ \hline 1638 \end{array}
$$

If reversing the factors does not give the same product, one of the products is not correct.

) **Multiplying with Decimals**

You multiply decimals the same way you multiply whole numbers. The only difference is that you must correctly place a decimal point in the product. Compare these two multiplication problems.

$$
\begin{array}{r} 37 \\ \times 45 \\ \hline 1665 \end{array}
\qquad
\begin{array}{r} 3.7 \\ \times 4.5 \\ \hline 16.65 \end{array}
$$

> The digits in the problems are the same. The steps are the same. But the place values are different because of the decimal points.

Placing the Decimal Point in the Product

 Decide where to place the decimal point in the product by using an estimate.

EXAMPLE 1: You fill a bag with 1.80 pounds of peanuts. The cost is $3.29 per pound. How much money do you spend?

To solve the problem, you can multiply 1.80 × 3.29.

PEANUTS
$3.29
PER
POUND

TRAIL MIX
$2.49
PER
POUND

❶ BEGIN BY MAKING AN ESTIMATE.	❷ MULTIPLY AS IF THE FACTORS WERE WHOLE NUMBERS.	❸ USE THE ESTIMATE TO PLACE THE DECIMAL POINT.
1.80 × 3.29 ↓ 2 × 3 = 6 **So the product will have only one digit left of the decimal.**	$$\begin{array}{r} 329 \\ \times 180 \\ \hline 59220 \end{array}$$	**The estimate was 6, so the decimal point should go after the 5:** 5.9220

The product is 5.9220. Since the answer needs to be in dollars and cents, round to the nearest cent. You pay $5.92.

Place the decimal point in the product by counting the number of places to the right of the decimal point in each factor. The total tells you how many places there will be to the right of the decimal point in the product.

EXAMPLE 2: Multiply 0.02×0.03.

❶ MULTIPLY AS IF THE FACTORS WERE WHOLE NUMBERS.	❷ COUNT THE PLACES TO THE RIGHT OF THE DECIMAL POINT IN EACH FACTOR. ADD.	❸ COUNT THE SAME NUMBER OF PLACES FROM RIGHT TO LEFT IN THE PRODUCT, THEN PLACE THE DECIMAL POINT. (SOMETIMES YOU'LL NEED TO FILL PLACES WITH ZEROS.)
$2 \times 3 = 6$	$0.02 \longrightarrow$ 2 decimal places $0.03 \longrightarrow +2$ decimal places 4 decimal places	0.0006 4 decimal places

So, $0.02 \times 0.03 = 0.0006$.

Multiplying with Fractions (160)

You can multiply fractions by fractions, by mixed numbers, or by whole numbers. To understand this kind of multiplication, think about the meaning of multiplication and the meaning of fractions.

EXAMPLE 1: a 3-mile path walked twice $\longrightarrow 3 \times 2 = 6$

The product is greater than 3.

EXAMPLE 2: a 3-mile path walked $\frac{1}{2}$ way $\longrightarrow 3 \times \frac{1}{2} = 1\frac{1}{2}$

The product is less than 3.

EXAMPLE 3: a $\frac{3}{4}$-mile path walked twice $\longrightarrow \frac{3}{4} \times 2 = 1\frac{1}{2}$

The product is greater than $\frac{3}{4}$.

EXAMPLE 4: a $\frac{3}{4}$-mile path walked $\frac{1}{2}$ way $\longrightarrow \frac{3}{4} \times \frac{1}{2} = \frac{3}{8}$

The product is less than $\frac{3}{4}$.

EXAMPLE 5: a $\frac{3}{4}$-mile path walked $1\frac{1}{2}$ times $\longrightarrow \frac{3}{4} \times 1\frac{1}{2} = 1\frac{1}{8}$

The product is greater than $\frac{3}{4}$.

161

Multiplying a Whole Number by a Fraction

When you multiply a whole number by a fraction less than 1, the product is less than the whole-number factor because you're only looking for part of it.

EXAMPLE: Your class has 18 students. In a survey, exactly two-thirds of the students say they like using a word processor better than writing by hand. How many students prefer using a word processor? (Hint: *of* signals multiplication.)

Fewer than 18 students prefer using a word processor. To solve the problem, you can multiply $\frac{2}{3} \times 18$.

ONE WAY You can find $\frac{2}{3} \times 18$ by drawing a picture.

$\frac{1}{3}$ of 18 ⟶

$\frac{1}{3}$ of 18 ⟶

$\frac{1}{3}$ of 18 ⟶

$\Big\}\frac{2}{3}$ **of 18**

So, $\frac{2}{3} \times 18 = 12$.

ANOTHER WAY You can multiply $\frac{2}{3} \times 18$ without drawing a picture.

MORE HELP
See 037

❶ WRITE THE WHOLE NUMBER AS A FRACTION.	❷ MULTIPLY THE NUMERATORS. MULTIPLY THE DENOMINATORS.	❸ WRITE THE PRODUCT IN SIMPLEST FORM.
$\frac{2}{3} \times 18$ ↓ $\frac{2}{3} \times \frac{18}{1}$	$\frac{2}{3} \times \frac{18}{1} = \frac{36}{3}$	$\frac{36 \div 3}{3 \div 3} = \frac{12}{1} = 12$

Either way, 12 students prefer using a word processor.

162

Multiplying a Fraction by a Fraction

When you multiply two fractions that are between 0 and 1, the product is smaller than *both* fractions.

EXAMPLE: A brownie recipe calls for $\frac{3}{4}$ cup of chopped walnuts. You only want to make $\frac{2}{3}$ as many brownies as the recipe makes. How many cups of chopped walnuts do you need?

Multiplying Mixed Numbers

When you multiply a positive mixed number by a fraction less than 1, the product is less than the mixed number.

EXAMPLE: In a cyclocross bicycle race, $\frac{1}{3}$ of the course is road. If a course is $1\frac{1}{4}$ miles long, how much is road?

(Source: The Sports Fan's Ultimate Book of Sports Comparisons)

To solve the problem, you can multiply $\frac{1}{3} \times 1\frac{1}{4}$.

 You can understand the multiplication by drawing a picture.

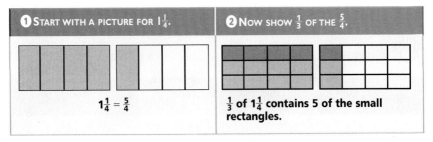

➊ START WITH A PICTURE FOR $1\frac{1}{4}$.	➋ NOW SHOW $\frac{1}{3}$ OF THE $\frac{5}{4}$.
$1\frac{1}{4} = \frac{5}{4}$	$\frac{1}{3}$ of $1\frac{1}{4}$ contains 5 of the small rectangles.

Each small rectangle is $\frac{1}{12}$ of a whole. So, $\frac{1}{3} \times 1\frac{1}{4} = \frac{5}{12}$.

 You can multiply $\frac{1}{3} \times 1\frac{1}{4}$ without drawing a picture.

MORE HELP
See 033, 037

➊ WRITE THE MIXED NUMBER AS A FRACTION.	➋ MULTIPLY THE NUMERATORS. MULTIPLY THE DENOMINATORS.	➌ WRITE THE PRODUCT IN SIMPLEST FORM.
$1\frac{1}{4} = \frac{4}{4} + \frac{1}{4} = \frac{5}{4}$	$\frac{1}{3} \times \frac{5}{4} = \frac{5}{12}$	$\frac{5}{12}$ is already in simplest form.

Either way, $\frac{5}{12}$ mile of the course is road.

Multiplying with Negative Numbers

Sometimes when you multiply, one or both factors are negative.

CASE 1 To understand how to multiply a positive number by a negative number, look at the following pattern. The pattern shows that when two factors have different signs, the product is negative.

You want to know what $\frac{2}{3}$ of $\frac{3}{4}$ is equal to. To solve the problem, you can multiply $\frac{2}{3} \times \frac{3}{4}$.

 ONE WAY You can understand the multiplication by drawing a picture.

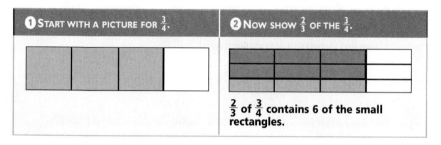

❶ START WITH A PICTURE FOR $\frac{3}{4}$.	❷ NOW SHOW $\frac{2}{3}$ OF THE $\frac{3}{4}$.
	$\frac{2}{3}$ of $\frac{3}{4}$ contains 6 of the small rectangles.

Each small rectangle is $\frac{1}{12}$ of the whole. So, $\frac{2}{3} \times \frac{3}{4} = \frac{6}{12}$, or $\frac{1}{2}$.

 ANOTHER WAY You can multiply $\frac{2}{3} \times \frac{3}{4}$ without drawing a picture.

❶ MULTIPLY THE NUMERATORS. MULTIPLY THE DENOMINATORS.	❷ WRITE THE PRODUCT IN SIMPLEST FORM.
$\frac{2}{3} \times \frac{3}{4} = \frac{6}{12}$	$\frac{6 \div 6}{12 \div 6} = \frac{1}{2}$

MORE HELP
See 037, 214

Either way, you need $\frac{1}{2}$ cup of chopped walnuts.

Shortcut

Here's a shortcut you can use to multiply fractions. Simplify the numerators and denominators *before* multiplying the fractions.

Divide the numerator of one fraction and the denominator of the other by a common factor. Then multiply.

$$\frac{\overset{1}{\cancel{2}}}{\underset{1}{\cancel{3}}} \times \frac{\overset{1}{\cancel{3}}}{\underset{2}{\cancel{4}}} = \frac{1}{2}$$

Divide the 3s by 3.

Divide 2 and 4 by 2.

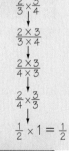

This process is sometimes called **canceling**. Here's why it works.

$$\frac{2}{3} \times \frac{3}{4}$$
↓
$$\frac{2 \times 3}{3 \times 4}$$
↓
$$\frac{2 \times 3}{4 \times 3}$$
↓
$$\frac{2}{4} \times \frac{3}{3}$$
↓
$$\frac{1}{2} \times 1 = \frac{1}{2}$$

$$4 \times 2 = 8$$
$$4 \times 1 = 4$$
$$4 \times 0 = 0$$
$$4 \times {}^-1 = {}^-4$$
$$4 \times {}^-2 = {}^-8$$

So, to find a product when two factors have different signs, multiply their absolute values. Then give the product a negative sign.

It makes sense that $4 \times {}^-2 = {}^-8$ because if you lose 2 yards on each football play for 4 plays, you lose 8 yards.

CASE 2 To understand how to multiply two negative numbers, you can use a pattern similar to the one that was used for factors with unlike signs.

The pattern shows that when two factors are negative, the product is positive.

So, to find a product when two factors have the same signs, multiply their absolute values. The product is positive.

$$2 \times {}^-4 = {}^-8$$
$$1 \times {}^-4 = {}^-4$$
$$0 \times {}^-4 = 0$$
$${}^-1 \times {}^-4 = 4$$
$${}^-2 \times {}^-4 = 8$$

If signs are the same, the product is positive. If signs are different, the product is negative.

Shortcut

You can also use absolute value and follow some simple rules to multiply signed numbers.

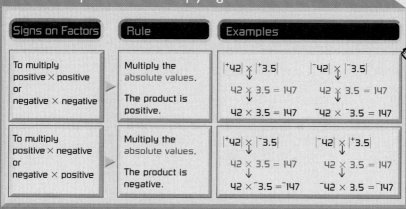

Signs on Factors	Rule	Examples	
To multiply positive × positive or negative × negative	Multiply the absolute values. The product is positive.	$\|{}^+42\| \times \|{}^+3.5\|$ $42 \times 3.5 = 147$ $42 \times 3.5 = 147$	$\|{}^-42\| \times \|{}^-3.5\|$ $42 \times 3.5 = 147$ ${}^-42 \times {}^-3.5 = 147$
To multiply positive × negative or negative × positive	Multiply the absolute values. The product is negative.	$\|{}^+42\| \times \|{}^-3.5\|$ $42 \times 3.5 = 147$ $42 \times {}^-3.5 = {}^-147$	$\|{}^-42\| \times \|{}^+3.5\|$ $42 \times 3.5 = 147$ ${}^-42 \times 3.5 = {}^-147$

MORE HELP
See 050

165) Using a Calculator to Multiply

You can use a calculator to multiply whole numbers, decimals, or signed numbers. Locate the following keys on your calculator:

- $\boxed{\times}$

- $\boxed{=}$

- $\boxed{.}$

- $\boxed{+/-}$

EXAMPLE 1: Use a calculator to multiply 36×204.

$\boxed{3}\ \boxed{6}\ \boxed{\times}\ \boxed{2}\ \boxed{0}\ \boxed{4}\ \boxed{=}\ \boxed{7344.}$

EXAMPLE 2: Use a calculator to multiply 7.2×23.4.

$\boxed{7}\ \boxed{.}\ \boxed{2}\ \boxed{\times}\ \boxed{2}\ \boxed{3}\ \boxed{.}\ \boxed{4}\ \boxed{=}\ \boxed{168.48}$

EXAMPLE 3: Use a calculator to multiply $^{-}25 \times 431$.

$\boxed{2}\ \boxed{5}\ \boxed{+/-}\ \boxed{\times}\ \boxed{4}\ \boxed{3}\ \boxed{1}\ \boxed{=}\ \boxed{-10775.}$

166 MATH ALERT Too Many Places for the Display

Sometimes your product will have more places than the calculator display will hold. There are many ways your particular calculator might handle this problem. Check the calculator instruction book to find out whether the calculator has a way to display a too-large or too-small number.

Using the Constant Function to Multiply

The **constant key** stores an operation and a number. For example, if you press $\boxed{\times}$ $\boxed{2}$ $\boxed{\text{Cons}}$, the calculator will remember the $\times 2$.

EXAMPLE: Use the constant key to show $6 \times 2 \times 2 \times 2 \times 2$. Clear the memory.

Then press:

$\boxed{\times}$ $\boxed{2}$ $\boxed{\text{Cons}}$ $\boxed{6}$ $\boxed{\text{Cons}}$ $\boxed{\text{Cons}}$ $\boxed{\text{Cons}}$ $\boxed{\text{Cons}}$ $\boxed{96.}$

Some calculators have displays that tell you how many times you've pressed $\boxed{\text{Cons}}$. For example, suppose you press $\boxed{\times}$ $\boxed{2}$ $\boxed{\text{Cons}}$. Then you press $\boxed{4}$ and press $\boxed{\text{Cons}}$ 3 times. The display might look like this: $\boxed{^{\text{CONS}}_{\times} 3 \quad 32.}$.

Some calculators have the constant function but not the $\boxed{\text{Cons}}$ key. Check the directions for your calculator.

Special Keys for Fractions

Some calculators have special keys that you can use to work with fractions. For example:

■ $\boxed{/}$ makes fractions.
  To show $\frac{6}{8}$, press $\boxed{6}$ $\boxed{/}$ $\boxed{8}$ $\boxed{6/8.}$.

■ $\boxed{\text{Simp}}$ simplifies fractions.
  To simplify $\frac{6}{8}$, press $\boxed{6}$ $\boxed{/}$ $\boxed{8}$ $\boxed{\text{Simp}}$ $\boxed{=}$ $\boxed{3/4.}$.

■ $\boxed{\text{Ab/c}}$ shows a fraction as a mixed number.
  To show $\frac{9}{7}$ as a mixed number, press $\boxed{9}$ $\boxed{/}$ $\boxed{7}$ $\boxed{\text{Ab/c}}$ $\boxed{1\,u\,2/7.}$.

■ $\boxed{\text{Unit}}$ is used to show a mixed number.
  To enter $1\frac{3}{8}$, press $\boxed{1}$ $\boxed{\text{Unit}}$ $\boxed{3}$ $\boxed{/}$ $\boxed{8}$ $\boxed{1\,u\,3/8.}$.

■ $\boxed{(}$ and $\boxed{)}$ group entries when you want to be sure of the order of calculations.

MORE HELP
See 207

Your calculator may have different keys. Check the directions.

Multiplying Fractions with Fraction Keys

EXAMPLE 1: Multiply $\frac{5}{6} \times \frac{2}{3}$.

$$\boxed{5}\;\boxed{/}\;\boxed{6}\;\boxed{\times}\;\boxed{2}\;\boxed{/}\;\boxed{3}\;\boxed{=}\quad_{N/D\to n/d}\quad 10/18$$

$$\boxed{\text{Simp}}\;\boxed{=}\quad 5/9$$

So, $\frac{5}{6} \times \frac{2}{3} = \frac{5}{9}$.

If you are not sure whether the answer is in simplest form, press $\boxed{\text{Simp}}$ and $\boxed{=}$. If the fraction does not change, it is in simplest form.

EXAMPLE 2: Multiply $4\frac{8}{9} \times 2\frac{2}{3}$.

$$\boxed{4}\;\boxed{\text{Unit}}\;\boxed{8}\;\boxed{/}\;\boxed{9}\;\boxed{\times}\;\boxed{2}\;\boxed{\text{Unit}}\;\boxed{2}\;\boxed{/}\;\boxed{3}\;\boxed{=}\quad 352/27$$

$$\boxed{\text{Ab/c}}\quad 13\;u\;1/27$$

So, $4\frac{8}{9} \times 2\frac{2}{3} = 13\frac{1}{27}$.

Multiplying Fractions Without Fraction Keys

MORE HELP
See 022–024

Even if your calculator doesn't have special keys for fractions, you can still use it to multiply fractions. Use the division key as if it were the fraction bar. Your answer will be a decimal. If your calculator does not have grouping symbols, test it before you trust it to multiply fractions.

EXAMPLE 1: Multiply $\frac{3}{4} \times \frac{3}{5}$.

Press:

$$\boxed{(}\;\boxed{3}\;\boxed{\div}\;\boxed{4}\;\boxed{)}\;\boxed{\times}\;\boxed{(}\;\boxed{3}\;\boxed{\div}\;\boxed{5}\;\boxed{)}\;\boxed{=}\quad 0.45$$

So, $\frac{3}{4} \times \frac{3}{5} = 0.45$.

EXAMPLE 2: Multiply $\frac{2}{9} \times \frac{3}{8}$.

Press:

$$\boxed{(}\;\boxed{2}\;\boxed{\div}\;\boxed{9}\;\boxed{)}\;\boxed{\times}\;\boxed{(}\;\boxed{3}\;\boxed{\div}\;\boxed{8}\;\boxed{)}\;\boxed{=}\quad 0.0833333$$

Since the decimal is a repeating decimal, write the product as $0.08\overline{3}$.

 Division

Division is the opposite of multiplication, and you use multiplication every time you divide. Terms you may hear used in division are **dividend**, **divisor**, and **quotient**.

$$\text{divisor} \longrightarrow 2\overline{)14} \quad \begin{array}{l} \longleftarrow \textbf{quotient} \\ \longleftarrow \textbf{dividend} \end{array}$$

There are two reasons to divide.

CASE 1 When you know the original amount and the number of shares, you divide to find the size of each share.

EXAMPLE 1: Five hungry people want omelets for breakfast. You have a dozen eggs. How many eggs are needed for each omelet? You have the original amount (12 eggs) and the number of shares (5). You need to know the size of one share ($12 \div 5$).

$12 \div 5 = 2.4$

That's about $2\frac{1}{2}$ eggs for each omelet.

CASE 2 When you know the original amount and the size of one share, you divide to find the number of shares.

EXAMPLE 2: You want to know how many 8-ounce sodas are in a 4-quart dispenser. You can figure this out using either ounces or quarts. Try quarts. You have the original amount (4 quarts) and the size of one share ($\frac{1}{4}$ quart is the same as 8 ounces). You need to know how many shares ($4 \div \frac{1}{4}$).

$4 \div \frac{1}{4} = 16$

So, sixteen 8-ounce sodas are in a 4-quart dispenser.

172

MATH ALERT Dividing with Measures

If you are dividing with measures, ALWAYS be sure you're using the SAME size unit. You can divide quarts by quarts or grams by grams but NEVER inches by feet.

173

Mental Division

You probably divide in your head without even thinking about it. If you and some friends are forming teams, you might divide in your head to see how many players will be on each team or how many teams you will make. Or, if you are buying a package of markers and you want to find out how much you are paying for each, you might divide mentally.

174

Dividing with Easy Numbers

You may find that some numbers are easy to divide by in your head.

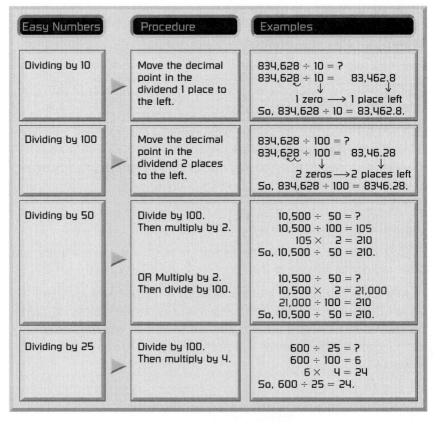

Easy Numbers	Procedure	Examples
Dividing by 10	Move the decimal point in the dividend 1 place to the left.	$834{,}628 \div 10 = ?$ $834{,}628 \div 10 = 83{,}462.8$ 1 zero → 1 place left So, $834{,}628 \div 10 = 83{,}462.8$.
Dividing by 100	Move the decimal point in the dividend 2 places to the left.	$834{,}628 \div 100 = ?$ $834{,}628 \div 100 = 83{,}46.28$ 2 zeros → 2 places left So, $834{,}628 \div 100 = 8346.28$.
Dividing by 50	Divide by 100. Then multiply by 2.	$10{,}500 \div 50 = ?$ $10{,}500 \div 100 = 105$ $105 \times 2 = 210$ So, $10{,}500 \div 50 = 210$.
	OR Multiply by 2. Then divide by 100.	$10{,}500 \div 50 = ?$ $10{,}500 \times 2 = 21{,}000$ $21{,}000 \div 100 = 210$ So, $10{,}500 \div 50 = 210$.
Dividing by 25	Divide by 100. Then multiply by 4.	$600 \div 25 = ?$ $600 \div 100 = 6$ $6 \times 4 = 24$ So, $600 \div 25 = 24$.

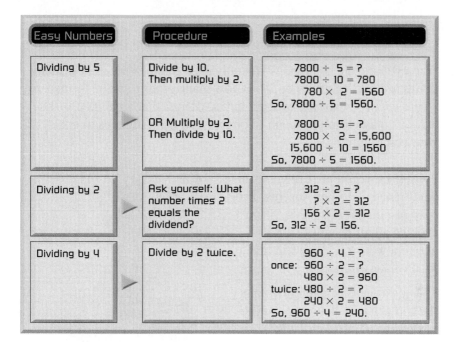

Easy Numbers	Procedure	Examples
Dividing by 5	Divide by 10. Then multiply by 2.	7800 ÷ 5 = ? 7800 ÷ 10 = 780 780 × 2 = 1560 So, 7800 ÷ 5 = 1560.
	OR Multiply by 2. Then divide by 10.	7800 ÷ 5 = ? 7800 × 2 = 15,600 15,600 ÷ 10 = 1560 So, 7800 ÷ 5 = 1560.
Dividing by 2	Ask yourself: What number times 2 equals the dividend?	312 ÷ 2 = ? ? × 2 = 312 156 × 2 = 312 So, 312 ÷ 2 = 156.
Dividing by 4	Divide by 2 twice.	960 ÷ 4 = ? once: 960 ÷ 2 = ? 480 × 2 = 960 twice: 480 ÷ 2 = ? 240 × 2 = 480 So, 960 ÷ 4 = 240.

Dividing with Tens

When you're dividing with tens or multiples of 10, you can often compute in your head.

Look at this pattern:

$320,000 \div 4 = 80,000$
$320,000 \div 40 = 8,000$
$320,000 \div 400 = 800$
$320,000 \div 4000 = 80$
$320,000 \div 40,000 = 8$

The pattern shows that a basic fact (like $32 \div 4 = 8$) can help you divide with multiples of 10.

Divide the basic fact. Then count the zeros on the end of the **dividend**. Subtract the number of zeros on the end of the **divisor**. The difference tells you how many zeros are on the end of the **quotient**.

EXAMPLE: If you and 29 friends won the $12,000,000 lottery, how much would each of you win?

To solve the problem, you can divide: $12,000,000 \div 30$

$12,000,000 \div 30 \longrightarrow 400,000$

$12 \div 3 = 4$

6 zeros − **1 zero** $\longrightarrow$ **5 zeros**

So, each of you would win $400,000!

Estimating Quotients

When you divide, sometimes you only need to know *about* how many things are in each group or *about* how many groups can be formed. So, sometimes you can *estimate* quotients. (Recall that a quotient is the answer to a division problem.) You can also use estimates to check your computation.

EXAMPLE 1: You are driving from San Francisco to Los Angeles. The road distance is 403 miles. If you average about 50 miles an hour, about how long will the trip take?

(Source: Information Please Almanac)

The question asks *about* how long the trip will take. Since one of the key pieces of information is approximate (average speed), you do not need an exact answer. An estimate is enough.

$400 \div 50 = 8$

So, the trip will take about 8 hours.

EXAMPLE 2: You use your calculator to divide $7125 \div 83$. The display shows 85.84337349 . To check this, you can estimate the quotient and compare. If your estimate is not close, you should compute again.

$7200 \div 80 = 90$

So, your answer is reasonable.

Using Multiples of 10 to Estimate Quotients

MORE HELP
See 144

You can use what you know about multiplying with multiples of 10 (like 30, 300, or 3000) to help you estimate quotients.

Why can you use multiplication to help you estimate quotients? Because multiplication is the *opposite* of division. For each division equation, there is a multiplication equation that uses the same numbers.

$12 \div 4 = ? \longrightarrow ? \times 4 = 12$
$3 \times 4 = 12$
So, $12 \div 4 = 3$

EXAMPLE 1: Estimate $525 \div 8$.　Think: $? \times 8$ is about 525.

dividend ——↑　↑—— divisor

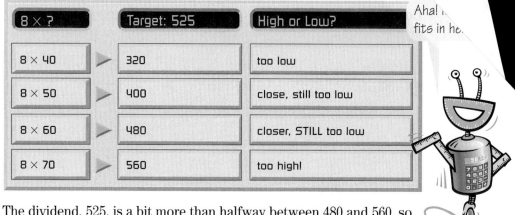

8 × ?	Target: 525	High or Low?
8 × 40	320	too low
8 × 50	400	close, still too low
8 × 60	480	closer, STILL too low
8 × 70	560	too high!

Aha! fits in he.

The dividend, 525, is a bit more than halfway between 480 and 560, so the quotient is a bit more than halfway between 60 and 70.

EXAMPLE 2: Estimate $4 \div 23$.

23 × ?	Target: 4	High or Low?
23 × 1	23	too high, think decimals
23 × 0.1	2.3	too low
23 × 0.2	4.6	too high

So, the quotient of $4 \div 23$ is between 0.1 and 0.2, closer to 0.2.

EXAMPLE 3: Estimate $0.006 \div 0.3$.

0.3 × ?	Target: 0.006	High or Low?
0.3 × 0.1	0.03	too high
0.3 × 0.01	0.003	too low
0.3 × 0.02	0.006	It's just right.

So, the quotient of $0.006 \div 0.3$ is exactly 0.02.

...ompatible Numbers to
...ate Quotients

...mpatible numbers are numbers that work well together. In division, they are number pairs that are easy to divide. You can use compatible numbers to estimate quotients.

EXAMPLE: In 2000, the population of Tokyo was about 8,200,000. Tokyo's area is 223 square miles. In 2000 about how many people were there for each square mile? *(Source: World Almanac)*

MORE HELP
See 173–175

You can estimate: 8,200,000 ÷ 223.
Find numbers close to 8,200,000 and 223.

> Use the basic fact
> 8 ÷ 2 = 4 to help you.

$$8,200,000 \div 223$$

$$8,000,000 \div 200 = 40,000$$

6 zeros − **2 zeros** = **4 zeros**

So, 8,200,000 ÷ 223 is about 40,000. In 2000, Tokyo had about 40,000 people per square mile.

> Wow! New York City had about 26,000 people per square mile in 2000.

Dividing with Whole Numbers

Long division might frighten some people, but behind all those rows of numbers there are just two simple steps that you repeat over and over: multiply and subtract.

The basic steps in division are:

MORE HELP
See 177, 178

1. *Multiply to estimate.* Look at the dividend. Find the first place that the divisor can divide. Use mental multiplication to get close to the dividend without going over.

2. *Subtract and compare.* Subtract the product you found in Step 1 from the dividend to see what remains to be divided.

3. *Repeat Steps 1 and 2* until there's not enough left to divide.

Using the Division Algorithm

Here's one way to record division.

EXAMPLE: You've got 525 players. It takes 8 players to form an International Tug of War team. How many teams can you make?

To solve the problem, divide 525 ÷ 8.

Start with the hundreds.
$$500 \div 8 = ?$$
Multiply to estimate.
$$8 \times 100 = 800$$
That's too much. So, don't write anything in the hundreds place.

Divide the tens.
$$520 \div 8 = ?$$
Multiply to estimate.
$$8 \times 6 \text{ tens} = 480$$
$$8 \times ? \qquad = 525$$
$$8 \times 7 \text{ tens} = 560$$
So, the quotient is between 60 and 70.
Write a 6 in the tens place and 480 under the dividend.
Subtract and compare.
$$525 - 480 = 45$$
You've now got 60 teams with 45 players left!
45 > 8, so you can keep dividing.

Divide the ones.
$$45 \div 8 = ?$$
Multiply to estimate.
$$8 \times 5 = 40$$
$$8 \times ? = 45$$
$$8 \times 6 = 48$$
45 is between 8×5 and 8×6.
Write a 5 in the ones place and 40 under the dividend.
Subtract and compare.
$$45 - 40 = 5$$
You've now formed 65 teams but 5 players are still left. 5 < 8, so you can't divide any more unless you use decimals.
The remainder is 5.

```
        Hundreds
           Tens
              Ones

           6 5 R 5
       _____
     8 ) 5 2 5
       - 4 8 0
       _____
           4 5
         - 4 0
         _____
             5
```

The quotient is more than 65 but less than 66. You need whole teams, so the answer to the question is, *You can make 65 teams of 8 if you have 525 players.* Maybe the remaining 5 people can sub.

MATH ALERT Zeros in the Quotient

Sometimes you need to show that there is nothing in a place in your quotient. Pay attention to place value and your estimates, and you won't accidentally forget a zero.

EXAMPLE: Total production in the henhouse today was 1316 eggs. How many boxes of one dozen eggs can be packed today?

See 004–007

Start with the thousands.
  $1000 \div 12 = ?$
Multiply to estimate.
  $12 \times 1 \text{ thousand} = 12,000$
  That's too much. So, don't write anything in the thousands place.

Divide the hundreds.
  $1300 \div 12 = ?$
Multiply to estimate.
  $12 \times 1 \text{ hundred} = 1200$
  $12 \times ? = 1316$
  $12 \times 2 \text{ hundreds} = 2400$
  So, the quotient is between 100 and 200.
  Write a 1 in the hundreds place and 1200 under the dividend.

Subtract and compare.
  $1316 - 1200 = 116$, so 116 is all that remains of the dividend. $116 > 12$, so you can keep dividing.

Divide the tens.
  $11 \text{ tens} \div 12 = ?$
Multiply to estimate.
  $12 \times 1 \text{ ten} = 120$. That's too much.
  Write 0 in the tens place to show that there are no tens in the quotient.

Divide the ones.
  $116 \div 12 = ?$
Multiply to estimate.
  $12 \times 9 \text{ ones} = 108$
  $12 \times ? = 116$
  $12 \times 10 \text{ ones} = 120$
  116 is between 12×9 and 12×10.
  Write a 9 in the ones place and 108 under the dividend.

Subtract and compare.
  $116 - 108 = 8$, so 8 is all that remains of the dividend. $8 < 12$, so you can't divide anymore unless you use decimals.
  The remainder is 8.

```
         Thousands
            Hundreds
               Tens
                  Ones

            1  0  9 R8
      12)1  3  1  6
        -1  2  0  0
         ─────────
            1  1  6
           -1  0  8
            ─────────
                  8
```

The quotient is more than 109, but the answer to the question is, *109 boxes of one dozen eggs can be packed today.*

Interpreting Quotients and Remainders

When your quotient is not a whole number, the question you're answering will give you a clue about what the remainder means.

CASE 1 If you're sharing something that can be divided into parts smaller than one, then you might write your remainder as a fraction:

$$\frac{\text{remainder}}{\text{divisor}}$$

EXAMPLE 1: If $525 was shared among 8 people, how much money would each person have? Since $525 \div 8 = 65$ with a remainder of 5, or $65\frac{5}{8}$, each person would have $\$65\frac{5}{8}$, or about $65.62.

CASE 2 Sometimes the remainder means that the answer to the problem is larger than the quotient.

EXAMPLE 2: How many times will the 8-person Zero Gravity ride run to serve the 525 people in line? Since $525 \div 8 = 65\frac{5}{8}$, this means that you can't fit all of the people on 65 runs, and $\frac{5}{8}$ of a run doesn't make sense. You will need 66 runs—one of those runs may carry only 5 people.

Maybe 3 of the runs will carry only 7 people—can you think of other solutions?

CASE 3 Sometimes, to answer the question, you use the quotient and ignore the remainder.

EXAMPLE 3: How many 8-oz bags of jelly beans can you *fill* with 52.5 ounces of the candies? Since $52.5 \div 8 = 6.5625$, you *could* say that you can fill 6.5625 bags but you can really only *fill* 6 bags.

CASE 4 Sometimes the remainder *is* the answer!

EXAMPLE 4: You have 525 yards of crepe paper to decorate the gym. If you cut as many 8-yard strips as possible for streamers, how much will be left to decorate the table?

$525 \div 8 = 65\frac{5}{8}$. Look at the fraction. $\frac{5}{8}$ means the last strip is only 5 of the needed 8 yards long. That means the answer to your question is *5 yards of crepe paper will be left for the table.*

Checking Division by Multiplying

Even if you think you divided correctly, you should always check your answer. Checking helps you make sure that you correctly recorded each step in the division, and that you hit the right calculator keys.

MORE HELP
See 152–157

One way to check your division is to use multiplication. This is because multiplication "undoes" division. If you multiply the quotient by the divisor and add any remainder, the answer should be the dividend.

EXAMPLE 1: Check whether dividing 17 players into groups of 3 gives 5 groups with 2 players left over.

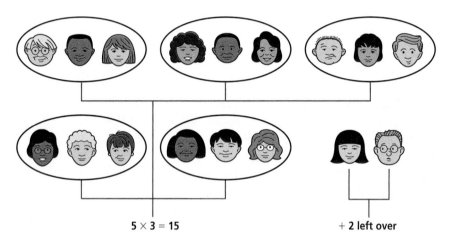

$5 \times 3 = 15$ $+ 2$ left over

EXAMPLE 2: Is 52 R3 a correct answer for $1251 \div 24$? To check, multiply the quotient by the divisor and add the remainder.

$$52 \times 24 = 1248$$

quotient ⌐ divisor

$$1248 + 3 = 1251$$

└ remainder

Since 1251 is the original dividend, the division is correct.

EXAMPLE 3: Does $3371 \div 73 = 47.82$? To check, multiply the quotient by the divisor.

$73 \times 47.82 = 3490.86$

Since $3490.86 \neq 3371$, you should do the division again.

Dividing with Decimals   184

You divide decimals the same way you divide whole numbers. The only difference is that you place a decimal point in the quotient. Compare these two division problems.

$$
\begin{array}{r}
34 \\
19\overline{)646} \\
-570 \\
\hline
76 \\
-76 \\
\hline
0
\end{array}
\qquad
\begin{array}{r}
3.4 \\
19\overline{)64.6} \\
-57\ 0 \\
\hline
7\ 6 \\
-7\ 6 \\
\hline
0
\end{array}
$$

The digits in the problems are the same. The steps are the same. But the place values are different because of the decimal points.

Dividing Decimals by Whole Numbers   185

When you divide a decimal by a whole number, you place the decimal point for the quotient *directly above* the decimal point in the dividend. Then you divide the same way you divide whole numbers.

EXAMPLE: You and three friends go to a restaurant. The bill is $26.88. If you split the bill equally, how much does each person pay?

To solve the problem, you can divide 26.88 ÷ 4.

❶ WRITE THE DECIMAL POINT FOR THE QUOTIENT DIRECTLY ABOVE THE DECIMAL POINT IN THE DIVIDEND.	**❷ DIVIDE THE SAME WAY YOU DIVIDE WHOLE NUMBERS.**
$$\begin{array}{r} . \\ 4\overline{)26.88} \end{array}$$	$$\begin{array}{r} 6.72 \\ 4\overline{)26.88} \\ -24\ 00 \\ \hline 2\ 88 \\ -2\ 80 \\ \hline 8 \\ -8 \\ \hline 0 \end{array}$$

The quotient is 6.72. You each pay $6.72.

Dividing by Decimals

 ONE WAY Divide by a decimal by multiplying the divisor and the dividend by the same power of 10. You choose the power of 10 that turns your divisor into a whole number.

EXAMPLE 1: A guinea pig weighs 24 ounces. A pygmy shrew weighs 0.16 ounce. How many times heavier is a guinea pig than a pygmy shrew? *(Source: The Sizeaurus)*

To solve the problem, you can divide $24 \div 0.16$.

Multiply the divisor by a power of 10 to make it a whole number.
$0.16 \times 100 = 16$
Move the decimal point 2 places to show this.

Multiply the dividend by the same power of 10.
$24 \times 100 = 2400$
Move the decimal point 2 places to show this. (Sometimes you'll need to fill in the extra places with zeros.)

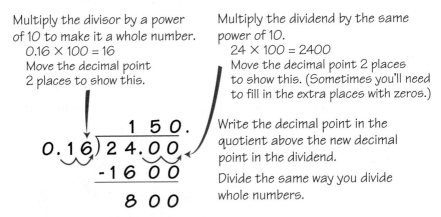

Write the decimal point in the quotient above the new decimal point in the dividend.

Divide the same way you divide whole numbers.

A guinea pig is 150 times heavier than a pygmy shrew.

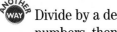 **ANOTHER WAY** Divide by a decimal by dividing as if you were dividing whole numbers, then estimating the quotient to place the decimal point.

EXAMPLE 2: Divide $972.5 \div 0.4$.

❶ DIVIDE AS IF YOU HAD WHOLE NUMBERS.	❷ ESTIMATE THE QUOTIENT.	❸ USE THE ESTIMATE TO PLACE THE DECIMAL POINT.
$\dfrac{243125}{4)972500}$ **With decimals, keep adding zeros onto the dividend until you think your quotient will answer the question.**	$972.5 \div 0.4$ ↓ $1000 \div 0.5 = 2000$	$972.5 \div 0.4 = 2431.25$ ↓ **The estimate, 2000, is close to 2431, so place the decimal point after the 1.**

So, $972.5 \div 0.4 = 2431.25$.

Dividing with Fractions 187

You can divide with fractions or mixed numbers. To understand what doing this kind of division means, think about the meaning of division and the meaning of fractions.

EXAMPLE 1: 2-inch pieces cut from a 3-inch ribbon⟶ $3 \div 2$

The quotient is less than 3.

EXAMPLE 2: $\frac{1}{2}$-inch pieces cut from a 3-inch ribbon⟶ $3 \div \frac{1}{2}$

The quotient is greater than 3.

EXAMPLE 3: 3-inch pieces cut from a $\frac{1}{2}$-inch ribbon⟶ $\frac{1}{2} \div 3$

The quotient is less than $\frac{1}{2}$.

> The quotient may be a fraction, but the answer is 0—you can't get any 3-inch pieces from a ribbon so short!

EXAMPLE 4: $\frac{1}{2}$-inch pieces cut from a $3\frac{1}{4}$-inch ribbon⟶ $3\frac{1}{4} \div \frac{1}{2}$

The quotient is greater than $3\frac{1}{4}$.

Reciprocals 188

Reciprocals are number pairs that have a product of 1. Here are a few:

MORE HELP
See 160–164

$$5 = \frac{5}{1} \qquad 3\frac{1}{2} = \frac{7}{2}$$

$\frac{3}{8}$ and $\frac{8}{3}$

$\frac{3}{8} \times \frac{8}{3} = \frac{24}{24} = 1$

5 and $\frac{1}{5}$

$\frac{5}{1} \times \frac{1}{5} = \frac{5}{5} = 1$

$3\frac{1}{2}$ and $\frac{2}{7}$

$\frac{7}{2} \times \frac{2}{7} = \frac{14}{14} = 1$

As you can see, it's easy to find the reciprocal of any number. If you have a fraction, just flip it over to find the reciprocal. If you have a whole number or a mixed number, rewrite it as a fraction, then flip that fraction upside down.

Dividing a Whole Number by a Fraction

EXAMPLE: You have 4 pounds of trail mix. You want to put it in bags so that there is $\frac{2}{3}$ pound in each bag. How many bags can you fill?

To solve the problem, you can divide $4 \div \frac{2}{3}$.

 ONE WAY You can divide by drawing a picture.

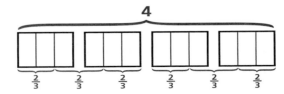

There are six $\frac{2}{3}$s in 4. So, $4 \div \frac{2}{3} = 6$.

 ANOTHER WAY You can divide $4 \div \frac{2}{3}$ without drawing a picture.

MORE HELP
See 037, 042, 188

❶ WRITE THE WHOLE NUMBER AS A FRACTION.	❷ MULTIPLY BY THE RECIPROCAL OF THE DIVISOR.	❸ WRITE THE PRODUCT IN SIMPLEST FORM.
$4 \longrightarrow \frac{4}{1}$	$\frac{4}{1} \div \frac{2}{3}$ $\downarrow$ $\frac{4}{1} \times \frac{3}{2} = \frac{12}{2}$	$\frac{12 \div 2}{2 \div 2} = \frac{6}{1} = 6$

Either way, you can fill six $\frac{2}{3}$-pound bags.

You can use what you know about algebra to understand the steps for dividing fractions. Division **expressions** can be written in fraction form. So, $4 \div \frac{2}{3}$ can be written as a **complex fraction**: $4 \div \frac{2}{3} \longrightarrow \frac{4}{\frac{2}{3}}$

You can multiply both the numerator and the denominator by the reciprocal of the denominator.

$\frac{\frac{3}{2}}{\frac{3}{2}}$ is just another name for one. Choose $\frac{3}{2}$ to multiply the numerator and denominator because it is the reciprocal of the denominator. If the denominator were $\frac{19}{25}$, you'd choose $\frac{25}{19}$ to multiply the numerator and denominator.

$$\frac{4}{\frac{2}{3}} \times \frac{\frac{3}{2}}{\frac{3}{2}} = \frac{4 \times \frac{3}{2}}{\frac{2}{3} \times \frac{3}{2}} = \frac{4 \times \frac{3}{2}}{\frac{6}{6}} = \frac{4 \times \frac{3}{2}}{1} = 4 \times \frac{3}{2}$$

Dividing a Fraction by a Whole Number

EXAMPLE: Three gold prospectors had a tough day. At the end of that day, they had panned only $\frac{7}{8}$ ounce of gold from a stream. If they split their gold into equal shares, what is each prospector's share?

To solve the problem, you can divide $\frac{7}{8} \div 3$.

 You can divide by drawing a picture.

Show $\frac{7}{8}$ by coloring $\frac{7}{8}$ of a rectangle.

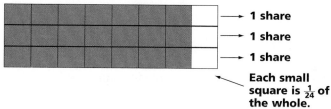

$$\frac{7}{8}$$

To find $\frac{7}{8} \div 3$, divide the rectangle into 3 equal rows.

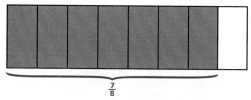

→ **1 share**

→ **1 share**

→ **1 share**

↖ **Each small square is $\frac{1}{24}$ of the whole.**

So, $\frac{7}{8} \div 3 = \frac{7}{24}$.

 You can divide $\frac{7}{8} \div 3$ without drawing a picture.

MORE HELP
See 037

❶ WRITE THE WHOLE NUMBER AS A FRACTION.	❷ MULTIPLY BY THE RECIPROCAL OF THE DIVISOR.	❸ WRITE THE PRODUCT IN SIMPLEST FORM.
$3 \longrightarrow \frac{3}{1}$	$\frac{7}{8} \div \frac{3}{1}$ $\downarrow$ $\frac{7}{8} \times \frac{1}{3} = \frac{7}{24}$	$\frac{7}{24}$ is already in simplest form.

Either way, each prospector's share is $\frac{7}{24}$ ounce of gold.

Dividing a Fraction by a Fraction

When working with measurement, you may need to divide a fraction by a fraction.

EXAMPLE: You have $\frac{3}{4}$ yard of ribbon. How many $\frac{1}{8}$-yard pieces can you cut the ribbon into?

To solve the problem, you can divide $\frac{3}{4} \div \frac{1}{8}$.

 Understand the division by drawing a picture.

Show a rectangle divided into both fourths and eighths.

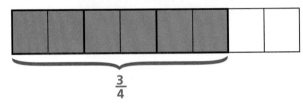

$$\frac{3}{4}$$

Count the number of $\frac{1}{8}$s in $\frac{3}{4}$.

There are six $\frac{1}{8}$s in $\frac{3}{4}$. So, $\frac{3}{4} \div \frac{1}{8} = 6$.

 Divide $\frac{3}{4} \div \frac{1}{8}$ without drawing a picture.

MORE HELP
See 037

❶ MULTIPLY BY THE RECIPROCAL OF THE DIVISOR.	❷ WRITE THE PRODUCT IN SIMPLEST FORM.
$\frac{3}{4} \div \frac{1}{8}$ $\downarrow$ $\frac{3}{4} \times \frac{8}{1} = \frac{24}{4}$	$\frac{24 \div 4}{4 \div 4} = \frac{6}{1} = 6$

Either way, you can cut the ribbon into six $\frac{1}{8}$-yard pieces.

Dividing Mixed Numbers

You can use what you know about dividing fractions to divide mixed numbers.

EXAMPLE: You have a $4\frac{3}{4}$-foot-long board. How many $1\frac{1}{2}$-foot shelves can you cut from this?

To solve the problem, you can divide $4\frac{3}{4} \div 1\frac{1}{2}$.

 You can understand the division by drawing a picture.

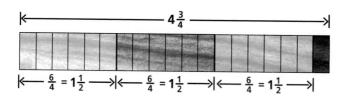

There are three $1\frac{1}{2}$-foot lengths in $4\frac{3}{4}$ feet. There is another $\frac{1}{4}$ foot left over. $\frac{1}{4}$ foot is only $\frac{1}{6}$ of $1\frac{1}{2}$ feet, since it takes 6 fourths to make $1\frac{1}{2}$.

 You can divide $4\frac{3}{4} \div 1\frac{1}{2}$ without drawing a picture.

① WRITE THE MIXED NUMBERS AS FRACTIONS.	② MULTIPLY BY THE RECIPROCAL OF THE DIVISOR.	③ WRITE THE PRODUCT IN SIMPLEST FORM.
$4\frac{3}{4} \div 1\frac{1}{2}$ $4 \quad \frac{3}{4} \div 1 \quad \frac{1}{2}$ $\frac{19}{4} \div \frac{3}{2}$	$\frac{19}{4} \div \frac{3}{2}$ $\frac{19}{4} \times \frac{2}{3} = \frac{38}{12}$	$\frac{38}{12} = 38 \div 12 = 3\frac{2}{12} = 3\frac{1}{6}$

MORE HELP
See 033,182

Either way, the quotient is $3\frac{1}{6}$. You can cut 3 shelves from the board with $\frac{1}{6}$ of a $1\frac{1}{2}$-foot shelf left over.

Dividing with Negative Numbers

You can use what you know about the relationship between multiplication and division, and what you know about multiplying negative numbers, to help you divide with negative numbers.

To understand how to divide with negative numbers, look at the pattern below.

MORE HELP
See 050, 164

MULTIPLICATION EQUATION	RELATED DIVISION EQUATION
$7 \times 4 = 28$	$28 \div 4 = 7$
$^-7 \times 4 = ^-28$	$^-28 \div 4 = ^-7$
$7 \times ^-4 = ^-28$	$^-28 \div ^-4 = 7$
$^-7 \times ^-4 = 28$	$28 \div ^-4 = ^-7$

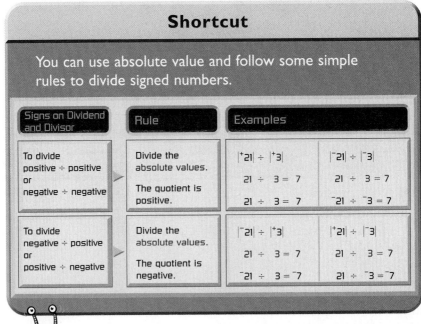

Shortcut

You can use absolute value and follow some simple rules to divide signed numbers.

Signs on Dividend and Divisor	Rule	Examples	
To divide positive ÷ positive or negative ÷ negative	Divide the absolute values. The quotient is positive.	$\|^+21\| \div \|^+3\|$ $21 \div 3 = 7$ $21 \div 3 = 7$	$\|^-21\| \div \|^-3\|$ $21 \div 3 = 7$ $^-21 \div ^-3 = 7$
To divide negative ÷ positive or positive ÷ negative	Divide the absolute values. The quotient is negative.	$\|^-21\| \div \|^+3\|$ $21 \div 3 = 7$ $^-21 \div 3 = ^-7$	$\|^+21\| \div \|^-3\|$ $21 \div 3 = 7$ $21 \div ^-3 = ^-7$

If the signs are the same, the quotient is positive.
If the signs are different, the quotient is negative.

Using a Calculator to Divide

To use a calculator to divide whole numbers, decimals, or signed numbers, locate these keys on your calculator:

- $\div$
- $=$
- $.$
- $+/-$

EXAMPLE 1: Use a calculator to divide ⁻676 ÷ 13.

| 6 | 7 | 6 | +/- | ÷ | 1 | 3 | = | *-52.* |

EXAMPLE 2: Use a calculator to divide 8.8128 ÷ 2.04.

| 8 | . | 8 | 1 | 2 | 8 | ÷ | 2 | . | 0 | 4 | = | *4.32* |

Interpreting Calculator Remainders

Sometimes when you use a calculator to divide a whole number by a whole number, your answer will be a decimal.

EXAMPLE 1: Divide 22 ÷ 5.

MORE HELP
See 182

| 2 | 2 | ÷ | 5 | = | *4.4* |

The 0.4 of the 4.4 can also be shown as a fraction ($\frac{4}{10}$) or a remainder. ($\frac{4}{10} = \frac{2}{5}$, so the remainder is 2.) How you interpret the quotient and remainder depends on the problem that you are trying to answer.

Some calculators have a key such as $\boxed{\text{INT÷}}$ that gives you an integer part of the quotient with a remainder, instead of expressing the remainder as a decimal.

EXAMPLE 2: Divide 22 ÷ 5.

| 2 | 2 | INT÷ | 5 | = | Q *4* R *2* |

The Q shows that the integer part of the quotient is 4. The R shows that the remainder is 2.

196 !

MATH ALERT Too Many Places for the Display

Sometimes your quotient will have more decimal places than the calculator display will hold. There are many ways your particular calculator might handle this problem. Check the calculator instruction book to find out.

- Does the calculator truncate (cut off) or round the answer? (Try pressing [2] [÷] [3]. If the display ends in a 6, it truncated the answer. If the display ends in 7, it rounded the answer.)

- Does the calculator have a way to display a too-large or too-small number in scientific notation?

197

Special Keys for Fractions

Some calculators have special keys that you can use to work with fractions. For example:

- [/] makes fractions.
  To enter $\frac{6}{8}$, press [6] [/] [8] ⬚ 6/8 ⬚.

- [Simp] simplifies fractions.
  To simplify $\frac{6}{8}$, press [6] [/] [8] [Simp] [=] ⬚ 3/4 ⬚.

- [Ab/c] shows a fraction as a mixed number.
  To show $\frac{9}{7}$ as a mixed number, press [9] [/] [7] [Ab/c] ⬚ 1 u 2/7 ⬚.

- [Unit] is used to show a mixed number.
  To enter $1\frac{3}{8}$, press [1] [Unit] [3] [/] [8] ⬚ 1 u 3/8 ⬚.

MORE HELP
See 207

- [( ] and [ )] group entries when you want to be sure of the order of calculations.

Your calculator may have different keys. Check the directions.
If your calculator has no grouping symbols *and* no fraction function, you should probably not use it to compute with fractions.

Dividing Fractions with Fraction Keys

EXAMPLE 1: Use a calculator to divide $\frac{3}{4} \div \frac{7}{8}$.

$$\boxed{3}\ \boxed{/}\ \boxed{4}\ \boxed{\div}\ \boxed{7}\ \boxed{/}\ \boxed{8}\ \boxed{=}\quad _{N/D\to n/d}\ \ 24/28$$

$$\boxed{\text{Simp}}\ \boxed{=}\quad _{N/D\to n/d}\ \ 12/14$$

$$\boxed{\text{Simp}}\ \boxed{=}\quad 6/7$$

If you are not sure whether the answer is in simplest form, press $\boxed{\text{Simp}}$ and $\boxed{=}$. If the fraction does not change, it is in simplest form.

EXAMPLE 2: Use a calculator to divide $3\frac{2}{3} \div \frac{4}{9}$.

$$\boxed{3}\ \boxed{\text{Unit}}\ \boxed{2}\ \boxed{/}\ \boxed{3}\ \boxed{\div}\ \boxed{4}\ \boxed{/}\ \boxed{9}\ \boxed{=}\quad _{N/D\to n/d}\ \ 99/12$$

$$\boxed{\text{Ab/c}}\quad _{N/D\to n/d}\ 8\ u\ 3/12$$

$$\boxed{\text{Simp}}\ \boxed{=}\quad 8\ u\ 1/4$$

Use $\boxed{\text{Ab/c}}$ when the display shows a fraction greater than 1.

Dividing Fractions Without Fraction Keys

Even if your calculator doesn't have special keys for fractions, you can still use it to divide fractions. Your answer will be a decimal. If your answer needs to be a fraction, you may be better off not using a calculator this way.

EXAMPLE 1: Divide $\frac{5}{8} \div \frac{1}{4}$.

$$\boxed{(}\ \boxed{5}\ \boxed{\div}\ \boxed{8}\ \boxed{)}\ \boxed{\div}\ \boxed{(}\ \boxed{1}\ \boxed{\div}\ \boxed{4}\ \boxed{)}\ \boxed{=}\quad 2.5$$

MORE HELP
See 022–024

EXAMPLE 2: Divide $\frac{5}{9} \div \frac{2}{3}$.

$$\boxed{(}\ \boxed{5}\ \boxed{\div}\ \boxed{9}\ \boxed{)}\ \boxed{\div}\ \boxed{(}\ \boxed{2}\ \boxed{\div}\ \boxed{3}\ \boxed{)}\ \boxed{=}\quad 0.8333333$$

Since the decimal is a repeating decimal, write the number as $0.8\overline{3}$.

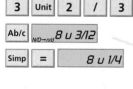

Algebra

Things change.

A basketball rises and falls.

The more you work, the more you earn.

To deal with things that vary, mathematicians invented algebra.

Did you ever read a paragraph that said so many things that it was hard to follow? Mathematics problems in plain English can be like that. Fortunately, we have algebra. Algebra provides tools for stating, simplifying, and picturing relationships.

Algebraic Notation

Algebraic notation is a key part of the language of mathematics.

■ When you want to talk about a number, even when you don't know what the number is, you can use algebraic notation.

■ When you want to talk about the relationship between changing quantities, you can use algebraic notation.

■ When you want to be sure everybody expresses a term, rule, or result in the same way, you can use algebraic notation.

202) Variables and Constants

A **constant** is a quantity that stays the same, like the number of days in a week. A **variable** is a quantity that can change, like your age.

Constants	**Variables**
number of cents in a quarter	number of inches tall a kid is
number of inches in a foot	amount of time you spend on homework in a month
number of months in a year	number of cents in your pocket

When you write equations, you can use a letter to stand for a variable. You can choose any letter you like—sometimes the first letters of the important words make the meaning of the equation easier to remember.

Distance = rate × time

$d = rt$

Area = length × width

$A = lw$

> To avoid confusion with variables, you don't often use the × symbol to show multiplication. Instead, to show that d is the product of r and t, you can write: $d = rt$, $d = r(t)$, or $d = r \cdot t$.

Expressions and Equations 203

An **expression** is like a phrase: It has no equals sign. An **equation** is a mathematical statement that says two expressions are equal to each other. The equation $A = lw$ says that the number that names the *a*rea of some figure is equal to the number you can find by multiplying the *l*ength by the *w*idth of the same figure.

EXAMPLE: Write equations for the area of this rectangle.

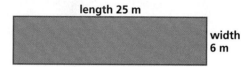

length 25 m

width
6 m

CASE 1 In the equation $A = lw$, A and lw are algebraic expressions.

CASE 2 In the equation $A = 25 \times 6$, A is an algebraic expression and 25×6 is a numerical expression.

CASE 3 In the equation $150 = 25 \times 6$, 150 and 25×6 are numerical expressions.

Writing Algebraic Expressions 204

When an algebraic expression has parts that are added (or subtracted, since subtracting is the same as adding the opposite of a number), each part is called a **term**.

EXAMPLES:

WORDS	ALGEBRAIC EXPRESSION
gift price plus tax (tax rate of 7% multiplied by gift price) plus $3 gift-wrapping charge	p + $0.07p$ + 3 term term term (price) (tax) (wrapping charge)
3, 6, 9, 12, ... The fifth number of the pattern is 3×5, so the *n*th number of the pattern is ...	$3n$ ⟶ *n*th number of pattern
the total number of people at the square dance divided by 8	$\dfrac{n}{8}$ ⟶ **number of square dance teams** **With variables, division is usually written in fraction form.**

Writing Algebraic Equations

An equation is just mathematical shorthand that shows the equal relationship between two expressions. You may know the numbers or you may only know how the numbers are related. Either way, you can translate words into symbols so that finding any missing information is easier.

EXAMPLES:

WORDS	ALGEBRAIC EQUATION
The perimeter of the school property is the sum of the lengths of its 4 sides.	$P = s + t + u + v$ (P stands for the perimeter. The lengths of the 4 sides are s, t, u, and v.)
The difference between the price of the bicycle and $100 is $27.	$100 - b = 27$
Albert Einstein discovered that the energy of an object could be determined by multiplying the mass of the object by the square of the speed of light.	$E = mc^2$
80% of the class of 45 students participated in the school play.	$0.8 \times 45 = n$

Evaluating Algebraic Expressions

To **evaluate** an algebraic expression, you substitute a number for the variable and carry out the computation.

EXAMPLE: Hair grows at the rate of about 0.4 inch per month. So, if m is the number of months, $0.4m$ is an expression for the number of inches hair grows in m months. Use this expression to find the number of inches hair grows in 12 months.

(Source: The Random House Book/Source of 1001 Questions and Answers About the Human Body)

To solve the problem, you evaluate the expression $0.4m$ when $m = 12$. Substitute 12 for m and compute.

$0.4m$

$0.4(12) = 4.8$ Remember, $0.4(12)$ means "0.4 times 12."

So, in 12 months hair grows about 4.8 inches.

Order of Operations

Order of operations is just what it sounds like: the order in which you perform operations in an expression.

MORE HELP
See 220

EXAMPLE: Evaluate $4 + 5 \times 6 \div 10$.

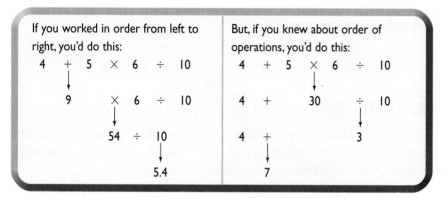

$4 + 5 \times 6 \div 10$ really does equal 7. The order of operations ensures that everyone doing the problem will get the same answer.

Using Symbols to Show Order of Operations

You can use parentheses and brackets to group calculations to be sure that some calculations are done in a special order. The fraction bar also groups calculations.

CASE 1 You can sometimes use parentheses to group terms.

EXAMPLE 1: Show the product of 5 and $r^2 + 6$.

Use parentheses to group $r^2 + 6$: $5(r^2 + 6)$. You can evaluate $r^2 + 6$ before multiplying by 5. Or you can use the Distributive Property and multiply each term by 5.

CASE 2 When more than one set of parentheses is needed, you can use nested parentheses (( )), parentheses in brackets [( )], or braces {( )} to group terms.

EXAMPLE 2: Show that $5(r^2 + 6) + 4r$ is to be multiplied by $7r$.

Write $7r[5(r^2 + 6) + 4r]$.

MORE ▶

You can evaluate the two terms inside the brackets before multiplying by $7r$. Or you can use the Distributive Property and multiply each term by $7r$.

CASE 3 The fraction bar sometimes comes in handy to show grouping.

EXAMPLE 3: Show the expression $6x^2 + 8$ being divided by 25.

Since the fraction bar can indicate division, it almost always replaces $\div$ in algebraic expressions: $\frac{6x^2 + 8}{25}$

You can evaluate the numerator before you divide by 25. Or you can use the Distributive Property and multiply both terms by $\frac{1}{25}$.

209

Rules for Order of Operations

To make sure that everyone finds the same answer when they complete a calculation or evaluate an algebraic expression, mathematicians have created rules called order of operations.

- First, do the operations within grouping symbols: $(\ ), [\ ], \frac{x}{y}$

MORE HELP
See 070–084

- Second, do powers or roots: x^y or $\sqrt{x}$

- Third, multiply or divide in order from left to right: $\times$ or $\div$

- Fourth, add or subtract in order from left to right: $+$ or $-$

EXAMPLE: Evaluate: $20 - \frac{16}{n} + (n - 3)^2$ for $n = 8$

$$20 - \frac{16}{n} + (n - 3)^2$$

Substitute 8 for _n_ $\longrightarrow$ $20 - \frac{16}{8} + (8-3)^2$

Deal with the grouping symbols $\longrightarrow$ $20 - \frac{16}{8} + (5)^2$

Do all powers and roots $\longrightarrow$ $20 - \frac{16}{8} + 25$

Multiply or divide left to right $\longrightarrow$ $20 - 2 + 25$

Add or subtract left to right $\longrightarrow$ $18 + 25$

43

Sometimes a silly sentence will help you remember the order of operations: Gary's Parents Rarely Make Dinner After Seven.

Order of Operations on the Calculator

Some calculators automatically follow the rules for order of operations. This is known as the algebraic ordering system. Other calculators carry out operations in the order that you enter them, even if that order is different from the rules.

EXAMPLE: Check your calculator for order of operations with this expression: $18 + 9 \div \sqrt{9}$.

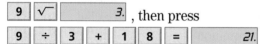

If your display shows ⎢   21.⎥, your calculator has order of operations. If it shows ⎢   9.⎥, it doesn't. Once you know how your calculator computes, then you can enter the calculations so they are done in the correct order. For example, to find $18 + 9 \div \sqrt{9}$ on a calculator that does not follow the rules for order of operations. You can press

To enter $\sqrt{9}$ into a calculator, first press ⎢9⎥, then ⎢√⎥.

⎢9⎥⎢√⎥⎢ 3.⎥ , then press

⎢9⎥⎢÷⎥⎢3⎥⎢+⎥⎢1⎥⎢8⎥⎢=⎥⎢ 21.⎥

OR, use grouping symbols:

When you enter ⎢(⎥, the calculator waits until you enter ⎢)⎥ before calculating what's between the grouping symbols.

211  # Properties

When you're working with real numbers, there are some things that are always true about how they behave. These things are called **properties**. Most of them are common-sense, but some of them aren't so obvious.

212) ## Commutative Properties

Sometimes order matters: You don't put on your socks after your shoes. But sometimes order doesn't matter: you *could* put on your shoes before your belt.

> Commutative sounds like commute. That means "go back and forth." Addition and multiplication work either backward or forward.

213 ### Commutative Property of Addition

The **Commutative Property of Addition** is sometimes called the Order Property of Addition. It states that changing the order of addends does not change the sum. So, $a + b = b + a$.

How can knowing this property help you? One way is that you can use it to make it easier to add.

EXAMPLE 1: Add 26 + 18.

$$26 + 18 = 44 \qquad 18 + 26 = 44$$
$$\text{So, } 26 + 18 = 18 + 26.$$

EXAMPLE 2: Add 25 + 147 + 75.

If you followed the order of operations rules, you'd add 25 + 147, then add 75. But you can use the Commutative Property to switch the order of 147 and 75.

$$25 + 147 + 75 = 25 + 75 + 147$$
$$= 100 + 147$$
$$= 247$$

MORE HELP
See 093

> Adding 25 + 75 = 100, then 100 + 147 = 247, is pretty easy!

Commutative Property of Multiplication

214

The **Commutative Property of Multiplication** is also called the Order Property of Multiplication. It states that changing the order of factors does not change the product. So, $a \times b = b \times a$.

$$5 \times 3 = 15$$

$$3 \times 5 = 15$$

EXAMPLE: Multiply 5 × 167 × 2.

If you followed the order of operations rules, you'd multiply 5 × 167, then multiply by 2. But you can use the Commutative Property to switch the order of 167 and 2 to make it easier to multiply.

$$5 \times 167 \times 2 = 5 \times 2 \times 167$$
$$= 10 \times 167$$
$$= 1670$$

> Multiply 5 × 2 = 10, then 10 × 167 = 1670.

215

MATH ALERT Subtraction and Division Are Not Commutative

Is $8 - 2$ equal to $2 - 8$? Is $8 \div 2$ equal to $2 \div 8$? No.

So, subtraction and division are *not* commutative.

CASE 1 BUT, you can rewrite a subtraction expression as addition and then use the Commutative Property of Addition.

EXAMPLE 1: Rewrite $8 - 2$ as a commutative expression.

$$8 - 2 = 6$$
$$\downarrow$$

Subtracting 2 is the same as adding ⁻2. $\quad 8 + {}^{-}2 = 6$
$$\downarrow$$

Addition is commutative. $\quad {}^{-}2 + 8 = 6$

CASE 2 You can also rewrite a division expression as multiplication and then use the Commutative Property of Multiplication.

EXAMPLE 2: Rewrite $8 \div 2$ as a commutative expression.

$$8 \div 2 = 4$$
$$\downarrow$$

MORE HELP
See 188

Dividing by 2 is the same as multiplying by $\frac{1}{2}$. $\quad 8 \times \frac{1}{2} = 4$
$$\downarrow$$

Multiplication is commutative. $\quad \frac{1}{2} \times 8 = 4$

---

216 **Associative Properties**

If you have a bunch of chores to do, you might save time by grouping them in a certain way. It makes sense to change the litter in the cat box, take out the trash, then wash up for dinner rather than to wash up *before* doing your other chores!

> You associate with friends in groups. The associative properties are all about the ways you can group addends and factors.

217 **Associative Property of Addition**

The **Associative Property of Addition** states that changing the grouping of addends does not change the sum. So, $(a + b) + c = a + (b + c)$. Note that the order of the addends stays the same.

How can knowing this property help you? One way is that you can use it to make things easier to add.

EXAMPLE: Add $88 + 49 + 21$.

MORE HELP
See 207–210

If you followed the order of operations rules, you'd add $88 + 49$ and then add 21. But you can use the Associative Property to change the grouping so you can add $49 + 21$ first.

$$(88 + 49) + 21 = 88 + (49 + 21)$$
$$= 88 + 70$$
$$= 158$$

Associative Property of Multiplication

218

The **Associative Property of Multiplication** states that changing the grouping of factors does not change the product. So, $(a \times b) \times c = a \times (b \times c)$.

You can use this property to make it easier to multiply.

EXAMPLE: Multiply $82 \times 25 \times 4$.

If you followed the order of operations rules, you'd multiply 82×25, then multiply by 4. But you can use the Associative Property to change the grouping so you can multiply 25×4 first.

$$(82 \times 25) \times 4 = 82 \times (25 \times 4)$$
$$= 82 \times 100$$
$$= 8200$$

Distributive Property

219

When you distribute things, you spread them out. The Distributive Property lets you *spread out* numbers so they're easier to work with.

Distributive Property of Multiplication

220

The **Distributive Property of Multiplication** states that for a, b, and c,
$$a(b + c) = (ab) + (ac)$$
$$a(b - c) = (ab) - (ac)$$

You can use this property to help you multiply in your head.

MORE ▶

EXAMPLE 1: Find the number of solar cells in an 8×23 array.

$8 \times 23 = 8 \times (20 + 3)$

$\qquad = (8 \times 20) + (8 \times 3)$

$\qquad = 160 + 24$

$\qquad = 184$

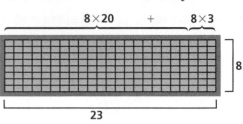

So, there are 184 solar cells in an 8×23 array.

EXAMPLE 2: Multiply 6×99.

$6 \times 99 = 6 \times (100 - 1)$

$\qquad = (6 \times 100) - (6 \times 1)$

$\qquad = 600 - 6$

$\qquad = 594$

99 is the same as $100 - 1$. It's easier to multiply by 100 and 1 than it is to multiply by 99.

Making Division Distributive

221

MORE HELP
See 188

The Distributive Property of Multiplication says that $a(b + c) = ab + ac$. Since dividing by a number is the same as multiplying by its reciprocal, you can say that $(b + c) \div a = \frac{1}{a}(b + c)$.

So, $(b + c) \div a = \frac{1}{a}(b + c) = \frac{b}{a} + \frac{c}{a}$.

EXAMPLE 1: Divide $(15 + 3) \div 5$.

$(15 + 3) \div 5 = \frac{1}{5}(15 + 3)$

$\qquad = \frac{1}{5}(15) + \frac{1}{5}(3)$

$\qquad = 3 + \frac{3}{5}$

$\qquad = 3\frac{3}{5}$

EXAMPLE 2: Divide $(15 - 3) \div 5$.

$(15 - 3) \div 5 = \frac{1}{5}(15 - 3)$

$\qquad = \frac{1}{5}(15) - \frac{1}{5}(3)$

$\qquad = 3 - \frac{3}{5}$

$\qquad = 2\frac{2}{5}$

222 | **Identity Elements**

Identity elements are numbers that combine with other numbers without changing them. These properties are just common sense.

CASE 1 The Identity Element for Addition is 0 because $a + 0 = a$ and $0 + a = a$.

$5 + 0 = 5$
$0 + 5 = 5$

CASE 2 The Identity Element for Multiplication is 1 because $a \times 1 = a$ and $1 \times a = a$.

$5 \times 1 = 5$
$1 \times 5 = 5$

MATH ALERT No Identity Elements for Division and Subtraction

Is $a - 0$ always a? Yes.
Is $0 - a$ always a? Not unless $a = 0$.

Subtraction is not commutative. It doesn't work the same way when the numbers are reversed. So, you can't say that zero is an identity element for subtraction as it is for addition.

Is $a \div 1$ always a? Yes.
Is $1 \div a$ always a? Not unless $a = 1$.

Division is not commutative. It also doesn't work the same way when the numbers are reversed. So, you can't say that 1 is an identity element for division as it is for multiplication.

Inverse Elements

Inverse elements are numbers that combine with other numbers and result in identity elements—1 or zero.

MORE HELP
See 046–047,
187–192

CASE 1 Additive Inverse
A number added to its additive inverse always equals 0:

8 and ⁻8 are additive inverses.	$8 + {}^-8 = 0$
$\frac{3}{5}$ and $-\frac{3}{5}$ are additive inverses.	$\frac{3}{5} + {}^-\frac{3}{5} = 0$
⁻7.2 and 7.2 are additive inverses.	$^-7.2 + 7.2 = 0$

CASE 2 Multiplicative Inverse (usually called the **reciprocal**)
A number multiplied by its reciprocal always equals 1:

3 and $\frac{1}{3}$ are reciprocals.	$3 \times \frac{1}{3} = 1$
$^-\frac{3}{8}$ and $^-\frac{8}{3}$ are reciprocals.	$^-\frac{3}{8} \times {}^-\frac{8}{3} = 1$
4.6 and $\frac{1}{4.6}$ are reciprocals.	$4.6 \times \frac{1}{4.6} = 1$

225) Zero Property

In multiplication, $a \times 0 = 0$ and $0 \times a = 0$. This is the **Zero Property of Multiplication**.

$5 \times 0 = 0$
$0 \times 5 = 0$

5 sets of zero give a total of zero.

226 ● MATH ALERT Don't Try to Divide by Zero

If you think about division as undoing multiplication, you'll see why we don't divide by zero.

EXAMPLE: Try to divide $245 \div 0$.

To divide, think of the related multiplication equation.

$245 \div 0 = ?$ asks the same question as $? \times 0 = 245$.

When you think about it this way, you can see that you're really stuck because any number times zero is zero! So, mathematicians say that division by zero is undefined.

227) Equality Properties

The **equality properties** let you compute with expressions on both sides of an equation. They help you keep an equation in balance.

228 Addition Property of Equality

The **Addition Property of Equality** says that if $a = b$, then $a + c = b + c$. Think of an equation as a balanced scale.

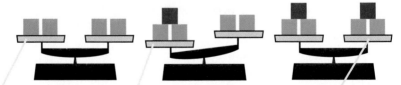

The amount in one pan balances the amount in the other pan.
$2 = 2$

If you add something to the pan on the left, the scale becomes unbalanced.
$2 + 1 \neq 2$

BUT, if you add the same thing to the pan on the right, the scale balances again!
$2 + 1 = 2 + 1$

You can also subtract the same number from both sides of an equation without putting it out of balance.

Multiplication Property of Equality

The **Multiplication Property of Equality** says that if $a = b$, then $ac = bc$.

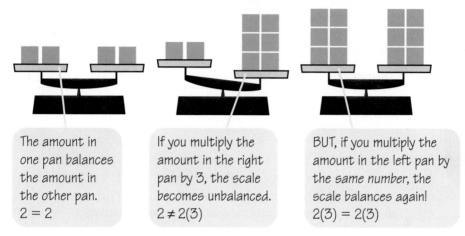

| The amount in one pan balances the amount in the other pan. $2 = 2$ | If you multiply the amount in the right pan by 3, the scale becomes unbalanced. $2 \neq 2(3)$ | BUT, if you multiply the amount in the left pan by the same number, the scale balances again! $2(3) = 2(3)$ |

Since dividing by a number is the same as multiplying by its reciprocal, you can also divide both sides of an equation by the same number without putting it out of balance.

Density Property

The **Density Property** states that between every two rational numbers there is another rational number.

EXAMPLE: Find a rational number between $\frac{1}{4}$ and $\frac{1}{2}$.

You can understand the Density Property by thinking of a number line. No matter how densely packed the number line is, more numbers can always be plotted between the numbers that are already there.

 Relations and Functions

If you say everybody in the eighth-grade class belongs to an eighth-grade club, you're describing a relation. For every eighth-grader you name, you can point to at least one club. And, for every eighth-grade club you name, you can point to at least one class member.

If you described one of these clubs by calling it The Club That John Belongs To, you might have a hard time making yourself understood if John belongs to more than one club. But, if John belongs to *only* one club, this relation is always clear and we call the relation a function.

232) Relations

A **relation** is a set of ordered pairs. These can be pairs of things (like shoes) or people (like tennis partners) or people and things (like ballplayers and their teams) or numbers (like 3 and 6).

MORE HELP
See 067, 246

Here are several ways to show a relation.
- a word description
- a table
- a list of ordered pairs
- an algebraic rule or equation
- a graph
- arrow diagrams—any way that shows how the elements in two sets are related

EXAMPLE 1: How can you show the relation between a set of creatures (cow, horse, chicken, ant, spider, centipede) and the number of legs each creature has?

The first value in an ordered pair comes from a set of elements called the **domain**. The second value in the ordered pair comes from a set of elements called the **range**. The domain contains values of the **independent variable**. The range contains values of the **dependent variable**.

Domain: cow, horse, chicken, ant, spider, centipede
Range: even whole numbers—2, 4, 6. . .

You can show this relation in different ways.

 Use a table to show a relation.

CREATURE	cow	horse	chicken	ant	spider	centipede
NUMBER OF LEGS	4	4	2	6	8	even numbers from 30 to 350

 List the ordered pairs to show a relation.

(cow, 4), (horse, 4), (chicken, 2), (ant, 6), (spider, 8), (centipede, 30), (centipede, 32), (centipede, 34), . . . , (centipede, 350)

 Use an arrow diagram to show a relation.

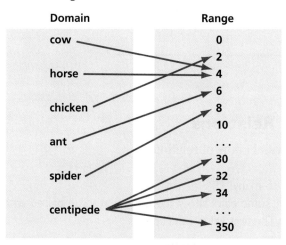

EXAMPLE 2: How can you show the following relation: *The second number is two more than the first number?*

 Use a table to show a relation.

x = first number y = second number

x	0	1	2	3	4	5	6	7	8
y	2	3	4	5	6	7	8	9	10

 Use an equation to show a relation.

$y = x + 2$

MORE ▶

List the ordered pairs to show a relation.

(0, 2), (1, 3), (2, 4), (3, 5), (4, 6), (5, 7), (6, 8), (7, 9), (8, 10) . . .

 Use a graph to show a relation.

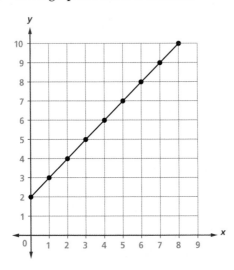

233 Kinds of Relations

There are several kinds of relations.

CASE 1 One-to-many
In this relation, some pairs show the same first value paired with different second values. The first value can repeat.

EXAMPLE 1: The relation containing the pairs (centipede, 30), (centipede, 32), (centipede, 34) , ... (centipede, 350) is *one-to-many* because there are many possibilities for the number of legs on a centipede.

CASE 2 Many-to-one
A *many-to-one* relation shows different first values paired with the same second value. The second value can repeat.

EXAMPLE 2: The relation containing the pairs (cow, 4) and (horse, 4) is *many-to-one* because two creatures are paired with the same number of legs.

CASE 3 Many-to-many

In a *many-to-many* relation, a first value may be paired with different second values and a second value may be paired with different first values. The first value can repeat and the second value can repeat.

EXAMPLE 3: The relation containing numbers paired with their multiples, (2, 2), (2, 4), (2, 6), (2, 8), (4, 4), and (4, 8), is *many-to-many* because the numbers 2 and 4 repeat and the multiples 4 and 8 repeat.

CASE 4 One-to-one

A *one-to-one* relation shows that each first value is paired with only one second value and each second value is paired with only one first value. No first values can repeat and no second values can repeat.

EXAMPLE 4: The relation where the second number is two more than the first number is *one-to-one*. This is because any first number in a pair may be paired with just one second number that is 2 more, and any second number in a pair may be paired with just one first number that is 2 less.

Functions 234

A **function** is a special kind of relation. It is a rule or correspondence from one set (domain) to another set (range). Like a relation, it is a set of ordered pairs. However, in a function, each first value may be paired with one and only one second value. So, a function is a relation that is *many-to-one* or *one-to-one*.

MORE HELP
See 233

EXAMPLE 1: In some theaters, admission price is a *function* of your age. In these theaters, people of different ages may be charged a different price and there is only one price for each age group. This function is a *many-to-one* relation.

EXAMPLE 2: At the post office, price is a *function* of the number of 32-cent stamps you buy. For each number of stamps, there is one price. Also, for each price, there is one number of 32-cent stamps. This function is a *one-to-one* relation.

NUMBER OF 32-CENT STAMPS	1	2	3	4	5	6
PRICE	$0.32	$0.64	$0.96	$1.28	$1.60	$1.92

MORE ▶

EXAMPLE 3: You own a painting business. Through experience, you've found the relationship shown by the following table and graph. Is this relation a function?

Painting a 2000-Square-Foot Space

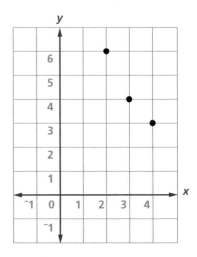

NUMBER OF PEOPLE WORKING (x)	2	3	4
DAYS NEEDED FOR JOB (y)	6	4	3

Sure enough, for every number of people working, there is a unique number of days needed to complete the job. So, this relation is a function. The number of days needed to complete the job is a *function* of the number of people working.

EXAMPLE 4: The water pressure on a scuba diver increases as the diver goes deeper. This relationship may be described by the equation $p = 0.43d$. The table and graph below give water pressure on a diver at different depths. Is this relation a function? *(Source: Engineering Formulas)*

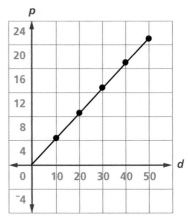

DEPTH (d) IN FEET	PRESSURE (p) PER SQUARE INCH
10	4.3
20	8.6
30	12.9
40	17.2
50	21.5

This relation is a function because for every depth, there is exactly one value of pressure. We say that water pressure is a function of depth.

Discrete and Continuous Functions

Think about filling a swimming pool. Until the pool is full, the water level will keep rising. The water level in this case is rising continuously and we say that the water level is a **continuous function** of the rate the water is entering the pool.

Now think about looking at time-lapse photographs of a flower opening. You can only look at the photos that are actually shot—these are discrete moments in time that have been captured, but none of the moments in between are available for you to look at. The photos are a discrete function of the time interval between the shots.

Some functions are **discrete**. In the graphs for discrete functions, even if the points look like you could connect them with a line, you don't.

EXAMPLE 1: This discrete graph is composed of separate distinct points.

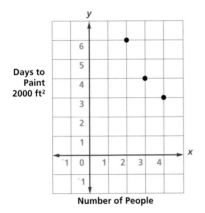

Days to Paint 2000 ft²

Number of People

If you connected the dots to make a line, you'd be saying that all the points between the ones you plotted tell how long it would take this number of people to paint 2000 ft². That means the point $(2\frac{1}{2}, 5)$ would work. But it might be silly to say that $2\frac{1}{2}$ people would get the job done in 5 days.

EXAMPLE 2: In this continuous graph there are no gaps.

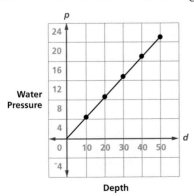

Water Pressure

Depth

This is a continuous function. You can connect the points you found and know that any other points on the graph also answer the question: What is the water pressure at this depth?

Dependent and Independent Variables in Functions

We say that water coming out of a tap is a function of turning the tap on. When a function consists of a set of ordered pairs of the form (x, y), we say that y is a function of x. In this case, x is the **independent variable** and y is the **dependent variable**. This means that you can choose a value for x, but as soon as you do, the value for y may change because *the value of y depends on the value of x*.

EXAMPLE: If you apply the function rule $y = 2x + 1$ to the x-values 1, 2, 3, and 4, what are the y-values? Use ordered pairs to describe your answer:

X-VALUE	FUNCTION RULE: MULTIPLY BY 2, THEN ADD 1	Y-VALUE
1	2 (1) + 1	3
2	2 (2) + 1	5
3	2 (3) + 1	7
4	2 (4) + 1	9

Four ordered pairs of the function $y = 2x + 1$ are:
$(1, 3), (2, 5), (3, 7), (4, 9)$

The $y = (2x)^2 - 5$ Machine

Equations

When you think of algebra, you probably think of equations. Equations can be simple or complex. They can have one variable or many. They can have one solution or many. They can be graphed. What's interesting about equations is that there's lots you can say about them just by looking at them, even before you start solving them. What you can say just by looking will help you reach a reasonable solution more quickly.

Simplifying and Solving Equations

There are several different methods you can use for making equations easier to solve.

Combining Like Terms to Simplify Equations

One way to simplify an equation is to combine like terms. Think about adding 3 boys, 4 girls, 2 more boys, and 5 more girls. If you combine the *boy* terms and the *girl* terms, you have a simpler expression: 5 boys + 9 girls.

In algebra, **like terms** are terms that have the same variable raised to the same power. $5x^2$ and $7x^2$ are like terms. $3y^2$ and $3y$ are *not* like terms because y^2 and y have different powers.

EXAMPLE 1: Simplify $7k - 5k + m = 16$ by combining like terms.

$$7k - 5k + m = 16$$

Combine like terms: $7k - 5k = 2k$ ⟶ $2k + m = 16$

EXAMPLE 2: Simplify $4x^2 + 2x^2 + 3x - x = 30$ by combining like terms.

$$4x^2 + 2x^2 + 3x - x = 30$$

Combine like terms: $4x^2 + 2x^2 = 6x^2$ ⟶ $6x^2 + 3x - x = 30$

Combine like terms: $3x - x = 2x$ ⟶ $6x^2 + 2x = 30$

240

Using Properties to Simplify Equations

You can use the Commutative, Associative, and Distributive Properties to simplify equations.

> It's much easier to work with subtracted terms if you make them into added terms: $-{}^+t = +{}^-t$ and $-{}^-t = +{}^+t$.

MORE HELP
See 213–214, 217–219

EXAMPLE 1: Simplify $11k - 5(3k + 4) = 64$.

$$11k - 5(3k + 4) = 64$$

$$11k + {}^-5(3k + 4) = 64$$

Use the Distributive Property:
$^-5(3k + 4) = {}^-15k + {}^-20$ ⟶ $11k + {}^-15k + {}^-20 = 64$

Combine like terms: $11k + {}^-15k = {}^-4k$ ⟶ $^-4k + {}^-20 = 64$

EXAMPLE 2: Simplify $8x + 7 + 4x = y$.

$$8x + 7 + 4x = y$$

Use the Associative Property to group addends ⟶ $8x + (7 + 4x) = y$

Use the Commutative Property to switch addends ⟶ $8x + (4x + 7) = y$

Use the Associative Property to group like terms ⟶ $(8x + 4x) + 7 = y$

Combine like terms: $8x + 4x = 12x$ ⟶ $12x + 7 = y$

241

Using Properties to Solve Equations

Think about weighing 5 apples and 9 oranges on the scale at the market. What do you need to do to find the weight of just one apple? You need to remove all the fruit except for the one apple. This idea works with equations, too. You can find the value of a variable when it's on one side of the equation. We call this **isolating** the variable.

MORE HELP
See 227–229

When you are looking for a solution to an equation, you want to find values for any variables that will make the equation true. To do this, isolate the variable for which you need a value. You can use what you know about the Addition and Multiplication Properties of Equality.

The following examples may seem like they take a lot of work to find an answer that you can get just by thinking. But these methods do save a lot of time when the equations are complicated.

CASE 1 Some equations can be solved in one step.

EXAMPLE 1: Lauren is 17 years older than Sheila. Lauren is 35. How old is Sheila? Use an equation to solve the problem.

WORDS	ALGEBRAIC EXPRESSION OR EQUATION
Sheila's age	a
Lauren is 17 years older than Sheila. Lauren is 35.	$a + 17 = 35$

To find Sheila's age, solve for a in the equation.

To isolate a, undo the addition in $a + 17$ ⟶ $a + 17 = 35$

The Addition Property of Equality lets
you subtract 17 from both sides ⟶ $a + 17 - 17 = 35 - 17$

Simplify ⟶ $a + 0 = 18$

So, Sheila is 18 years old. $a = 18$

EXAMPLE 2: Solve $\frac{n}{6} = 54$.

To isolate n, undo the division in $\frac{n}{6}$ ⟶ $\frac{n}{6} = 54$

The Multiplication Property of Equality
lets you multiply both sides by 6 ⟶ $\frac{n}{6} \times 6 = 54 \times 6$

Simplify ⟶ $n = 324$

CASE 2 It may take more than one step to simplify and solve an equation.

EXAMPLE 3: Your friend gave you half a sack of oranges. After you gave 3 oranges to me, you had 19 oranges. If you bought a whole sack, would you have enough to share with all the kids in your class?

WORDS	ALGEBRAIC EXPRESSION OR EQUATION
oranges in a full sack	s
oranges in a half sack	$\frac{s}{2}$
oranges left after you gave me 3	$\frac{s}{2} - 3 = 19$

MORE ▶

To answer the question, first solve for s in the equation: $\frac{s}{2} - 3 = 19$

$$\frac{s}{2} - 3 = 19$$

To isolate s, first undo the subtraction by adding 3 to both sides of the equation $\longrightarrow$ $\frac{s}{2} - 3 + 3 = 19 + 3$

Simplify $\longrightarrow$ $\frac{s}{2} = 22$

Next, undo the division by multiplying both sides of the equation by 2 $\longrightarrow$ $\frac{s}{2} \times 2 = 22 \times 2$

Simplify $\longrightarrow$ $s = 44$

There are 44 oranges in a full sack. You could share with the entire grade if there are no more than $44 + 19 = 63$ students in that grade.

How do you decide what to undo first? Undoing is working backward, so follow the order of operations backward and you'll untangle even the most complicated equations.

242 Checking Solutions to Equations

To see if a number is a solution for an equation, replace the variable with the number you think is the solution.

EXAMPLE 1: Is $x = 13$ a solution to $3x + 26 = 65$?

$$3x + 26 = 65$$

Replace x with 13 $\longrightarrow$ $3(13) + 26 = 65$

Simplify $\longrightarrow$ $39 + 26 = 65$

This statement is true $\longrightarrow$ $65 = 65$

Replacing x with 13 makes a true statement ($65 = 65$). So, $x = 13$ is a **solution** to $3x + 26 = 65$.

EXAMPLE 2: Is $x = 21$ a solution to $\frac{x}{3} - 4 = 4$?

$$\frac{x}{3} - 4 = 4$$

Replace x with 21 $\longrightarrow$ $\frac{21}{3} - 4 = 4$

Simplify $\longrightarrow$ $7 - 4 = 4$

This statement is false $\longrightarrow$ $3 = 4$

Replacing x with 21 makes a false statement ($3 = 4$). So, $x = 21$ is *not* a solution to $\frac{x}{3} - 4 = 4$.

Making Tables of Values from Equations

You can think of many pairs of numbers with a sum of 80. That means there is more than one solution to the equation $x + y = 80$. When an equation has two variables, there can be many pairs of numbers that make the equation true. A **table of values** will show some of these pairs.

EXAMPLE: If you weigh 100 pounds on Earth, you would weigh 140 pounds on Neptune. The force of gravity on Neptune is 1.4 times as great as on Earth. This means that on Neptune, an object weighs 1.4 times as much as on Earth. In algebra shorthand, you can simply write it this way: $n = 1.4e$, where **n** = the weight of an object on **Neptune** and **e** = the weight of the same object on **Earth**. *(Source: Planets)*

To complete a table of values for $n = 1.4e$, substitute each value for e in the equation. Then write the answer in the table.

WEIGHT ON EARTH IN POUNDS (e)	80	100	120	140
WEIGHT ON NEPTUNE IN POUNDS (n)	112	140	168	196

If $e = 80$, then
$n = 1.4 \times 80$, or 112

Writing Equations from Tables of Values

Suppose you have a table of values for two variables. You can analyze that table to see if there is a relationship between the two variables. Then you can write an equation that describes that relationship. Scientists often find relationships this way. They make measurements and then try to find the simplest way to describe how the measurements are related.

EXAMPLE: Write an equation that describes the relationship between the variables in the table.

HOURS WORKED (h)	1	2	3	4
DOLLARS EARNED (d)	5.25	10.5	15.75	21

The table shows that for each hour worked, $5.25 is earned. The total number of dollars is 5.25 times the number of hours. So, $d = 5.25h$.

Graphing Equations

MORE HELP
See 235

A graph is a picture of an equation. The graphs of some equations are straight lines—these are **linear equations**. The graphs of other equations can be curves or other interesting shapes—these are **nonlinear equations**.

246 **Is the Equation Linear or Nonlinear?**

 ONE WAY You can tell whether an equation is linear or nonlinear by graphing it on a graphing calculator.

MORE HELP
See 247–250, 253

EXAMPLE: Graph: $y = 2x + 1$

Press: Y=

Next to Y₁ =, press: 2 X/T + 1

Press: Graph

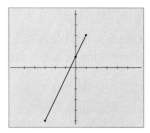

The equation $y = 2x + 1$ is linear because its graph is a straight line.

ANOTHER WAY You can also tell whether an equation is linear by just looking at the equation. A linear equation contains one or two variables, each in the first power. If either variable is raised to a power other than 0 or 1, its graph is not linear.

CASE 1 Here are some linear equations:

$$y = 3x + 5 \qquad\qquad C = \pi d$$
$$y = \tfrac{1}{2}(x) - 9 \qquad\qquad y = 4$$

CASE 2 Here are some equations that are not linear equations. If you graphed them, they would not be straight lines.

$A = \pi r^2$ ——This is not a linear equation because r^2 is a variable raised to the second power.

$y = \tfrac{3}{x} + 9$ ——This is not a linear equation because $y = \tfrac{3}{x} + 9$ is the same as $y = 3x^{-1} + 9$. The variable is raised to the ⁻1 power.

Using a Table to Graph a Linear Equation

You can use a table of values to graph a linear equation.

EXAMPLE: Here's a math puzzle about counting vehicles by counting their wheels. Let's say that there are motorcycles and cars in a parking lot and that there are 24 wheels altogether. Write an equation and draw a graph to show the different possible combinations of motorcycles and cars in the lot.

1. First, write an equation.

WORDS	EXPRESSION OR EQUATION
Multiply 2 wheels by the number of motorcycles	$2m$
Multiply 4 wheels by the number of cars	$4c$
Sum of motorcycle wheels and car wheels is 24	$2m + 4c = 24$

2. Next, make a table of values (remember, $2m + 4c$ must equal 24).

m	c
12	0
10	1
8	2

You really only need to find two points in order to define the line of the graph.

3. Then plot the points on the graph.

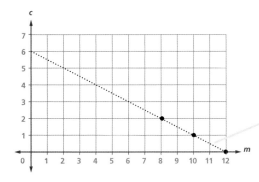

There can't be any half-motorcycles or half-cars, so this is a discrete graph, but you can dot in the line to find other ordered pairs that are whole numbers.

MORE HELP
See 235

So, there are 7 possible combinations of motorcycles and cars: 12 and 0, 10 and 1, 8 and 2, 6 and 3, 4 and 4, 2 and 5, and 0 and 6.

Slope

Sometimes, on mountain roads, you'll see signs warning truckers about very steep hills. Often the sign uses a percent to show how steep (0% would be flat and 100% would be a cliff) and a picture to show whether it's steep going up or down.

5% grade

8% grade

MORE HELP
See 108, 136

You can use the same idea to measure the steepness of a line. A line (like line *a* below) that moves upward from left to right has a **positive slope**. A line (like line *b* below) that moves downward from left to right has a **negative slope**. If a line is flat from left to right, it has a slope of 0 and if it's straight up and down, it has no slope at all.

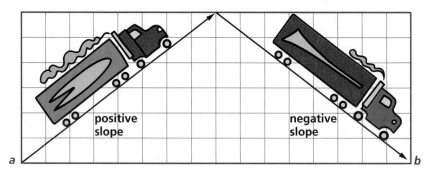

positive slope

negative slope

a

b

What can you find out by looking at a slope? You can see the rate at which the quantity represented by *y* is increasing or decreasing. For example, in this graph, the slope of the line for rental charges at Quick Computers is steeper than the slope of the line for rental charges at Computer Time. This means that the charges at Quick Computers are piling up at a faster rate than the charges at Computer Time.

Cost of Rental
(in dollars)

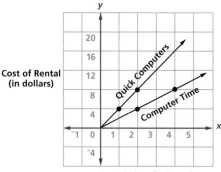

Rental Time (in hours)

To find the number that represents the slope of a line, you need to find how the value of y is changing as the value of x changes.

EXAMPLE 1: Find the slope of the line for $y = 2x - 1$.

Look at line c. Point to (1, 1) and follow the line to the right to (2, 3). The line moves up to the right, so the slope is positive. When the y-value changes by 2, the x-value changes by 1. These changes are in the ratio of $\frac{2}{1}$, so the slope of line c is 2.

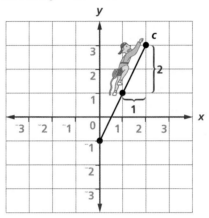

EXAMPLE 2: Find the slope of the line for $y = {}^-3x + 4$.

Look at point (0, 4), then choose another point to the right (like 2, $^-2$). The line moves down to the right, so the slope is negative. To find the slope, you need to find the change in the y-value between your two points and the change in the x-value between the *same two points.*

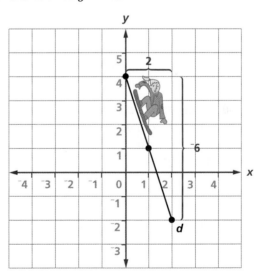

$$\text{Slope} = \frac{\text{change in } y\text{-value}}{\text{change in } x\text{-value}} = \frac{(\text{second } y - \text{first } y)}{(\text{second } x - \text{first } x)} = \frac{({}^-2 - 4)}{(2 - 0)} = \frac{{}^-6}{2} = {}^-3$$

A short way to write (second y − first y) is ($y_2 - y_1$).

MORE ▶

EXAMPLE 3: What is the slope of line e?

Choose any pair of points on line e. You'll notice that the point on the right is downward from the point on the left. This means you have a line with negative slope. Now calculate the slope:

$$\text{Slope} = \frac{(y_2 - y_1)}{(x_2 - x_1)}$$

No matter what points you chose, the slope should be $\frac{-1}{2}$.

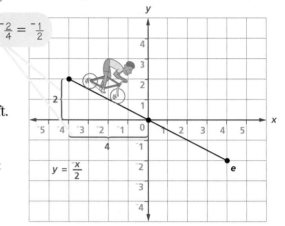

$$\frac{-2}{4} = \frac{-1}{2}$$

$$y = \frac{x}{2}$$

Using the Slope and a Point to Graph a Linear Equation

If you know the slope of a line and any point on the line, you can graph that line on the coordinate plane.

EXAMPLE: Graph the line with slope of $\frac{1}{2}$ that passes through the point $(1, 3)$.

To draw the graph, start by marking the point: $(1, 3)$. Then use the definition of slope to find another point.

Since slope $= \frac{1}{2}$:

$$\frac{\text{change in } y\text{-value}}{\text{change in } x\text{-value}} = \frac{1}{2}$$

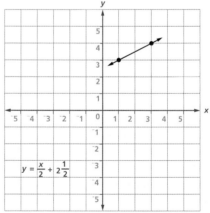

$$y = \frac{x}{2} + 2\frac{1}{2}$$

So, for each increase of 2 in the x-value, the y-value increases 1. To graph another point add 2 to the x-value of $(1, 3)$ and 1 to the y-value of $(1, 3)$. Graph the point $(3, 4)$. Continue graphing points until it is easy for you to draw a line through them.

Using Slope-Intercept Form to Graph a Linear Equation

Look at the graphs of this set of equations. Notice that all of the equations have the same form: $y = \frac{1}{2}x + b$, where b is some number. What makes this form *really* useful is that b is where the line crosses the y-axis. It's always the y-value for the point $(0, y)$. This point is called the **y-intercept**.

When a linear equation is in the form $y = mx + b$, you can tell the slope and y-intercept just by looking at the equation. In this form, m is the slope and b is the y-intercept.

$$y = \tfrac{1}{2}(x) + 2$$

The slope is $\frac{1}{2}$

The y-intercept is 2

The point of the y-intercept is $(0, 2)$.

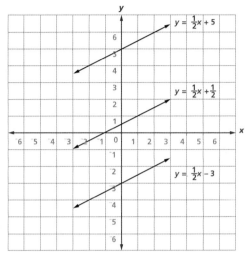

EXAMPLE: Find the slope and the y-intercept of $y = 5x - 4$. Graph the equation.

$$y = 5x - 4$$

slope

y-intercept

$y = mx + b$
$m = $ slope and
$b = $ y-intercept

So, $y = 5x + {}^{-}4$

For $y = 5x - 4$, the slope is 5 and the y-intercept is $^{-}4$.

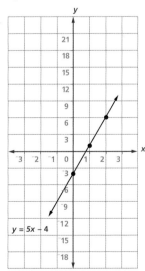

$y = 5x - 4$

Graphs of Parabolas

If you throw a ball into the air, you can graph its height from time zero, when you let go, to some time later, when you catch it. The graph will be in a shape called a **parabola**.

When a nonlinear function has a variable that is squared, it is called a **quadratic function**. Here are some quadratic functions:

$$y = 3x^2 \qquad\qquad y = 3x^2 + 9x + 1 \qquad\qquad \text{Area of a circle} = \pi r^2$$

Quadratic functions have a degree of 2 and the exponents are positive. The graph of a quadratic function is a parabola. The standard form for the equation of a parabola is $y = ax^2 + bx + c$, where a, b, and c are constants and $a \neq 0$.

As these parabolas show, some parabolas open upward and some open downward.

When a parabola opens upward, it has a *minimum* value. An example would be a graph of a high-diver's progress into a pool and back to the surface. The minimum value, or **lower bound**, is the lowest point the diver reaches.	When a parabola opens downward, it has a *maximum* value. An example would be a graph showing the arc of a ball thrown into the air. The maximum value, or **upper bound**, is the top of the arc.
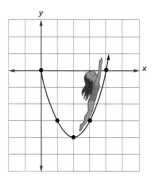	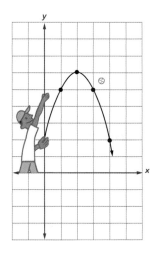

Graphing a Parabola Using a Table of Values

252

You can use a table of values to graph a parabola.

EXAMPLE: You launch a model rocket. The launch speed is 100 feet per second. The relationship between the height of the rocket (y) and the amount of time that has passed since the launch (x) at any moment in its flight can be found by using the formula $y = {^-}16x^2 + 100x$. Graph the height of the rocket. Then use the graph to estimate when the rocket would hit the ground if the parachute didn't open.

x (TIME IN SECONDS)	y (HEIGHT IN FEET)
0	0
1	84
2	136
3	156
4	144
5	100
6	24
7	${^-}84$

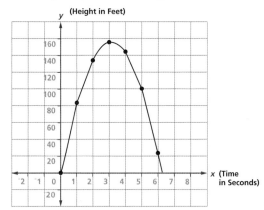

The graph intersects the x-axis at somewhere between 6 and 7. So the rocket will hit the ground at some time between 6 and 7 seconds.

Graphing an Equation with a Graphing Calculator

253

Graphing calculators come with special keys and a screen that allow you to graph an equation. For example:

- **Y=** allows you to enter the equation you want graphed.
- **X/T** represents the variable x (or sometimes t).
- **Range** allows you to enter the range of x-values (say ${^-}5$ to 5) and the range of y-values (say ${^-}3$ to 10) and the intervals between notches on the axis (say by 1s, 2s, 10s, and so on).
- **Graph** displays a graph of your equation with the range of values that you entered.
- **>** positions the cursor at the next entry to be made.

MORE ▶

EXAMPLE: Graph $y = 3x - 5$ on the graphing calculator.

On the display, you should see:

Press: Y=

```
Y1 =
Y2 =
Y3 =
Y4 =
```

Press: 3 X/T − 5

```
Y1 = 3x-5
Y2 =
Y3 =
Y4 =
```

Press: Range

```
RANGE
Xmin =
Xmax =
Xscl =
Ymin =
Ymax =
Yscl =
```

Press: − 5 >

Press: 5 >

Press: 1 >

Press: − 2 0 >

Press: 2 0 >

Press: 2

```
RANGE
Xmin = -5
Xmax = 5
Xscl = 1
Ymin = -20
Ymax = 20
Yscl = 2
```

Press: Graph

254) Simple Systems of Equations

When you graph an equation, all the points on the line are named by pairs of numbers that are solutions to the equation. Sometimes you need to find a pair of numbers that is a solution to 2 or more *different* equations. We call these equations a **system of equations**. The point where the lines intersect is a solution to all the equations, and a solution to the system of equations.

Using a Graph to Solve a System of Equations

One way to solve a system of equations is to graph the equations.

EXAMPLE: The ads show the rates of two companies that sell Internet service. Will the two companies ever charge the same amount of money for a given amount of time?

MORE HELP
See 247–250

1. Write an equation for each company. Let x = number of hours and y = total cost. These equations represent the cost of each plan for different amounts of time:

   The Highway: $y = 2x + 4$ Super Server: $y = x + 10$

2. Graph the equations on the same coordinate plane.

3. Find the point where the two lines intersect. They intersect at (6, 16). This means that (6, 16) is a solution to both equations. At this point, the cost for 6 hours is $16 for both plans.

Check the answer. Substitute $x = 6$ and $y = 16$ in both equations.

The Highway	Super Server
$y = 2x + 4$	$y = x + 10$
$16 = 2(6) + 4$	$16 = 6 + 10$
$16 = 12 + 4$	$16 = 16$
$16 = 16$	

The solution (6, 16) checks in both equations.

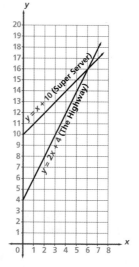

MATH ALERT Parallel and Collinear Systems

If graphed lines are parallel, they have no intersection point, and so there is no solution for the system of their equations. If the lines have two or more points in common, they are in fact the same line (or collinear), and the solution to their system of equations would be all the points on the line.

MORE HELP
See 324

 Inequalities

The most you have to spend on T-shirts from the discount catalog is $40. This means that the cost for all your T-shirts plus the shipping and handling charge must be less than or equal to $40. That is an **inequality statement**. In algebra, we have a shorter way to write the same thing: $7t + 5 \le 40$. The symbol $\le$ means "less than or equal to."

If you wanted to spend exactly $40, there is only one way to do it—order 5 shirts. But since you are interested in keeping your spending to $40 or less, there are several ways to do it. Assuming you want to buy any T-shirts at all, you can buy 1, 2, 3, 4, or 5 shirts.

258) Solving Inequalities with One Variable

MORE HELP
See 239–240

If you know how to simplify and solve equations, you know how to simplify inequalities. All you need to do is combine like terms and use what you know about the properties of addition, subtraction, multiplication, and division.

Inequalities have more than one solution.

CASE I Sometimes only one step is needed to simplify an inequality.

EXAMPLE 1: According to fire laws, Rocco's Restaurant can have no more than 104 people in it at one time. Right now, there are 95 people in the restaurant. A group of people enters, but the total number of people in the restaurant still does not go over the limit. How many people are in the group?

 Think about this problem using a number line.

You know that 104 is the maximum number of people allowed in the restaurant. You also know that 95 people are there when a new group of customers arrives. You can count the number of places left in the restaurant.

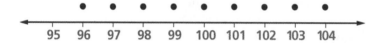

 Think about the problem using algebra.

To solve an inequality for a variable such as x, take the same steps that you do to solve an equation. You can use addition or subtraction to isolate the variable in an inequality the same way you would in an equation.

Let n = the number of people who come in.

The inequality $n + 95 \leq 104$ represents the situation. To find the number of people who come in, find n:

$$n + 95 \leq 104$$

Subtract 95 from both sides ⟶ $n + 95 - 95 \leq 104 - 95$

$$n \leq 9$$

Either way, any new group must have 9 or fewer people.

MORE ▶

CASE 2 Sometimes it takes more than one step to simplify an inequality.

EXAMPLE 2: Solve: $4x - 8 \geq 28$

$$4x - 8 \geq 28$$

Add 8 to both sides ⟶ $4x - 8 + 8 \geq 28 + 8$

$$4x \geq 36$$

Divide both sides by 4 ⟶ $4x \div 4 \geq 36 \div 4$

$$x \geq 9$$

So, any number greater than or equal to 9 is a solution.

259

MATH ALERT Be Careful with Negative Numbers in Inequalities

Sometimes you have to multiply or divide to isolate the variable. With inequalities, just as with equations, you can multiply or divide both sides by the same number. But with inequalities you *must* follow these rules:

- If you multiply or divide both sides of the inequality by the same *positive number*, the direction of the inequality does not change.
- If you multiply or divide both sides of the inequality by the same *negative number*, the direction of the inequality reverses.

This is where it gets tricky. If you leave the inequality sign alone, you'll be saying numbers greater than ⁻5 solve the inequality. ⁻4 is greater than ⁻5, so try it out: Is ⁻4 × ⁻4 > 20? Oops, it's not! In case you forget the rule about flopping the inequality sign, always try out a few possible solutions to be sure you've got it right.

EXAMPLE: $^-4n > 20$

$$^-4n > 20$$
$$^-4n \div {}^-4 > 20 \div {}^-4$$
$$\downarrow$$
$$n < {}^-5$$

So, any number less than ⁻5, but not including ⁻5, is a solution.

260

Checking Solutions to Inequalities

It's a good idea to check your work when you solve an inequality. The best way to check is to substitute a sample number or two into the original inequality. You should also look carefully at the original question to be sure you're not including some numbers that work in the inequality but make no sense in the real world.

EXAMPLE: The Surprise Dock charges a $10 fee plus $5 per hour to rent windsurfers. What might you tell the clerk when she asks how many whole hours you'll want? An inequality that expresses the relationship between the $24 in your pocket and the possible fees is $5h + 10 \leq 24$. Solve and check the inequality and answer the question.

Solve: $$5h + 10 \leq 24$$

Subtract 10 from both sides ⟶ $5h + 10 - 10 \leq 24 - 10$

$$5h \leq 14$$

Divide both sides by 5 ⟶ $5h \div 5 \leq 14 \div 5$

$$h \leq 2.8$$

Check: Try two numbers less than 2.8, like 2 and ¯1, as h in the original inequality.

Is $5 \times 2 + 10 \leq 24$?   Yes, 20 is less than or equal to 24.

Is $5 \times \ ^{-}1 + 10 \leq 24$?   Yes, 5 is less than or equal to 24.

Now answer the question:

Can you really say that every number less than or equal to 2.8 gives a number of whole windsurfing hours you can pay for? No, you can't. First, negative time is impossible, so the answer can't be less than 0. Second, since you pay for whole hours, the answer can only be a whole number.

So, the answer to the question is, *You can pay for 1 or 2 hours of windsurfing.*

Solving Inequalities with Two Variables   261

When an inequality has two variables, you can graph its solutions on the coordinate plane. When the inequality is a linear inequality (neither variable has a power greater than one), the solutions will be all of the points on one side of a boundary line. You can find the boundary line by graphing the linear equation that is related to the inequality.

MORE ▶

EXAMPLE I: You have 10 minutes to complete a quiz that contains two parts, a multiple-choice part and a short-answer part. How much time can you spend on each part?

Let x represent the time spent on the multiple-choice part and let y represent time on the short-answer part. Since you can spend up to 10 minutes on the entire quiz, $x + y \leq 10$ represents this situation.

To solve the problem, you can graph the inequality $x + y \leq 10$.

1. Graph the related linear equation $x + y = 10$

x	0	2	4	6	8	10
y	10	8	6	4	2	0

Since solutions of $x + y \leq 10$ include the solutions of $x + y = 10$, draw a *solid line* for $x + y = 10$. This shows that the points on the line are part of the solution.

2. Pick a point on one side of the line. Check to see if it is a solution of the inequality: $x + y \leq 10$

Try point (2, 5).
Is $2 + 5 \leq 10$?
$7 \leq 10$ is true, so (2, 5) is a solution.

3. Shade the part of the graph on the same side of the line as (2, 5). All the points in that part are solutions to the inequality.

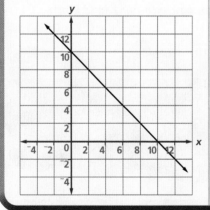

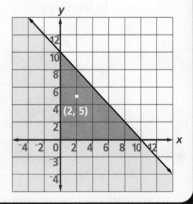

When you answer the question, be careful! You can only spend a positive amount of time on a task. There are many possible solutions to the question: How much time can you spend on each part? Use any point in the darker shaded region, where both times are positive.

EXAMPLE 2: Use a graph to solve the inequality $y > x + 2$.

1. Graph the related linear equation $y = x + 2$

x	-2	0	2	4
y	0	2	4	6

Since solutions of $y > x + 2$ do *not* include the solutions of $y = x + 2$, draw a *dashed line* for $y = x + 2$. This shows that the points on the line are not part of the solution.

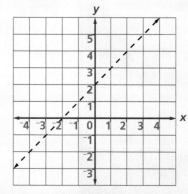

2. Pick a point on one side of the line. Check to see if it is a solution of the inequality: $y > x + 2$

Try point $(3, 3)$.
Is $3 > 3 + 2$?
No, so $(3, 3)$ is not a solution.

3. Shade the part of the graph on the side of the line that *does not have* $(3, 3)$. All the points in that part are solutions to the inequality.

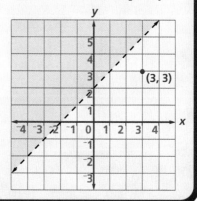

So all the points in the shaded region and not on the line are solutions.

Use a solid line when points on the line are solutions. Use a dashed line when they are not.

Graphs and Statistics

King Kong's work would have been much easier had he presented his wishes in a clear, concise manner.

Bananas Needed

Days

Will it rain tomorrow? Which batteries really last longest? How healthy or unhealthy is my lunch? Many questions like these don't have simple answers. In an uncertain world, statistics are tools for helping us answer the big questions. Statistics are generalizations about lots of pieces of information—data that somebody has sorted, analyzed, displayed, and based conclusions on.

When you look for information to help make important decisions, you will often find that information in the form of graphs. Many major newspapers regularly use graphs to help readers compare amounts and see trends. You need to use what you know about how data are gathered and displayed when you decide whether or not the graphs have anything useful to say to you.

Gathering Data

When you measure your height, you are collecting information. When you ask friends about their favorite TV shows, you are also collecting information. These collected pieces of information are called **data**. You often rely on data to make decisions such as what CD to buy or who makes the best burger. Voters rely on data to help them decide how to vote on candidates and issues. Car buyers rely on data to help them decide which car is safest or most reliable.

The more you know about how to gather and record data properly, the better you'll be at judging data gathered by others.

264 Taking Samples

When you want to get information about a large group, such as the students at your school or all the fish in a lake, it's often impossible to survey or examine every member of the group. So you take a **sample**.

For the results of the sample to be as close to the truth as possible, the sample you choose must closely represent the *whole* group. That is why it is very important to consider the *kind* of members in the sample and the *number* of members in the sample.

265 Populations

When you are studying or gathering information about a group, that group is called the **population**. The population can be limited to a specific group, such as eighth-graders in a school, or it can include the entire population of this country! Populations can also be animals, insects, or even plants.

Sample Size

When you are taking a sample in order to get an idea about the whole population, you need to get *enough* data to be sure your conclusions are accurate.

EXAMPLE: You want to use a toothpaste recommended by dentists. What question should you ask the advertisers who say two out of three dentists recommend Brand X?

You should ask how many dentists were surveyed. A **sample size** of 300 or 3000 dentists would make the results much more reliable than a sample size of only 3 dentists.

Random Samples

A **random sample** is a select group that closely represents the whole population. That means if the population you're studying is students in your town, you can't just sample your friends or students who live nearby, you need to *randomly select* students from the entire town—all neighborhoods, all ages, all schools, and so on.

EXAMPLE: You want to know what foods most middle-school and high-school students like. How can you choose a random sample?

Whom would you ask? The members of the boys' soccer teams? But that wouldn't include any girls. The students at your middle school? But that wouldn't include older teenagers. So, if you're being honest, you'll ask people who represent the entire population of middle school and high school students, including boys and girls and people from different cultures and neighborhoods.

One way to do this is to have a person stand outside the main entrance door of each middle school and high school from 7:45 A.M. to 8:45 A.M. on the same day and survey every twentieth student. The random sample would be the combined number of students surveyed at each school.

Recording Data

When you are gathering data, whether you get it from the Internet or from talking to people, you need a way to keep track of that data. It helps if you collect information in an organized way. If you don't, you may miss something important about the data, or you may have difficulty putting it in a form (like a graph) that makes interpreting the data easy.

Using a table or a chart helps you to clarify what you're looking for and lets you record your data.

EXAMPLE: You're wondering what the precipitation amount is in different towns in different months. You make a grid with the months listed across the top and the towns along the side. Now, as you gather each bit of information, you have someplace to record it.

Tallies

You've probably been doing tallies since kindergarten. They're an easy way to keep track of things as you are counting them. Tallies are really helpful when you're counting events as they happen, and you can't keep track of the data in your head. Tallies are not really helpful when the data are already collected and written down where you can count them.

EXAMPLE: You're counting cars to see whether a busy intersection needs a stoplight. You could list equal time intervals so the person collecting the data could tally the number of cars headed in each direction in each time interval.

TIME	NUMBER OF CARS EAST/WEST	NUMBER OF CARS NORTH/SOUTH
6–8 A.M.	JHT JHT JHT III	JHT JHT I
8–10 A.M.	JHT JHT JHT JHT JHT I	JHT JHT JHT III
10–12 noon	JHT JHT III	III
12 noon–2 P.M.		
2–4 P.M.		
4–6 P.M.		
6–8 P.M.		
8–10 P.M.		

Organizing and Summarizing Data with Statistics

You are going on a trip in April. In order to know how to pack, you look up the climate data for your destination. You may find that a reference book or an Internet site shows a single temperature that is a 30-year average temperature. If you didn't have statistics as a way of summarizing data, you would have to look at all the high and low temperatures for each day in April for the last 30 years and try to make sense of 1800 numbers!

Fortunately, we have several ways to find a single number that summarizes a whole bunch of numbers. You can

- find the average high and low for each day (60 numbers),
- find the average overall temperature for each day (30 numbers), and
- find the average overall temperature for the month (1 number) to give you a sense of what to expect.

Summaries of data may tell you what's typical in the set of data, how much variation there is in the data, or where your favorite bit of data fits in with the whole set.

) **Arranging Data**

One of the first steps after gathering numerical data is to arrange the numbers in order from least to greatest. In this way, it is very easy to see the **minimum** (lowest) **value** and the **maximum** (highest) **value**.

EXAMPLE: By the end of the basketball season, the players on the Sixth Grade Spurs had scored the following numbers of points: 32, 45, 17, 18, 59, 38, 78, 48, 65, 31. What was the worst score? The best score?

Arrange the scores from least to greatest:
17, 18, 31, 32, 38, 45, 48, 59, 65, 78

The minimum score (the worst) was 17. The maximum score (the best) was 78.

272

Range

A singer who can sing very high and very low notes is said to have a wide range. A shortstop who can cover a lot of ground has a large range. In statistics, the **range** is the difference between the greatest and least numbers in a set of data. Knowing the range can help you decide whether the differences among your data are important.

EXAMPLE: The table shows some of the top money-making movies of all time as of February 2003. What can you say about the range of the top-10 earners compared to the range of the next 139 earners?

MOVIE	AMOUNT EARNED IN THE U.S. (ROUNDED TO THE NEAREST MILLION DOLLARS)
1. Titanic	601,000,000
2. Star Wars	461,000,000
3. E.T. the Extra Terrestrial	435,000,000
4. Star Wars: Episode I	431,000,000
5. Spider-Man	404,000,000
6. Jurassic Park	357,000,000
7. Forrest Gump	329,000,000
8. The Lord of the Rings: The Two Towers	328,000,000
9. The Lion King	326,000,000
10. Harry Potter and the Sorcerer's Stone	318,000,000
✳✳✳✳✳✳✳✳✳✳✳✳✳✳✳✳✳✳✳✳✳✳✳✳✳✳✳✳	✳✳✳✳✳✳✳✳✳✳✳✳✳✳✳✳✳✳✳✳✳✳✳✳
149. The Nutty Professor	129,000,000

(Source: www.us.imdb.com/Charts/usatopmovies)

The range of earnings for the top 10 movies is about $283,000,000 ($601,000,000 − $318,000,000 = $283,000,000). What makes these data really interesting is that the earnings drop $283 million from number 1 to number 10, then drop only another $189 million from number 10 to number 149.

Types of Average 273

If you were to pick a number that best describes all the data in a set, what number would you pick? People most often choose a number somewhere in the middle of the data ordered from least to greatest, or a number with a lot of data clustered around it. This number is known as an **average**, or a **measure of central tendency**.

There are three types of average: mean, median, and mode.

Sets of data can have really different looks. The three main ways to describe average are useful in these different situations:

1. For sets of data with no very high or low numbers, *mean* works well.

2. For data sets with a couple of points much higher or lower than most of the others, *median* may be a good choice.

3. For sets of data with many identical data points, *mode* may be a better description.

Look at the question you are trying to answer to decide which type of average to use.

Mean 274

What does the word *mean* mean? In math, the **mean** is an average. It is found by adding all the values in a set and dividing by the number of values.

CASE I When all the data are close to each other, the mean is close to all the data.

EXAMPLE 1: In five basketball games, you score 17, 20, 14, 18, and 16 points. What is your average points per game (the mean of your scores)?

MORE ▶

ONE WAY Find the mean by evening out the scores.

❶ MAKE A STACK OF COUNTERS FOR EACH SCORE.	❷ MOVE COUNTERS FROM STACK TO STACK UNTIL EACH STACK HAS THE SAME NUMBER OF COUNTERS.
17 20 14 18 16	17 17 17 17 17

 ANOTHER WAY Find the mean by computing it.

❶ ADD TO FIND THE TOTAL OF THE NUMBERS.	❷ DIVIDE THE TOTAL BY THE NUMBER OF ADDENDS.
$17 + 20 + 14 + 18 + 16 = 85$	$85 ÷ 5 = 17$

Either way, you scored an average of 17 points per game.

CASE 2 When one piece of data is much bigger or much smaller than the rest, it can move the mean away from the main group of data.

EXAMPLE 2: What would happen to the mean if you scored 50 points at the next game?

❶ ADD TO FIND THE TOTAL OF THE NUMBERS.	❷ DIVIDE THE TOTAL BY THE NUMBER OF ADDENDS.
$17 + 20 + 14 + 18 + 16 + 50 = 135$	$135 ÷ 6 = 22\frac{1}{2}$

MORE HELP
See 283

Just one unusually high-scoring game brought your average points-per-game up by more than 5 points! It made the mean bigger than any of the other data points. So the mean no longer describes a typical number in the set of numbers.

275

Median

The **median** is another type of average. It is the number that falls exactly in the middle of a set of data when the data are arranged in order from least to greatest.

CASE 1 When there is an odd number of data points, the median is the middle number.

EXAMPLE 1: During one 7-hour shift, The Sandwich Barn kept track of the number of customers served each hour.

If there aren't any big gaps in the middle of the data but there are outliers at either end, the median may be the best number to use to describe the data.

MORE HELP
See 283

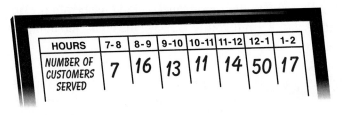

HOURS	7-8	8-9	9-10	10-11	11-12	12-1	1-2
NUMBER OF CUSTOMERS SERVED	7	16	13	11	14	50	17

What is the median number of customers per hour? Why is the median a good average for these data?

❶ ARRANGE THE NUMBERS IN ORDER FROM LEAST TO GREATEST.	❷ FIND THE MIDDLE NUMBER.
7, 11, 13, 14, 16, 17, 50	7, 11, 13, 14, 16, 17, 50

The median for the set of data is 14. So the typical number of customers in an hour is 14. The mean for this set of data is about 18.29. The slow first hour and the very hectic lunch hour are not typical of the rest of the shift and they do not affect the median as much as they affect the mean.

MORE HELP
See 274

CASE 2 An even number of numbers in a set of data has two middle numbers. In this case you need to find the mean of the two numbers. This creates a *fake* middle number for the set of data.

EXAMPLE 2: Rolando is The Sandwich Barn's best customer. They have even named a sandwich after him! Last week he went there six times and spent the amounts shown at the right. What is Rolando's typical lunch bill (the median amount)?

Clearly, $25.90 is not typical of Rolando's lunchtime spending. So it's nice that this number doesn't affect the median very much.

❶ ARRANGE THE NUMBERS IN ORDER FROM LEAST TO GREATEST. FIND THE TWO MIDDLE NUMBERS.	❷ FIND THE MEAN OF THE TWO MIDDLE NUMBERS.
3.95, 4.26, 4.58, 5.02, 5.36, 25.90	(4.58 + 5.02) ÷ 2 = 4.80

Rolando's typical bill is about $4.80.

Mode

Sometimes, the best way to describe what is typical about a set of data is to use the value that occurs most often. This value is called the **mode**. For example, in the set of data 2, 3, 5, 5, 6, the mode is 5.

CASE 1 Sometimes there is one value that occurs more often than any other.

EXAMPLE 1: According to the American Trucking Association's Web site, the 50 states and Washington, D.C., have different maximum speed limits for trucks:

MAXIMUM SPEED LIMITS	NUMBER OF STATES
55 mph	7
60 mph	2
65 mph	21
70 mph	13
75 mph	8

(Source: www.trucking.org)

If you look at the data, far more states have a 65 mph speed limit for trucks than have any other speed limit. So you could say the typical maximum speed limit for trucks is 65 mph.

CASE 2 Sometimes there is more than one value that occurs most often. In this case, all these highest values are modes for the set of data.

EXAMPLE 2: According to Weather Post at *The Washington Post*'s Web site, Sacramento, California, has an interesting pattern for average daily temperatures:

AVERAGE DAILY TEMPERATURE	NUMBER OF MONTHS
in the 40s	2
in the 50s	4
in the 60s	2
in the 70s	4

(Source: www.washingtonpost.com)

You could say that Sacramento, California, has a **bimodal** (two modes) weather pattern because there are 4 months with averages in the 50s *and* 4 months with averages in the 70s.

CASE 3 Sometimes there is no value that occurs more often than the others. In this case, there is no mode.

When there is no mode, it might be a good idea to use the mean or median to describe the set of data.

Dividing Data Into Equal Parts   (277

Sometimes it's easiest to understand a set of data if you divide it into equal-size groups. **Quartiles** group the data set into quarters, and **percentiles** group it into hundredths.

Quartiles

278

Suppose you take a test and want to compare your score to other scores. You can use quartiles to find out whether your score is in the top quarter of the scores. The median splits a set of data into 2 parts. Along with the median, quartiles split a set of data into 4 parts.

MORE HELP
See 275

EXAMPLE: The 22 test scores for your class are listed to the right. The bold, blue score is your score. Is your score in the top one-fourth of your class?

73	69	58	45	39
71	55	57	43	60
68	73	49	36	59
58	45	51	56	64
44	50			

You can use quartiles to solve the problem.

1. Arrange the data in order from greatest to least.

2. Find the median of the data:
$(57 + 56) \div 2 = 56.5$

3. Find the median of the upper half of the data. Examine the top 11 scores and find the middle number. This is the upper quartile. The *upper quartile* is 64 because scores of 64 or higher are in the *top quarter*.

4. Find the median of the lower half of the data. Examine the bottom 11 scores and find the middle number. This is the lower quartile. The *lower quartile* is 45 because scores of 45 or lower are in the *bottom quarter*.

Notice how the median and the quartiles separate the data into 4 parts. Your score, **60**, is not in the top quarter of the scores.

```
73
73
71
69
68
64
----
60
59
58
58
57
----
56
55
51
50
49
----
45
45
44
43
39
36
```

The upper quartile is also called the **third quartile.**

The median is 56.5. This is also called the **second quartile.**

The lower quartile is also called the **first quartile.**

Percentiles

Suppose you heard someone say that your score on a test is in the
82nd percentile. What would that mean?

Percentiles tell you what percent of a group of numbers is less than or
equal to a given number. If your score is in the 82nd percentile, it means
that 82 percent of the scores are less than or equal to your score.

Percentiles are used very
often with standardized test
scores to make it easy to
picture how well a person or a
group of people did compared
to other test-takers.

EXAMPLE: Your local newspaper
has reported these standardized
test scores for your class. You
happen to know that your score
was 150. What was your percentile
ranking?

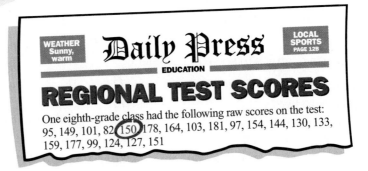

WEATHER Sunny, warm

Daily Press

LOCAL SPORTS PAGE 12B

EDUCATION

REGIONAL TEST SCORES

One eighth-grade class had the following raw scores on the test:
95, 149, 101, 82, 150, 178, 164, 103, 181, 97, 154, 144, 130, 133,
159, 177, 99, 124, 127, 151

To find your percentile ranking, follow these steps:

1. Arrange the data in order from least to greatest:
82, 95, 97, 99, 101, 103, 124, 127, 130, 133, 144, 149, 150, 151, 154, 159,
164, 177, 178, 181

2. Find the total number of scores:
$n = 20$

3. Find how many scores are less than or equal to yours:
82, 95, 97, 99, 101, 103, 124, 127, 130, 133, 144, 149, **150**, 151, 154, 159,
164, 177, 178, 181
13 of the 20 scores are less than or equal to 150.

MORE HELP
See 425, 426

4. Find out what percent 13 is of 20:
$13 \div 20 = 0.65$
65% of the scores are less than or equal to yours.

So your score is in the 65th percentile. Your score is at least as good as
the scores of 65% of your classmates.

Variability of Data   280

Data are a lot like fish. The word *data* and the word *fish* are plural. There are many kinds of data and many kinds of fish. Some data, like some fish, cluster together and some spread way out. Pieces of data in a set are related in some way, just as fish in a school are related.

Most data can be plotted on a graph of some sort, which means you usually have two bits of information in a relation that makes up a piece of data, a **data point**. The two bits might be two numbers (4, $6.50), or a word and a number (January, 25°), or even a phrase and an interval of numbers (boys' heights, 5' 6"–6' 0"). In order to make a graph, you need to know not only the bits of information that make up each piece of data but also something about the way the data spread out. Range, average deviation, standard deviation, and outliers are all measures of the variability of data.

MORE HELP
See 272

Average Deviation   281

Before distributing the tests, your teacher tells you that the mean score on the math test was 60. If most kids in the class received scores around 60, there's a high chance your score is also very close to 60. However, if there is a wide range of scores, it's more likely that your score is quite a bit higher (or lower) than 60.

When you use mean to talk about what's typical about a set of data, it helps to be able to say by how much most of the numbers in the set tend to differ from the mean. **Average deviation** can give you this information. A low average deviation tells you that the data tend to cluster around the mean—there is not much difference between most numbers in the set and the mean. A higher average deviation tells you that the data are more spread out.

MORE ▶

MORE HELP
See 301

EXAMPLE: The **line plots** below show the heights in inches of players on two women's college basketball teams. On which team is there more variation in the heights of the players?

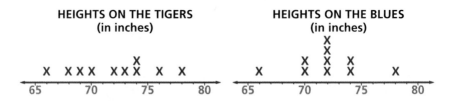

To solve the problem, you can find the average deviation for each team.

1. Find the mean of the data.

2. Deviations are like distance—always positive. So, find the positive difference, or deviation, of each value from the mean. The mean of the deviations is the average deviation.

That's interesting. The range in heights is the same, but the heights of the Tigers are spread out more.

TIGERS		BLUES	
Mean height = 720 in. ÷ 10 = 72 in.		Mean height = 720 in. ÷ 10 = 72 in.	
Height	Deviation from Mean	Height	Deviation from Mean
66	6	66	6
68	4	70	2
69	3	70	2
70	2	72	0
72 ← mean	0	72 } mean	0
73	1	72	0
74	2	72	0
74	2	74	2
76	4	74	2
78	6	78	6
720	30	720	20

Mean deviation = 30 ÷ 10 = 3
So, the average deviation on the Tigers is 3 in.

Mean deviation = 20 ÷ 10 = 2
So, the average deviation on the Blues is 2 in.

The average deviation on the Tigers is more than the average deviation on the Blues. This means that on the Tigers, the heights differ more from the mean than on the Blues.

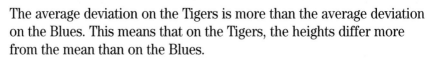

Standard Deviation

Standard deviation is another way to describe how data in a set tend to differ from the mean. To find the standard deviation:

MORE HELP
See 076, 079

1. Find the mean.
2. Find the deviation of each data point from the mean.
3. Find the square of the deviation of each data point.
4. Find the mean of these squares. This is called the variance.
5. Then find the square root of the variance. This is the standard deviation.

EXAMPLE: Compare the average deviation with the standard deviation for the heights of the Tigers.

HEIGHTS OF TIGERS MEAN HEIGHT: 72 IN.	66	68	69	70	72	73	74	74	76	78
DEVIATION		6	4	3	2	0	1	2	2	4	6
DEVIATION SQUARED		36	16	9	4	0	1	4	4	16	36
VARIANCE = MEAN OF SQUARES OF DEVIATIONS: 126 ÷ 10 = 12.6 IN.
STANDARD DEVIATION = SQUARE ROOT OF VARIANCE, ABOUT 3.55 IN.

You can see that the standard deviation is different than the average deviation. Scientists use standard deviation to talk about data that have a *normal* distribution. That is, there are more data points in the middle and fewer on the ends. In a normal distribution, 68% of the data points should be no more than one standard deviation on either side of the mean.

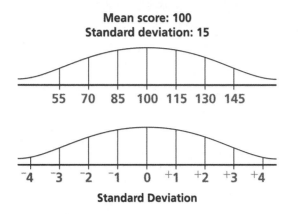

Mean score: 100
Standard deviation: 15

55 70 85 100 115 130 145

⁻4 ⁻3 ⁻2 ⁻1 0 ⁺1 ⁺2 ⁺3 ⁺4
Standard Deviation

Outliers

Did you ever have a video-game score that was incredibly better or worse than all your other scores? In statistics, a piece of data that seems to float too far out at one end of the range is called an **outlier**. Outliers can affect how you interpret your data.

EXAMPLE: A dynamometer is a tool that measures hand strength. Suppose 10 students in a gym class use a dynamometer. They get the results below. Does the set of data contain any outliers?

MORE HELP
See 301–303

To decide if there are any outliers, place the numbers on a line plot. Then check the least and the greatest numbers to see if they are much less or much greater than the next closest number.

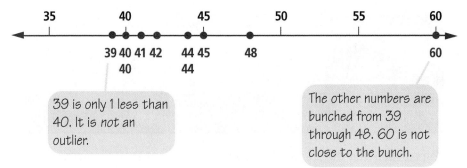

35   40   45   50   55   60

39 40 41 42   44 45   48   60
   40   44

39 is only 1 less than 40. It is *not* an outlier.

The other numbers are bunched from 39 through 48. 60 is not close to the bunch.

Since 60 is not close to the bunch, 60 is an outlier.

How can identifying outliers help you? Suppose that the data above only contained the top 5 dynamometer scores and that you wanted to use the mean or the median to give someone an idea of the typical score. Because the outlier increases the mean, you might decide that the median is a more typical score.

Displaying Data in Tables and Graphs

It seems harder and harder to cross the intersection near your house. Suppose you know that the average daily traffic at your intersection was 490 vehicles in 1990, 570 vehicles in 1994, 1060 vehicles in 1998, and 2000 vehicles in 2002. Suppose you also know how many new houses were built near the intersection each year from 1991 to 2002. You want to get a stoplight installed at that corner, but the information alone usually does not convince voters and other town decision makers.

Organizing and displaying data clearly is a convincing way to show information, especially if you want to prove a point. From the displays you can see trends, make predictions, and easily compare and contrast ideas. And if you know how to read graphs carefully, you can even tell whether someone's trying to fool you!

Suppose you have lots of data about a topic. You want to organize the data so that any piece of data can be found easily. One way to do it is to make a table.

EXAMPLE: You have the following data about the 2000 Summer Olympics:

WEATHER
Cloudy,
T-storms

Daily Press

THEATER,
MOVIES
PAGE 1C

SPECIAL

SUMMER OLYMPICS WRAPUP

The 2000 Summer Olympics are now over and some of the medal counts are quite impressive. The U.S. Olympians brought home 40 gold medals, 24 silvers, and 33 bronze medals. Russian athletes also did quite well, with 32 gold, 28 silver, and 28 bronze. China's count was 28 gold, 16 silver, and 15 bronze medals.

(Source: World Almanac)

You can organize the data into a table that makes it easy to find and compare specific pieces of data.

To read the table, you find the country name in the far-left column, then move along that row until you find the column for the medal you want information about. For example, to find the number of bronze medals won by Russia, you move along the row for Russia until you find the total in the column for bronze. The number is 28.

2000 SUMMER OLYMPICS MEDAL COUNT				
COUNTRY	GOLD	SILVER	BRONZE	TOTAL
United States	40	24	33	97
Russia	32	28	28	88
China	28	16	15	59

Frequency Tables

A frequency table is a way to show how often an item, a number, or a range of numbers occurs. Here are two different ways to use a frequency table to show data. The one you use depends on the type of data you have to show.

CASE 1 When you are counting responses, keep track of each response.

EXAMPLE 1: A teacher asks her class, "What's the main reason you use your computer: Internet, games, word processing, or something else?" The results are at the right.

INTERNET, INTERNET, GAMES, WORD PROCESSING, GAMES, WORD PROCESSING, SOMETHING ELSE, WORD PROCESSING, INTERNET, GAMES, GAMES, INTERNET, GAMES, INTERNET, WORD PROCESSING, SOMETHING ELSE, INTERNET, INTERNET

To make a frequency table, first list each item in the data. Then count and record the number of times each item occurs. Using a tally can help you count.

COMPUTER USE	TALLY	FREQUENCY
Internet	卌 II	7
word processing	IIII	4
games	卌	5
something else	II	2

CASE 2 Another way to make a frequency table is to group data into intervals. This is called a **grouped frequency table**.

MORE HELP
See 289

EXAMPLE 2: Suppose the television show *Not You!* gets the following ratings over a 20-week period:

15.3, 12.2, 13.4, 15.6, 18.9, 20.2, 21.3, 22.4, 25.9, 20.1, 18.8, 17.4, 19.1, 17.2, 18.1, 19.3, 17.2, 14.3, 12.1, 15.3

1. Choose a range that includes all the data (in this case 10–29.9).
2. Divide that range into equal intervals (10–14.9, 15–19.9, etc.).
3. Count the number of data points in each interval. A tally can help you count the data.

RATINGS FOR *NOT YOU!*		
INTERVAL	TALLY	FREQUENCY
10–14.9	IIII	4
15–19.9	卌 卌 I	11
20–24.9	IIII	4
25–29.9	I	1

Making Graphs

When you make a bar graph, a line graph, or a histogram, you start with a grid, a set of crossed lines. To make that grid a graph you need to give meaning to the lines. You can do that by finding ways to make the lines refer to important parts of your data—numbers or categories. This requires you to choose labels and intervals for your data.

288

Labeling the Axes

The **axes** on a graph are the reference lines. They most often are a horizontal line and a vertical line that cross where one or both axes are zero. When there are no negative numbers in your graph, the axes are usually the bottom and left-hand borders of the graph. How you label the axes depends on the data you have and what you want your graph to show.

EXAMPLE: Suppose you want to make a line graph that shows the average cost of tuition and fees for 4-year private colleges in each of 5 years. How would you label the two axes?

Since you want to show the cost for each year, one axis would list the years. The other axis would list the costs. At the right are the two possibilities.

A bar graph might use either of the two options. The top option would produce a graph with horizontal bars. The bottom would produce a graph with vertical bars.

On line graphs, time is usually shown on the horizontal axis.

AVERAGE COST OF TUITION AND FEES

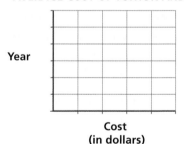

Year

Cost
(in dollars)

AVERAGE COST OF TUITION AND FEES

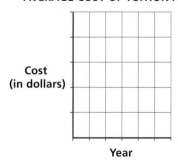

Cost
(in dollars)

Year

Choosing the Scales

Suppose you are making a graph. After you label the axes, choose the **scale**—the numbers running along a side of the graph. The difference between numbers from one grid line to another is the **interval**. The interval will depend on the range of your data.

CASE 1 When you can, you should choose simple scales, with the numbers starting at zero and increasing by ones or other equal intervals.

EXAMPLE 1: Choose the scales for a graph of these data.

TEMPERATURES IN IOWA CITY, IOWA												
MONTH	J	F	M	A	M	J	J	A	S	O	N	D
AVERAGE HIGH TEMPERATURE (°C)	⁻1	1	9	17	23	28	30	29	25	19	9	1

(Source: www.washingtonpost.com)

You can list the months across the horizontal axis and the temperatures along the vertical axis. The range of temperatures is from ⁻1 to 30.

You can choose the interval between grid lines.

■ Choosing an interval of 1 will make a tall, skinny graph.
■ Choosing an interval of 2 will make a more squarish graph.
■ Choosing an interval of 10 will make a short, wide graph.

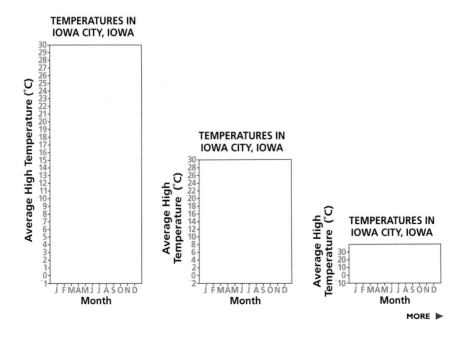

MORE ▶

CASE 2 Sometimes there just isn't enough paper to make your scale start at zero and still have small intervals that are useful.

EXAMPLE 2: Show the scale you would use to make a line graph that shows the average cost of tuition and fees for 4-year private colleges in each of the years from 1991 to 1995. The data are shown in the table below.

AVERAGE COST OF TUITION AND FEES FOR 4-YEAR PRIVATE COLLEGES				
1991	1992	1993	1994	1995
$8389	$9053	$9553	$10,100	$10,698

(Source: Digest of Education Statistics, U.S. Center for Education Statistics)

After you choose your axes—Year and Cost—choose a scale that will let you plot all the costs. That means you need a scale that lets you plot numbers that range from 8389 to 10,698—the lowest and highest costs.

A scale that starts at zero and counts by ones or tens to 10,698 would be impractical. Even counting by hundreds you would need 107 lines to show 10,698! So, what scale can you use?

The scale to the right is one solution. Since the minimum value is $8389, you can use a jagged line to break the scale and show that you are not plotting values between 0 and 8000. After that, you can use intervals of 500 from 8000 to 12,000. By rounding the data to the nearest hundred, you can estimate where to plot each point on the graph.

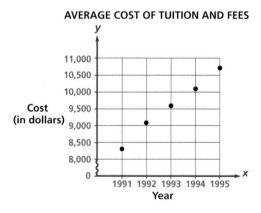

AVERAGE COST OF TUITION AND FEES

MATH ALERT Broken Scales Can Exaggerate Changes

You need to be very careful when you break the scale in a graph. Use a jagged line to show the break in the scale. You can easily mislead your reader into thinking that the data show more serious change than they do. Look again at the average annual cost of tuition and fees for 4-year private colleges.

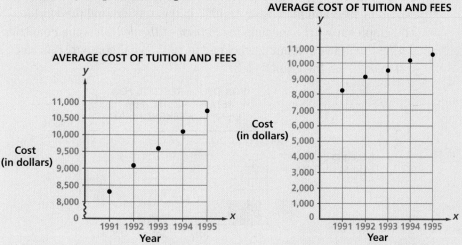

When you don't break the scale, it doesn't look like costs are rising quite as fast!

Graphs That Compare

Some graphs do a great job of illustrating how data compare. For example, they may show:

- the same kind of data at different times or places (like scoring records for one team in different years);
- different kinds of data at the same time or place (like scoring records for two different teams in the same year);
- the different kinds of data that make up 100% of one group of data (like all the different ages of students in your class).

The most popular graphs for comparing data are **bar graphs**, **pictographs**, **histograms**, and **circle graphs**.

Single-Bar Graphs

A **bar graph** uses the length of solid bars to represent numbers and compare data. With just one glance at a bar graph, you can see how quantities compare.

EXAMPLE: Many movies made in the United States are also popular in other countries. One such movie is *Return of the Jedi*. It was first shown in 1983 and then again in 1997 in theaters around the world. The graph shows the receipts for *Return of the Jedi* in some countries during the movie's opening weekend in 1997. What comparisons can you make from the graph?

BOX OFFICE RECEIPTS FOR
RETURN OF THE JEDI,
OPENING WEEKEND, 1997

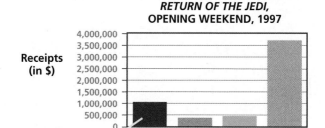

Receipts (in $)

Country

(Source: Variety)

MORE HELP
See 288–289

To make the bar graph, estimate where each amount would fall on the vertical axis, then draw a bar to that height.

The tallest bar is for the United Kingdom and Ireland. So, *Return of the Jedi* made the most money in the United Kingdom and Ireland.

Where was *Return of the Jedi* most popular? To answer this, you need more information— how many people live in each country and what the ticket price was in each country.

Double-Bar Graphs

Sometimes, to compare sets of data, a bar graph with pairs of bars works better than a bar graph with individual bars. This kind of graph is called a **double-bar graph**.

EXAMPLE: The following table shows statistics for the home-run leaders in the American and National Leagues for 1998–2002. The graph shows the information from the table. What comparisons can you make between the two leagues?

HOME-RUN LEADERS		
YEAR	AMERICAN LEAGUE LEADER	NATIONAL LEAGUE LEADER
1998	56	70
1999	48	65
2000	47	50
2001	52	73
2002	57	49

(Source: World Almanac)

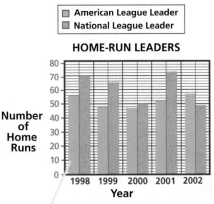

The double-bar graph was made by taking the numbers for each league for each year, estimating about where those numbers would fall on the vertical axis, and drawing a pair of bars for those heights.

MORE HELP
See 288–289

The graph tells you lots of interesting things about the years 1998–2002. The National League leaders in 1998 and 2001 had 70 or more home runs, but the league leader in 2002 had only 49 home runs.

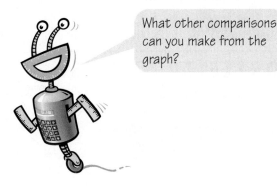

What other comparisons can you make from the graph?

Pictographs

Do you want to compare data, but do it in a way that's more eye-catching than a bar graph? You could make a **pictograph**—a graph that uses pictures or symbols to compare data. Newspapers and magazines often use this kind of graph to jazz up their pages.

EXAMPLE: You take a random survey to find out what kinds of TV shows students in your school like best. The results are in the table. Make a pictograph that shows the results.

FAVORITE KINDS OF TV SHOWS	
KIND OF SHOW	VOTES
Information	25
Drama	45
Comedy	50
Sports	40

To make a pictograph, follow these steps:

1. Title your graph.

2. List the items in your data that are being measured in some way.

3. Choose a symbol for your data and draw a **key** to show what each symbol represents. In this graph, one TV stands for 10 votes.

4. Draw the appropriate number of symbols next to each item.

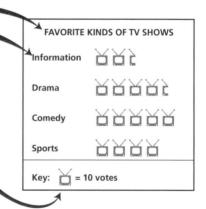

Histograms

Sometimes you want to show how often data fall into different ranges, or intervals. One way to show this is to use a **histogram**.

EXAMPLE: Each week, *Billboard 200*™ lists the 200 top-selling albums. It also shows how many weeks each album has been on the Top-200 Chart. As of March 8, 2003, the top 25 albums had been on the chart these numbers of weeks: 1, 3, 52, 26, 66, 1, 38, 6, 3, 2, 13, 15, 8, 15, 21, 10, 61, 40, 11, 14, 35, 26, 14, 17, 17. *(Source: Billboard)*

Show the results on a histogram. Then tell which interval has the greatest number of albums.

MORE HELP
See 286

Before making a histogram, it is helpful to first make a frequency table. Be sure to choose a range that contains all the data and divide it into equal intervals. In this table, intervals of 20 from 1 through 80 are used.

NUMBER OF WEEKS ON TOP-200 CHART (AS OF MARCH 8, 2003)	
NUMBER OF WEEKS	FREQUENCY
1–20	16
21–40	6
41–60	1
61–80	2

Once you have a frequency table, you can use it to make the histogram. Making a histogram is just like making a bar graph, except that each bar represents an interval, and there are no spaces between the bars.

The interval with the most albums is 1–20. This means that most of the top-25 albums don't stay on the Top-200 Chart list for more than 20 weeks.

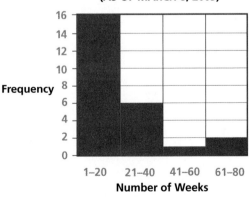

NUMBER OF WEEKS ON TOP-200 CHART (AS OF MARCH 8, 2003)

Circle Graphs

You can use a **circle graph** to show how a whole is broken into parts.

EXAMPLE: The table shows how all electricity is generated in the United States. It gives the percent of the total electricity that each source contributes.

SOURCES OF ELECTRICITY IN THE UNITED STATES	
SOURCE	PERCENTAGE
Oil	11%
Hydropower	13%
Gas	22%
Nuclear	12%
Coal	40%
Other	2%

(Source: Electric Power Annual, 1999)

Make a circle graph of the data.

1. Draw a circle. Mark the center.

2. You know the percent of the total electricity that comes from each source, so you find

MORE HELP
See 340

that percent of 360° (since 360° is the whole circle).

11% of electricity comes from oil.

11% of 360° is 39.6, so you use a bit more than 39° of the circle for oil.

3. Use a protractor to draw a central angle with the degree measure you've assigned to each source.

4. Label and title your graph.

39°

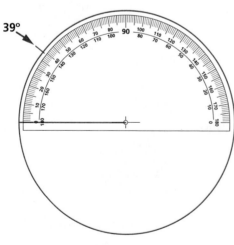

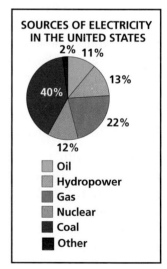

SOURCES OF ELECTRICITY IN THE UNITED STATES
2% 11%
13%
40%
22%
12%

☐ Oil
☐ Hydropower
☐ Gas
☐ Nuclear
■ Coal
■ Other

11% of 360 = 0.11 × 360 = 39.6

Graphs That Show Change Over Time 297

Some graphs are best at showing how things change over time.
You can show one thing changing. Or you can compare how several
things change over the same time period. The most widely used graphs
for showing change over time are **line graphs**.

Single-Line Graphs 298

By looking at the line in a line graph, you can tell whether something is
increasing, decreasing, or staying the same over time.

EXAMPLE: In the 1990s, in-line
skating was one of the fastest
growing sports in the U.S. The
table at the right shows how
many in-line skaters there were
from 1991 through 2001. The
graph shows the information
in the table. During which years
did the number of in-line skaters
grow the most?

IN-LINE SKATERS IN THE U.S.	
YEAR	NUMBER OF SKATERS (TO THE NEAREST 100,000)
1991	7,300,000
1993	12,400,000
1995	23,900,000
1997	26,600,000
1999	24,100,000
2001	19,200,000

(Source: National Sporting Goods Association)

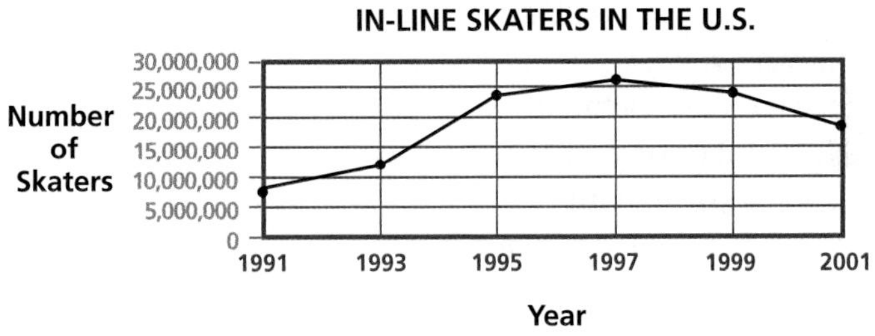

MORE HELP
See 248,
288–289

To find the
year in which
in-line skating
increased the
most, find the
steepest line
segment. The
steepest line
segment runs
from 1993–1995. So the number of in-line skaters increased the most
from 1993 to 1995.

IN-LINE SKATERS IN THE U.S.

Number of Skaters
(30,000,000 / 25,000,000 / 20,000,000 / 15,000,000 / 10,000,000 / 5,000,000 / 0)

Year (1991 / 1993 / 1995 / 1997 / 1999 / 2001)

299   Multiple-Line Graphs

Suppose you want to compare two or more quantities that are increasing or decreasing over time. You can use a multiple-line graph, in which each line shows one set of data.

EXAMPLE: People's interest in different sports is changing. The table shows the number of people who play softball and those who play soccer. The graph shows the information from the table. What trends does the graph show?

SOCCER VERSUS SOFTBALL		
YEAR	SOCCER (IN MILLIONS)	SOFTBALL (IN MILLIONS)
1991	10	19.6
1993	10.3	17.9
1995	12	17.6
1997	13.7	16.3
1999	13.2	14.7
2001	13.9	13.2

(Source: National Sporting Goods Association)

MORE HELP
See 288–289, 298, 310

The line for soccer is moving upwards. So the popularity of soccer is increasing. The line for softball is moving downward. If both trends continue, the number of people playing soccer will exceed the number playing softball.

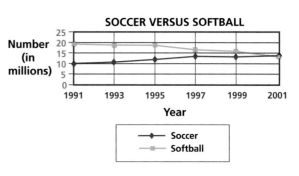

300   Graphs That Show How Data Are Clustered

Some graphs do a very good job at letting you see how data group or cluster together. These graphs can illustrate:

- whether some events are related to other events (such as your age in relation to your height), or
- whether the data are mostly bunched up or spread way out (such as the heights of basketball players versus the heights of everyone else).

MORE HELP
See 295

The graphs that show data groupings are generally called plots. This is because you usually just show the individual data points, not bars or connected lines.

Line Plots

Sometimes, instead of comparing data or showing trends, you want to show the spread of the data. You can do this with a **line plot**. When you look at a line plot, you can quickly identify the range, the mode, and any outliers of the data. Often, line plots are used when you want to see the mode—how often one number occurs in a set of data.

MORE HELP
See 272, 276, 283

EXAMPLE: Sixteen students estimated how much television they watched each week, to the nearest hour. Here are their results:
14, 16, 12, 14, 14, 11, 20, 12, 8, 10, 16, 15, 17, 5, 15, 10

Show these results on a line plot. Then identify the mode of the data and any outliers that you see.

To make a line plot:

1. Title your plot.

2. Draw a horizontal line segment on grid paper.

3. Make a scale of numbers below the line. The numbers should include the greatest value and the least value in the set of data.

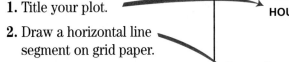
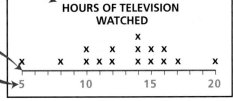

4. For each piece of data, draw an X above the corresponding number.

The most X's are above 14. So, the mode is 14. Both 5 and 20 are separated from the rest of the data. So, 5 and 20 are outliers.

Box-and-Whisker Plots

Suppose you have a large set of data and you want a display that gives a general idea of how the data cluster together. A **box-and-whisker plot** displays the median, the quartiles, and outliers of a set of data, but does not display any other specific values.

EXAMPLE: The Federal Highway Administration keeps track of the average miles per gallon for vehicles driven in each state. The table to the right shows the data for the Midwestern States region for 1998. Use the data to make a box-and-whisker plot.

AVERAGE MILEAGE IN THE MIDWESTERN STATES REGION	
STATE	MILES PER GALLON
Illinois	17.03
Indiana	16.65
Iowa	14.09
Kansas	15.58
Michigan	16.34
Minnesota	16.46
Missouri	16.21
Nebraska	14.32
North Dakota	14.27
Ohio	16.19
South Dakota	13.80
Wisconsin	17.81

(Source: Federal Highway Administration)

To make a box-and-whisker plot:

1. Write the data in order from least to greatest.
   13.80, 14.09, 14.27, 14.32, 15.58, 16.19, 16.21, 16.34, 16.46, 16.65, 17.03, 17.81

2. Draw a number line that can show the data in equal intervals.

MORE HELP
See 275, 277, 278

3. Mark the median: 16.20
4. Mark the median of the upper half (the upper quartile): 16.555
5. Mark the median of the lower half (the lower quartile): 14.295
6. Mark the upper extreme (the greatest number): 17.81
7. Mark the lower extreme (the lowest number): 13.80
8. Draw a box between the lower quartile and the upper quartile. Split the box by drawing a vertical line through the median. Draw two "whiskers" from the quartiles to the extremes.

AVERAGE MILEAGE IN THE MIDWESTERN STATES REGION

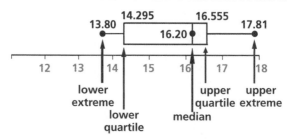

Stem-and-Leaf Plots

Stem-and-leaf plots allow you to see easily the greatest, least, and median values in a set of data. Like histograms and grouped frequency tables, they give you a quick way of checking how many pieces of data fall in various ranges. But they also let you see something the two other displays don't: the value of every piece of data.

EXAMPLE: As of 2001, the following are the ages, in chronological order, at which U.S. Presidents were inaugurated:
57, 61, 57, 57, 58, 57, 61, 54, 68, 51, 49, 64, 50, 48, 65, 52, 56, 46, 54, 49, 50, 47, 55, 55, 54, 42, 51, 56, 55, 51, 54, 51, 60, 62, 43, 55, 56, 61, 52, 69, 64, 46, 54
(Source: World Almanac)

Use a stem-and-leaf plot to help you summarize the data.

To make a stem-and-leaf plot:

1. Title your plot.
2. Write the data in order from least to greatest:
   42, 43, 46, 46, 47, 48, 49, 49, 50, 50, 51, 51, 51, 51, 52, 52, 54, 54, 54, 54, 54, 55, 55, 55, 55, 56, 56, 56, 57, 57, 57, 57, 58, 60, 61, 61, 61, 62, 64, 64, 65, 68, 69
3. Find the least and greatest values: 42 and 69
4. Choose stem values that will include the extreme values. For this graph, it makes sense to use tens: 4 tens, 5 tens, and 6 tens.
5. Write the tens vertically from least to greatest. Draw a vertical line to the right of the stem values.
6. Separate each number into **stems** (tens) and **leaves** (ones). Write each leaf to the right of its stem in order from least to greatest.
7. Write a key that explains how to read the stems and leaves.

AGES OF U.S. PRESIDENTS WHEN INAUGURATED

Stem	Leaves
4	2, 3, 6, 6, 7, 8, 9, 9
5	0, 0, 1, 1, 1, 1, 2, 2, 4, 4, 4, 4, 4, 5, 5, 5, 5, 6, 6, 6, 7, 7, 7, 7, 8
6	0, 1, 1, 1, 2, 4, 4, 5, 8, 9

Key: 4|2 represents 42 years.

You can see from the plot that:

- all the U.S. Presidents entered office in their 40s, 50s, and 60s;
- most of them were inaugurated during their 50s (actually mostly between 54 and 58);
- more Presidents were sworn in while in their 60s than while in their 40s.

Double Stem-and-Leaf Plots

You can use a **double stem-and-leaf plot** (also called a **back-to-back stem-and-leaf plot**) to compare two sets of data.

EXAMPLE: The double stem-and-leaf plot below compares tall buildings in Chicago and New York. For each city, the plot shows the heights of buildings that are 700 feet tall or greater. The heights are rounded to the nearest 10 feet.

Use the plot to answer these questions:

■ How tall is the tallest building in each city?
■ Which city has more buildings over 1000 feet?

In a double stem-and-leaf plot, the stem is in the middle. The leaves are on either side. Read from the middle to the left for Chicago. Read from the middle to the right for New York. In this plot, the stem shows the thousands and hundreds digits of the heights. The leaves show the tens digits.

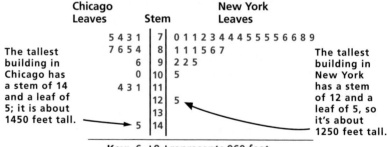

HEIGHTS OF BUILDINGS OVER 700 FEET TALL IN CHICAGO AND NEW YORK

Chicago Leaves	Stem	New York Leaves
5 4 3 1	7	0 1 1 2 3 4 4 4 5 5 5 5 6 6 8 9
7 6 5 4	8	1 1 1 5 6 7
6	9	2 2 5
0	10	5
4 3 1	11	
	12	5
	13	
5	14	

The tallest building in Chicago has a stem of 14 and a leaf of 5; it is about 1450 feet tall.

The tallest building in New York has a stem of 12 and a leaf of 5, so it's about 1250 feet tall.

Key: 6 | 9 | represents 960 feet.
|10| 5 represents 1050 feet.

(Source: World Almanac)

To find the number of buildings that are 1000 feet or taller, look at the stems for 10–14. Chicago has more buildings that are over 1000 feet tall.

Scatter Plots

Suppose you want to analyze two sets of data to see how closely they are related. One way to do it is to use a **scatter plot** (also called a **scattergram**). On a scatter plot, you plot corresponding numbers from two sets of data as ordered pairs. You then decide if they are related by determining how close they come to forming a straight line.

MORE HELP
See 308,
318–319

EXAMPLE: A student kept track of the number of hours she studied for tests and the grade on each test. The results are in the table. Make a scatter plot for the table. Then describe the relationship between the amount of time she studied and the grade she received.

STUDY TIME (IN HOURS)	1.5	1	3	2.5	1.5	4	3.5
GRADE	75	71	88	86	80	97	92

To make a scatter plot:

1. Title your plot.
2. Decide which set of numbers you will plot on each axis and label the axes.
3. Choose a scale for each axis.
4. Plot corresponding numbers as ordered pairs. For example, in the table above, plot (1.5, 75), (1, 71) (3, 88), and so on.

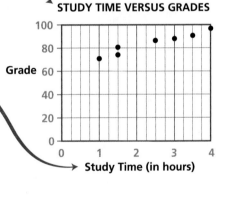

STUDY TIME VERSUS GRADES

Grade

Study Time (in hours)

The dots on the scatter plot are close to forming a straight line. So, there is a strong positive correlation between the number of hours the student studied and her test grades. It seems that the more she studied, the better her grades.

Line of Best Fit

When the dots on a scatter plot come close to forming a straight line, you can draw a **line of best fit**. This line, which is sometimes called a **trend line**, is the line that comes closest to connecting the points on a scatter plot. You can use this line to make predictions.

EXAMPLE: Richard runs 8 miles. After every 2 miles, he checks the time. The scatter plot shows his results. Draw a line of best fit on the scatter plot.

The black dashed line is the line of best fit. It rises 10 minutes for each mile. So you could say that Richard runs about 10-minute miles.

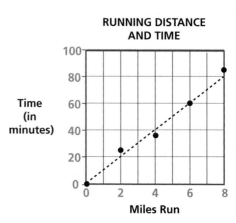

RUNNING DISTANCE AND TIME

Time (in minutes)

Miles Run

Interpreting Data

Does smoking cause cancer? What will be the population of your town in 10 years? Who has the most popular new album?

After the data have been sorted, re-sorted, averaged, tabled, and graphed, you can still do more with the information. You can look for:

■ how data are (or are not) related;
■ trends, what new data might come in at a later time;
■ what could have happened if . . . ; and
■ what did happen between the lines.

Correlations

Did you ever wonder whether people who drive red cars really get more tickets than others? Questions like this can be answered by analyzing two sets of data (in this case, the average number of tickets all drivers get and the average number of tickets red-car drivers get).

When you analyze the data, you are trying to decide:

■ whether there is a correlation between the two sets of data (if not, red-car drivers would get the same number of tickets as anyone else);
■ whether the correlation is weak or strong (if red-car drivers get more tickets, do they get many more or only a few more?); and
■ whether the correlation is positive (red-car drivers get more tickets) or negative (red-car drivers get fewer tickets).

MORE ▶

One way to figure out the correlation is to plot the data in a scatter plot. The closer the points come to forming a straight, slanted line, the stronger the correlation is. But, if the line is horizontal or vertical, that means no matter what happens to one variable, the other never changes. This makes it hard to determine correlation.

CASE 1 If you were to plot average January temperature against the land area of U.S. cities, you would probably see **no correlation** and the plot would look like this:

CASE 2 If you were to plot average age against weekly TV viewing time, you would probably see a somewhat **positive correlation** and the plot would look like this:

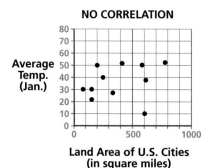

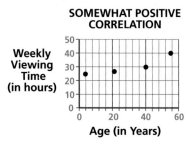

CASE 3 If you plotted grade level against average age, you would see a **strong positive correlation** and the plot would look like this:

CASE 4 There's a somewhat **negative correlation** between age in years and school enrollment. A scatter plot comparing these two sets of data might look like this:

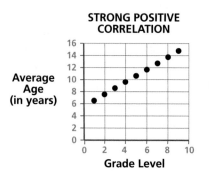

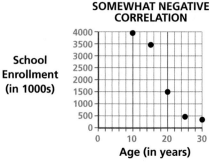

EXAMPLE: The table shows the average heights for girls of various ages. The scatter plot shows the data from the table. How strong is the correlation between age and height?

AGE (IN YEARS)	AVERAGE HEIGHT (IN INCHES)
8	49
10	53
12	58
14	63
16	64

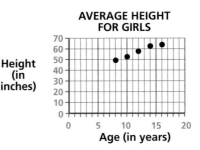

AVERAGE HEIGHT FOR GIRLS

Height (in inches)

Age (in years)

(Source: World Book Encyclopedia)

The dots on the scatter plot are close to forming a straight line that moves up from left to right. So there is a strong positive correlation between age and height, at least at these ages.

309

MATH ALERT Correlation Versus Cause and Effect

When you find correlations, be careful not to draw conclusions about cause and effect. A strong correlation only tells you that two sets of data are related. It does not tell you *why* the two sets of data are related, or if the changes in one set of data are causing changes in the other set of data. For example, you would probably find some correlation between children's heights and the sizes of their vocabularies. But this does not mean that learning words makes children taller. The correlation is there because both height and vocabulary are related to age.

Trends

Suppose you work for a big video store. You want to know if sales are increasing, decreasing, or staying the same in your store. You are trying to identify **trends**. One good way to identify trends is to plot data in graphs.

EXAMPLE: The double-line graph shows the money spent on video tapes and DVDs in the United States during various years. What trends does the graph show?

To determine the trends, look at the direction of each line.

■ The line for DVD sales rises. So, the amount spent on DVDs is increasing.
■ The line for video sales rises from 1997 to 1998, but declines from 1998 to 2003.

(Source: Pricewaterhouse Coopers LLP)

Video Tape and DVD Sales

■ DVDs   ● Videos

Extrapolation

Sometimes you can make predictions by extending a graph beyond the range of the data you already have. This is called **extrapolation**.

EXAMPLE: You invent "The Fabulous No-Fat Fudge Bar" and survey 50 people to see how many of them would buy it at various prices. Use the data to predict how many people out of 50 would buy the fudge bar if the price was $2.75.

PRICE	BUYERS
$1.25	32
$1.50	29
$1.75	24
$2.00	21
$2.25	16
$2.50	12

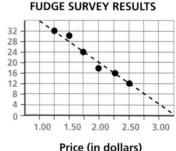

FUDGE SURVEY RESULTS

Number of Buyers (out of 50)

Price (in dollars)

MORE HELP
See 305–306

As the graph shows, the points are close to a line that shows the number of buyers decreasing by 4 for each $0.25 added to the price. So, you would predict the number of buyers would decrease to 8 if you increased the price from $2.50 to $2.75.

MATH ALERT Use Common Sense When Extrapolating

When you use extrapolation to make predictions, be careful. Sometimes a relationship that seems to exist may change as you get more information or you get close to some limit.

For example, suppose a runner checks her time as she completes each mile of a 5-mile run. The graph of the data shows that the points are close to a line where each mile takes about 9 minutes. Can she predict how long it would take her to run 50 miles? She could use the relation:

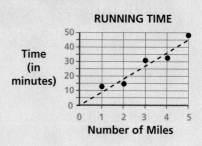

RUNNING TIME

Time (in minutes)

Number of Miles

Total time = 9 minutes × number of miles

But because 50 miles is so *much* farther than she usually runs, her pace may slow down significantly.

Interpolation

Sometimes you use a graph or relation to find an unknown value *between* data points you already know. This is called **interpolation**.

EXAMPLE: Use the data to estimate how many inches of snow had fallen at the end of the first $2\frac{1}{2}$ hours of the blizzard.

MORE HELP
See 305–306

LENGTH OF BLIZZARD (IN HOURS)	TOTAL SNOWFALL (IN INCHES)
1	2
2	4
3	5.8
4	8
5	10.2
6	11.7

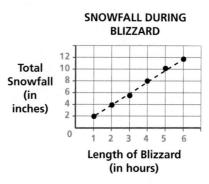

SNOWFALL DURING BLIZZARD

Total Snowfall (in inches)

Length of Blizzard (in hours)

As the graph shows, the points are close to a line that shows the number of inches increasing by about 2 for each hour. Based on these data, you would expect that about 5 inches fell in $2\frac{1}{2}$ hours.

Geometry

Mathematics is a language we use to describe our world. Numbers and computation help us talk about "how many" and "how big" and to make some comparisons. Geometry is all about the space around us and the objects and shapes in that space.

When you give directions, play soccer, bake, or build, you rely on ideas such as straight, curved, turn, round, and corner. Geometry is an important part of mathematics because it is an important part of our lives.

When you study geometry, you will probably be asked to construct various geometric figures. You can find steps for geometric constructions in the Almanac section of this book.

Elements of Geometric Figures

Points, lines, curves, and planes are ideas constructed in mathematicians' imaginations. But imagine all the pictures you can draw with just points, lines, and curves. There is no limit! You can make squares and circles and houses and trees and anything you can think of. These simple elements form the building blocks of geometry, and they help us to talk about shape, position, direction, and how forms relate to each other.

316   Points

In geometry, **points** are places in space. They have no dimensions—you can't touch them or measure them—but you can name where they are and you can draw a representation of one.

Where two lines intersect (cross), there is a point.

If you name any two points, there is a line that will pass through both of them.

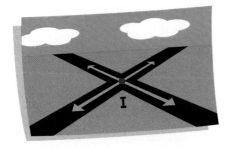

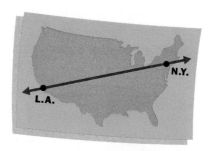

If you name any three points that are not on the same line (that is, they are not **collinear**), then:

MORE HELP
See 317, 321, 348, 370

- they can be the endpoints of a triangle;

- there is a circle that can contain them all;

- and there is a plane that can contain them all.

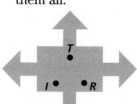

Planes

317

In geometry, planes are more like the Great Plains than like airplanes! A **plane** is a collection of points that forms a flat surface infinitely wide and infinitely long. We say that points and lines *lie* in a plane.

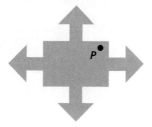

MORE ▶

CASE 1 Planes can intersect each other, and where they do, there is a line. This intersection is called a **dihedral angle**. The corners of rooms, where the walls come together, are dihedral angles.

MORE HELP
See 324

CASE 2 Two planes can be parallel to each other, and when they are, a line in one is either parallel or skew to a line in the other.

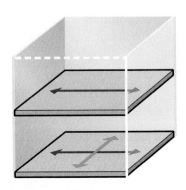

318 Coordinate Geometry

A grid is very useful. In some towns, streets are laid out in a grid and it is *very* easy to tell someone how to get from one place to another.

Descartes, who first used this system, was a seventeenth-century mathematician.

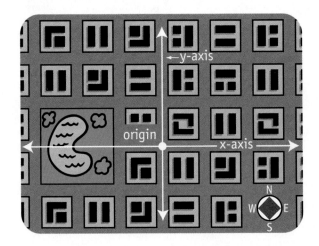

A **coordinate grid**, or **Cartesian Coordinate System**, is a way to locate points in a plane. To draw a picture of a coordinate grid, draw a horizontal number line, called the x-**axis**, and a vertical number line, the y-**axis**. These two lines intersect at a point called the **origin**. The x-axis and y-axis divide the coordinate plane into four sections called **quadrants**.

You can name any point on this plane with 2 numbers (called **coordinates**). The first number is for the distance from the origin along the x-axis, the x-coordinate. The second is for the distance along the y-axis, the y-coordinate. Since the pair is always named in order (first x, then y), it's called an **ordered pair**.

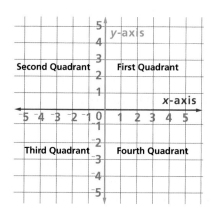

Write: (x, y)

Say: *point x y*

Points in the First Quadrant

When both numbers in an ordered pair (x, y) are positive, the ordered pair is in the first quadrant.

CASE 1 Sometimes you have the coordinates of a point and you need to place the point (plot it) on the grid. When you're plotting a point, start at $(0, 0)$, the origin, and let the x-coordinate tell you how far to move horizontally. Then, let the y-coordinate tell you how far to move vertically.

EXAMPLE 1: Plot the point $(1, 1.5)$.

Some people use *Humvee* as a quick reminder that the Horizontal coordinate is always before the Vertical coordinate.

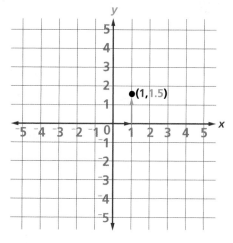

CASE 2 Sometimes you have the point and need to name it.

EXAMPLE 2: The grid shows the locations of different spots in a town. What ordered pair describes the location of the movie theater?

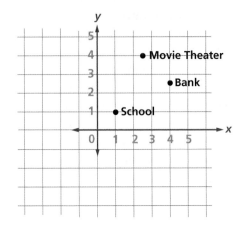

To find the location, start at the origin, (0, 0). To reach the movie theater, count 2.5 units to the right (horizontal), then 4 units up (vertical). So, the movie theater is at (2.5, 4) or $(2\frac{1}{2}, 4)$.

320 ▶

Points in All Four Quadrants

When one or both of the numbers in an ordered pair (x, y) is negative, the point is not in the first quadrant.

The sign of the coordinate tells the direction to move from the origin.

- A positive x-coordinate means go right.
- A negative x-coordinate means go left.

- A positive y-coordinate means go up.
- A negative y-coordinate means go down.

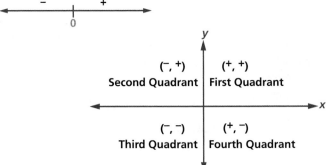

The absolute value of the coordinate tells the number of units to move.

EXAMPLE 1: Plot point A at ($^-$4, $^-$2).

EXAMPLE 2: Plot point B at ($^-$4, 2).

EXAMPLE 3: Plot point C at (4, $^-$2).

EXAMPLE 4: Plot point D at (4, 2).

EXAMPLE 5: The grid shows the location of three sailboats, A, B, and C. Give an ordered pair for each sailboat.

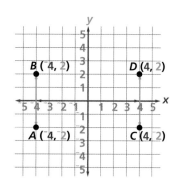

MORE HELP
See 050–051

To find the ordered pair for each sailboat, start at the origin, (0, 0). Look along the horizontal (x) axis and then along the vertical (y) axis to find the coordinates in order.

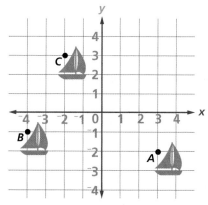

Sailboat A is at (3, $^-$2).

Sailboat B is at ($^-$4, $^-$1).

Sailboat C is at ($^-$2, 3).

Lines

In mathematics, a **line** is a *straight* path of points that has no endpoints. It has length but not width. If you have two points, you can always draw a line that contains them both. So mathematicians say that two points *determine* a line. The symbol ⟷ indicates a line.

To name a line, you can use a single lowercase letter or you can name any two points on the line with capital letters and then name the line with those letters.

Write: $\overleftrightarrow{FG}$, $\overleftrightarrow{GF}$, or a

Say: *line F G, line G F, or line a*

The arrowheads indicate that the line continues indefinitely in both directions.

Rays

You know a ray of sunshine starts at the sun and heads outward. In mathematics, a **ray** is half of a line that has one endpoint and continues indefinitely in one direction. You name a ray with its endpoint and one other point on the ray. The symbol $\longrightarrow$ indicates a ray.

Write: $\overrightarrow{OP}$
Say: *ray O P*

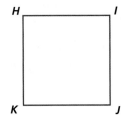

Another name for ray is half-line.

EXAMPLE: Name the rays with endpoint I.

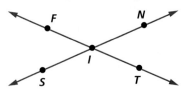

$\overrightarrow{IF}$, $\overrightarrow{IN}$, $\overrightarrow{IT}$, and $\overrightarrow{IS}$ are rays with endpoint I.

Line Segments

A **line segment** is a part of a line that has two endpoints and includes all of the points between those endpoints. To name a line segment, use the endpoints. The symbol $\overline{}$ indicates a line segment.

Write: $\overline{FS}$
Say: *line segment F S* or *segment F S*

EXAMPLE: Name the line segments that form the square at the right.

The segments are $\overline{HI}$, $\overline{IJ}$, $\overline{JK}$, and $\overline{KH}$.

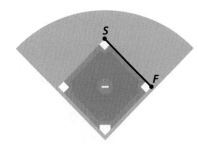

Parallel, Intersecting, and Skew Lines

Parallel lines are lines that are in the same plane and never cross because they are always the same distance apart. They have no points in common. The symbol ‖ indicates parallel lines.

Intersecting lines are lines that *do* cross. They either have one point or all points in common. If they have all points in common, they are the same line. If two lines intersect, then there is one plane that can contain them.

Skew lines are lines that are neither parallel nor intersecting. There is no *one* plane that can contain skew lines (no matter how you look at them).

MORE HELP
See 317

Segments of parallel, intersecting, and skew lines are parallel, intersecting, and skew as well.

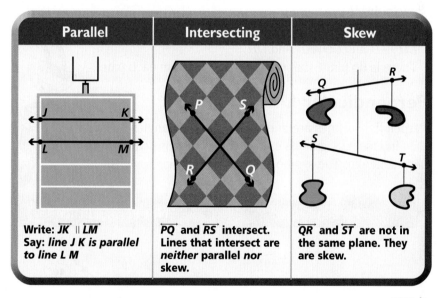

Parallel	Intersecting	Skew
Write: $\overleftrightarrow{JK}$ ‖ $\overleftrightarrow{LM}$ Say: *line J K is parallel to line L M*	$\overleftrightarrow{PQ}$ and $\overleftrightarrow{RS}$ intersect. Lines that intersect are *neither* parallel *nor* skew.	$\overleftrightarrow{QR}$ and $\overleftrightarrow{ST}$ are not in the same plane. They are skew.

MORE ▶

EXAMPLE: Name one pair of parallel lines, one pair of intersecting lines, and one pair of skew lines in this cube.

There are many solutions to this problem:

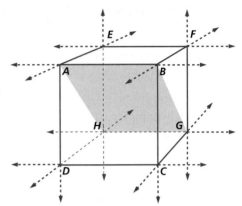

■ Some parallel pairs are: $\overleftrightarrow{AB}$ and $\overleftrightarrow{DC}$, $\overleftrightarrow{AB}$ and $\overleftrightarrow{EF}$, and $\overleftrightarrow{AB}$ and $\overleftrightarrow{HG}$. There is a plane that contains each pair, and each pair has no points in common.

■ Some intersecting pairs are: $\overleftrightarrow{AB}$ and $\overleftrightarrow{AD}$, $\overleftrightarrow{AB}$ and $\overleftrightarrow{AE}$, and $\overleftrightarrow{AB}$ and $\overleftrightarrow{BC}$. Each pair has one point in common.

We know the parallel pairs are parallel because a cube's faces are squares. The opposite sides in a square are parallel.

■ Some skew pairs are: $\overleftrightarrow{AB}$ and $\overleftrightarrow{EH}$, $\overleftrightarrow{AB}$ and $\overleftrightarrow{CG}$, $\overleftrightarrow{AB}$ and $\overleftrightarrow{DH}$. There is no plane that contains both lines in each pair.

Perpendicular Lines

Perpendicular lines are lines that form right angles where they intersect. Segments of perpendicular lines can also be perpendicular. The symbol ⊥ indicates perpendicular lines.

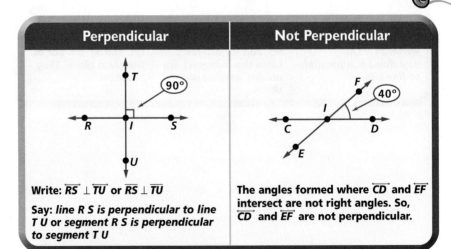

Perpendicular	Not Perpendicular
Write: $\overleftrightarrow{RS} \perp \overleftrightarrow{TU}$ or $\overline{RS} \perp \overline{TU}$ Say: *line R S is perpendicular to line T U or segment R S is perpendicular to segment T U*	The angles formed where $\overleftrightarrow{CD}$ and $\overleftrightarrow{EF}$ intersect are not right angles. So, $\overleftrightarrow{CD}$ and $\overleftrightarrow{EF}$ are not perpendicular.

If you see a square corner drawn at the intersection of two lines or segments, that indicates they are perpendicular and form 90° angles. If you don't see the little square corner and no other clue tells you that the lines are perpendicular, then don't assume they are—measure to be sure.

EXAMPLE: Name the perpendicular segments in this figure. *AEHD* is a square. *ABCD* and *EFGH* are rectangles. *ABFE* and *DCGH* are congruent.

"∟" indicates a right angle.

MORE HELP
See 317, 331, 363–364, 381–383

Here are a few of the pairs of perpendicular segments.

■ Since *AEHD* is a square, $\overline{AE} \perp \overline{AD}$, $\overline{AE} \perp \overline{EH}$, $\overline{AD} \perp \overline{DH}$, and $\overline{DH} \perp \overline{EH}$.
■ *ABFE* and *DCGH* are congruent. So, because $\overline{AE} \perp \overline{AB}$, $\overline{DH}$ must be perpendicular to $\overline{DC}$.
■ Since ∠*CBF* is a right angle, $\overline{BC} \perp \overline{BF}$.

Perpendicular Bisectors

326

A **perpendicular bisector** of a line segment is a line, line segment, ray, or plane that forms a right angle with a line segment and divides that line segment into two congruent parts.

MORE HELP
See 325

EXAMPLE: Is $\overleftrightarrow{CD}$ the perpendicular bisector of $\overline{AB}$? Is $\overleftrightarrow{GH}$ the perpendicular bisector of $\overline{EF}$?

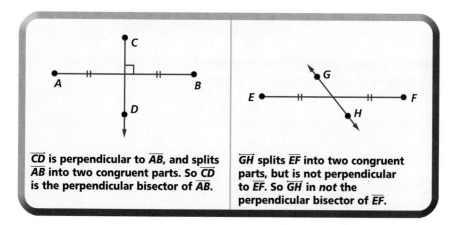

$\overleftrightarrow{CD}$ is perpendicular to $\overline{AB}$, and splits $\overline{AB}$ into two congruent parts. So $\overleftrightarrow{CD}$ is the perpendicular bisector of $\overline{AB}$.

$\overleftrightarrow{GH}$ splits $\overline{EF}$ into two congruent parts, but is not perpendicular to $\overline{EF}$. So $\overleftrightarrow{GH}$ in *not* the perpendicular bisector of $\overline{EF}$.

If a line or a line segment could be bent, you would have a curve.

A curve can be open or closed.

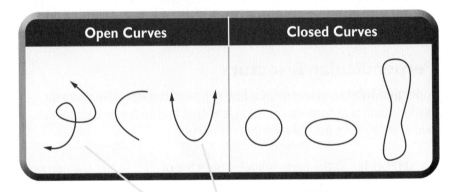

The arrowheads mean the curve continues indefinitely.

MORE HELP
See 251, 370

There are many special kinds of curves. Some of them, such as parabolas and circles, can be described by equations.

Angles

328

You are making a quilt, a skating ramp, or a flag for a school play. What kind of corners should you form to make everything fit right? You are searching the skies for a comet or setting yourself for a game-winning basket. How much should you turn? How much arc should you use? These questions are about angles—identifying them, measuring them, drawing them, describing them, and using them.

Turn to the Almanac section of this book to learn how to use a protractor to measure angles.

Parts of Angles

329

Angles are formed by two rays with a common endpoint, called the **vertex**. You can find angles where lines and line segments intersect, within circles and polygons, and, occasionally, on their own. The symbol ∠ indicates an angle.

You can name an angle in three ways:

- using a three-letter name in this order: point on one ray, vertex, point on other ray, such as ∠*BAG*
- using a one-letter name: vertex (when there is only one angle with this vertex in a diagram), such as ∠*A*
- using a numerical name when the number is within rays of the angle, such as ∠1.

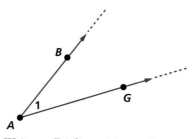

Write: ∠*BAG* or ∠*A* or ∠1
Say: *angle B A G* or *angle A* or *angle 1*

330) Measuring Angles

When you spin around to face backward, you say you "did a 180." This is a very mathematical use of angle measurement! An angle is a turn around a point and the size of the angle is the measure of how far one side is turned from the other side: 0° is no turn, 90° is a right-angle turn, 180° is straight backward, and 360° is back facing forward again.

331) Naming Different-Size Angles

Angles are named for the way they relate to 90° or 180°.

MORE HELP
See 512

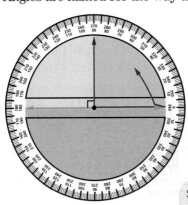

Moving counterclockwise from 0°:

< 90°	Acute
= 90°	**Right**
> 90° and < 180°	Obtuse
= 180°	Straight
>180° and < 360°	Reflex

Some people remember the way angles are named as they get bigger with this silly sentence:
A Riddle **O**ften **S**ounds **R**idiculous.

332) Angle Relationships

Angles are like puzzle pieces. When they can fit together in specific ways, or when they have special sums, they have special names.

333 Congruent Angles

When two angles have the same angle measure, we say they are **congruent**.

This means either angle can fit exactly over the other angle.

Write: $\angle CON \cong \angle GRU$
Say: *angle C O N is congruent to angle G R U*

Supplementary Angles

If the sum of the measures of two angles is 180°, then the two angles are **supplementary**. If two angles form a straight line, then they are supplementary.

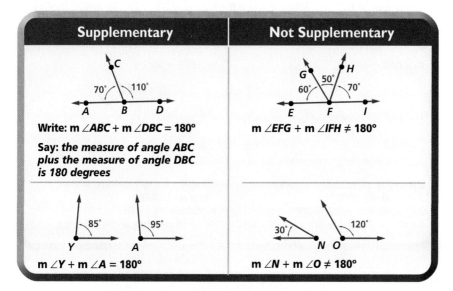

Supplementary	Not Supplementary
Write: m ∠ABC + m ∠DBC = 180°	m ∠EFG + m ∠IFH ≠ 180°
Say: *the measure of angle ABC plus the measure of angle DBC is 180 degrees*	
m ∠Y + m ∠A = 180°	m ∠N + m ∠O ≠ 180°

Complementary Angles

If the sum of the measures of two angles is 90°, then the angles are **complementary**.

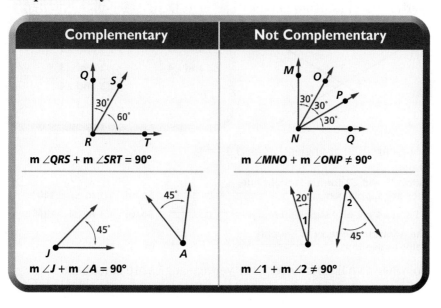

Complementary	Not Complementary
m ∠QRS + m ∠SRT = 90°	m ∠MNO + m ∠ONP ≠ 90°
m ∠J + m ∠A = 90°	m ∠1 + m ∠2 ≠ 90°

336 Angle Bisectors

An **angle bisector** is a ray that separates an angle into two congruent angles.

EXAMPLE: Is $\overrightarrow{BD}$ the angle bisector of $\angle ABC$? Is $\overrightarrow{FH}$ the angle bisector of $\angle EFG$?

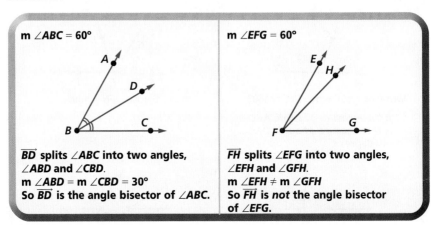

m $\angle ABC = 60°$

m $\angle EFG = 60°$

$\overrightarrow{BD}$ **splits** $\angle ABC$ **into two angles,** $\angle ABD$ **and** $\angle CBD$.
m $\angle ABD$ = m $\angle CBD$ = 30°
So $\overrightarrow{BD}$ is the angle bisector of $\angle ABC$.

$\overrightarrow{FH}$ **splits** $\angle EFG$ **into two angles,** $\angle EFH$ **and** $\angle GFH$.
m $\angle EFH$ ≠ m $\angle GFH$
So $\overrightarrow{FH}$ is **not** the angle bisector of $\angle EFG$.

337 Angles Formed by Intersecting Lines

When two lines intersect, they form two types of angle pairs: vertical angles and adjacent supplementary angles. If you know the measure of just one of these four angles, you can use it to figure out the measures of the other three.

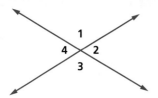

Vertical Angles	Supplementary Angles
$\angle 1$ and $\angle 3$	$\angle 1$ and $\angle 2$
$\angle 2$ and $\angle 4$	$\angle 2$ and $\angle 3$
	$\angle 3$ and $\angle 4$
	$\angle 4$ and $\angle 1$

Look carefully at angles 1, 2, and 4.

Since $\angle 1$ and $\angle 2$ form a straight line, they are supplementary————————→ So, m $\angle 1$ + m $\angle 2$ = 180°

$\angle 1$ and $\angle 4$ are also supplementary————————→ So, m $\angle 1$ + m $\angle 4$ = 180°

MORE HELP
See 228 **The Addition Property of Equality helps us see that**————————→ m $\angle 2$ = m $\angle 4$

So, when two lines intersect, the vertical angles are congruent.

EXAMPLE: m ∠5 = 50°. Find the measures of angles 6, 7, and 8.

Since ∠5 and ∠7 are vertical angles, they are congruent. So, if m ∠5 = 50°, m ∠7 = 50°.

∠5 and ∠6 are supplementary angles. So are ∠5 and ∠8. Their sums are 180°.

If m ∠5 = 50°, then m ∠6 = 130°, and m ∠8 = 130°.

Angles Formed by Lines Cut by a Transversal

338

A **transversal** is a line that intersects two or more other lines.

CASE 1 When a transversal intersects two lines, it forms eight angles.

■ **Corresponding angles** are in the same position from one line to the other. So, there are four pairs of corresponding angles: ∠1 and ∠5; ∠2 and ∠6; ∠3 and ∠7; and ∠4 and ∠8.

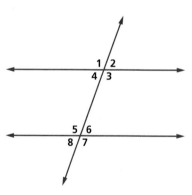

■ **Alternate exterior angles** are on opposite sides of the transversal and on the *outside* of the lines it intersects. So, there are 2 pairs of alternate exterior angles: ∠1 and ∠7; and ∠2 and ∠8.

■ **Alternate interior angles** are on opposite sides of the transversal and on the *inside* of the lines it intersects. So there are 2 pairs of alternate interior angles: ∠4 and ∠6, ∠3 and ∠5.

CASE 2 If the two intersected lines are *parallel*, the angles that are formed by the transversal have special relationships.

■ Corresponding angles are congruent.
■ Alternate exterior angles are congruent.
■ Alternate interior angles are congruent.

You believe this is true because if you could slide one of the parallel lines along the transversal, it would fit exactly over the other parallel line, with all angles matching.

MORE ▶

EXAMPLE: In the figure below, a transversal intersects two parallel lines, and m ∠1 = 110°. Use this measure to find the measures of angles 2–8.

∠1 and ∠5 are corresponding angles.
If m ∠1 = 110°, then m ∠5 = 110°.

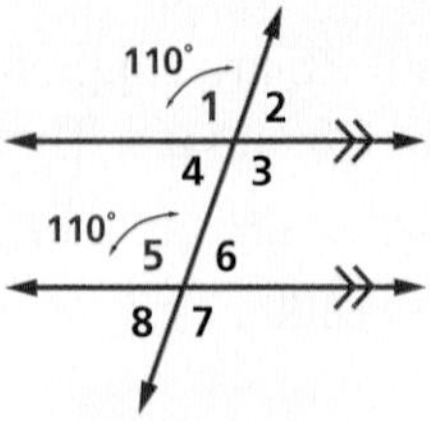

∠1 and ∠7 are alternate exterior angles.
If m ∠1 = 110°, then m ∠7 = 110°.

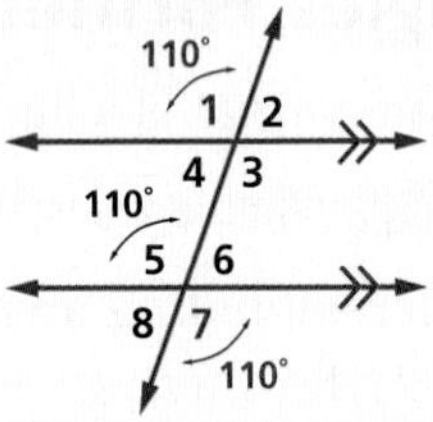

∠5 and ∠3 are alternate interior angles.
If m ∠5 = 110°, then m ∠3 = 110°.

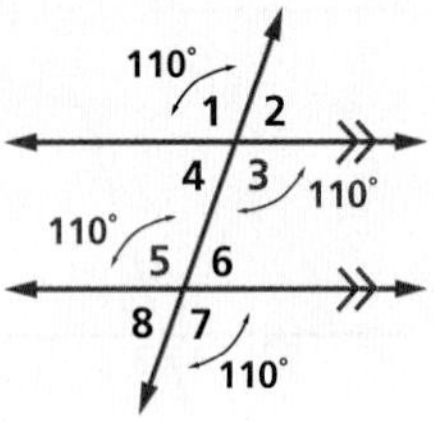

Each of the remaining angles is supplementary to one of the angles you already know.
So, ∠2, ∠4, ∠6, and ∠8 each have a measure of 70° (180° − 110° = 70°).

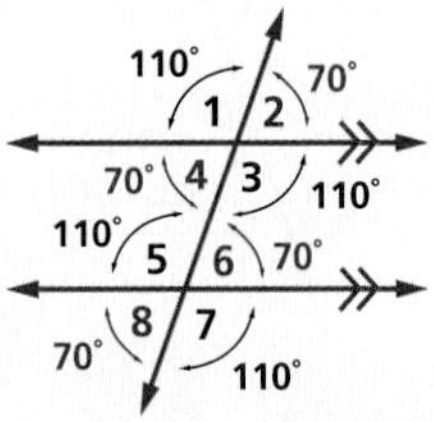

Angles in Polygons and Circles

Polygons are simple, closed figures made up of line segments. Where the sides of the polygons intersect, angles are formed. The angles can be on the inside of the figure or on the outside. In a circle, central angles are formed by intersecting diameters or radii.

MORE HELP
See 370

Central Angles

MORE HELP
See 345, 370

340

CASE 1 If you draw radii out from the center of a circle, you are forming **central angles** in that circle. Remember, turning completely around is turning 360°. So, adding the measures of all the central angles in any circle gives a sum of 360°.

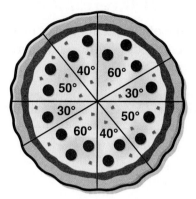

40° + 50° + 30° + 60° + 40° + 50° + 30° + 60° = 360°

CASE 2 Now look at central angles in polygons. Choose a point in the interior of a polygon. If you draw segments from this point to each of the vertices of the polygon, these segments will form angles at the interior point. The sum of the measures of these angles is *always* 360°.

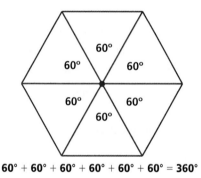

60° + 60° + 60° + 60° + 60° + 60° = 360°

Interior Angles

341

Most of the time, when someone asks you to measure an angle in a polygon, they're referring to an **interior angle**. This is an angle formed by sides of the polygon and *inside* the figure.

EXAMPLE: How many interior angles are in the pentagon? How many in the octagon?

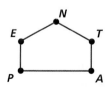   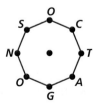

There are five interior angles in the pentagon, ∠P, ∠E, ∠N, ∠T, and ∠A. There are eight interior angles in the octagon, ∠O, ∠C, ∠T, ∠A, ∠G, ∠O, ∠N, and ∠S. So, there are as many interior angles in a polygon as there are sides.

Sums of Interior Angles of Polygons

The sum of the interior angles of a polygon varies depending on the number of sides. Fortunately, there is a pattern to the way this sum changes.

POLYGON	NUMBER OF SIDES	SUM OF ANGLES
Triangle	3	$180° \times 1 = 180°$
Quadrilateral	4	$180° \times 2 = 360°$
Pentagon	5	$180° \times 3 = 540°$
Hexagon	6	$180° \times 4 = 720°$
Septagon	7	$180° \times 5 = 900°$
Octagon	8	$180° \times 6 = 1080°$

Each additional side adds 180° to the sum of the interior angles. So you could subtract 2 from the number of sides, then multiply by 180 to find the sum of interior angles for any polygon:

$180(n - 2)$ = degrees in the interior angles of a polygon with n sides

Exterior Angles

To see an exterior angle, you need to extend one of the sides of the polygon. Then you can measure the angle between that extension and the other side. There are *two* exterior angles for every vertex in a polygon.

EXAMPLE: Look at the two exterior angles at vertex A. What can you say about these angles?

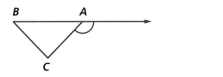
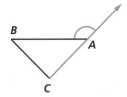

MORE HELP
See 334

Each exterior angle is supplementary to the same interior angle. So the two exterior angles at any vertex of a polygon are congruent.

▶ Plane Figures

Have you ever made shadow pictures on a wall? Those images you project onto the wall are flat. Squares, triangles, and other plane figures are flat, too. They are called **plane figures** because they lie in a single plane.

In geometry, a **plane** is a 2-dimensional surface that is perfectly flat and infinitely large. Even though they are perfectly flat, planes and plane figures are useful in our 3-dimensional world. Think about city maps, diagrams of basketball plays, and computer animation games.

Plane figures come in a variety of shapes and sizes, but they can be grouped according to the number, size, and position of their sides and angles. Plane figures can be measured and moved and bent and patterned and scaled up or down.

Polygons

A **polygon** is a closed figure whose sides are all line segments.

A diagonal of a polygon is a line segment with endpoints that are two non-adjacent vertices.

Non-adjacent vertices are not next to each other.

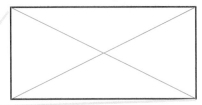

In a **convex polygon** all the diagonals are inside the figure. In a **concave polygon** one or more diagonals are outside or partly outside the figure.

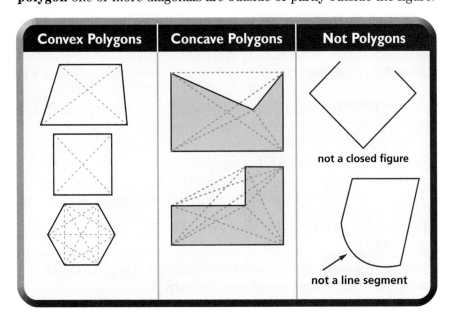

Convex Polygons	Concave Polygons	Not Polygons

not a closed figure

not a line segment

Perimeter

The distance around a polygon is called the **perimeter**. To find the perimeter of any polygon, add the lengths of its sides.

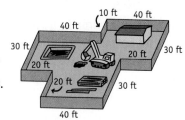

EXAMPLE: This construction site is fenced so that no one will enter. How long is the fence?

To find the length of the fence, find the perimeter of the site.

Add: $30 + 40 + 10 + 40 + 30 + 20 + 30 + 40 + 20 + 20 = 280$

The fence is 280 feet long.

Area

The **area** of a figure is the number of square units inside the figure.

If you know how to find the area of a rectangle, you can find the area of *any* polygon, no matter how strange it looks.

EXAMPLE: Find the area of the figure at the right. In this grid, each square represents 1 ft².

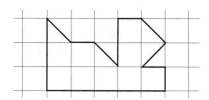

 You can find the area of an irregular polygon by breaking the figure into smaller rectangles or triangles, finding the area of each smaller figure, and then adding.

In this figure, you can count all the half squares and all the whole squares:

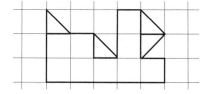

$$\begin{array}{r} 2 \quad \text{(4 half squares)} \\ + 9 \quad \text{(9 whole squares)} \\ \hline 11 \quad \text{whole squares} \end{array}$$

 You can also find the area of an irregular polygon by finding a larger rectangle that fits around it and then subtracting the area of the part that you must take away to get back to the original figure.

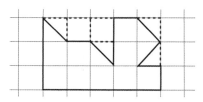

In this figure, the area of the rectangle that contains the figure is 15 ft². Subtract 2 whole squares and 4 half squares:

$$15 - 4 = 11$$

Either way, the area of the figure is 11 ft².

Triangles

When you look at bridges, towers, or space stations, you see many triangles. Triangles are popular in construction because they are rigid. If you press on a triangle and try to form a different one with the same sides but different angles, you can't. The sides go together in only one way. This is *not* true of quadrilaterals and other polygons.

MORE HELP
See 323

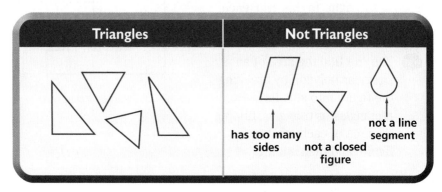

Triangles	Not Triangles
	has too many sides not a closed figure not a line segment

349 ## Parts of Triangles

The **height**, or **altitude**, of a triangle is a line segment that starts at any vertex and is perpendicular to the opposite side of the triangle (called the **base**). *The same triangle can have 3 different height and base pairs.* But the product of height and base will be the same!

MORE HELP
See 325, 356

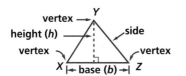

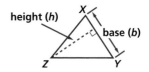

To name a triangle, use the vertices.

Write: $\triangle XYZ$
Say: *triangle X Y Z*

To name a triangle or any other figure, name the vertices in either clockwise or counterclockwise order. Often the vertices are in alphabetical order. You could also call this triangle $\triangle YZX$ or $\triangle ZXY$ or . . .

Triangle Inequality Theorem

You've probably heard the saying that the shortest distance between any two points is a straight line. (The saying should say line segment, not line.) You can use a triangle to see that this statement is true.

The shortest route from *A* to *C* is directly from *A* to *C*, not from *A* to *B* to *C*.

The shortest route from *B* to *C* is directly from *B* to *C*, not from *B* to *A* to *C*.

The shortest route from *A* to *B* is directly from *A* to *B*, not from *A* to *C* to *B*.

You can combine all three of these statements into one: the sum of the lengths of any two sides of a triangle is greater than the length of the third side. This is called the **Triangle Inequality Theorem**. If you don't believe this, try to make a triangle with 2-inch, 2-inch, and 4-inch sides.

Using Angle Size to Classify Triangles

In any triangle, the sum of the angle measures is always 180°. The name of a triangle tells you about the triangle's angles, sides, or both. Here are some names that are based on the angles of a triangle.

Name	Description	Example
Acute Triangle	All angles < 90°.	
Equiangular Triangle An equiangular triangle is also equilateral.	All angles = 60°.	60° 60° 60° Angles with the same markings are congruent.
Obtuse Triangle	One angle > 90°.	
Right Triangle	One angle = 90°.	90° Right angles are marked with └ .

MORE HELP
See 331

352 Using Side Length to Classify Triangles

Here are some triangle names that are based on the lengths of sides.

MORE HELP
See 381

Name	Description	Example
Equilateral Triangle	All sides congruent	Sides marked the same way are congruent.
Isosceles Triangle	Two sides congruent	
Scalene Triangle	No sides congruent	

353 Overlapping Classifications of Triangles

All triangles can be classified by their sides (equilateral, isosceles, scalene), by their angles (acute, right, obtuse), or both. This means that every triangle can be described in more than one way.

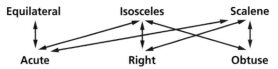

To read the diagram above, think about the phrases *is always, may be,* or *is never.* For example, a right triangle *may be* either scalene or isosceles, but *is never* acute, equilateral, or obtuse.

EXAMPLE: Classify each triangle in more than one way.

  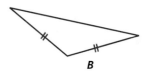

Triangle *A* is a right triangle. It is also a scalene triangle.

Triangle *B* is an obtuse triangle. It is also an isosceles triangle.

Perimeter of Triangles

To find the perimeter of any triangle, add the lengths of the sides.

EXAMPLE 1: Find the length of the rope around the garden.

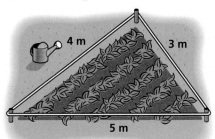

4 m   3 m

5 m

To find the perimeter, add:

3 m + 4 m + 5 m = 12 m

The length of the rope around the garden (its perimeter) is 12 m.

EXAMPLE 2: Find the perimeter of this equilateral triangle.

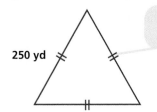

250 yd

Sides marked the same way are congruent.

 ONE WAY You can find the sum of the lengths of the sides:
250 + 250 + 250 = 750

 ANOTHER WAY You can multiply the length of one side by 3:
3 × 250 = 750

Either way, the perimeter of the triangle is 750 yd.

MATH ALERT Adding Mixed Measures

Sometimes when you compute with measures, you add measures that have different units. You can do this by simplifying the sum after you add the units that are the same.

EXAMPLE: Find the perimeter of the triangle.

```
   8 ft    8 in.
  16 ft    3 in.
+ 18 ft    5 in.
─────────────────
  42 ft   16 in.
```

16 ft 3 in.

8 ft 8 in.

18 ft 5 in.

⟶ **42 ft 16 in.** = 42 ft + (12 in. + 4 in.)

= (42 ft + 1 ft) + 4 in.

= 43 ft 4 in.

So, the perimeter is 43 ft 4 in.

Area of Triangles

CASE I A right triangle is half of a rectangle.

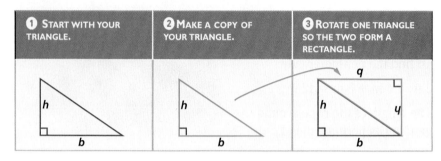

❶ START WITH YOUR TRIANGLE.	❷ MAKE A COPY OF YOUR TRIANGLE.	❸ ROTATE ONE TRIANGLE SO THE TWO FORM A RECTANGLE.

MORE HELP
See 366–367

Since the area of a rectangle is its length times its width, the area of this rectangle is bh. So, the formula for the area of a triangle is $\frac{1}{2}bh$.

EXAMPLE 1: Use the formula to find the area of $\triangle FGH$.

$$A = \frac{1}{2}bh$$
$$= \frac{1}{2}(4)(3)$$
$$= 6$$

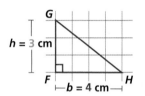

So, the area of $\triangle FGH$ is 6 cm².

CASE 2 Any triangle is half of a parallelogram.

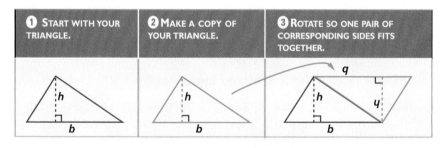

❶ START WITH YOUR TRIANGLE.	❷ MAKE A COPY OF YOUR TRIANGLE.	❸ ROTATE SO ONE PAIR OF CORRESPONDING SIDES FITS TOGETHER.

Since the area of a parallelogram is the length of its base times its height, the area of this parallelogram is bh. So, the area of your triangle is $\frac{1}{2}bh$.

MORE HELP
See 366–367

EXAMPLE 2: Use the formula to find the area of $\triangle ABC$.

$$A = \frac{1}{2}bh$$
$$= \frac{1}{2}(5)(2)$$
$$= 5$$

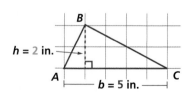

So, the area of $\triangle ABC$ is 5 in².

357

MATH ALERT Inches Times Inches Gives You Square Inches

When you multiply units of measure (like inches or centimeters) by other units of measure, you need to remember two very important things:

1. Always be sure the units are the same. For example, you can multiply inches times inches or feet times feet, but *never* inches times feet.

2. Always be sure that your answer has the right kind of unit. For example, if you've multiplied inches times inches, you're finding area, and area is in square inches. (2×2 is *2 squared*, inches × inches is *inches squared*.)

Special Characteristics of Right Triangles

358

The words *hypotenuse* and *leg* describe sides of right triangles *only*.

What's so special about a right triangle? For one thing, no matter how large or small your right triangle is, if one angle measures $30°$, then one leg will be $\frac{1}{2}$ as long as the hypotenuse. Such relationships are called **trigonometric ratios**. Surveyors, astronomers, and engineers use trigonometric ratios (trig ratios) to find distances or angles that are impossible or impractical to measure directly.

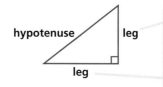

The legs are the two shorter sides. They are always adjacent to (next to) the right angle.

Some people use a silly phrase to remember these ratios:
SOH CAH TOA

MORE HELP
See 371, 380

Name of Ratio	Ratio	
sine of ∠A (sin A)	length of leg opposite ∠A / length of hypotenuse	SOH
cosine of ∠A (cos A)	length of leg adjacent to ∠A / length of hypotenuse	CAH
tangent of ∠A (tan A)	length of leg opposite ∠A / length of leg adjacent to ∠A	TOA

Pythagorean Theorem

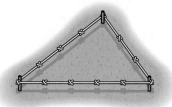

In ancient Egypt, farmers wanted to make square corners for their fields. Around 2000 B.C., they discovered the 3-4-5 right triangle. Field workers made a loop of rope and knotted it into 12 equal spaces. Then they put the rope around stakes to make a triangle that had sides of 3, 4, and 5 units. The angle opposite the longest side was always a square corner—a right angle. *(Source: World Book Encyclopedia)*

Later, the ancient Greeks studied the 3-4-5 right triangle. They found a special relationship, the **Pythagorean theorem**. This relationship is true for *any* right triangle.

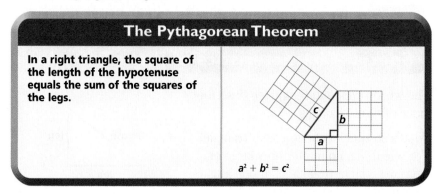

The Pythagorean Theorem

In a right triangle, the square of the length of the hypotenuse equals the sum of the squares of the legs.

$a^2 + b^2 = c^2$

CASE I Any time you know the lengths of two sides of a right triangle, you can use the Pythagorean theorem to find the length of the third side.

EXAMPLE 1: City blocks border a triangular park as shown in the diagram at the right. The north-south street and the east-west street meet at a right angle. About how many blocks long is the diagonal street? (The city blocks have about the same lengths.)

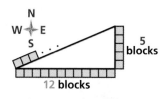

To find the length of the diagonal street, use the Pythagorean theorem.

$$a^2 + b^2 = c^2$$
$$5^2 + 12^2 = c^2$$
$$25 + 144 = c^2$$
$$169 = c^2$$
$$\sqrt{169} = c$$
$$13 = c$$

So, the length of the diagonal street is about 13 blocks.

CASE 2 You can also use the Pythagorean theorem to tell whether you can make a right triangle from three given line segments.

EXAMPLE 2: Can you make a right triangle with sides 6 m, 8 m, and 12 m?

$$a^2 + b^2 = c^2$$

Does $6^2 + 8^2 = 12^2$?

$$36 + 64 \neq 144$$

So, you cannot make a right triangle with sides 6 m, 8 m, and 12 m.

But, you could make one with sides of 6, 8, and 10 meters (multiples of 3, 4, and 5). *And* you could make a non-right triangle with sides of 6, 8, and 12 meters.

30°-60°-90° Triangles

360

Some right triangles have special ratios. The 30°-60°-90° triangle is one of those right triangles.

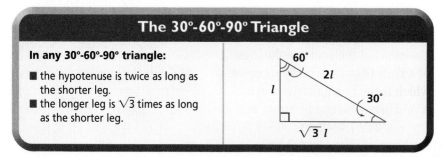

The 30°-60°-90° Triangle

In any 30°-60°-90° triangle:

- the hypotenuse is twice as long as the shorter leg.
- the longer leg is $\sqrt{3}$ times as long as the shorter leg.

This is the same as saying the sine of 30° is $\frac{1}{2}$ and the tangent of 60° is $\sqrt{3}$.

EXAMPLE: Look at the diagram. How high does the ladder reach?

The 20-ft ladder is the hypotenuse. The shorter leg is $\frac{1}{2}$ the length of the ladder, or 10 ft. The longer leg is $\sqrt{3}$ times as long as the shorter leg.

Since $\sqrt{3} \approx 1.7321$ and $10\sqrt{3} \approx 17.321$, the ladder reaches about 17.3 ft.

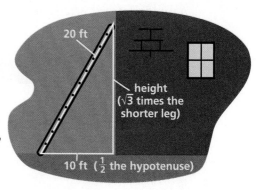

45°-45°-90° Triangles

The 45°-45°-90° triangle is a right triangle whose sides have special ratios.

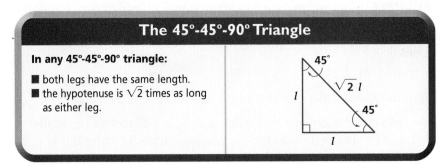

The 45°-45°-90° Triangle	
In any 45°-45°-90° triangle: ■ both legs have the same length. ■ the hypotenuse is $\sqrt{2}$ times as long as either leg.	

This is the same as saying the sine and cosine of 45° are both $\frac{1}{\sqrt{2}}$ and the tangent of 45° is 1.

EXAMPLE: The diagram shows a roof. Suppose you have to replace a beam that joins the two sides of the roof. How long is the beam?

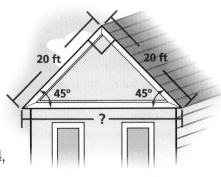

The sides of the roof are the legs of a right triangle. The hypotenuse, which is the beam that you need, is $\sqrt{2}$ times as long as either leg. Since $\sqrt{2} \approx 1.4142$ and $20\sqrt{2} \approx 28.284$, the beam is about 28.3 ft long.

Quadrilaterals

A **quadrilateral** is a closed 2-dimensional figure with four sides that are line segments.

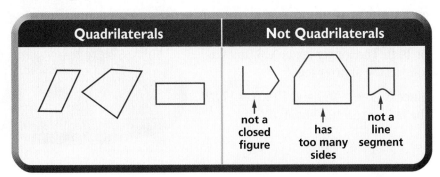

Quadrilaterals	Not Quadrilaterals
	not a closed figure has too many sides not a line segment

Classifying Quadrilaterals

Some quadrilaterals have special traits, so they have special names.

MORE HELP
See 324, 331,
341, 381–383

Name	Description	Example
Trapezoid	Exactly one pair of parallel sides	Sides marked with the same number of arrow notches are parallel.
Parallelogram	Opposite sides the same length and parallel	Sides marked the same way are congruent.
Rectangle	Parallelogram with four right angles	Angles marked with square corners are right angles.
Rhombus	Parallelogram with four congruent sides	
Square	Rhombus with four right angles; a special rectangle	

The parallelogram is special in two ways:

■ its opposite angles are congruent, and
■ its diagonals bisect each other.

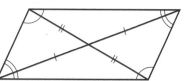

MORE ▶

The rhombus has more special features:

■ its diagonals bisect the angles they connect,
■ its diagonals are perpendicular, and
■ it is a parallelogram.

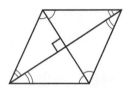

Overlapping Classifications of Quadrilaterals

Suppose a friend tells you that she's designed a school flag shaped like a parallelogram. Can you tell which of these shapes her flag would be?

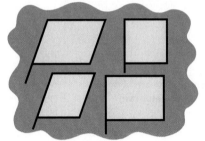

Her flag could be any of the shapes, because a square, a rhombus, and a rectangle are all parallelograms, too.

You can think of quadrilaterals as a family. Some members of the family can be classified in more than one way, like your cousin who is also your aunt's son.

Many quadrilaterals can be described using more than one name. This diagram shows the relationships among different quadrilaterals.

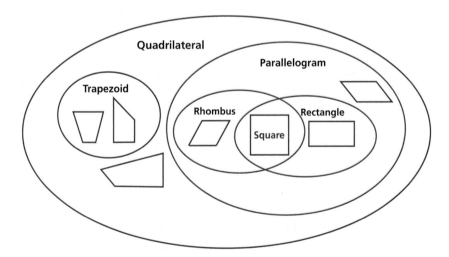

To read this Venn diagram, think about the phrases *is always, may be,* or *is never.* For example, a rhombus also *may be* a square, but a rhombus *is never* a trapezoid.

Perimeter of Quadrilaterals

The distance around a polygon is called the **perimeter**.

CASE 1 To find the perimeter of any quadrilateral, add the lengths of its sides.

EXAMPLE 1: Find the length of fencing needed to enclose the yard.

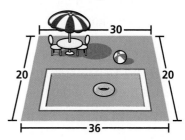

To find the perimeter, add:

$20 + 30 + 20 + 36 = 106$

The perimeter of the yard is 106 feet. So, you need 106 feet of fencing.

CASE 2 For quadrilaterals with congruent sides, you can use a formula to find the perimeter.

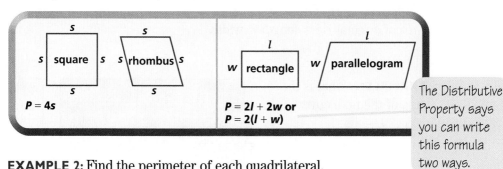

The Distributive Property says you can write this formula two ways.

EXAMPLE 2: Find the perimeter of each quadrilateral.

rhombus
$s = 2$ cm

$P = 4s$
$= 4(2)$
$= 8$

So, the perimeter of the rhombus is 8 cm.

$w = 2$ in. rectangle $l = 6$ in.

$P = (2l) + (2w)$
$= (2 \times 6) + (2 \times 2)$
$= 12 + 4$
$= 16$

So, the perimeter of the rectangle is 16 in.

Area of Rectangles

The area of a rectangle is measured in square units.

 ONE WAY You can find the area of a rectangle by counting the number of square units inside.

EXAMPLE 1: In the grid, each square is 1 square foot (ft²). What is the area of the rug?

There are 24 squares. So, the area is 24 ft².

 ANOTHER WAY You can also find the area of a rectangle by using a formula.

Area of a rectangle = length × width
$$A = lw$$

EXAMPLE 2: What is the area of the pool cover?

$$A = lw$$
$$= 8 \times 5$$
$$= 40$$

So, the area of the pool cover is 40 square meters, or 40 m².

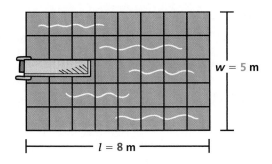

$w = 5$ m

$l = 8$ m

Area of Parallelograms

You can use what you know about rectangles to find the area of a parallelogram. If you cut up a parallelogram, you can rearrange the pieces to make a rectangle. Since you don't need to throw away any pieces of the parallelogram, the area doesn't change between the parallelogram and the rectangle. Since the area of a rectangle is its length times its width, the area of this rectangle is *bh*. The formula for the area of the parallelogram is also *bh*.

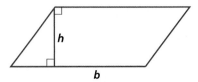

h

b

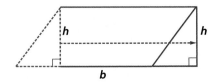

h

h

b

EXAMPLE: Use the formula to find the area of this parallelogram.

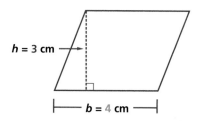

$h = 3$ cm

$b = 4$ cm

$A = bh$

$= (4)(3)$

$= 12$

So, the area of this parallelogram is 12 cm².

Area of Trapezoids

368

You can use the formulas for the area of a rectangle and a triangle to see why the formula for finding the area of a trapezoid works.

If you cut up any trapezoid, you can rearrange the pieces to make a rectangle and a triangle. Since you don't throw away any pieces of the trapezoid, you can add the areas of the rectangle and the triangle to find the area of the trapezoid.

Since the height of a trapezoid is perpendicular to the parallel sides, cut off the right triangles to get a rectangle.

The area of a rectangle is its length times its width, so the area of this rectangle is b_1h.

Push the two triangles together at their right angles. The base of the new triangle is what's left after you cut the length of b_1 off of b_2. So the area of this triangle is $\frac{1}{2}(b_2 - b_1)h$.

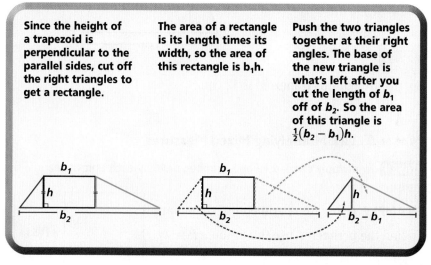

MORE ▶

MORE HELP
See 220, 239

The formula for the area of a trapezoid uses algebra to combine the formulas for the area of the rectangle and the area of the triangle.

Area of rectangle + Area of triangle
↓

$$b_1h + \tfrac{1}{2}(b_2 - b_1)h$$

Use the Distributive Property ──────────→ $b_1h + \tfrac{1}{2}b_2h - \tfrac{1}{2}b_1h$

$$h(b_1 + \tfrac{1}{2}b_2 - \tfrac{1}{2}b_1)$$

Combine like terms ──────────→ $h(\tfrac{1}{2}b_1 + \tfrac{1}{2}b_2)$

Use the Distributive Property again ──────────→ $\tfrac{1}{2}h(b_1 + b_2)$

So, the formula for the area of a trapezoid is $\tfrac{1}{2}h(b_1 + b_2)$.

EXAMPLE: Use the formula to find the area of this trapezoid.

$$A = \tfrac{1}{2}(b_1 + b_2)h$$
$$= \tfrac{1}{2}(3 + 5)3$$
$$= \tfrac{1}{2}(8)3$$
$$= 12$$

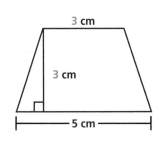

3 cm

3 cm

5 cm

So, the area of this trapezoid is 12 cm.²

369

MATH ALERT Multiplying Mixed Measures

CASE I To multiply a measure by a number, multiply each unit of the measure separately.

EXAMPLE I: Find the perimeter of the square.

To find the perimeter, use the formula $P = 4s$.

3 ft 5 in.

$$\begin{array}{r} 3 \text{ ft } 5 \text{ in.} \\ \times \quad 4 \\ \hline 12 \text{ ft } 20 \text{ in.} \end{array}$$ ──────→ **12 ft 20 in.** = **12 ft + (12 in. + 8 in.)**
= **(12 ft + 1 ft) + 8 in.**
= **13 ft 8 in.**

So, the perimeter is 13 ft 8 in.

CASE 2 To multiply a measure by a measure, be sure all measures are in the same units before you begin multiplying.

EXAMPLE 2: Find the area of the square.

2 ft 6 in.

To find the area of the square, use the formula: $A = s^2$

Multiply inches	or		**Multiply feet**	
2 ft 6 in. ⟶ 30 in.			$2\frac{1}{2}$ ft	or	2.5 ft
× 2 ft 6 in. ⟶ × 30 in.			× $2\frac{1}{2}$ ft		× 2.5 ft
900 in.²			$6\frac{1}{4}$ ft²		6.25 ft²

So, the area of the square is 900 in.², or $6\frac{1}{4}$ ft², or 6.25 ft².

Circles 370

Think about a dog on a leash. The leash is attached to a stake in the middle of a large yard. Unless there are trees in the way, the dog can get to any spot in the yard that's within a circle with a radius as long as the leash.

A **circle** is a set of points, all of which are the same distance from a given point. That point is the **center** of the circle. You can use the center to name a circle.

Write: ⊙*A*

Say: *circle A*

A chord is any line segment that joins two points on a circle.

center

A diameter is a chord that passes through the center of the circle and has endpoints on the circle.

A

A radius is any line segment from the center of the circle to a point on the circle.

Circles make great wheels because no matter how they're turned, the center stays the same distance from the ground.

Tangents

CASE 1 A tangent is a ratio.

MORE HELP
See 358

In right triangles, the tangent of an acute angle is the ratio of the length of the opposite leg to the length of the adjacent leg.

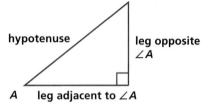

hypotenuse

leg opposite ∠A

A   leg adjacent to ∠A

tangent of $\angle A = \dfrac{\text{length of leg opposite } \angle A}{\text{length of leg adjacent to } \angle A}$

CASE 2 A tangent is also a line that intersects a circle at just one point.

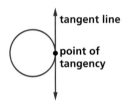

tangent line

point of tangency

How are the two meanings of tangent related? If you use a circle with a radius of 1 unit, you can see.

- Draw a tangent line to the circle at point *B*.
- Draw a radius from the center *C* to the point *B*. The tangent line forms a right angle with the radius *CB*.
- Draw a 35° angle with sides *CB* and *CA* to form right triangle *ABC*.

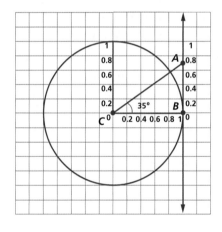

Note the position of point *A* on the graph.
- Find the length of *BA*: 0.7 units
- Find the tangent ratio for ∠*BCA*:

$\dfrac{\text{opposite}}{\text{adjacent}} = \dfrac{0.7}{1} = 0.7$

Compare the length of *BA* to the tangent ratio for ∠*BCA*.
They are the same! This relationship is true even when angle *C* is not 35° and the sides of the right triangle are different lengths.

Circumference

Circles are so special that they have their own name for perimeter: **circumference**.

The circumference of a circle is given by these formulas:

$C = \pi d$ or $C = 2\pi r$

That makes sense because the diameter is twice the radius.

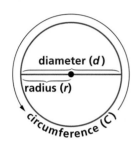

EXAMPLE: In the Olympics, a men's discus has a diameter of 22 cm. Find the circumference of the discus.

MORE HELP
See 158–159

(Source: The Ultimate Throwing Page on the World Wide Web)

When numbers are approximate, use ≈ instead of =.

$$C = \pi d$$
$$\approx 3.14 \times 22$$
$$\approx 69.08$$

So, the circumference of the discus is about 69.08 cm.

Pi

For all circles, the ratio of the circumference to the diameter ($\frac{C}{d}$) is always the same. This ratio is called **π (pi)**. The value of π is *approximately* 3.14, or $\frac{22}{7}$.

MORE HELP
See 025

Arcs

MORE HELP
See 296

Each section of a circle graph has an angle with the center of the circle as its vertex. These angles are called **central angles**. Central angles split the circle into **arcs**. An arc greater than a semicircle is a **major arc**. An arc less than a semicircle is a **minor arc**.

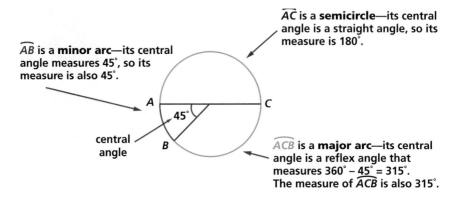

$\overline{AC}$ is a **semicircle**—its central angle is a straight angle, so its measure is 180°.

$\overarc{AB}$ is a **minor arc**—its central angle measures 45°, so its measure is also 45°.

central angle

$\overarc{ACB}$ is a **major arc**—its central angle is a reflex angle that measures 360° − 45° = 315°. The measure of $\overarc{ACB}$ is also 315°.

You name a minor arc by its endpoints. To name a major arc, you need a third point so that you don't confuse it with the minor arc.

Write: $\overarc{ACB}$

Say: *arc A C B*

EXAMPLE: Find the measures of the arcs in this circle graph.

BASKETBALL PARTICIPATION
(ages 17 and younger)

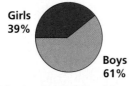

Girls
39%

Boys
61%

(Source: 1993 American Basketball Council Survey)

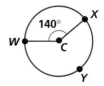

The measure of an arc is the measure of its central angle. So, the minor arc, $\overarc{WX}$, has a measure of 140°. The major arc, $\overarc{WYX}$, has a measure of 360° − 140° = 220°.

Area of a Circle

You can see how the formula for the area of a circle works by cutting a circle into wedges and rearranging them into a shape that is like a parallelogram.

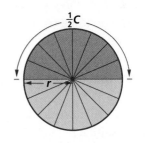

The formula for the area of a parallelogram is its base times its height. So, for this figure, the area is $\frac{1}{2}C \cdot r$.

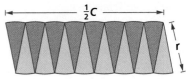

Since $C = 2\pi r$,

$$A = \frac{1}{2} \cdot C \cdot r$$
$$= \frac{1}{2} \cdot 2\pi r \cdot r$$
$$= \pi r^2$$

So, the formula for the area of a circle is $A = \pi r^2$.

EXAMPLE: Use the formula to find the area of the circle.

$$A = \pi r^2$$
$$\approx 3.14(5^2)$$
$$\approx 3.14(25)$$
$$\approx 78.5$$

So, the area of the circle is about 78.5 cm².

Similarity

Usually, when people say that two things are similar, they mean that the things are alike. In geometry, **similar** figures are alike in a very specific way—they have the same shape, and may or may not have the same size as well. Here are three drawings: the original drawing, an enlargement of the original, and a reduction of the original. Because all three drawings show the same shape, the figures are similar.

MORE ▶

Two similar polygons have:
- corresponding (or matching) angles that are congruent.
- corresponding (or matching) sides that are proportional.

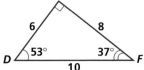

The ratios of pairs of corresponding sides are equal.

EXAMPLE 1: Are $\triangle ABC$ and $\triangle DEF$ similar?

In these triangles:

$\angle A \cong \angle D$; $\angle B \cong \angle E$; $\angle C \cong \angle F$
($\cong$ means "is congruent to")

$$\frac{\overline{AB}}{\overline{DE}} = \frac{\overline{BC}}{\overline{EF}} = \frac{\overline{CA}}{\overline{FD}}$$

$$\frac{3}{6} = \frac{4}{8} = \frac{5}{10} = \frac{1}{2}$$

With triangles, it is enough to show that all corresponding angles are congruent OR that all pairs of corresponding sides have the same ratio.

$\triangle ABC$ and $\triangle DEF$ have corresponding angles that are congruent and corresponding sides that are proportional. So, $\triangle ABC$ and $\triangle DEF$ are similar.

Write: $\triangle ABC \sim \triangle DEF$.

Say: *triangle A B C is similar to triangle D E F*

EXAMPLE 2: These two rectangles are similar. Use what you know about similarity to find x.

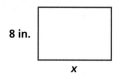

8 in.

x

12 in.

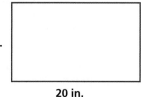

20 in.

You know that pairs of corresponding sides in similar figures have equal ratios.

MORE HELP
See 428–429

❶ WRITE A PROPORTION.	❷ SOLVE THE PROPORTION.
$\frac{8}{12} = \frac{x}{20}$	$13\frac{1}{3} = x$

So, the missing dimension is $13\frac{1}{3}$ in.

Here's a list of some figures that are *always* similar to each other.

Figures That Are Always Similar	
Description	**Examples**
all equilateral triangles	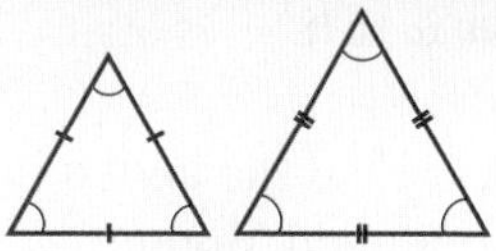
all 45°-45°-90° triangles	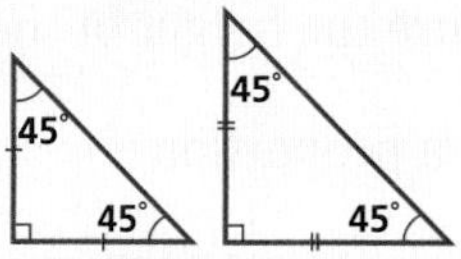
all 30°-60°-90° triangles	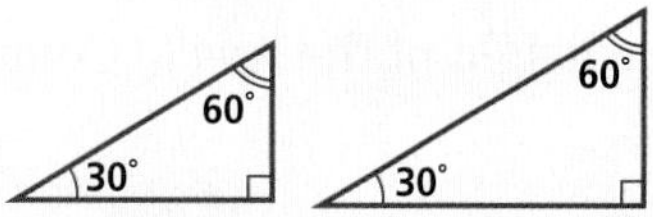
all squares	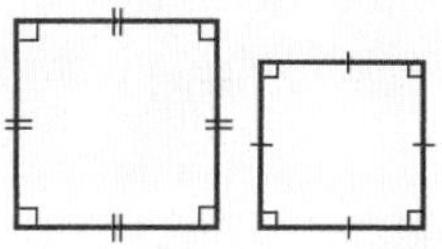
all circles	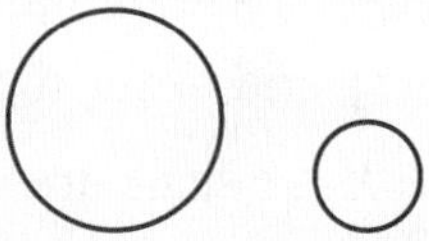
any two regular polygons that have the same number of sides	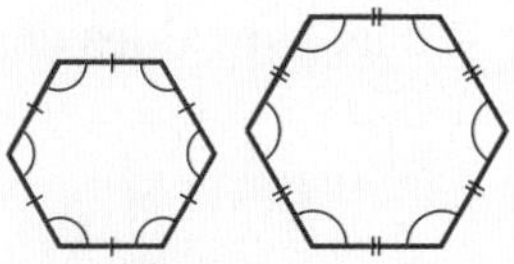 All the sides and angles of a regular polygon are congruent.

Scale Drawings

377

A **scale drawing** is a drawing that is the same shape but not the same size as the object it shows. Scale drawings often show objects that are too large or too small to be shown in their actual sizes. Blueprints and maps are examples of scale drawings.

MORE ▶

This scale drawing shows the *Apollo* Command Module that went to the moon.

MORE HELP
See 428–429

Scale: $\frac{1}{2}$ in. = 10 ft
The scale $\frac{1}{2}$ in. = 10 ft is a ratio. Corresponding parts of the drawing and the module are in the ratio of $\frac{1}{2}$ in. to 10 ft.

EXAMPLE: Find the actual height of the *Apollo* Command Module.

1. Measure the height of the drawing. It is about $1\frac{3}{4}$ in.

2. Write a proportion

$$\left.\begin{array}{c}\text{height in drawing} \longrightarrow \\ \text{actual height} \longrightarrow\end{array}\right. \frac{1\frac{3}{4}}{x} \approx \frac{\frac{1}{2}}{10}\left.\right\}\text{scale}$$

3. Solve the proportion $\longrightarrow$ $x \approx 35$

So, the height of the *Apollo* Command Module is about 35 ft.

When you work with ratios you *don't* absolutely have to make all your units the same, but you *do* have to remember which units are correct in your answer.

378

MATH ALERT Changing the Scale Changes the Size a Lot!

You can use a grid to see the effects of changing the scale of a figure.

EXAMPLE: Make scale drawings of a rectangle with sides of 6 in. and 8 in. First, you use a scale of 1 unit = 1 in. Then, you use a scale of 1 unit = 2 in. How does changing the scale change the drawing?

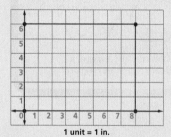

1 unit = 1 in.

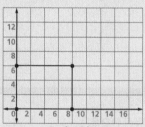

1 unit = 2 in.

In this scale, to show sides of 6 in. and 8 in., draw sides of 6 units and 8 units. The area is 48 square units.

Area = (8)(6)
= 48 square units

Doubling the scale shortens the length of each side by half: the sides are now 3 units and 4 units.

Area = (4)(3)
= 12 square units

The area of this rectangle is $\frac{1}{4}$ of the area of the one at the left.

Indirect Measurement: Proportions

Can you imagine using a tape measure to find the width of a raging river? In this type of situation, you can use similar figures to measure distance. This type of calculation is called **indirect measurement**.

EXAMPLE: Find the height (h) of the tree.

MORE HELP
See 428–429

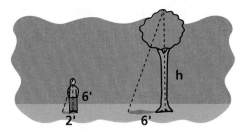

Using shadows in proportions this way is called shadow reckoning.

1. Write a proportion⎯⎯⎯⎯⎯⎯⎯⎯ $\dfrac{\text{man's shadow}}{\text{tree's shadow}} \rightarrow \dfrac{2}{6} = \dfrac{6}{h} \leftarrow \dfrac{\text{man's height}}{\text{tree's height}}$

2. Solve the proportion ⎯⎯⎯⎯⎯⎯ $h = 18$

The height of the tree is 18 ft.

Indirect Measurement: Trigonometric Ratios

Imagine using a tape measure to find the height of a skyscraper or the distance across a galaxy. Sometimes, you can use trigonometric ratios to find distances that are difficult to measure.

EXAMPLE: A 55-ft cable connects a point on the ground to the top of a pole. The cable makes a 60° angle with the ground. Find the height of the pole to the nearest foot.

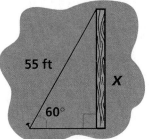

55 ft

x

60°

The pole is the side opposite the 60° angle of the right triangle. The cable is the hypotenuse. So you can use the sine ratio and the values in the diagram to find the height.

MORE HELP
See 358

$$\text{Sin } A = \frac{\text{opposite}}{\text{hypotenuse}}$$

1. Write an equation for the sine of 60°⎯⎯⎯⎯⎯→ $\text{Sin } 60° = \frac{x}{55}$

2. Look up sine of 60° in item 541 of the Almanac→ $0.866 \approx \frac{x}{55}$

3. Solve the equation ⎯⎯⎯⎯⎯⎯⎯⎯⎯→ $47.63 \approx x$

The height of the pole is about 48 ft.

The ratios found in trig tables are almost all rounded. When you calculate with approximate numbers, use ≈ instead of =.

Congruence

Figures that have the same shape and size are **congruent**. Sides are congruent if they are the same length. Angles are congruent if they have the same number of degrees.

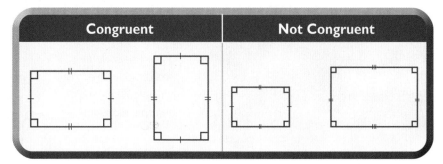

Congruent	Not Congruent

How do you know if two figures are congruent? All the corresponding parts of the two figures must be congruent.

EXAMPLE: Are $\triangle MNO$ and $\triangle PQR$ congruent?

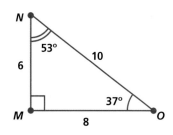 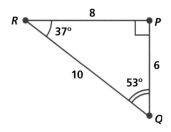

In these triangles:

$\angle M \cong \angle P$; $\angle N \cong \angle Q$; $\angle O \cong \angle R$ — The three pairs of corresponding angles are congruent.

$\overline{MN} \cong \overline{PQ}$; $\overline{NO} \cong \overline{QR}$; $\overline{OM} \cong \overline{RP}$

Write: $\angle M \cong \angle P$ — The three pairs of corresponding sides are congruent.

Say: *angle M is congruent to angle P*

$\triangle MNO$ and $\triangle PQR$ have corresponding angles that are congruent and corresponding sides that are congruent. So, $\triangle MNO$ and $\triangle PQR$ are congruent.

If you know that two figures are congruent, then you also know that their corresponding parts are congruent.

Marking Figures to Show Congruence

Parts of figures can be marked to show they are congruent.

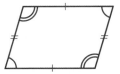 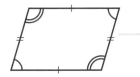

All sides with a single mark (—┼—) are congruent. All sides with a double mark (—╫—) are congruent. This applies to angles, too.

Showing Congruence

You can use what you know about similarity and about properties of figures to tell whether two figures, or some of their parts, are congruent.

EXAMPLE 1: These two figures are similar. Are they congruent?

You can see that:

■ The corresponding angles are congruent.

■ One pair of corresponding sides is congruent.

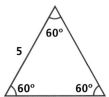 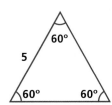

MORE HELP
See 376

Since the triangles are equiangular, they are also equilateral. So, if one pair of corresponding sides is congruent, all pairs of corresponding sides must be congruent.

So, the two triangles are congruent.

EXAMPLE 2: These two pentagons are similar. Are they congruent?

Corresponding angles are congruent, but not all corresponding sides are congruent.

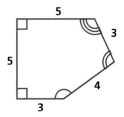 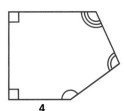

So, these pentagons are not congruent.

Transformations

Suppose you trace a figure on a piece of paper. You then move the figure and trace it again. You have just made a **transformation** of the first figure.

Anytime you move, shrink, or enlarge a figure, you make a transformation of that figure. You can move a figure by sliding (translation), turning (rotation), or flipping (reflection). You can also change the size of a figure (dilation).

If the figure you are moving is labeled with letters, such as X, Y, and Z, you can label the corresponding points on the **transformation image** (the second figure) with the same letters and a prime sign.

Write: X', Y', Z'

Say: X prime, Y prime, Z prime

△XYZ was flipped over the line to form △X'Y'Z'.

Translations

A **translation** is also called a **slide**. That's because in a translation, every point in the figure slides the same distance in the same direction. You can use a **slide arrow** to show the direction and distance of the movement.

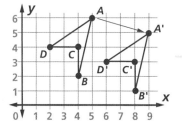

The slide arrow shows that the slide moves figure ABCD 4 units right and 1 unit down.

Rotations

When something rotates, it turns. In geometry, **rotating** a figure means turning the figure around a point. The point can be on the figure or it can be some other point. This point is called the **turn center**, or **point of rotation**.

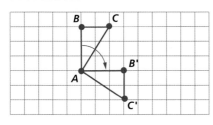

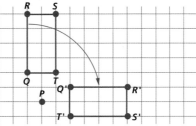

The point of rotation is *A*.   The point of rotation is *P*.

When you rotate a figure, you can describe the rotation by giving the direction (clockwise or counterclockwise) and the angle that the figure is rotated around the point of rotation.

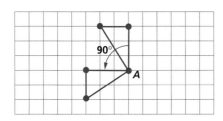

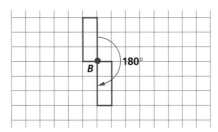

This figure was rotated 90° counterclockwise about point *A*.

This figure was rotated 180° clockwise about point *B*.

Turn Symmetry

A figure that rotates onto itself before turning 360° has **turn symmetry**.

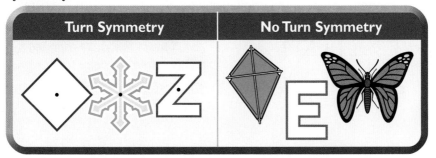

MORE ▶

EXAMPLE 1: Does rectangle *ABCD* have turn symmetry?

A half-turn (180°) about point *P* rotates *ABCD* onto itself.

So, *ABCD* has turn symmetry.

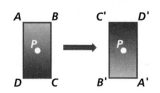

When a figure fits onto itself after rotating exactly 180° it also has **point symmetry.** So, a rectangle has point symmetry as well as turn symmetry.

EXAMPLE 2: Does trapezoid *LMNO* have turn symmetry?

There are no corresponding sides or angles of *LMNO* that are congruent. So, the only way to rotate it onto itself is to turn it 360°.

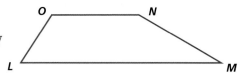

So, *LMNO* does not have turn symmetry.

388

Reflections

The reflection that you see in a rearview mirror is a reverse image of what you're looking at.

In geometry, a **reflection** is a transformation in which a figure is flipped over a line. That's why it's also called a **flip**. Each point in a reflection image is the same distance from the line as the corresponding point in the original shape.

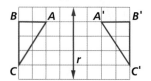

A and A' are both 2 units from line r.
B and B' are both 4 units from line r.
C and C' are both 4 units from line r.

Line Symmetry

If you can fold a figure so that it has two parts that match exactly, that figure has **line symmetry**, which is often just called symmetry. The fold line is called the **line of symmetry**. A figure can have no lines of symmetry, one line of symmetry, or more than one line of symmetry.

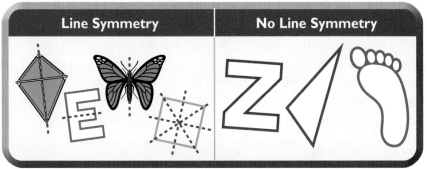

Line Symmetry	No Line Symmetry

Dilations

A **dilation** is a transformation that moves a figure and changes its size to create a similar figure. Here's how to make a dilation.

❶ Draw a triangle XYZ. Draw a point C outside the triangle. C is the center of dilation.	❷ Draw $\overline{CX}, \overline{CY},$ and $\overline{CZ}$. Choose a factor by which you want to increase the size of $\triangle XYZ$. We used 2 here.	❸ Draw points $X', Y',$ and Z' so that $CX' = 2CX, CY' = 2CY,$ and $CZ' = 2CZ$. Connect X', Y' and Z'.

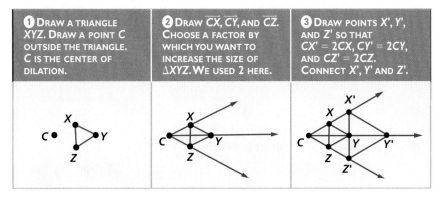

So, $\triangle X'Y'Z'$ is a dilation of $\triangle XYZ$.

The picture to the right is an example of a **tessellation**. In a tessellation, a figure or pattern of figures is repeated to cover a flat surface. For an arrangement to be a tessellation, the shapes must fit together so that there are no overlapping shapes or gaps between the shapes.

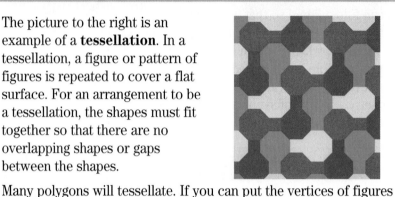

Many polygons will tessellate. If you can put the vertices of figures right next to each other around a point so there are no gaps and no overlaps, the figures will tessellate. That means that the sums of the angles around any one point must equal 360°.

MORE HELP
See 342

Here are a few examples:

Figure	Tessellate?	Example
rectangles	tessellate	
equilateral triangles	tessellate	
rectangles with equilateral triangles.	tessellate	
regular pentagons	don't tessellate	

Tessellations that involve more than one type of shape are called **semi-regular tessellations**. The octagon-square combination is an example of a semi-regular tessellation.

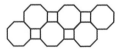

Topology

Suppose you copy a picture onto a piece of play putty. If you stretch it, the picture becomes distorted.

The pictures on the two pieces of play putty are topologically equivalent. This means that one figure can be made by stretching, shrinking, or bending the other.

If you can make a figure into another by stretching, shrinking, or bending it *and* without connecting or disconnecting points, then the two figures are topologically equivalent. If you fold or cut a figure to make another, you have created two figures that are *not* topologically equivalent.

Topologically Equivalent to an S	Not Topologically Equivalent to an S
Z 1 2 3 5 7	A X O 4 6 8 9

Can you find more topologically equivalent figures?

While congruent geometric figures must have congruent sides and angles, you can see that topologically equivalent figures do not have to have congruent segments, curves, or angles. So, all polygons are topologically equivalent to each other.

 Solid Figures

Imagine a world where people built things without paying attention to shape. What would it be like if the wheels on your bike or in-line skates were made out of prisms instead of cylinders? What would it be like to eat off a table that didn't have a flat surface? What would it be like to live in a house that's a sphere instead of a prism or where the floors are spherical instead of flat?

Some geometric terms you may hear used are *face*, *edge*, and *vertices*.

A **face** is a flat surface of a solid figure.

An **edge** is the line segment at which two faces of a solid figure meet.

Vertices are the corner points of a solid figure.

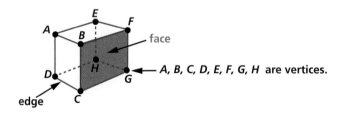

Prisms

Some very common shapes are types of prisms.

A **polyhedron** is a 3-dimensional closed figure with faces that are polygons. Polyhedrons with at least two faces that are congruent and parallel are called **prisms**.

MORE HELP
See 324, 331

CASE 1 The congruent and parallel faces are the bases of this prism. The bases are hexagons and the lateral faces are rectangles. Because the altitude of this prism is one of its edges, this is a **right prism**.

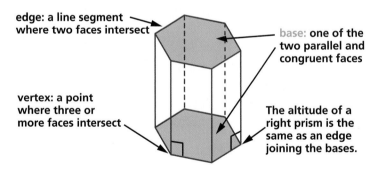

edge: a line segment where two faces intersect

base: **one of the two parallel and congruent faces**

vertex: a point where three or more faces intersect

The altitude of a right prism is the same as an edge joining the bases.

CASE 2 The bases of this prism are hexagons and the faces are parallelograms. Because the altitude of this prism is not one of its edges, this is an **oblique prism**.

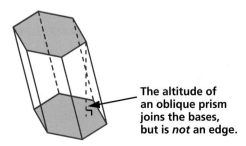

The altitude of an oblique prism joins the bases, but is *not* an edge.

MORE ▶

There are many different kinds of prisms. A prism is named according to the shape of its bases.

Name	Shape of Bases	Number of Lateral Faces	Examples
triangular prism	triangle	3	
rectangular prism	rectangle	4	
pentagonal prism	pentagon	5	
hexagonal prism	hexagon	6	
octagonal prism	octagon	8	

Nets of Prisms

A net is a closed plane figure that can be folded into a closed 3-dimensional figure.

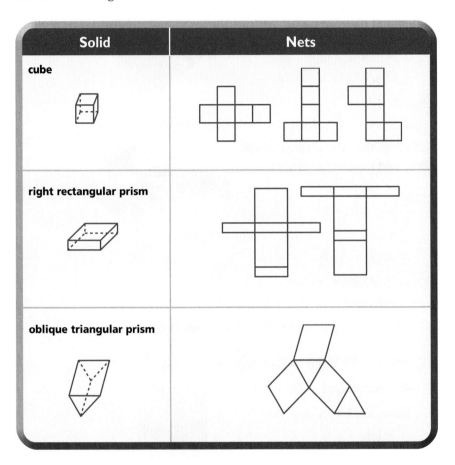

Solid	Nets
cube	
right rectangular prism	
oblique triangular prism	

Surface Area of Prisms

The **surface area** of a prism is the sum of the areas of all the faces, including the bases. You can use a net to find a general formula for the surface area of *any* prism.

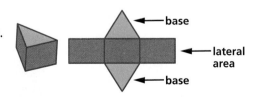

base

lateral area

base

MORE HELP
See 347

To find the surface area (*SA*), find the area of both bases (2*B*). Add the sum of the areas of the lateral faces—the lateral area (*LA*): $SA = 2B + LA$

MORE ▶

EXAMPLE 1: You want to paint a set of blocks. The hardware store can tell you how much paint to buy, but first you need to find the surface area of each block. What is the surface area of the triangular block below?

Use the formula $SA = 2B + LA$

The bases are triangles, so:

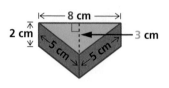

$$B = \tfrac{1}{2}bh$$
$$= \tfrac{1}{2}(8 \cdot 3)$$
$$= 12$$

$2B = 24$ So, the bases have a surface area of 24 cm².

Unfolded, the lateral faces would make one long rectangle, so:

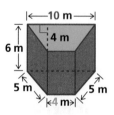

$$LA = lw$$
$$= (5 + 8 + 5) \cdot 2$$
$$= 36$$ So, the lateral area is 36 cm².

$$SA = 2B + LA$$
$$= 24 \text{ cm}^2 + 36 \text{ cm}^2$$
$$= 60 \text{ cm}^2$$

So, the surface area of the triangular prism is 60 cm².

EXAMPLE 2: Find the surface area of the prism.

Use the formula $SA = 2B + LA$

MORE HELP
See 368

The bases are trapezoids, so:

$$B = \tfrac{1}{2}(b_1 + b_2)h$$
$$= \tfrac{1}{2}(4 + 10)4$$
$$= 28$$

$2B = 56$ So the bases have a surface area of 56 m².

The lateral surface unfolds into a rectangle, so:

$$LA = lw$$
$$= (5 + 10 + 5 + 4) \cdot 6$$
$$= 24 \cdot 6$$
$$= 144$$

So, the lateral area is 144 m².

$$SA = 2B + LA$$
$$= 56 \text{ m}^2 + 144 \text{ m}^2$$
$$= 200 \text{ m}^2$$

So, the surface area of the prism is 200 m².

Volume of Prisms

The **volume** of a prism is the amount of space inside the prism. Volume is measured in **cubic units**, which means it tells you how many cubes of a given size it takes to fill the prism.

You can use this diagram to see why the formula for the volume of any prism works.

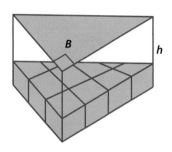

To find the volume (V) of a prism, multiply the number of cubic units needed to cover the base (B) by the number of layers (h).

So, for any prism,

$$V = Bh \longleftarrow \text{number of layers}$$

volume of a prism ⎯┘ └⎯ number of cubic units needed to cover the base

> Don't be confused by the use of *h* in formulas to name both the height of a solid and the height of each face.

CASE 1 The volume formula works for right prisms.

EXAMPLE 1: Find the volume of this prism.

$$V = Bh$$

The bases are triangles, so:

$B = \frac{1}{2}bh$ **The *b* and *h* are the base and height of the *triangle*.**

$$= \frac{1}{2}(15 \cdot 4)$$
$$= 30 \quad \text{So, the area of the base is 30 cm}^2.$$

$V = Bh$ **This *h* is the height of the *prism*.**

$$= 30 \cdot 5$$
$$= 150$$

So, the volume of the prism is 150 cm³.

MORE ▶

CASE 2 The formula works just as well when the prism is oblique.

EXAMPLE 2: Find the volume of this oblique rectangular prism.

$V = Bh$

The base is a rectangle, so:

$B = lw$

$= 5 \cdot 2$

$= 10$

The area of the base is 10 m².

$V = Bh$ **This height (h) is**
            the height of the
$= 10 \cdot 4$ **prism.**

$= 40$

So, the volume of this prism is 40 m³.

h = 4 m

w = 2 m

l = 5 m

398

MATH ALERT Volume Is Measured in Cubic Units

When you multiply units of measure by other units of measure, you need to remember two very important things:

1. Always be sure the units are the same. (You can multiply inches times inches or feet times feet, but never inches times feet.)

2. Always be sure that your answer has the right kind of unit. If you've multiplied inches times inches times inches again, you're finding volume, and volume is measured in cubes.
   - $2 \times 2 \times 2$ is *2 cubed* (2^3)
   - inches $\times$ inches $\times$ inches is *inches cubed* (in.³)

399   **Cubes and Rectangular Prisms**

A prism with bases that are rectangles is called a **rectangular prism**. A prism in which all the faces are congruent squares is called a **cube**.

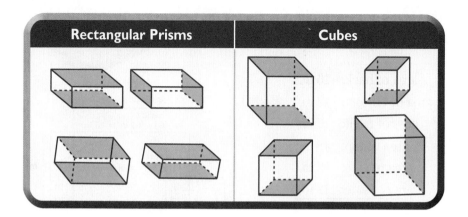

| Rectangular Prisms | Cubes |

Drawing Cubes and Rectangular Prisms

400

To make a sketch of a cube or rectangular prism look realistic, you should think about perspective. Lined, squared, or dot paper might help you.

EXAMPLE: Sketch a rectangular prism.

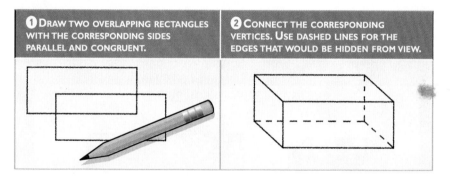

| ❶ DRAW TWO OVERLAPPING RECTANGLES WITH THE CORRESPONDING SIDES PARALLEL AND CONGRUENT. | ❷ CONNECT THE CORRESPONDING VERTICES. USE DASHED LINES FOR THE EDGES THAT WOULD BE HIDDEN FROM VIEW. |

MORE HELP
See 381–383

Surface Area of Cubes and Rectangular Prisms

401

Suppose you wanted to know the amount of self-adhesive paper you would need to cover a box. The area of each face of the box would tell you how much sticky paper covers that face. Adding the areas of all the faces would give you the area of the entire surface of the box (the surface area).

MORE ▶

EXAMPLE 1: Find the surface area of the box.

The net can help you find the area of each face.

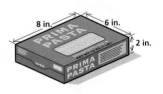

area of back:	16 in.²
area of bottom:	48 in.²
area of front:	16 in.²
area of top:	48 in.²
area of side:	12 in.²
area of side:	12 in.²
sum:	152 in.²

MORE HELP
See 324, 366, 381

So, the surface area of the box is 152 in.²

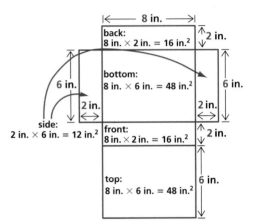

Shortcut

Since a rectangular prism has three pairs of congruent sides, you can find the surface area with this formula:

$$SA = 2lw + 2lh + 2wh$$

There is a formula for finding the surface area of a cube. In a cube, all six faces have the same area. So, you only need to find the area of one face, then multiply by 6: $SA = 6s^2$.

EXAMPLE 2: Find the surface area of the cube.

$$SA = 6s^2$$
$$= 6 \cdot 8 \cdot 8$$
$$= 384$$

So, the surface area of the cube is 384 in².

Volume of Cubes and Rectangular Prisms

The **volume** of a prism is the amount of space inside the prism.

To find the volume of a cube or a rectangular prism, think about a model.

> Remember: Volume should always be measured in cubic units.

EXAMPLE: Find the volume of each prism. Each cube is a 1-cm cube.

Cube	Rectangular Prism
There are 2 layers of centimeter cubes. There are 4 centimeter cubes in each layer. So, the volume is 8 cm³.	There are 2 layers of centimeter cubes. There are 6 centimeter cubes in each layer. So, the volume is 12 cm³.

Shortcut

To find the volume of a rectangular prism, multiply the length by the width by the height of the prism. The formula for volume of a rectangular prism is $V = lwh$. If you think about filling a right rectangular prism with cubes, you can see why the formula works.

Rectangular Prism

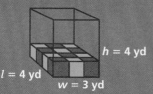

$h = 4$ yd
$l = 4$ yd
$w = 3$ yd

One layer contains $l \cdot w$ 1-yard cubes. There are h layers.
So, volume $= lwh$
$= 4 \cdot 3 \cdot 4$
$= 48$
The volume of this prism is 48 yd³.

Cube

$s = 3$ yd

One layer contains $s \cdot s$ 1-yard cubes. There are s layers.
So, volume $= s^3$
$= 3 \cdot 3 \cdot 3$
$= 27$
The volume of this cube is 27 yd³.

Pyramids

What do you think of when you hear the word *pyramid*? You may have heard of a few famous monuments that are pyramids.

In geometry, a **pyramid** is a polyhedron with a single base that is a polygon and faces that are triangles.

This pyramid is a **regular pyramid**. Its vertex is directly above the center of its base, which is a regular polygon.

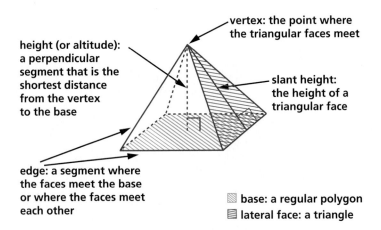

vertex: the point where the triangular faces meet

height (or altitude): a perpendicular segment that is the shortest distance from the vertex to the base

slant height: the height of a triangular face

edge: a segment where the faces meet the base or where the faces meet each other

base: a regular polygon
lateral face: a triangle

This pyramid is an **oblique pyramid**. Its vertex is *not* directly above the center of its base, so the altitude of the pyramid is a perpendicular segment from the vertex to the plane that the base lies in.

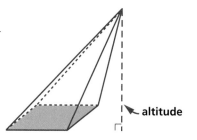

altitude

Types of Pyramids

404

A pyramid is named according to the shape of its base.

Name	Shape of Base	Number of Lateral Faces	Examples
triangular pyramid	triangle	3	
square pyramid	square	4	
hexagonal pyramid	hexagon	6	
octagonal pyramid	octagon	8	

405

Drawing Pyramids

You can sketch a pyramid by first drawing the base and then connecting the vertices of the base to the vertex of the pyramid. Grid paper or dot paper may help you.

To show a right square pyramid (and not an *oblique* square pyramid), center the vertex over the square.

EXAMPLE: Draw a square pyramid.

① DRAW A SQUARE STANDING ON ONE CORNER. DRAW A POINT THAT IS ABOVE THE SQUARE.	**②** CONNECT EACH VERTEX OF THE SQUARE TO THE POINT ABOVE THE SQUARE. USE DASHED LINES FOR THE EDGES THAT WOULD BE HIDDEN FROM YOUR VIEW.

406

Nets of Pyramids

You can unfold a pyramid so that you show all its faces. This unfolded figure is called a **net**.

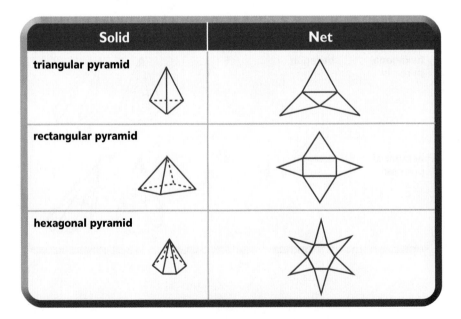

Solid	Net
triangular pyramid	
rectangular pyramid	
hexagonal pyramid	

Surface Area of Pyramids

The **surface area** of a pyramid is the sum of the areas of all of the faces, including the base. You can use a net to find a general formula that will help you find the surface area of *any* pyramid.

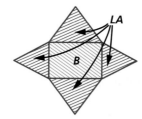

To find the surface area (SA), you need to find the area of the base (B) and the lateral area (LA), then add: $SA = B + LA$

MORE HELP
See 366

EXAMPLE 1: Find the surface area of the right square pyramid.

Use the formula: $SA = B + LA$

The base is a square, so:

$B = s^2$

$\quad = 5^2$

$\quad = 25$ So, the area of the base is 25 cm².

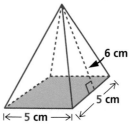

There are four congruent lateral faces. Find the areas of the triangles.

$LA = 4(\frac{1}{2}bh)$

$\quad = 4(\frac{1}{2} \cdot 5 \cdot 6)$

$\quad = 60$ So, the lateral area is 60 cm².

$SA = B + LA$

$\quad = 25 \text{ cm}^2 + 60 \text{ cm}^2$

$\quad = 85 \text{ cm}^2$

So, the surface area of the pyramid is 85 cm².

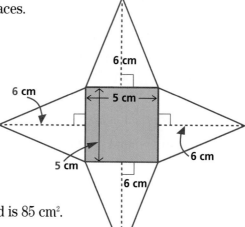

EXAMPLE 2: Find the surface area of the pyramid. The base and the lateral faces are congruent triangles.

Use the formula: $SA = B + LA$

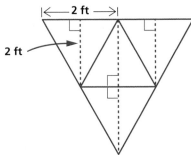

The base is a triangle, so:

$B = \frac{1}{2}bh$

$\quad = \frac{1}{2} \cdot 2 \cdot 2$

$\quad = 2 \qquad$ So, the area of the base is 2 ft².

Each of the three lateral faces has the same dimensions and area as the base. So, the lateral area is three times the area of the base.

$LA = 3B$

$\quad = 3 \cdot 2$

$\quad = 6 \qquad$ So, the lateral area is 6 ft².

$SA = B + LA$

$\quad = 2 \text{ ft}^2 + 6 \text{ ft}^2$

$\quad = 8 \text{ ft}^2$

So, the surface area of the pyramid is 8 ft².

Volume of Pyramids

The volume of a pyramid is the amount of space inside the pyramid. Volume is measured in cubic units, which means it tells you how many cubes of a given size it takes to fill the pyramid.

MORE HELP
See 366

The volume (V) of a pyramid is $\frac{1}{3}$ the volume of a prism with the same base area (B) and height (h).

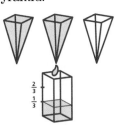

Volume of prism $= Bh$

Volume of pyramid $= \frac{1}{3}Bh$

EXAMPLE: Find the volume of the square pyramid.

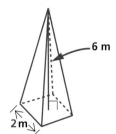

$V = \frac{1}{3}Bh$

$\quad = \frac{1}{3}(2 \cdot 2) \cdot 6$

$\quad = 8$

So, the volume of the pyramid is 8 m³.

Cylinders 409

Most cans are cylinders. So are paper rolls, mailing tubes, and drain pipes.

In geometry, a cylinder is a solid figure that has two circular bases. These bases are congruent and parallel.

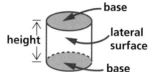

Drawing Cylinders 410

Here's how to make a 3-dimensional sketch of a cylinder.

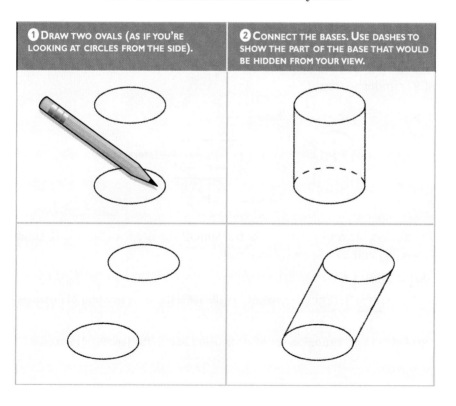

| ❶ DRAW TWO OVALS (AS IF YOU'RE LOOKING AT CIRCLES FROM THE SIDE). | ❷ CONNECT THE BASES. USE DASHES TO SHOW THE PART OF THE BASE THAT WOULD BE HIDDEN FROM YOUR VIEW. |

411

Nets of Cylinders

You can unroll a cylinder so that it shows its two bases and its lateral surface. The lateral surface unrolls into a rectangle.

cylinder   **net of cylinder**

If you want to see for yourself that the cylinder's side unrolls into a rectangle, peel the label off of any cylindrical can.

412

Surface Area of Cylinders

You can use a net to help you see why the formula for the surface area of a cylinder works.

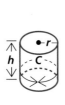 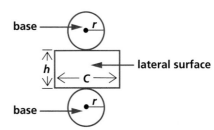

MORE HELP
See 370, 372, 375

The surface area of a cylinder is the sum of the areas of its two circular bases (B) and its lateral surface (LA).

$$SA = 2B + LA$$
$$= 2(\underbrace{\pi r^2}) + (\underbrace{2\pi r})h \longleftarrow \text{height of cylinder is the same as width of rectangle}$$

       ↑   ↑

area of circle   **circumference of circle unrolled into the length of rectangle**

EXAMPLE: About how much metal was used to make this tuna can?

To find the answer, find the surface area of the can.

$$SA = 2B + LA$$
$$= 2\pi r^2 + 2\pi rh$$
$$\approx 2 \cdot 3.14 \cdot 4.3^2 + 2 \cdot 3.14 \cdot 4.3 \cdot 3.8$$
$$\approx 218.73$$

r = 4.3 cm

h = 3.8 cm

SEA KING
CHUNK LIGHT TUNA

Since 3.14 is an approximation for π, use ≈ instead of =.

The surface area of the can is about 218.73 cm². So, a little less than 219 cm² of metal was used to make the can.

Volume of Cylinders

413

The volume of a cylinder is the amount of space inside the cylinder. Volume is measured in cubic units.

Use this diagram to help you understand why the formula for the volume of a cylinder works.

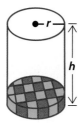

r

h

To find the volume (V) of a cylinder, multiply the number of cubic units needed to cover one layer by the number of layers. So, for any cylinder:

$$V = Bh$$
$$V = \underbrace{\pi r^2}h \longleftarrow \text{height of the cylinder}$$

area of the circular base

EXAMPLE: Find the volume of the juice can.

$$V = Bh$$
$$= \pi r^2 h$$
$$\approx 3.14 \cdot 1.5^2 \cdot 6$$
$$\approx 42.39$$

r = 1.5 in.

THE WILD ONE!

Splash

h = 6 in.

ORANGE SODA

12 FL OZ

So, the volume of this can is a bit more than 42 in³.

Cones

You've probably seen lots of objects that are shaped like cones.

In geometry, a **cone** is a 3-dimensional figure with one circular base. A curved surface connects the base to the vertex.

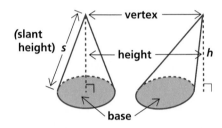

Drawing Cones

Here's how to sketch a cone.

❶ DRAW AN OVAL TO SHOW THE CIRCULAR BASE AS IT WOULD LOOK FROM THE SIDE. DRAW A POINT ABOVE THE BASE.	❷ DRAW TWO LINE SEGMENTS TO CONNECT THE BASE AND THE POINT. USE DASHES TO SHOW THE PART OF THE BASE THAT WOULD BE HIDDEN FROM YOUR VIEW.

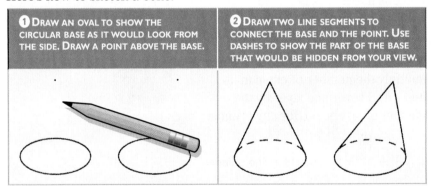

Nets of Cones

You can unroll a cone so that it shows its base and its lateral surface.

cone   net of cone

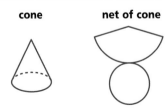

Surface Area of Cones

Use a net to help you see why the formula for the surface area of a right cone works.

The **surface area** of a cone is the sum of the area of its base (B) and its lateral area (LA).

MORE HELP
See 375

$$SA = B + LA$$

B is a circle, so:

$$B = \pi r^2$$

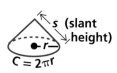

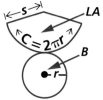

To find LA, imagine cutting the lateral surface into wedges and arranging the wedges to form a figure like a parallelogram. The base of the new figure is πr and the height is s (the **slant height** of the curved surface.) So, $LA = \pi rs$.

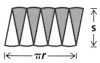

$$SA = B + LA$$

$$= \pi r^2 + \pi rs$$

EXAMPLE: If you're designing tents for backpackers, you need to keep them light. To decide what fabrics are acceptable to backpackers, you need to know the amount of fabric it takes to construct a tent. How much fabric is required to construct this tent?

To find the answer, find the surface area of the tent.

$$SA = B + LA$$

$$= \pi r^2 + \pi rs$$

$$\approx (3.14 \cdot 8^2) + (3.14 \cdot 8 \cdot 10)$$

$$\approx 452.16$$

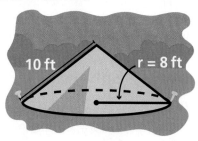

The surface area of the tent is about 452 ft².

418   Volume of Cones

Volume is measured in cubic units. The volume of a cone (V) is $\frac{1}{3}$ the volume of a cylinder with the same base area (B) and height (h).

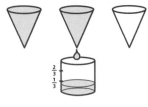

$$V_{cylinder} = Bh$$
$$= \pi r^2 \cdot h \; \leftarrow \text{height of cylinder}$$

$\uparrow$
area of circular base

$$V_{cone} = \tfrac{1}{3}Bh$$
$$= \tfrac{1}{3} \cdot \pi r^2 \cdot h \; \leftarrow \text{height of cone}$$

$\uparrow$
area of circular base

EXAMPLE: Find the volume of this snow-cone holder.

$$V = \tfrac{1}{3} Bh$$
$$= \tfrac{1}{3} \cdot \pi r^2 h$$
$$\approx \tfrac{1}{3} \cdot \tfrac{22}{7} \cdot 3^2 \cdot 6$$
$$\approx 56\tfrac{4}{7}$$

The volume of the snow-cone holder is a little less than 57 cm³.

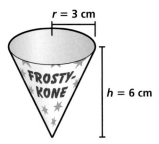

r = 3 cm
FROSTY-KONE
h = 6 cm

419   Spheres

A sphere is a 3-dimensional figure. All of the points on the surface of the sphere are the same distance from the center.

center — radius

420   Drawing Spheres

Here's how to sketch a sphere.

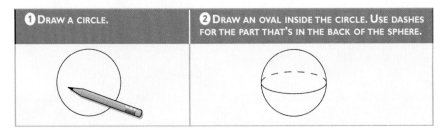

| ❶ DRAW A CIRCLE. | ❷ DRAW AN OVAL INSIDE THE CIRCLE. USE DASHES FOR THE PART THAT'S IN THE BACK OF THE SPHERE. |

Surface Area of Spheres

421

The area of the circle that contains the center of the sphere is πr^2. It would take exactly 4 of these circles to wrap the sphere completely. $SA = 4\pi r^2$.

MORE HELP
See 375

EXAMPLE: Suppose you want to produce basketballs. What's the least amount of material you would need for each one?

Find the surface area of the basketball.

$$SA = 4\pi r^2$$
$$\approx 4 \cdot 3.14 \cdot 4.89^2$$
$$\approx 300.34$$

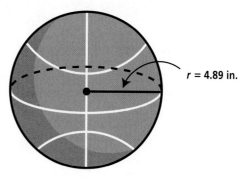

$r = 4.89$ in.

So, you need a bit more than 300 in.² of material to make a basketball.

(Source: The Sports Fan's Ultimate Book of Sports Comparisons)

Volume of Spheres

422

Volume is measured in cubic units. A circle on the sphere with the same center as the sphere has an area of πr^2. Imagine this same circle as the base of a cylinder that exactly contains the sphere.

The volume of this cylinder would be the area of its base times its height, which is $\pi r^2 \cdot 2r$, or $2\pi r^3$.

The sphere doesn't fill the whole cylinder. In fact, its volume is $\frac{2}{3}$ of the volume of the cylinder:

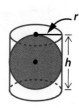

$h = 2r$

side view

r

h

$$\tfrac{2}{3}(2\pi r^3) = \tfrac{4}{3}\pi r^3$$

So, for a sphere:

$$V = \tfrac{4}{3}\pi r^3$$

EXAMPLE: Find the volume of water in this spherical rooting glass.

$$V = \tfrac{4}{3}\pi r^3$$
$$\approx \tfrac{4}{3} \cdot \tfrac{22}{7} \cdot 3^3$$
$$\approx 113\tfrac{1}{7}$$

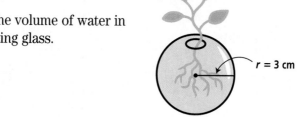

$r = 3$ cm

The volume of the water is a bit more than 113 cm³.

423

Ratio, Proportion, and Percent

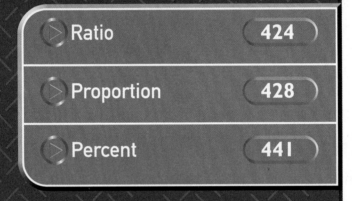

Did anyone ever tell you that you were blowing things way out of proportion? This is a very mathematical statement! It means that they thought you were reacting to something in a manner that was too extreme for the circumstances. Like crying over spilled milk. Or skipping a party because you didn't have new clothes to wear.

Ratios help us keep things in proportion. If a lemonade recipe calls for 4 cups of water, 1 cup of lemon juice, and 1 cup of sugar, then twice as much lemonade would mean using twice as much of *each* ingredient: 8 cups of water, 2 cups of lemon juice, and 2 cups of sugar. You get the idea—everything in proportion means the lemonade tastes the same no matter how much you make.

Ratio

You can compare two quantities two different ways:

 ONE WAY You can subtract to find the difference.

EXAMPLE 1: Katie has 30 CDs and Bryan has 20 CDs. How much bigger is Katie's CD collection than Bryan's?

Number of CDs Katie has − Number of CDs Bryan has

$$30 - 20 = 10$$

Katie has 10 more CDs than Bryan.

 ANOTHER WAY Or, you can use a ratio.

EXAMPLE 2: $\dfrac{\text{number of CDs Katie has}}{\text{number of CDs Bryan has}} = \dfrac{30}{20}$

Katie has $\frac{30}{20}$, or $1\frac{1}{2}$ times as many CDs as Bryan.

MORE HELP
See 028–029

Ratios compare two numbers. They are pretty interesting because, even though they can be written in fraction form, they do not have to follow fraction rules.

CASE 1 You can use a ratio to compare part of something to all of it. This ratio is most like a regular fraction.

EXAMPLE 3: The ratio of Katie's classical CDs to all of her CDs is 3 to 30 ($\frac{3}{30}$, or $\frac{1}{10}$).

Katie's CD List

Rock..............13

Country........14

Classical.......3

CASE 2 You can use a ratio to compare one part to another part.

EXAMPLE 4: The ratio of Katie's classical CDs to her country CDs is 3 to 14 ($\frac{3}{14}$).

CASE 3 You can use a ratio to compare all of something to all of something else.

EXAMPLE 5: The ratio of Katie's CD collection to Bryan's CD collection is 30 to 20 ($\frac{30}{20}$, or $\frac{3}{2}$).

Ways to Write Ratios 425

There are several different ways to write ratios.

EXAMPLE: A brand of candy comes in five colors: red, green, blue, yellow, and pink. There are two sizes of packages: small and large.

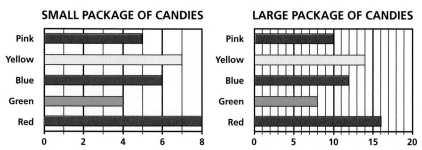

SMALL PACKAGE OF CANDIES   LARGE PACKAGE OF CANDIES

Here are some ways you can write ratios that show comparisons of the candy.

WAYS TO WRITE	COMPARE CANDIES IN SMALL PACKAGE (RED TO ALL).	COMPARE CANDIES IN LARGE PACKAGE (RED TO YELLOW).	COMPARE SMALL PACKAGE TO LARGE PACKAGE (ALL TO ALL).
Use *to*	8 to 30	16 to 14	30 to 60
Use a colon	8:30	16:14	30:60
Use fraction form	$\frac{8}{30}$, or $\frac{4}{15}$	$\frac{16}{14}$, or $\frac{8}{7}$	$\frac{30}{60}$, or $\frac{1}{2}$
Use decimal form	0.27	1.14	0.5

426

MATH ALERT Ratios Differ from Fractions

A ratio can be written in fraction form, with a numerator and a denominator. It can also be simplified the same way fractions are simplified (the ratio 8 to 16, or $\frac{8}{16}$, is equivalent to the ratio 1 to 2, or $\frac{1}{2}$). However, ratios don't always follow the same rules as fractions.

MORE HELP
See 028–029

The denominators of fractions and ratios are chosen differently. A fraction's denominator *always* tells you how a whole is divided (like a pizza divided into eighths). With ratios, the denominator *may* tell you:

■ how a whole is divided, or
■ the number of parts in another whole, or
■ a different part of the whole than the numerator describes (like the ratio of red candies to yellow candies in the same bag of candy).

Ratios also don't follow fraction rules when it comes to units. A fraction compares things that have the same units (like 3 pizza slices on your plate compared to 8 slices in a whole pizza). A ratio may compare things with like units or with unlike units (like 30 miles to 1 gallon).

Finally, we don't add or subtract ratios as we add or subtract fractions.

427 **Trigonometric Ratios**

MORE HELP
See 358, 380

In right triangles there are special relationships between the angle measures and side lengths. These relationships are called **trigonometric ratios**. You've probably heard of some of these ratios:

$$\text{sine ratio} = \frac{\text{side opposite angle}}{\text{hypotenuse}}$$

$$\text{cosine ratio} = \frac{\text{side adjacent to angle}}{\text{hypotenuse}}$$

$$\text{tangent ratio} = \frac{\text{side opposite angle}}{\text{side adjacent to angle}}$$

To find more about these ratios, see items 358 and 380.

⊘ Proportion

Think about your school pictures. You may get some wallet-size photos, some 4×5 photos for the relatives, and an 8×10 photo to frame and hang up in the living room. These different-size pictures are all pictures of you. Each picture looks like you because the features of your face are still in the same proportion to one another.

When a photograph is taken, the camera and the developer shrink (or enlarge) the image proportionally. That is, all dimensions are increased or decreased by the same factor. So, if your face is $2\frac{1}{2}$ inches from hairline to chin in the 4×5 photo, it will be twice as long (5 inches) in the photo with dimensions twice as large (8×10). It will be half as long ($1\frac{1}{4}$ inches) in a photo with dimensions half as large ($2 \times 2\frac{1}{2}$).

 $1\frac{1}{4}$ in.

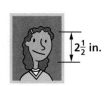 $2\frac{1}{2}$ in.

 5 in.

Ways to Write Proportions

A **proportion** is an equation showing that two ratios are equal. There are different ways to write proportions.

In an official United States flag, the ratio of the length to the width must be 19 to 10. So, if a souvenir maker makes a U.S. flag that is 57 cm long, in order for it to be an official U.S. flag, its width must be 30 cm.

(Source: The Flag Book of the United States)

To write proportions about this relationship, some common element must tie the numerators together. Another common element ties denominators together.

- Both numerators could relate to one dimension such as length, while both denominators relate to another dimension such as width.

$$\frac{\text{length of souvenir}}{\text{width of souvenir}} = \frac{\text{official length}}{\text{official width}}$$

- OR both numerators could relate to the scale lengths, while both denominators relate to the actual lengths.

$$\frac{\text{length of souvenir}}{\text{official length}} = \frac{\text{width of souvenir}}{\text{official width}}$$

WAYS TO WRITE	COMPARE OFFICIAL RATIO TO RATIO OF SOUVENIR FLAG DIMENSIONS.	COMPARE RATIO OF LENGTHS TO RATIO OF WIDTHS.
Use *to*	19 to 10 = 57 to 30	19 to 57 = 10 to 30
Use a colon	19:10 = 57:30	19:57 = 10:30
Use fraction form	$\frac{19}{10} = \frac{57}{30}$	$\frac{19}{57} = \frac{10}{30}$
Use decimal form	1.9 = 1.9	$0.\overline{3} = 0.\overline{3}$

The colon notation is read the same way you read analogies in English.

Write: $a{:}b = c{:}d$

Say: *a is to b as c is to d.*

Direct Proportion

When two quantities are proportional, a change in one quantity corresponds to a predictable change in the other. In a **direct proportion**, both quantities increase by the same factor, or both quantities decrease by the same factor.

EXAMPLE 1: You work for $5.00 per hour. As hours increase, total earnings increase by the same factor. So, *hours* and *total earnings* are directly proportional.

EXAMPLE 2: In the produce section of the supermarket, prices are usually listed by the pound. A pound of apples may cost $0.90. But you don't have to buy a whole pound. As the *weight* of the apples decreases, the *price* you'll pay decreases by the same factor. So, weight and price are directly proportional.

Inverse Proportion 431

In an **inverse proportion**, when one quantity *increases* by a certain factor, the other quantity *decreases* by the same factor, and vice versa. For example, if you multiply one quantity by 2, the other is divided by 2 (or multiplied by $\frac{1}{2}$).

EXAMPLE: You run 5 miles every morning. As your speed increases from 6 miles an hour to 8 miles an hour, the amount of time it takes to run the 5 miles decreases from $\frac{5}{6}$ hour (50 minutes) to $\frac{5}{8}$ hour (37.5 minutes). $\frac{4}{3}$ of the original speed gives the new speed ($6 \cdot \frac{4}{3} = 8$). $\frac{3}{4}$ of the original time gives the new time ($\frac{5}{6} \cdot \frac{3}{4} = \frac{5}{8}$). *Speed* and *time* are inversely proportional.

> $\frac{3}{4}$ is the inverse of $\frac{4}{3}$.

Constant of Proportionality 432

When a quantity is always a particular multiple of another quantity, the factor is called a **constant of proportionality**.

EXAMPLE: Apples are $0.90 per pound. To find what you'll pay for your bag of apples, multiply 0.9 by the number of pounds. No matter what the number of pounds is, 0.9 is the constant factor you use to find the price.

You can express the relationship among cost, price, and number of apples with an equation.

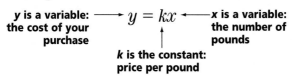

y is a variable: the cost of your purchase → $y = kx$ ← **x is a variable:** the number of pounds

k is the constant: price per pound

433) Terms

In the proportion $a{:}b = c{:}d$, a and d are the **extreme terms** and b and c are the **mean terms**. The product of the extreme terms equals the product of the mean terms, $ad = bc$.

MORE HELP
See 037, 229

Why is this so?

Rewrite the proportion using fractions $\longrightarrow$ $\frac{a}{b} = \frac{c}{d}$

Multiply both sides of the equation by **bd** $\longrightarrow$ $\frac{a}{b}(bd) = (bd)\frac{c}{d}$

Simplify the fractions $\longrightarrow$ $\frac{a\not{b}d}{\not{b}} = \frac{b\not{d}c}{\not{d}}$

$$ad = bc$$

EXAMPLE: Is $5{:}8 = 10{:}16$ a true proportion?

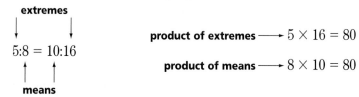

extremes

$5{:}8 = 10{:}16$

means

product of extremes $\longrightarrow$ $5 \times 16 = 80$

product of means $\longrightarrow$ $8 \times 10 = 80$

So, $5{:}8 = 10{:}16$ is a true proportion.

434) Using Proportions to Solve Problems

When you mix paint, to keep the color the same for any quantity of paint, you keep all the ingredients in the same ratio. Sometimes you don't have all the elements of a proportion, so you need to solve an equation to find the missing piece.

MORE HELP
See 036

 ONE WAY You can solve a proportion by finding equivalent fractions.

EXAMPLE 1: You have 2 gallons of latex paint that will cover 800 ft². You have 2400 ft² of walls and ceilings to paint. How many more gallons of paint do you need?

You can use a proportion to solve the problem.

$$\frac{\text{gallons}}{\text{square feet}} \longrightarrow \frac{2}{800} = \frac{x}{2400}$$
$$x = 6$$

$800 \times 3 = 2400,$ so

$$\frac{2}{800} = \frac{2 \times 3}{800 \times 3} = \frac{6}{2400}$$

You can also use what you know about the product of the extremes and the product of the means to solve a proportion.

gallons: feet² = gallons: feet²

$$2{:}800 = x{:}2400$$
$$2 \cdot 2400 = 800 \cdot x$$
$$4800 = 800x$$
$$6 = x$$

The relationship between the extremes and the means is sometimes called the **Rule of Three** because if you know any three terms you can find the fourth.

 You can also solve a proportion by using cross products.

MORE HELP
See 036

$$\text{gallons} \longrightarrow \frac{2}{800} \diagup \frac{x}{2400} \quad \frac{800x}{4800}$$
$$\text{square feet} \longrightarrow$$

$$4800 = 800x$$
$$6 = x$$

Finding cross products is the same as multiplying the extremes by the means!

No matter what way you choose to solve the proportion, you need 6 gallons of paint altogether. So, you need 4 more gallons.

Rate   435

A **rate** is a special ratio. Its denominator is always 1. Rates are easy to use in proportions because they involve less computing than ratios with denominators that are not 1. Rates you may be familiar with include:

Rate		Ratio
miles per hour (mph)	▷	$\dfrac{\text{number of miles}}{1 \text{ hour}}$
revolutions per minute (rpm)	▷	$\dfrac{\text{number of turns of a wheel}}{1 \text{ minute}}$
miles per gallon (mpg)	▷	$\dfrac{\text{number of miles driven}}{1 \text{ gallon}}$
annual percentage rate (APR)	▷	$\dfrac{\text{percent interest charged}}{1 \text{ year}}$

MORE ▶

EXAMPLE: You're traveling 60 miles per hour. How many miles do you go in two hours?

 You could set up and solve a proportion.

$$\frac{\text{miles}}{\text{hours}} \longrightarrow \frac{60}{1} = \frac{x}{2}$$
$$120 = x$$

 You can also multiply the rate times the time to get the distance.

$60 \cdot 2 = 120$

Either way, you travel 120 miles in two hours.

436 Using Conversion Factors

When you travel to another country, you exchange U.S. dollars for local money—Japanese yen, Mexican pesos, Euros, or whatever currency is used where you are going. When you exchange money, a **currency exchange rate** is used to figure out how much foreign money you will get for your dollars. These rates change every day.

This table shows some exchange rates on Thursday, March 13, 2003.

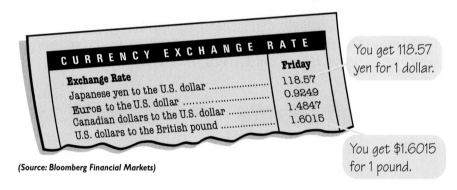

(Source: Bloomberg Financial Markets)

EXAMPLE 1: Suppose on March 13, 2003, you exchanged $1000 for Japanese yen. How many yen should you have received?

You can use a proportion to solve this problem.

$$\frac{\text{yen}}{\text{dollars}} \longrightarrow \frac{118.57}{1} = \frac{x}{1000} \longleftarrow \frac{\text{yen}}{\text{dollars}}$$
$$118{,}570 = 1x$$

Your variable was in the numerator, so its unit is *Japanese yen*. You should have received 118,570 yen for 1000 U.S. dollars.

EXAMPLE 2: Suppose on March 13, 2003, you exchanged $1000 for British pounds. How many pounds should you have received?

To keep track of the units, it helps to write the ratio in words next to the numerical ratios.

Set up and solve a proportion.

$$\text{dollars} \longrightarrow \frac{1.6015}{1} = \frac{1000}{x} \longleftarrow \text{dollars}$$
$$\text{pounds} \longrightarrow \qquad\qquad\qquad \longleftarrow \text{pounds}$$

$$1.6015x = 1000$$

$$x = 1000 \div 1.6015$$

$$\approx 624.41$$

Your variable was in the denominator, so its unit is *British pounds*. You should have received 624.41 pounds for 1000 U.S. dollars.

Multiple-Step Conversions

437

Sometimes when you convert from one unit to another, such as from inches to miles or from days to seconds, you have to make more than one conversion to get the answer.

EXAMPLE: How many seconds are in a day?

Time	
1 day (d)	**= 24 hours (h)**
1 hour	**= 60 minutes (min)**
1 minute	**= 60 seconds (s)**

1. First find the number of minutes in 24 hours.

$$\text{minutes} \longrightarrow \frac{60}{1} = \frac{x}{24} \longleftarrow \text{minutes}$$
$$\text{hours} \longrightarrow \qquad\qquad \longleftarrow \text{hours}$$

There are 1440 minutes in 24 hours.

2. Then find the number of seconds in 1440 minutes.

$$\text{seconds} \longrightarrow \frac{60}{1} = \frac{x}{1440} \longleftarrow \text{seconds}$$
$$\text{minutes} \longrightarrow \qquad\qquad \longleftarrow \text{minutes}$$

There are 86,400 seconds in 1440 minutes. So, there are 86,400 seconds in a day.

Shortcut

Since you're using rates, if you're careful with the units, you can just set up a series of multiplications to do multiple conversions:

days · 24 hours in a day · 60 minutes in an hour · 60 seconds in a minute = seconds in that many days

$$d \cdot \quad 24 \quad \cdot \quad 60 \quad \cdot \quad 60 \quad = \quad s$$

Unit Price

What do the numbers on this label mean?

Nt Wt (lb) means net weight in pounds—the total weight of the cheese. The net weight is 0.77 lb.

$/lb means the price per pound of the cheese. The price for one unit of an item is called unit price. The unit price of this cheese is $4.02 per pound.

Total price = unit price × number of units. The total price of the cheese is $3.0954, or $3.10.

The **unit price** is the rate $\frac{\text{price}}{\text{one unit}}$.

To find the unit price of any item, you can set up a proportion.

$$\frac{\text{price}}{\text{one unit}} = \frac{\text{total price}}{\text{units in the package}}$$

EXAMPLE: What is the unit price for each soap?

Sun Valley Soap
Unit price = 1.29 ÷ 5 = 0.258
This rounds to $0.26 per ounce.

Sabrina's Wonder Bar
Unit price = 0.99 ÷ 4 = 0.2475
This rounds to $0.25 per ounce.

MATH ALERT Comparing Unit Prices to Find the Better Buy

Sometimes comparing unit prices doesn't really tell you whether one item is a better buy than another. For example, though one brand of tuna might have a lower unit price, you may not like the taste, or it may come in a can that contains more than you can use.

Scale

MORE HELP
See 377

A **scale drawing** has the same shape but not necessarily the same size as the object it represents. The parts of an object in a scale drawing are proportional to the corresponding parts of the actual object. To find out more about scale, look at item 377.

Percent

A percent can tell you a lot about how significant a quantity is. What if someone told you that the humane society found homes for 6 more puppies this month than last month. Is that a big change? If you were also told that this is a 100% increase over last month, the answer is yes. But if this is a 1% increase over last month, then the increase of 6 puppies is not much of a difference.

Percents can also make it easier to compare quantities. What if you wanted to compare the population of girls at your school to the population of girls at another school. You could say $\frac{3}{5}$ of the students in your school are girls and $\frac{5}{8}$ of the students in the other school are girls. But if you use percents rather than fractions, the comparison would be more obvious: 60% is less than 62.5%.

Understanding Percent

Percent literally means "per hundred."

EXAMPLE 1: If you have 100 marbles and 25 of them are blue, 25% of the marbles are blue.

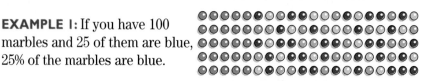

EXAMPLE 2: If you used 50 out of 200 postcard stamps, then you used 25% of your stamps.

EXAMPLE 3: If your class goal was to wash 50 cars in one day, and you really washed 100 cars, you achieved 200% of your goal!

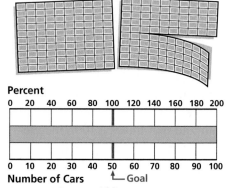

MORE HELP
See 043–044

A percent is like a ratio: It compares a number to 100.
A number followed by a **percent symbol (%)** has a denominator of 100, so it's easy to write as either a fraction or a decimal.

PERCENT	FRACTION	DECIMAL
25%	$\frac{25}{100}$	0.25
2%	$\frac{2}{100}$	0.02
0.5%	$\frac{0.5}{100} = \frac{5}{1000}$	0.005
$33\frac{1}{3}\%$	$\frac{33\frac{1}{3}}{100}$	$0.33\overline{3}$

To get the most out of a percent statement, think of it as an equation.

word equation: $a\%$ of a whole equals part of the whole
algebraic equation: $a\% \cdot b = c$

$$a\% \quad \cdot \quad b \quad = \quad c$$
$$\text{percent} \quad \text{of} \quad \text{whole} \quad \text{part}$$

There are three variables in the algebraic percent equation. If you know any two of those numbers, you can find the third using algebra or using a proportion.

Finding a Percent of a Number

In the percent equation $a\% \cdot b = c$, sometimes you need to find c, the percent of a number.

 To find a percent of a number, you can write and solve an equation.

EXAMPLE 1: The graph shows the 2003 sales tax rates for three states.

Suppose you live in North Dakota and you buy a bicycle that has a price of $175. How much is the sales tax?

2003 SALES TAX RATES

The graph shows that North Dakota has a 5% sales tax. You can use the equation $a\% \cdot$ the whole = the part. You know the percent and the whole. To find the part, the amount of sales tax on $175, you need to find 5% of 175.

❶ REWRITE THE TAX RATE AS A DECIMAL.	❷ MULTIPLY THE PRICE BY THE DECIMAL.
5% = 0.05	0.05 · 175 = 8.75

MORE HELP
See 026

5% of $175 is $8.75. So, you pay $8.75 in sales tax.

 You can also use a proportion to find a percent of a number.

EXAMPLE 2: Your restaurant bill without tax is $31. You decide to leave the waiter a 15% tip. How much should you leave?

❶ WRITE THE PROPORTION.	❷ SOLVE THE PROPORTION.
$\dfrac{\text{part}}{\text{whole}} \longrightarrow \dfrac{15}{100} = \dfrac{t}{31}$	$100t = 465$ $t = 4.65$

So, you should leave $4.65 for the waiter.

Finding What Percent One Number Is of Another

Sometimes you need to find a, the percent in $a\% \cdot b = c$.

 ONE WAY To find what percent one number is of another number, you can write and solve an equation.

MORE HELP
See 238, 434

EXAMPLE 1: A poll at Pierson Middle School asks students if they want a school uniform. The chart shows the results of the poll. What percent of the students do *not* want uniforms?

PIERSON MIDDLE SCHOOL UNIFORM POLL

YES_150
NO_350
?_____125

625 students were polled. 350 students do not want uniforms. Use the equation $a\%$ of the whole = the part. Since you know that 625 is the whole and 350 is the part, you just need to find the percent.

❶ WRITE AN EQUATION.	❷ SOLVE THE EQUATION.
$a\% \cdot b = c$ $\frac{a}{100} \cdot 625 = 350$	$\frac{a}{100} \cdot 625 = 350$ $6.25a = 350$ $a = 350 \div 6.25$ $a = 56$

So, 56% of the students do not want school uniforms.

 ANOTHER WAY You can also write and solve a proportion to find what percent one number is of another.

EXAMPLE 2: What percent of the students surveyed are undecided?

The poll shows that 125 of the students don't know whether they want school uniforms. The sum of the responses is 625.

❶ WRITE A PROPORTION.	❷ SOLVE THE PROPORTION.
$\frac{\text{part}}{\text{whole}} \longrightarrow \frac{p}{100} = \frac{125}{625}$	$\frac{p}{100} = \frac{125}{625}$ $625p = 100 \cdot 125$ $p = \frac{12{,}500}{625}$ $p = 20$

$\frac{p}{100} = \frac{20}{100}$, so 20% of the students are undecided.

Finding the Total When the Percent Is Known

445

In the percent equation, $a\% \cdot b = c$, sometimes you need to find b, the total.

ONE WAY To find the total number when you know a percent of that number, you can write and solve an equation.

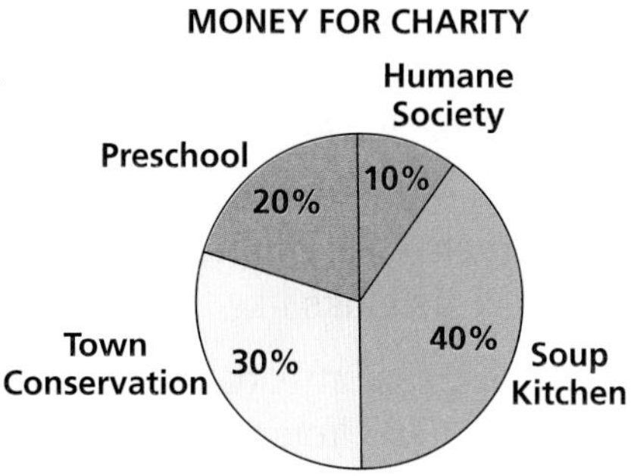

MONEY FOR CHARITY

Humane Society 10%
Preschool 20%
Town Conservation 30%
Soup Kitchen 40%

MORE HELP
See 238, 434

EXAMPLE 1: A class voted on how to donate money they raised for charity. The circle graph shows what they decided. The newspaper reports that the class donated $165 to the town conservation fund. How much money did the class raise?

The graph shows that 30% of the money goes to the town conservation fund. You know that in $a\%$ of the whole = the part, 30 is the percent, and 165 is the part. You're looking for the whole.

❶ WRITE AN EQUATION.	❷ SOLVE THE EQUATION.
$a\% \cdot b = c$ $0.3 \cdot b = 165$	$0.3 \cdot b = 165$ $b = 165 \div 0.3$ $b = 550$

So, the class raised $550 for charity.

ANOTHER WAY You can also write and solve a proportion to find the total when you know the percent.

EXAMPLE 2: 12 is 6% of what number?

❶ WRITE A PROPORTION.	❷ SOLVE THE PROPORTION.
part $\longrightarrow$ $\frac{6}{100} = \frac{12}{w}$ whole $\longrightarrow$	$\frac{6}{100} = \frac{12}{w}$ $6w = 100 \cdot 12$ $w = \frac{1200}{6}$ $w = 200$

So, 12 is 6% of 200.

Percent of Change

One of the most common uses for percent is to show change.

EXAMPLE: 2000 more people attended ball games this year than last. Compare the change in attendance if last year's attendance was 2000 to the change if last year's attendance was 200,000.

If last year's attendance was 2000 people, then a bar graph comparing the two years looks like the first graph.

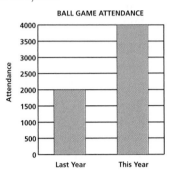

You can see that attendance doubled: It went up 100%! You could also say that this year's attendance is 200% of last year's.

But, if last year's attendance was 200,000 people, then a bar graph comparing the two years looks like the second graph.

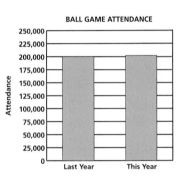

In this case, attendance went up $\frac{2000}{200,000}$, or 1%. You could also say that this year's attendance is 101% of last year's.

So, an increase in attendance of 2000 is a much bigger deal if the increase is from 2000 than if it's from 200,000.

Percent of Increase

Percent of increase compares the increase to the original number.

- A 100% increase is 2 times (double) the original amount.
- A 50% increase is $1\frac{1}{2}$ times the original amount.

EXAMPLE: You earn $6.00 per hour. Your boss tells you that you will get a 10% raise. What will be your new hourly rate?

MORE HELP
See 238

❶ WRITE AND SOLVE AN EQUATION.	❷ ADD THE INCREASE TO THE ORIGINAL AMOUNT.
10% of 6 = c 0.1 · 6 = 0.60	6 + 0.60 = 6.60

Shortcut

You can find the amount of increase faster if you remember that you add the percent of increase to 100%.

❶ ADD THE INCREASE TO 100%.	❷ WRITE AND SOLVE AN EQUATION.
old % + % increase = new % 100% + 10% = 110 %	110% of 6.00 = x 1.1 · 6 = 6.6

Either way, now you will earn $6.60 per hour.

Percent of Decrease

448

Percent of decrease compares the decrease to the original amount.

- A 100% decrease is a total loss.
- A 50% decrease means whatever it was, it's half gone.

> So, you can have a 200% increase, but a 200% decrease makes no sense!

EXAMPLE: Suppose you own a video store. During your first year, you rent about 120 videos per day. In the second year, the number of videos you rent drops by 15%. In the second year, about how many videos do you rent per day?

❶ WRITE AND SOLVE AN EQUATION.	❷ SUBTRACT THE DECREASE FROM THE ORIGINAL AMOUNT.
15% of 120 = c 0.15 · 120 = 18	120 − 18 = 102

Shortcut

You can find the amount of decrease faster by subtracting the percent of decrease from 100%. If you decrease an amount by 15%, you'll end up with 85% of the original amount.

❶ SUBTRACT THE % DECREASE FROM 100%.	❷ WRITE AND SOLVE AN EQUATION.
old % − % decrease = new % 100% − 15% = 85%	85% of 120 = x 0.85 · 120 = 102

Either way, you rented about 102 videos per day in the second year.

449

MATH ALERT Percent of Increase and Decrease

Be careful when you calculate two or more percent changes. For example, if a quantity increases and then decreases by the same percent, you will *not* end up with the original quantity.

MORE HELP
See 443

EXAMPLE 1: A camera store buys cameras from the factory for $130 each. The store normally sells the cameras for 50% more than they paid. If the store has a 50%-off sale, would the sale price be more than, less than, or the same as the price that the store paid?

50% of a larger number is more than 50% of a smaller number.

❶ FIND THE REGULAR PRICE.	❷ FIND THE SALE PRICE.
150% of 130 = regular price	50% of 195 = sale price
1.5 · 130 = 195	0.5 · 195 = 97.5
The regular price is $195.	The sale price is $97.50.

So, the sale price is less than the price the store paid for the camera.

EXAMPLE 2: Is a 10% discount followed by a 20% discount the same as a 30% discount? Check by using a regular price of $100.

REGULAR PRICE: $100 DISCOUNT: 10%, THEN 20% MORE	REGULAR PRICE: $100 DISCOUNT: 30%

Find 10% discount and sale price:
  100% − 10% = 90%
  90% of 100 = 90
Now use 90 as original amount.
Find the 20% discount and sale price:
  100% − 20% = 80%
  80% of 90 = 72
	Find 30% discount and sale price.
	  100% − 30% = 70%
	  70% of 100 = 70

Since 72 ≠ 70, a 10% decrease followed by a 20% decrease is *not* the same as a 30% decrease.

450 **Interest**

Interest is the amount that someone pays to use someone else's money. If you invest money in a savings account, the bank pays interest to you. If you borrow money from the bank, you pay interest on that money to the bank. The amount of money borrowed or invested is called the **principal**. The interest rate is the percent charged or paid during a given period of time.

Simple Interest

There are two different ways of calculating interest: simple and compound. When you pay **simple interest**, you pay interest only on the principal, not on interest that has already been paid.

EXAMPLE: Suppose you borrow $2000 at a simple interest rate of 12% per year. You agree to repay the loan at the end of 2 years. How much interest will you pay? How much will you pay to the bank in all?

To find the amount of interest that you will pay, you can use this formula:

interest (I) = principal (p) · annual rate of interest (r) · time in years (t)

$$I = prt$$
$$= (2000)(0.12)(2)$$
$$= 480$$

> $12\% = 0.12$

You will pay $480 in interest. Since the principal is $2000, you will pay $2000 + $480, or $2480, to the bank.

Compound Interest

Unlike simple interest, **compound interest** is paid on the principal *and* on interest that has already been paid.

 You can calculate compound interest by making a table.

EXAMPLE 1: Suppose you put $500 in a bank account that pays 8% annual interest and is compounded every month. After each 1-month period, the interest is added to the principal and you earn interest on the new total in your account. How much money will you have in the account at the end of 3 months?

> 3 months is three 1-month periods.

> The rate (r) is 8%, or 0.08. Since the time period is 1 month, which is $\frac{1}{12}$ year, $t \approx 0.083$.

PERIOD	PRINCIPAL (p)	INTEREST (I) $(I = prt)$	NEW TOTAL $(p + I)$
1st month	500.00	$(500.00)(0.08)(0.083) \approx 3.32$	503.32
2nd month	503.32	$(503.32)(0.08)(0.083) \approx 3.34$	506.66
3rd month	506.66	$(506.66)(0.08)(0.083) \approx 3.36$	510.02

So, at the end of 3 months, you will have $510.02 in the account.

MORE ▶

MORE HELP
See 207, 238

 You can also calculate compound interest by using a formula.

$$\text{Total Amount} = \text{Original Principal} \times (1 + \tfrac{\text{rate}}{\text{\# yearly compounds}})^{\text{\# yearly compounds} \times \text{years}}$$

$$A = P(1 + \tfrac{r}{n})^{nt}$$

EXAMPLE 2: Suppose you put $900 in a bank account that pays 6% annual interest. After each 3-month period, the interest is added to the principal and you earn interest on the new total in your account. How much money will you have in the account at the end of 1 year?

$$
\begin{aligned}
A &= P(1 + \tfrac{r}{n})^{nt} \\
&= 900(1 + \tfrac{0.06}{4})^{4 \cdot 1} \\
&\approx 955.227
\end{aligned}
$$

Since the account can't have parts of a cent, round the total to $955.23.

453 Credit Cards

When you use credit cards, you may pay compound interest without realizing it. So, your annual effective interest—the interest rate you actually pay for the year—may be greater than the simple annual percentage rate listed on the card. How can that be?

The answer comes from how your finance charges are computed. If you don't pay off your balance in full each month, you pay interest both on the unpaid balance *and* on the finance charges that are applied each day. When you pay interest on interest, interest is compounded. So, although the daily rate listed on the bill is accurate, the interest you pay over a year ends up being greater than the annual rate listed on the bill.

Daily Periodic Rate: the interest rate charged each day on the average daily balance (this is $\frac{1}{365}$ of the annual rate)

Average Daily Balance: the sum of the balance owed on each day of the billing period divided by the total number of days in the billing period. The average daily balance is $0 if all of the previous month's balance was paid.

Finance Charge: the total interest charged this month

Current Annual Percentage Rate: rate × 365 (rounded to the nearest hundredth)

CREDIT CARD STATEMENT

Number of Days This Billing Period	31
*Daily Periodic Rate	0.04288%
*Average Daily Balance	$379
=Finance Charge	$5.04
Current Annual Percentage Rate	15.650%

Computing with Percents Using a Calculator (454

Calculators are very useful when you need to compute with percents. Some calculators have a percent key % that you can use when you work with percents.

EXAMPLE: Find 15% of 420.

Remember to check how your calculator works. On some calculators, the percent *must* be the second factor in the multiplication. Some of these calculators do not require you to press = after using the % key.

Finding Percents Without a Percent Key

455

Even if your calculator doesn't have a percent key, you can still use the calculator to find a percent of a number. Enter the percent as a decimal, then multiply.

MORE HELP
See 026

EXAMPLE 1: Find 35% of 140.

Enter the percent as a decimal: 35% = 0.35

Multiply:

EXAMPLE 2: Find 125% of 75.

Enter the percent as a decimal: 125% = 1.25

Multiply:

Probability and Odds

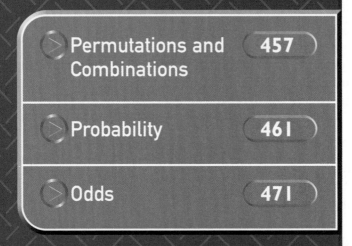

Everyone would like to be able to predict the future. Often, the best we can do is tell how likely something is to happen. When most people say things like "it's a sure thing," or "she's got a 50-50 chance of winning the race," or "odds are, that'll never happen," they're talking about probability and odds. Both probability and odds are ways of telling how likely it is that something will (or won't) happen.

Probability and odds are only useful when all possible outcomes are known, or when you are predicting a likely rate of occurence.

Permutations and Combinations

If you've ever played a board game and needed to toss two number cubes and get a 12 to win, you know it's not very likely. A 7 would be a lot easier. You can tell how much more likely it is to toss a 7 than a 12 by counting the different ways to get 7 and to get 12.

The different ways things can be arranged and grouped are called **permutations** and **combinations**. These are powerful tools in figuring out all the things that can happen in many kinds of probability situations.

458   Permutations

MORE HELP
See 466

A **permutation** is any arrangement of items or events. If you change the order of items or events, then you have another permutation. So, the word *ARE* is a permutation of the word *EAR*. The items are the same (the letters *A*, *E*, and *R*), but the order is different.

ONE WAY You can find all the possible permutations for a set of items by using a **tree diagram**.

EXAMPLE 1: Three friends rent and take turns riding a 2-seat bicycle. How many possible seating arrangements are there?

So, there are 6 possible permutations for seating arrangements.

You can use special notation to show the number of permutations. For the 2-seat bicycle situation,

Write: $_3P_2 = 6$

Say: *The number of permutations of 3 items taken 2 at a time is 6.*

MORE ▶

You can also use multiplication to find all the possible permutations for a set of items.

EXAMPLE 2: There are 6 runners in a race. How many different permutations are possible for the places in which the runners finish?

Once the winner has crossed the finish line, there are only 5 runners left who could be second.

For this situation, you are looking for permutations of 6 runners.

Write: $_6P_6$

MORE HELP
See 057, 459

Say: *permutations of six items taken six at a time*

6 choices for first place
   5 choices left for second place
      4 choices left for third place
         3 choices left for fourth place
            2 choices left for fifth place
               1 choice left for sixth place

$6 \times 5 \times 4 \times 3 \times 2 \times 1 = 720$

There are 720 possible orders in which the runners finish.

When you multiply a whole number by every positive whole number less than itself, you can use **factorial notation**.

Write: $6! = 6 \times 5 \times 4 \times 3 \times 2 \times 1$

Say: *six factorial equals six times five times four times three times two times one*

459 Counting Principle

The **counting principle** states that if a first event can occur in a ways, and a second event can occur in b ways, then the two events can occur together in $a \cdot b$ ways.

EXAMPLE 1: A team shirt comes in 4 colors, and in long or short sleeves. How many choices of shirts are there?

Choices = colors × sleeve lengths
    = 4 × 2
    = 8

So, there are 8 choices of shirts.

EXAMPLE 2: Six people are running in the class elections. The person with the most votes will be President. The person who comes in second will be Vice President. How many different teams of President and Vice President can be elected?

Number of different pairs = Choices for President × Choices left for Vice President

    = 6 × 5

    = 30

30 different pairs can be elected.

There are only 5 choices for Vice President because 1 of the 6 people has to be the President.

Combinations   460

A **combination** is a group of items or events. If you change the order of items or events, you do not change the group, and you do not make a new combination. So, a nickel, a dime, and a quarter is the same combination of coins as a dime, a quarter, and a nickel. Either way, the combination is worth 40¢.

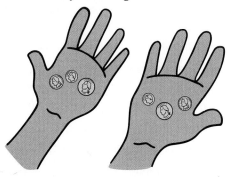

 ONE WAY To find all the possible combinations for a set of items, you can make a list.

EXAMPLE 1: Sheila has 4 different shirts. She wants to pack 2 of the 4 shirts for a trip. How many different combinations of 2 shirts can she pack?

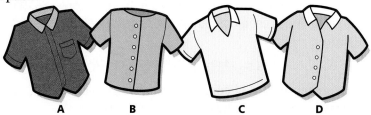

A   B   C   D

MORE ▶

① FIND THE PERMUTATIONS.	② FIND THE COMBINATIONS.
$_4P_2 = 4 \times 3 = 12$ Here are all the possible orders (permutations) Sheila may take the shirts from her drawer:	AB and BA are the same two shirts, so cross off BA. Cross off all the other duplicates.

AB	AC	AD
BA	BC	BD
CA	CB	CD
DA	DB	DC

AB	AC	AD
B̶A̶	BC	BD
C̶A̶	C̶B̶	CD
D̶A̶	D̶B̶	D̶C̶

So, there are 6 different possible combinations of 2 shirts.

You can use special notation to show combinations. For this situation:

Write: $_4C_2 = 6$

Say: *The number of combinations of 4 items taken 2 at a time is 6.*

 You can also compute to find all the possible combinations for a set of items.

EXAMPLE 2: The Sandwich Shop has 6 employees. Only 3 people need to be on duty at any one time. The manager wants to have a different group of people on duty every day for 2 weeks. Is this possible?

You want to know how many combinations of 3 can be made from a group of 6 ($_6C_3$). If this number is greater than or equal to 14, the number of days in 2 weeks, the answer to the question is *yes*.

MORE HELP
See 459

To find the number of possible combinations, start by finding the number of possible permutations.

6 choices for the first employee

  5 choices left for the second employee

    4 choices left for the third employee

$6 \times 5 \times 4 = 120$

Each group of 3 employees can be ordered in 3!, or 6, ways. So, the 120 permutations includes each combination 6 times (once for each possible order).

Number of combinations $= \frac{\text{number of permutations}}{\text{number of different orders}} = \frac{120}{6} = 20$

Since there are more than 14 combinations, it is possible to have a different group of people on duty every day for 2 weeks.

▶ Probability

It's helpful to know if something is likely or unlikely to happen. It's more useful if you can use a number to describe that likelihood. That number expresses **probability**.

Probability will help you decide how often something is likely to happen, but it will never help you to know exactly when that event will happen unless the probability is 0 (it will never happen) or 1 (it will always happen).

How Likely Is an Event?

The probability of an event can be a number from 0 through 1. It can be expressed as a fraction, a decimal, or a percent. If the probability of an event is 0, it is impossible. If an event is certain, it has a probability of 1. The more *unlikely* an event is, the closer its probability is to 0. The more *likely* an event is, the closer its probability is to 1.

PROBABILITY

	less often than not			more often than not	
0	$\frac{1}{4}$		$\frac{1}{2}$	$\frac{3}{4}$	1
0.0	0.25		0.5	0.75	1.0
0%	25%		50%	75%	100%
impossible	unlikely		as likely as unlikely	likely	certain

MORE ▶

EXAMPLE 1: The freezing point of fresh water at sea level is 32°F. When the temperature is 60°F, it is *impossible* for water to freeze. The probability of fresh water at sea level freezing at 60°F is 0.

EXAMPLE 2: The likelihood that 2 people in any group of 13 will have the same birthday is about 20%. Since the probability is closer to 0% than 100%, matching birthdays in a group of 13 is *unlikely* (but not impossible).

EXAMPLE 3: When you roll a cube with one of the digits 1–6 on each side, your chance of the number on top being even is $\frac{3}{6}$, or 0.5. So, getting an even number *is as likely as it is unlikely.*

EXAMPLE 4: The weather forecaster says there's a 75% chance of rain today. This means it's *likely* to rain today. It does not mean it *will* rain today. So, if it doesn't rain, don't say the forecaster was wrong!

EXAMPLE 5: It is *certain* that the sun will rise every day. So, the probability of the sun rising is 100%.

463) Sample Space

To calculate probability, you need to know all the different things that can happen. A **sample space** is a list of all the possible outcomes of an activity.

EXAMPLE: Suppose you spin the spinner. Make a sample space for a spin.

This spinner can land on 12 different regions.

To make the sample space, list all the possible outcomes of the spin.

So the sample space is:

20, 10, 100, spin again, 50, 500, 20, 10, 100, lose turn, 50, 500

Using Tree Diagrams to Find Sample Space

464

It may sometimes be easier to find all possible outcomes in a sample space by drawing a tree diagram and/or making an organized list.

EXAMPLE: An ice cream stand offers two flavors, chocolate and vanilla. You can get either a cup or a cone. You can have rainbow or chocolate sprinkles as a topping. How many possible combinations of flavors, containers, and toppings are there?

Make a tree diagram to show all of the possible combinations (outcomes) in the sample space.

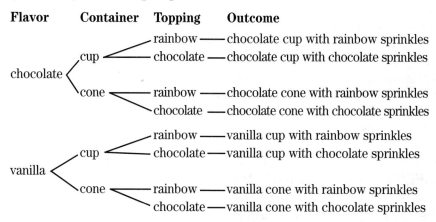

Flavor	Container	Topping	Outcome
chocolate	cup	rainbow	chocolate cup with rainbow sprinkles
		chocolate	chocolate cup with chocolate sprinkles
	cone	rainbow	chocolate cone with rainbow sprinkles
		chocolate	chocolate cone with chocolate sprinkles
vanilla	cup	rainbow	vanilla cup with rainbow sprinkles
		chocolate	vanilla cup with chocolate sprinkles
	cone	rainbow	vanilla cone with rainbow sprinkles
		chocolate	vanilla cone with chocolate sprinkles

So, the sample space contains 8 outcomes.

Probability of an Event

465

Have you ever tried to figure out just how likely it would be to spin a certain number on a spinner? We call *that* number a **favorable outcome**. *All* of the possible numbers are called **possible outcomes**. When you calculate the likelihood of an event, you are finding the probability of that event.

MORE HELP
See 026,
043–044, 425

Write: $P(\text{event}) = \dfrac{\text{number of favorable outcomes}}{\text{number of possible outcomes}}$

Say: *The probability of an event is the ratio of the number of favorable outcomes to the number of possible outcomes.*

MORE ▶

EXAMPLE: Suppose you are playing Concentration and need a 6 to win. These cards are the only ones left and they are face down. What is the probability you will pick a 6?

Each choice of card is equally likely to occur, so:

P(6 card) = $\frac{2}{5}$ ◄────── **number of sixes**
                 ◄────── **number of cards**

So, the probability of picking a 6 is $\frac{2}{5}$, or 0.4, or 40%.

This means it's less likely that you'll pick a 6 than some other card.

---

466 Theoretical and Experimental Probability

When you use a formula to find the probability of an event, you are finding the **theoretical probability**.

Theoretical Probability (event) = $\frac{\text{number of favorable outcomes}}{\text{number of possible outcomes}}$

You can also find the probability of an event by doing an experiment. When you do this, you are finding **experimental probability**.

Experimental Probability (event) = $\frac{\text{number of times favorable outcomes occur}}{\text{number of trials in the experiment}}$

You can use theoretical probability to predict the results of a probability experiment. In general, as the number of attempts in an experiment increases, experimental probability gets closer to theoretical probability.

MORE HELP
See 161, 286, 463–464

EXAMPLE: Suppose you toss a coin:

(a) What is the theoretical probability of the coin landing on heads?

P(heads) = $\frac{\text{number of sides with heads}}{\text{number of sides}}$ = $\frac{1}{2}$

(b) Use the theoretical probability to predict how many times the coin would land on heads if you tossed it 50 times.

You can predict the number of times an outcome will occur by multiplying its probability by the number of attempts.

P (heads) × number of tosses = $\frac{1}{2}$ × 50

$$= 25$$

So, the theoretical probability is that you will toss heads 25 times out of 50.

(c) Suppose you toss a coin 50 times and it lands on heads 29 times. The experimental probability is $\frac{29}{50}$, or 0.58. The theoretical probability is $\frac{1}{2}$, or 0.50. So, the experimental probability is fairly close to the theoretical probability.

Heads	Tails
IIII IIII IIII IIII IIII IIII	IIII IIII IIII IIII IIII IIII
IIII IIII IIII IIII	IIII IIII IIII IIII
IIII IIII IIII	I

467

MATH ALERT Experimental Probability Can Be Deceptive

When a probability experiment has very few attempts or pieces of data, the results can be deceptive. For example, if you rolled a 1–6 number cube three times and rolled a 6 two of the times, the experiment might lead you to say the probability of rolling a 6 would be $\frac{2}{3}$. But you know that you don't actually have a $\frac{2}{3}$ chance of rolling a 6 every time! This experimental probability of $\frac{2}{3}$ would probably drop if you continued to roll the number cube many times.

Probability of Compound Events

468

Suppose you and your brother both enter The Great Raffle! What's the chance of you or your brother winning? Drawing one of your raffle numbers is a **simple event**. Drawing one of your brother's numbers is a simple event. However, drawing one of your *or* your brother's numbers is a **compound event** because it combines at least two simple events. When you calculate the chance that one event *or* another event will occur, you are finding the probability of a compound event.

THE GREAT RAFFLE
GRAND PRIZE: A COMPUTER!
ONLY 500 TICKETS SOLD!
TICKETS ARE $10 00 EACH
DRAWING TO BE HELD NEXT WEEK!

When two events cannot both occur, they are called **mutually exclusive events**. In the situation above, if you and your brother do not share any raffle tickets, the outcomes *you win* and *your brother wins* are mutually exclusive. If two outcomes are mutually exclusive, you can use this formula to find the probability that one or the other will happen:

Probability(A or B) = Probability(A) + Probability(B)

MORE ▶

EXAMPLE: You pay for 3 raffle tickets. Your brother pays for 7 raffle tickets. 500 raffle tickets are sold, and only one winner will be drawn. What is the probability that you *or* your brother will win the raffle?

MORE HELP
See 026, 043,
043–044, 106

These two outcomes are mutually exclusive because you and your brother cannot both win.

$$P(\text{you win } or \text{ your brother wins}) = P(\text{you win}) + P(\text{your brother wins})$$
$$= \tfrac{3}{500} + \tfrac{7}{500}$$
$$= \tfrac{10}{500}$$

So, the probability of you or your brother winning is $\tfrac{10}{500}$, or 0.02, or 2%.

469

Independent and Dependent Events

Sometimes, you want to find the probability that two events will *both* occur. To do that, you should first think about how the events are related.

CASE I When the outcome of one event does not affect the outcome of another event, the two events are **independent**. If two events are independent, you can use this formula to find the probability of both events occurring:

Probability(A and B) = Probability(A) · Probability(B)

EXAMPLE I: Suppose a school poll shows that 16% of the students play soccer and 75% like pasta. Playing soccer does not affect whether a student likes pasta (and vice versa), so these two events are independent. What is the probability that a randomly chosen student plays soccer *and* likes pasta?

MORE HELP
See 026,
043–044

$$P(\text{plays soccer } and \text{ likes pasta}) = P(\text{plays soccer}) \cdot P(\text{likes pasta})$$
$$= 0.16 \cdot 0.75$$
$$= 0.12$$

So, the probability that a randomly chosen student in that school plays soccer and likes pasta is 0.12, or 12%.

CASE 2 When the outcome of one event affects the outcome of another event, the events are **dependent**. If two events are dependent, you can use this formula to find the probability of both events occurring:

> Probability(B given A) means the likelihood that B will happen when A happens.

Probability(A and B) = Probability(A) · Probability(B given A)

EXAMPLE 2: Suppose you are playing a Scrabble® game, and these 8 tiles are left. If you choose two tiles at random, what is the probability you will choose a Q, then another Q?

Since choosing one Q changes the number of tiles and the number of Qs that are left to choose from, the two choices are dependent events.

$$P(Q, \text{then } Q) = P(Q) \cdot P(Q, \text{given } Q)$$

$$\frac{\text{number of Qs}}{\text{number of tiles}} \longrightarrow \frac{2}{8} \cdot \frac{1}{7} \longleftarrow \frac{\text{number of Qs left after the first pick}}{\text{number of tiles left after the first pick}}$$

$$= \frac{1}{28}$$

So, the probability that you choose a Q, then another Q, is $\frac{1}{28}$, 0.0357. . ., or about 3.6%.

Complementary Events

Either there will be tacos on the school lunch menu today, or there won't. These are two mutually exclusive events. They are the only ones that can possibly occur, so they are called **complementary events**. If two events are complementary, the sum of their probabilities is 1.

EXAMPLE: Tell whether each pair of events is complementary:

(a) spinning an odd number or spinning an even number

Because there are no numbers on the spinner that are neither odd nor even, the two events are complementary.

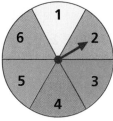

(b) spinning a 4 or spinning a 5

Because there are four other possible events (1, 2, 3, 6), the two events are *not* complementary.

 # Odds

Odds are just another way to express probability. For example, the probability of tossing a coin and having it land heads up is $\frac{1}{2}$ because there are two things that can happen—heads or tails—and heads should happen as often as tails does. But the odds of tossing a coin and having it land heads up are 1 to 1 because, of two things that can happen, 1 is favorable and 1 is unfavorable. The likelihood is the same (one event happens half the time and the other happens the other half of the time), but they're expressed differently.

Computing Odds

MORE HELP
See 188, 425

A ratio involving favorable outcomes and unfavorable outcomes for an event is called odds. Odds can be in favor of an event or against an event.

> So, the odds in favor of and against the same event are reciprocals of each other.

$$\text{Odds(in favor of an event)} = \frac{\text{number of favorable outcomes}}{\text{number of unfavorable outcomes}}$$

$$\text{Odds(against an event)} = \frac{\text{number of unfavorable outcomes}}{\text{number of favorable outcomes}}$$

EXAMPLE 1: It is the bottom of the ninth inning. Any hit or walk will win the game. The batter gets a hit or walk 1 out of every 3 times she is at bat. Give the odds in favor of the game being won in that time at bat.

Odds (in favor of a win during that at-bat)

$$= \frac{\text{number of favorable outcomes}}{\text{number of unfavorable outcomes}}$$

$$= \frac{1}{2}$$

> For each 3 at-bats, there is 1 hit or walk. So, there are 2 at-bats that are not hits or walks.

The odds in favor of winning the game in that at-bat are $\frac{1}{2}$, 1:2, or 1 to 2.

EXAMPLE 2: At a carnival, an average of 3 people in 10 win a prize at a ring toss. Give the odds *against* winning a prize.

$$\text{Odds(against winning)} = \frac{\text{number of unfavorable outcomes}}{\text{number of favorable outcomes}}$$

$$= \frac{7}{3}$$

> Out of each 10 people, there are 7 who do not win. There are 3 people who win.

The odds against winning a prize are $\frac{7}{3}$, 7:3, or 7 to 3.

Almanac 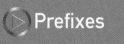 473

This almanac includes very useful tables and lists. It also has tips on how to solve problems, take notes in class, and take tests.

Prefixes

Prefixes are word beginnings that combine with words or suffixes to add consistent meaning.

Prefix	Definition	Example
bi-	two	biweekly: every two weeks
centi-, cent-	one hundredth	centimeter: a unit of length equal to one hundredth of a meter
co-	joint, jointly, together	coplanar: lying in the same plane
dec-, deca-, deka-	ten	decahedron: polyhedron with ten faces
deci-	one tenth	deciliter: one tenth of a liter
di-	two, twice, double	dihedral: two sided
dodeca-	twelve	dodecagon: polygon with 12 sides
equi-	equal, equally	equiangular: having all angles equal
giga-	one billion	gigabyte: one billion bytes
hecto-	100	hectometer: metric unit of length equal to 100 meters
hemi-	half	hemisphere: a half of a sphere
in-	not or without	inequality: not equal $6 \neq 7$ or $6 < 7$
inter-	between, mutual	intersecting: lines or planes that cross or meet
iso-, is-	equal	isosceles triangle: a triangle that has at least two congruent angles
kilo-	1000	kilogram: 1000 grams
mid-	middle	midpoint: point on a line segment that cuts it into two congruent segments

Prefix	Definition	Example
milli-	one thousandth	millimeter: one thousandth of a meter
nona-	ninth, nine	nonagon: polygon with nine sides
octa-, octo-, oct-	eight	octagon: polygon with eight sides
para-, par-	beside, alongside	parallel: being an equal distance apart at every point
penta-, pent-	five	pentagon: polygon with five sides
per-	for each	percent: a ratio that compares a number to 100
poly-	many	polyhedron: a many-sided 3-dimensional figure
quad-	four	quadrants: the four sections of a coordinate plane that are separated by the x- and y-axes
semi-	half	semiannually: happening once every half year
septi-, sept-	seven	septennial: occurring every seven years
sexa-, sex-	six	sexcentenary: pertaining to a six-hundred-year period
tri-	three	triangle: polygon with three sides

Suffixes

Suffixes are word endings that combine with prefixes or words to add consistent meaning.

Suffix	Definition	Examples
-centenary	of or pertaining to a 100-year period	tercentenary: of or pertaining to 300 years
-gon	figure having a specified number of interior angles	polygon: many-sided figure hexagon: 6-sided figure
-hedral	surfaces or faces of a given number	dihedral: formed by two plane faces
-hedron	figure having a given number of faces or surfaces	polyhedron: a solid where faces are polygons heptahedron: polyhedron with seven faces
-lateral	of, at, or relating to sides	equilateral: having all sides equal
-metry	science or process of measuring	geometry: mathematics of properties, measurement, and relationships of points, lines, angles, surfaces, and solids
-sect	cut or divide	bisect: cut or divide into two equal parts

Problem Solving

In general, problems are not supposed to be easy. So do what good mathematicians do. Keep on trying and think about strategies to help solve the problem. If what you try first doesn't work, don't worry, just look at what you've done and make another try. This happens all the time to the best problem solvers.

Guidelines for Solving Word Problems

1. **Read** the problem several times until it makes sense.
2. **Plan**. Think of a strategy that you can try.
3. **Solve**. Try your strategy. Don't give up. Keep trying different things. If one idea or strategy doesn't work, try another.
4. **Check** over what you have done to make sure it makes sense.

If you do not understand the problem, try these ideas:

- Read the problem again slowly.
- Picture in your mind what's happening in the problem. Study any illustrations, charts, or diagrams that are included in the problem.
- Take notes or draw pictures to help.
- Look up any words or symbols you don't know.

If you've tried a few things and you feel stuck, do something else for a little while, then come back to the problem.

After you find an answer, look back and ask yourself: Does my answer make sense? Does it really answer the problem? Is my computation correct? Can I do the problem another way to check and see if I get the same answer? Is my answer reasonable?

Problem-Solving Strategies

To solve a problem, try the following problem-solving strategies.

Guess, Check, and Revise

If you are putting a puzzle together, you might guess which pieces fit together and then check and revise until you find pieces that match. Guess, Check, and Revise can help you solve math problems.

PROBLEM

Ms. Lewis bought two types of books. The nature books cost $6.50 each and the novels cost $4.25 each. She spent a total of $38.50, but her receipt does not list each book separately. How many of each type of book did Ms. Lewis buy if she bought 8 books?

SOLUTION

Step 1: Understand the problem and think about a strategy.

You know:

■ the cost of each type of book ($6.50 and $4.25);
■ the total number of books (8);
■ the total cost ($38.50).

It may be hard to find the answer directly, but you do have enough information to tell whether an answer is correct. So, you can make a guess. If it's right, great. If it's not right, you can make a better guess.

Step 2: Try using the strategy.

GUESS (SUM MUST BE 8)	CHECK (TOTAL MUST BE $38.50)	EVALUATE AND REVISE
nature: 4 novels: 4 (4 + 4 = 8)	4(6.50) + 4(4.25) = 26.00 + 17.00 = 43	Too high! Make a guess that lowers the total.
nature: 3 novels: 5 (3 + 5 = 8)	3(6.50) + 5(4.25) = 19.50 + 21.25 = 40.75	You're going in the right direction.
nature: 2 novels: 6 (2 + 6 = 8)	2(6.50) + 6(4.25) = 13.00 + 25.50 = 38.50	Just right!

Step 3: Check your answer.

■ Is the total cost $38.50? Yes, 2($6.50) + 6($4.25) = $38.50.
■ Is the total number of books 8? Yes, 2 + 6 = 8 books.
■ Does the answer make sense? Yes, it does.

ANSWER

Ms. Lewis bought 2 nature books and 6 novels.

Work Backward

Often, you know how to get from one place (Point A) to another (Point B), such as from your home to school. To go back from Point B to Point A, or from school back home, you follow the same directions backward. You know the end and you know the steps in between. You want to find the beginning. You may use this strategy, Work Backward, to solve math problems.

PROBLEM

Natalie and 5 of her friends went to an ice cream shop. Each person ordered a single-scoop cone with sprinkles. Their bill for $8.70 included $0.36 sales tax. How much does one single-scoop cone with sprinkles cost before tax?

SOLUTION

Step 1: Understand the problem and think about a strategy.

You know:
- the final cost ($8.70);
- the amount of tax ($0.36).

You can use this information to work backward and find the total cost of the 6 cones. Then you can *keep* working backward to find the cost of one cone.

Step 2: Try using the strategy.

FINAL COST: **TAX:** **COST BEFORE TAX:**	8.70 − 0.36 8.34	Since the tax is added to the total cost of the 6 cones, subtract the tax from the total for the cost before tax.
COST OF EACH CONE:	1.39 6)8.34	There are 6 people: Natalie plus her 5 friends. So, to find the cost of one cone, divide the cost before tax by 6.

Step 3: Check your answer.

Cost of one single-scoop cone: 1.39
Multiply by total number of cones: ×   6
     8.34
Add the tax: + 0.36
Total Cost: 8.70

ANSWER

One single-scoop cone with sprinkles costs $1.39 plus tax.

Make a Table or an Organized List

If you are planning a big party you might want to make an organized list or use a table to keep track of the people, events, and prizes. This strategy can help you keep track when you're dealing with math problem-solving situations, too.

PROBLEM

There are 8 players in a tennis tournament. Each player must play one game with every other player. How many games will be played?

SOLUTION

Step 1: Understand the problem and think about a strategy.

You know:

- Players must play games in pairs.
- If you start with only 2 players, only 1 game is played.

Start with small numbers and look for a pattern.

Step 2: Try using the strategy.

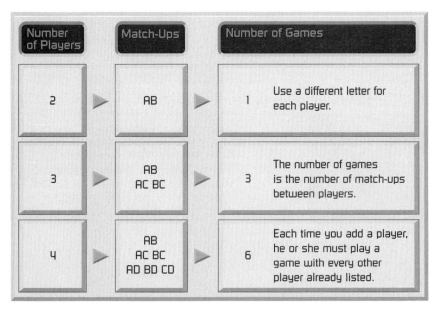

Number of Players	Match-Ups	Number of Games	
2	AB	1	Use a different letter for each player.
3	AB AC BC	3	The number of games is the number of match-ups between players.
4	AB AC BC AD BD CD	6	Each time you add a player, he or she must play a game with every other player already listed.

A pattern is beginning to appear. Each time a player is added, you take the previous total and add to it the number of games the new player must play.

Use the pattern to make and complete a table.

MORE HELP
See 481, 484

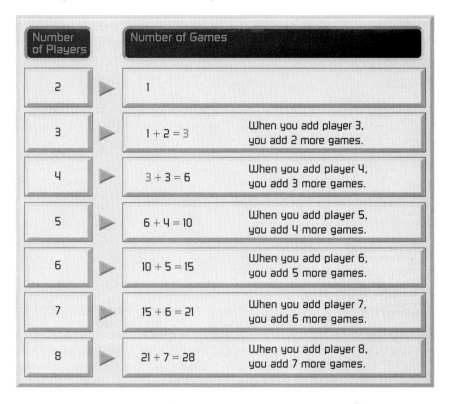

Number of Players	Number of Games	
2	1	
3	1 + 2 = 3	When you add player 3, you add 2 more games.
4	3 + 3 = 6	When you add player 4, you add 3 more games.
5	6 + 4 = 10	When you add player 5, you add 4 more games.
6	10 + 5 = 15	When you add player 6, you add 5 more games.
7	15 + 6 = 21	When you add player 7, you add 6 more games.
8	21 + 7 = 28	When you add player 8, you add 7 more games.

Step 3: Check your answer. Make sure your pattern works.

ANSWER
In the tennis tournament, 28 games will be played by 8 players.

Use Simpler Numbers

To solve a difficult math problem, you can start with a simpler problem with easier numbers to understand how to solve the more difficult problem.

PROBLEM

The Trailblazer Store buys hiking boots wholesale, then marks them up 67%. The hiking boots are now on sale for 33% off. If the wholesale price for hiking boots was $58, what is the sale price?

SOLUTION

Step 1: Understand the problem and think about a strategy.

It might be easier to find how simpler percents relate to an easier amount to figure out how to solve the problem. Try 70%, 30%, and $10.

Step 2: Try using the strategy.

REPHRASE THE QUESTION WITH SIMPLER NUMBERS.	A store marks up boots 70%. The boots are on sale for 30% off. The wholesale price is $10. What is the sale price?
FIND THE ORIGINAL PRICE OF THE BOOTS.	70% of 10 = $0.70 \times 10 = 7$ $10 + 7 = 17$ **Add the markup to the wholesale amount to find the original price.**
FIND THE DISCOUNT AND SALE PRICE.	30% of 17 = $0.30 \times 17 = 5.10$ $17 - 5.10 = 11.90$ **The sale price is the difference between the original price and the discount.**

Now that you've used easy numbers to plan a solution, you can follow the same steps with the real numbers and a calculator.

Original price:
$$67\% \text{ of } 58 =$$
$$0.67 \times 58 = 38.86$$
$$58 + 38.86 = 96.86$$

When you work with approximate numbers, use ≈ instead of =.

Sale price:
$$33\% \text{ of } 96.86 =$$
$$0.33 \times 96.86 \approx 31.96$$
$$96.86 - 31.96 \approx 64.90$$

Step 3: Check your answer.

Is the answer reasonable? Is your computation correct?
Did you match up the percents of each number correctly?

ANSWER

$64.90 is the sale price of the hiking boots.

Write an Equation

You may already be familiar with writing equations in algebra and geometry exercises. But you can also use this as a strategy to solve other kinds of problems.

PROBLEM

Eva walks the tightrope in a carnival show. The tightrope is 14 feet off the ground. The angle between the support wire and the ground is 45°. What is the length of the support wire to the nearest foot?

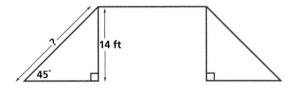

SOLUTION

Step 1: Understand the problem and think about a strategy.

- The triangle is a right triangle. You need to find the length of the hypotenuse.
- You can find the ratio of the opposite side to the hypotenuse of a right triangle in the trig tables—it is the sine ratio.

So, you can write an equation with the sine ratio and solve for the length of the hypotenuse.

MORE HELP
See 358, 359

Step 2: Try using the strategy.

WRITE AN EQUATION.	$\sin 45° = \dfrac{\text{opposite}}{\text{hypotenuse}}$	
SUBSTITUTE INFORMATION YOU KNOW OR CAN FIND.	$0.7071 \approx \dfrac{14}{x}$	**Look up the sine of 45° in the tables in item 541. Remember that this is a rounded number, so you need to use $\approx$ instead of $=$.**
SOLVE THE EQUATION.	$x \approx 19.8$	

Step 3: Check your answer.

Make sure that you correctly wrote and solved the equation.

ANSWER

To the nearest foot, the length of the support wire is 20 feet.

Make a Model or a Diagram

If you are planning to build a bookcase or picture frame, you might first draw a diagram to decide what materials you need or how you will organize the design. This strategy is also useful in solving math problems.

PROBLEM

Jenny has a photograph that is 8 inches long by 6 inches wide. She wants to make a frame for the photo. But she wants to put a mat between the photo and the frame. She wants the mat to be 2 inches wide on each side of the photo. How many inches of frame will Jenny need to construct?

SOLUTION

Step 1: Understand the problem and think about a strategy.

To understand how the information in the problem can be used to solve the problem, you can draw and label a diagram.

Step 2: Try using the strategy.

Draw and label a diagram.

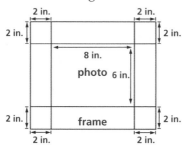

The dimensions of the larger rectangle are found by adding 2 inches to the length and the width on each side of the smaller rectangle.

$$l = 8 + 2 + 2 = \textbf{12 in.}$$
$$w = 6 + 2 + 2 = \textbf{10 in.}$$

Find the perimeter: $P = 2l + 2w = 2(12) + 2(10) = 44$

Step 3: Check your answer.

Make sure that you correctly drew and labeled the diagram.

ANSWER

Jenny needs 44 inches of frame.

Look for Patterns

Your dog often digs up the neighbor's flowers. If you notice that he only does this when you let him out before you feed him, you're noticing a pattern in his behavior. You can use the pattern to solve the problem: Feed him before you let him out! Looking for patterns can be a powerful tool in math problem solving, too.

PROBLEM

This 10 × 10 grid is made up of 100 individual squares. How many squares of *any size* are there in the 10 × 10 grid?

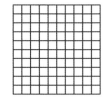

SOLUTION

Step 1: Understand the problem and think about a strategy.

To solve this problem, try to find a pattern. Start with a smaller grid and then work up to larger grids to try to find the pattern.

Step 2: Use the strategy to solve the problem.

Process	Diagram	Result
Start with a 1 × 1 grid.		A 1 × 1 grid has 1 square.
Try a 2 × 2 grid.		There are 5 squares in this grid: 1 × 1 squares: 4 2 × 2 squares: 1
Next try a 3 × 3 grid.		There are 14 squares in this grid: 1 × 1 squares: 9 2 × 2 squares: 4 3 × 3 squares: 1 **The number of squares in the grid seems to be the sum of consecutive squares!** $1^2 + 2^2 + 3^2 = 14$

Check your pattern on the next grid:

4 × 4 grid:

There are 30 squares in this grid:
1×1 squares: 16
2×2 squares: 9
3×3 squares: 4
4×4 squares: 1
$30 = 1^2 + 2^2 + 3^2 + 4^2$

Your pattern seems to be working. Use it to solve the problem.
$1^2 + 2^2 + 3^2 + 4^2 + 5^2 + 6^2 + 7^2 + 8^2 + 9^2 + 10^2 = 385$

Step 3: Check your answer.

Make sure you used the correct pattern. Check your computation.

ANSWER

There are 385 squares of any size in a 10 × 10 grid.

Make a Graph

You might make a circle graph to help you visualize your budget. You can also make other types of graphs to solve math problems.

PROBLEM

Tina has two different job offers to sell cookies. Sugarsnaps will pay her $30 at the end of her first month plus $0.75 for each box of cookies that she sells. Chips will pay her $15 at the end of her first month plus $1.00 for each box of cookies that she sells. How many boxes of cookies will Tina have to sell to earn the same amount from both jobs?

SOLUTION

Step 1: Understand the problem and think about a strategy.

You can make a graph to show how cookie sales will affect Tina's earnings. Use the same grid to plot points for each company.

Step 2: Try using the strategy.

Plot a few points for each company in ordered pairs of (boxes sold, earnings):

Sugarsnaps: (5, 33.75), (10, 37.50), (15, 41.25)

Chips: (5, 20), (10, 25), (15, 30)

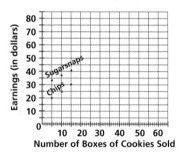

Notice that each set of points can be connected in a straight line. Draw the lines.

The lines intersect at the point (60, 75).

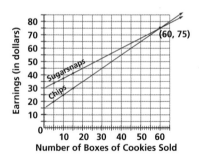

Tina will make more money at Sugarsnaps until she sells 60 boxes of cookies.

Step 3: Check your answer.

Look over your graph. Be sure you have plotted your points accurately.

ANSWER

Tina will earn $75 from both jobs when she sells 60 boxes of cookies.

Problem-Solving Skills

The following problem-solving skills can be used with any strategy.

Take Notes

You can take notes to keep track of what you spend shopping. This skill can also work for solving math problems.

PROBLEM

Ms. Wong opened a bank account with $500 at the beginning of the year. Each week she deposited $25 into the account. Each month she withdrew $45 from the account. She also made three withdrawals of $60. By the end of the year, interest payments of $35.76 had been added. What was Ms. Wong's account balance at the end of the year?

SOLUTION

Taking notes will help you organize the problem into parts that will be easier to solve. You need to find all deposits, interest payments, and withdrawals that Ms. Wong made for a year.

ORGANIZE YOUR NOTES BY RECORDING AMOUNTS PUT IN SEPARATELY FROM AMOUNTS TAKEN OUT OF THE ACCOUNT.	**Amounts put in:** To start: $500.00 52 deposits: $25.00 Interest: $35.76 **Amounts taken out:** 12 withdrawals: $45 3 withdrawals: $60	**Ms. Wong deposited $25 into her account every week for one year. (1 year = 52 weeks)** **Ms. Wong withdrew $45 every month for a year. (1 year = 12 months)**
FIND THE TOTAL OF THE MONEY ADDED TO THE ACCOUNT.	$ 500.00 1300.00 ‑‑‑‑‑‑‑‑‑ **52 × $25** + 35.76 $1835.76	
FIND THE TOTAL OF THE MONEY TAKEN FROM THE ACCOUNT.	$540 ‑‑‑‑‑‑‑‑‑ **12 × $45** + 180 ‑‑‑‑‑‑‑‑‑ **3 × $60** $720	
FIND THE DIFFERENCE.	$1835.76 − 720.00 $1115.76	

ANSWER

At the end of the year Ms. Wong had $1115.76 in her account.

Make a Plan

Suppose each of your teachers gives you a homework assignment. Where do you begin? If you make a plan for completing each assignment, the work will be a lot easier. Making a plan is also a good math problem-solving skill.

PROBLEM

A dance company performed 5 times last week at a hall that seats 12,000 people. Two performances were sold out. The others missed selling out by 540 tickets, 850 tickets, and 150 tickets. What was the average number of people at each performance?

SOLUTION

In this problem, you must find the average of a set of numbers. If you take the time to make a plan you can simplify the problem. One plan could be to find the average number of empty seats and then subtract from the total. This will give you the average number of people at each performance.

FIND THE NUMBER OF EMPTY SEATS AT EACH PERFORMANCE.	0, 0, 540, 850, and 150	**Because two of the performances were sold out, they had zero empty seats.**
FIND THE AVERAGE NUMBER OF EMPTY SEATS FOR THE 5 PERFORMANCES.	$(0 + 0 + 540 + 850 + 150) \div 5 = 308$	
SUBTRACT TO FIND THE AVERAGE NUMBER OF PEOPLE AT EACH PERFORMANCE.	$12,000 - 308 = 11,692$	**The average number of people at each performance is the difference between the capacity of the hall and the average number of empty seats.**

ANSWER

The average number of people at each performance was 11,692.

Ignore Unneeded Information

Have you ever read a magazine or newspaper article that gives you more details than you thought were necessary? Sometimes you have to read carefully to find the information that most interests you. This skill can also be applied to math problem solving.

PROBLEM

Carl likes to eat 3 peanut butter and banana sandwiches 5 days a week, but he needs to watch his protein intake. He uses 1 tablespoon of peanut butter, 1 medium banana, and 1 slice of whole grain bread per sandwich. How many grams of protein does one sandwich contain?

FOOD	PORTION	GRAMS OF PROTEIN
Banana	1 medium	1.3
Beans, kidney	$\frac{1}{2}$ c cooked	7.2
Bread, whole grain	1 slice	2.3
Broccoli	$\frac{1}{2}$ c	2.4
Cheese, American	1 slice	6.6
Oatmeal	1 c cooked	4.8
Peanut butter	1 T	4.0
Rice, brown	1 c cooked	4.9
Soybeans	1 c cooked	9.9
Spaghetti	$\frac{1}{2}$ c cooked	6.5

SOLUTION

You need to know how many:
- grams of protein are in 1 T peanut butter (4.0);
- grams of protein are in 1 medium banana (1.3);
- grams of protein are in 1 slice of whole grain bread (2.3).

You can ignore:
- the fact that Carl eats 3 sandwiches at a time;
- the fact that Carl eats these 5 days a week;
- the extra information in the table.

ANSWER

One sandwich contains $4.0 + 1.3 + 2.3 = 7.6$ grams of protein.

Find Needed Information

Have you ever been curious about something, such as the habitat of a favorite animal, and tried to find information about the subject? This skill can come in handy when you solve math problems.

PROBLEM

Mrs. Santiago believes these paper towels are equally good. Which paper towels are a better value?

SOLUTION

Not all problems have enough information to solve the problem. You cannot find the better value if you do not know the number of sheets on a roll of E-Z Clean paper towels.

> **QUESTIONS THAT YOU CAN ASK YOURSELF TO HELP FIND NEEDED INFORMATION INCLUDE:**
>
> What information could help solve the problem?
> Could I look up the information?
> Could I ask someone?
> Could I take a measurement?
> Can I use an estimate?

In this case, the information you need is hidden in the advertisement. One roll of E-Z Clean towels has 5 dozen sheets. You must compute to make that useful.

Think: 1 dozen   = 12 sheets,
so 5 dozen = 5 × 12, or 60 sheets

E-Z Clean: $1.23 ÷ 60   ≈ $0.02 per sheet
Wipeaway: $1.39 ÷ 100   ≈ $0.01 per sheet

ANSWER

Wipeaway paper towels are the better value.

Use Math Sense

Sometimes you may be involved in situations where you do not exactly know what the outcome will be, but you use your common sense to make a decision. In a similar way, you can use math sense to help solve math problems.

PROBLEM

It is 10 miles from Anderson Township to Bailey City. It is 5 miles from Bailey City to Carson Crossing. What can you tell about how far it is from Anderson Township to Carson Crossing?

SOLUTION

Let A stand for Anderson Township, B stand for Bailey City, and C stand for Carson Crossing.

MORE HELP
See 350

You know:

■ the distance from A to B
■ the distance from B to C

You don't know:

■ the distance from A to C
■ the direction from A to B
■ the direction from A to C

Use your math sense:
■ If A, B, C are in a straight line, then they can be arranged like this:

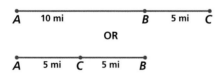

So, A could be 15 miles from C or A could be 5 miles from C.

■ If A, B, C are not in a straight line, they can be connected by the sides of a triangle:

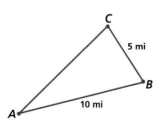

You know that the sum of the lengths of any two sides of a triangle must be greater than the length of the third side. So, you can say that the distance from A to C may be more than 5 but less than 15 miles.

ANSWER

The distance from Anderson Township to Carson Corners can be anywhere from 5 to 15 miles.

Logical Reasoning

Have you ever had to use your reasoning abilities to solve a mystery?
You can use this skill to solve math problems as well.

PROBLEM

Alex, Casey, Gina, and Jonah are four friends with pets. One friend has
a dog, one a cat, one a horse, and one a turtle. Gina is allergic to cats.
Alex has the largest pet. Casey does not have a turtle or a cat. What is
each friend's pet?

SOLUTION

To solve this problem, look at the clues and use logical reasoning to
figure out the clues. Read the clues carefully and keep track of what
you find in a table. As you figure out each clue, cross out the rest of
the boxes in that row and column.

	DOG	CAT	HORSE	TURTLE
ALEX	X	X	Alex has the largest pet, so it must be the horse.	X
CASEY	Since Alex has a horse and Casey doesn't have a turtle or a cat, he must have a dog.	X	X	X
GINA	X	X	X	Gina must have the turtle since she is allergic to cats and the horse and dog are taken.
JONAH	X	Since all the other pets are taken, Jonah must have the cat.	X	X

ANSWER

Alex has a horse, Casey has a dog, Gina has a turtle, and Jonah has a cat.

More Than One Answer

Have you ever bought soda from a machine that required exact change? You can find exact change for most amounts in more than one way—75¢ could be 3 quarters or 7 dimes and a nickel, or . . . . In a similar way, there may be more than one answer to a math problem.

PROBLEM

Jeremy says that he scored 6 baskets in a basketball game. He is also sure that he scored at least two 1-point baskets. Karen says that Jeremy scored 10 points. Ralph says that Jeremy scored 9 points. Who is right? Explain your solution.

SOLUTION

You know:
- Each basket in basketball scores 1, 2, or 3 points.
- At least two of the baskets were 1-pointers.

You don't know:
- What the value of the other 4 baskets was.

Karen's solution:
Suppose all of the remaining baskets were 2-point baskets.

So, Karen could be right.

$4 \times 2 = 8$

$1 + 1 + 8 = 10$

the two 1-point baskets Jeremy remembers

Ralph's solution:
Suppose one basket is a 3-point basket, one is a 2-point basket, and the other two are 1-point baskets.

So, Ralph could be right.

$1 + 1 + 3 + 2 + 1 + 1 = 9$

the two 1-point baskets Jeremy remembers

ANSWER

Both solutions could be correct. In fact, other solutions are possible, too.

Use More Than One Strategy to Solve

If you are painting a fence in your yard, there are many ways to go about it. You may choose from different materials, decide on a variety of places to start working, and even use different types of strokes to paint with. There is more than one way to plan for, execute, and finish the job. There may often be more than one way to solve a problem, too.

MORE HELP
See 478, 480, 492

PROBLEM

Two friends were born 61 days apart. They were born in two consecutive months. Which 2 months?

SOLUTION

Think—if they were born 61 days apart, the birthday of the first, plus 61, would give you the birthday of the second. So, you need at *least* 62 days in the 2 months. There are several ways that you could solve this problem. You should try the one that seems the easiest to you. If you are unsuccessful, try another way to solve the problem. In this case, you can use logical reasoning, you can make a list of the months and the number of days in each month, or you can use Guess, Check, and Revise.

METHOD	SOLUTION
Use logical reasoning.	In a month with 31 days, the last day is 30 days after the first one. So, find 2 consecutive months with 31 days in each month.
Make a list of the months and the number of days in each month.	Month Days January 31 February 28 (29) March 31 April 30 May 31 June 30 July 31 August 31 September 30 October 31 November 30 December 31 **Find a sum of 62: There are 62 days in July and August and in December and January.**
Use Guess, Check, and Revise.	Pick a month and count 61 days from the first of that month. If your first choice doesn't work, try another month.

ANSWER

The two friends could have been born in July and August or December and January.

Study Tips

Taking Notes and Keeping a Journal

Think how helpful notes can be to you. Notes should help you remember what you learned in class. They should also serve as a guide when you try exercises on your own. A math journal is a good place to record examples that you think are especially helpful as well as fun facts about mathematics. Write about new vocabulary, use symbols with examples, and draw diagrams or illustrations. Include descriptions of how mathematics is used in the world around you.

Wherever you take notes, have a good set of tools with you: a pencil or two with good erasers, a highlighter, and plenty of lined paper.

Why Take Notes?

The best reason to take notes is that you will forget a great deal of what the teacher or your classmates said after class is over. After several days, you will forget even more. Note-taking improves your understanding of new topics because it makes you listen carefully and focus on the key details.

498

How to Take Notes

Math notes can be written on cards that you keep in an envelope. This can be punched to hang on a ring in your loose-leaf binder. Or they can be written in a notebook. Date your notes so that you will know the order in which topics were introduced, studied, or reviewed in class.

Your notes can take different forms. They can be in outline form or paragraph form. They can be diagrams or concept maps.

499

Evaluating Your Notes

If your notes are hard to read or they're not complete, they won't be much use when you study for tests. So, if one way of taking notes isn't as helpful as you'd like it to be, try something new.

- If writing in paragraphs doesn't work, write in outline form instead.
- If you can't find what you need in your notes because they are too brief, try to fill in some of the details.
- If you have too many details, concentrate on only the most important points, or use a highlighter on those points.

500

Guidelines for Improving Note-Taking Skills

- **Be attentive.** Listen carefully as your teacher explains how to solve a problem or an equation or how to use a procedure. Carefully read explanations in your textbook or this handbook. Write down parts of the explanation that seem to particularly help you understand the problem and its solution.

- **Be concise.** Remember, taking good notes does not mean writing down everything the teacher says. Write only things that help you understand how to solve problems. Make sure you use words, not just symbols, to explain steps as you work through new problems. Use simple illustrations to clarify problems if you can.

- **Be organized.** Number all items presented in a list or a time order. Highlight items that you do not understand so that you can look them up or ask about them later. Review your notes within one day. Try to review all of your notes once a week.

Listening Skills
501

When the teacher works through the problem before your eyes, it all seems so easy. But, do you really understand the problem? It is important to try to listen as actively as possible. Try similar problems on your own as soon as possible.

Listen attentively. Think about what the teacher is saying and how the problem is being solved. Ask a question if you are uncertain about a particular step or part of a solution. By listening attentively, you will also be ready to respond if you are called upon to answer a question or solve a part of a problem.

Working Together
502

Learning to work together in a group is an important skill. Whether the project is with school, community, or family, the group that is able to work together will have good results. To make your group more effective, practice these good work habits.

■ **Cooperation**
The only way a group can cooperate and work together successfully is to use common courtesy and share a common goal. Everyone in the group should take part in the project and no one should be left out. Compliment and support group members. Practice disagreeing without putting someone down. For example, if you think someone's computation is wrong, you could say something like "Let's check that on a calculator," instead of "No way, you're definitely wrong!"

■ **Responsibility**
Success is learning and reaching the goals of the group. So, you need to be responsible for yourself and for the whole group. Do your assigned tasks carefully and help others do theirs.

■ **Listening**
Listen to group members as they explain the methods they used to solve a problem. For many problems there are alternate solutions, and you can learn a lot by listening to others explain their thinking.

MORE ▶

■ **Encouragement**

Offer and ask for help. Give words of encouragement and credit a job well done or a good suggestion. Persons in the group who feel their efforts are appreciated will contribute more and feel better about their contributions. Remember to be courteous.

■ **Decision Making**

The group often must decide what the project will be and when, where, and how to do it. Be sure to state your points clearly. But also be willing to follow a different but equally good group plan. Work together to delegate responsibility.

■ **Creativity**

Apply what you already know to learn new concepts, but be open-minded about new approaches and strategies. Look for rules, patterns, and strategies. Explore and make sense of new ideas as you work together to try to make new connections.

503) Managing Your Time

If you can't seem to get things done on time (or at all), you might want to practice time management. This will help you organize both your study time and your free time more efficiently since you should be spending less time on procrastination!

■ **Keep a Weekly Schedule**

A weekly planner helps you organize your assignments and plan for time to complete them. It allows you to plan ahead and prepare for exams, projects, or assignments. It allows you time to ask your teacher to explain things that you do not understand. Keep this schedule in your notebook or in your math journal.

	homework	tests
Mon.	PAGE 85 EX. 10-16	REVIEW NOTES
Tues.	PAGE 88 EX. 23-29	STUDY SESSION
Wed.	PAGE 92 EX. 15-28	REVIEW NOTES
Thur.	PAGE 96 EX. 12-20	STUDY FOR TEST!
Fri.		GEOMETRY TEST!

■ **Make a Daily List**

Write down things you need to do today and must do tomorrow. Number them in order of importance. Hang the list in a place where it is easy to check. Or, keep it in a special section of your math journal. Check off items as you complete them.

■ **Have a Homework Schedule**

Set aside a specific time for doing homework assignments. Allow yourself short breaks between each assignment. Do not make any break longer than 5 minutes, so you can finish your homework accurately and quickly.

■ **Set Goals**

Set realistic goals and reward yourself for completing tasks that you set for yourself. Do not be too hard on yourself. Try to learn from goals or tasks that you don't quite achieve. Reward yourself for reaching key goals.

■ **Get It Done and Turn It in on Time**

Go over all the directions your teacher has given you for completing an assignment. Pick an easy thing to do first, just to get started. Read the directions in your textbook carefully if it is being used for the assignment. Check your notes and your textbook to make sure that you know how to accurately complete an assignment. Keep a list of things you need to check on or ask your teacher about.

Keep completed assignments someplace where you can't possibly forget to take them to school:

- on the floor by the door;
- in the front pocket of your book bag;
- in a pouch on your bike;
- with your lunch or lunch money.

Using a Computer for Math

505   Spreadsheets

Computer spreadsheets can help you organize and analyze data quickly and efficiently. If data change, they automatically recalculate results. They are faster and produce fewer errors than paper worksheets.

506   Terminology

A document that is created with a spreadsheet program may be called either a **worksheet** or a **spreadsheet**.

A cell is a box where you can enter data. The cell address gives the location of the cell. The cell address includes the column letter followed by the row number. A2 refers to the cell in column A row 2.

When you type an entry into an active cell, it shows here. When you make that cell active again, what you entered before shows here.

Information is entered into the active cell. It has a dark border or looks shaded.

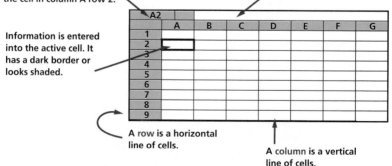

A row is a horizontal line of cells.

A column is a vertical line of cells.

You can enter three kinds of data into a cell.

- **Labels** are words or abbreviations. They may be entered into cells to identify information used in the spreadsheet.
- **Values** are numbers.
- **Formulas** or **functions** perform calculations on data. Functions are formulas that are built into spreadsheets to perform common calculations.

B8		= Sum (B1:B6)					
	A	B	C	D	E	F	G
1		89					
2		76					
3		92					
4		85					
5		90					
6		81					
7							
8	Sum:	513					
9							
10							

Sum is a function that adds a list of numbers.
Cell B8 contains this function: = Sum (B1:B6)
When you press Enter after typing a function or formula, the computer makes the calculation and puts the result in the cell. So, when you make cell B8 active again, the cell will have a number in it, but the entry window at the top of the spreadsheet will show what you typed.

What-if Analysis

507

A useful feature of spreadsheets is that you can see what happens if the data change. For example, if you double the length of the side of a rectangle, you can immediately see how the area will change. If you want to see how doubling the width changes the area, you just change the width. Or you can double both dimensions to compare to the original area. If you entered the correct formula in cells B4, C4, D4, and E4, the spreadsheet will automatically calculate the area.

B4		= B1 * B2					
	A	B	C	D	E	F	G
1	Length	8	16	8	16		
2	Width	6	6	12	12		
3							
4	Area	48	96	96	192		
5	New Area						
6							
7							
8							

Graphs

Another very useful tool in spreadsheets lets you create a graph from data in the spreadsheet. Spreadsheets usually let you make bar graphs, scatter plots, pie charts, line graphs, and 3-dimensional graphs. You select the graphing option to use and it makes the graph and creates a legend that explains the colors or symbols used in the graph.

The spreadsheet leads you through several steps to create the graph. It does not make your graph make sense—you need to do that by choosing the kind of graph that displays the kind of data you have. Suppose you want to graph the data about plant growth below.

B2								
	A	B	C	D	E	F	G	H	I
1	Week	1	2	3	4	5	6	7	8
2	Water Only	2	3	6	7	10	11	13	15
3	Plant Food	2	4	6	8	11	12	15	18
4									
5									

This is a spreadsheet. The first row and the first column are labels. The rest of the cells contain data.

You may decide to make a double-line graph from the data in the spreadsheet. This choice of a graph makes sense because a line graph is a good way to show change over time.

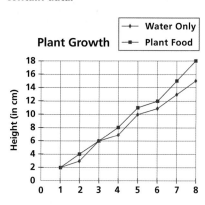

The computer *will* let you select a graph that doesn't make sense. If you selected a pie chart for these data, you'd get a circle graph like this.

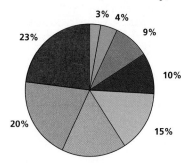

The graph does not make any sense. Remember, a useful graph summarizes the data and makes it easy to read and interpret. So, you must use your knowledge of graphs to select an appropriate graph type for the data.

Databases

A **database** is a collection of information. Databases include telephone books and dictionaries. The nice thing about computer databases is that they're fast, neat, and easy to change. Your electronic address book won't be full of crossouts like your paper one probably is.

You can use a database to collect, store, and organize information. A **file** is made up of a collection of **records**. You may think of these records as a set of index cards containing information about a subject.

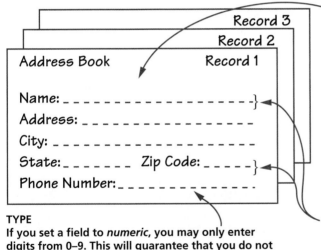

FIELD
Each piece of data is stored in a field. Each field has a name to distinguish it from other fields.

SIZE
Each field may also be limited in size, to conserve space in the computer. You can only type in as many characters as the size of the field allows. So, if you have a very long name, and the field is not long enough, some of the letters may get cut off!

TYPE
If you set a field to *numeric*, you may only enter digits from 0–9. This will guarantee that you do not write names in the *phone number* field.

MORE ▶

These features are part of most database programs.

■ **Browse** You can browse a database, or scan it for information, to get familiar with the database. If a database is very large, browsing may be limited to certain records.

■ **Search** If you know what you need, you can have the computer search for the records and display them on screen.

■ **Sort** A database can sort information using different orders. For example, you can sort names in alphabetical order or zip codes in numerical order.

■ **Query** The process of letting a computer know which records you need is called a query. It can be used with the browse, search, and sort features.

510   The Internet

The **Internet** is an interconnection of networks that enables computers to communicate with each other. For a home computer to access the Internet, it must have a modem. The **modem** connects the computer to the telephone or cable lines, which are then combined with Internet software installed on the computer to connect to a host server. The **server** offers various services to its users. In particular, a user may send and receive **electronic mail** (e-mail) or connect to the World Wide Web. Generally, computer users pay a monthly fee for the service.

The **World Wide Web (WWW)** is a system of resources available to computer users connected to the Internet. Users can interact with each other. They can also look up a variety of information, including magazine archives, library resources, current local and world news, and weather forecasts. A user can point to text or an item on the screen and immediately be linked to other Web pages on the server or even other servers on the network.

▶ Geometric Constructions

Protractor

A **protractor** is used to measure angles. Some protractors are semicircular and some are circular, but both kinds work the same way. Almost all protractors have two scales. To decide which scale to read, think about whether you're measuring an acute or obtuse angle.

MORE HELP
See 328–331

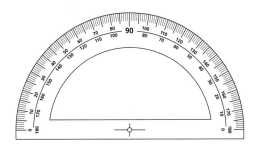

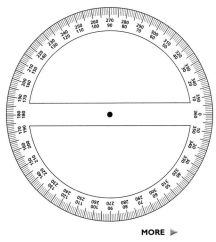

MORE ▶

EXAMPLE 1:

1. To measure this obtuse angle, choose one ray for the bottom.

2. Place the protractor on the angle. If the rays aren't long enough, extend them with your straightedge. Place the center point on the vertex. Place the 0° mark on the bottom ray.

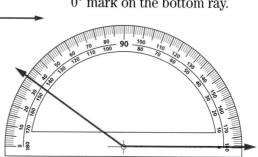

This obtuse angle measures 145°.

EXAMPLE 2:

1. To measure this acute angle, choose one ray for the bottom.

2. Place the protractor on the angle. If the rays aren't long enough, extend them with your straightedge. Place the center point on the vertex. Place the 0° mark on the bottom ray.

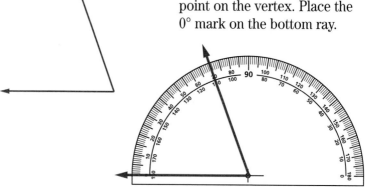

This acute angle measures 70°.

Compass

A **compass** is a tool for making circles or arcs. You can use the fact that a compass can be set for a specific radius to help you copy segments and angles. These segments and angles can help you make other geometric constructions.

You can set some compasses at the length you want your radius.

You can also set a compass by putting the point on one endpoint of a segment and moving the pencil until it is on the other end of the segment.

To make a circle or arc, hold the point steady where you want the center of your circle to be. Spin the pencil-end of the compass around that point.

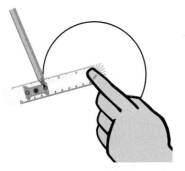

Constructions with Compass and Straightedge

A **straightedge** is just that: anything that will help you draw a straight line segment. A ruler is a straightedge, but you don't need the measurement marks of a ruler to do these constructions.

515   **Copying a Line Segment**

1. Use your straightedge to draw a line longer than $\overline{AB}$. Mark point A' somewhere on that line.

2. To copy $\overline{AB}$, set your compass to the length of $\overline{AB}$. Place the point of the compass on A' and draw an arc that intersects the line. Label the point of intersection B'.

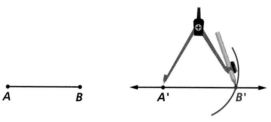

Since you set your compass to the length of $\overline{AB}$, B' is distance $\overline{AB}$ from A'. So, $\overline{AB} \cong \overline{A'B'}$.

516   **Constructing an Equilateral Triangle**

An equilateral triangle has all three sides the same length.

1. Use your straightedge to draw a line. Mark two points on your line and label them S and T.

2. Use $\overline{ST}$ to set your compass. Place the point of the compass on S and draw an arc that intersects your line twice.

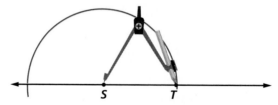

Think of $\overline{ST}$ as a distance. All points on this arc are distance $\overline{ST}$ from S.

3. Keep your compass setting the same. Place the point of the compass on *T* and draw an arc that intersects your line twice.

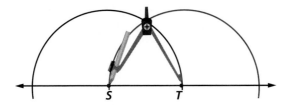

All points on this arc are distance $\overline{ST}$ from *T*.

4. Label the point where your two arcs intersect *R* and use your straightedge to draw $\overline{RS}$ and $\overline{RT}$.

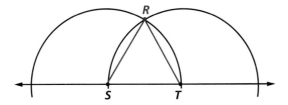

Since $\overline{RS}$, $\overline{RT}$, and $\overline{ST}$ are the same length radius, they must be congruent!

So, $\triangle RST$ is an equilateral triangle.

517

Copying an Angle

1. To construct an angle congruent to ∠*MNO*, draw a ray. Label the endpoint *Z*. Your goal is to find a point that will let you draw another ray from *Z* in a way that makes the two angles congruent.

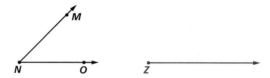

2. Place the point of your compass at *N* and draw an arc that intersects both rays of the angle. Label the points of intersection *X* and *Y*. Keeping this setting, place the point of your compass at *Z* and draw a long arc. Label the point of intersection *X'*.

 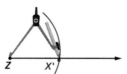

3. Place the point of your compass at *X* and the pencil at *Y* and set the compass. Keeping this setting, place the point of your compass at *X'* and draw an arc. Label the point of intersection *Y'*. Use your straightedge to draw a ray from *Z* through *Y'*.

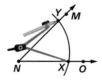 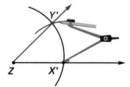

Point *Y'* is related to $\overrightarrow{ZY'}$ in exactly the same way as point *Y* is related to $\overrightarrow{NY}$. So, the ray through *Y'* makes ∠*Y'ZX'* congruent to ∠*MNO*.

518

Constructing Congruent Triangles

To construct a triangle congruent to △*FGH*, you must copy all three sides and arrange them into a triangle.

1. Draw a line. Mark a point on the line and label it *F'*.

2. Copy side $\overline{FH}$. Set your compass to the length of side $\overline{FH}$. Place the point of the compass on F' and draw an arc that intersects the line. Label the point of intersection H'.

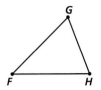 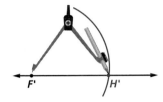

3. Copy $\angle F$. Use any compass setting that works.

MORE HELP
See 517

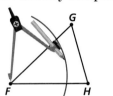 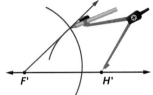

4. Copy side $\overline{FG}$ onto the new ray. Set your compass to the length of $\overline{FG}$. Label the new point G'.

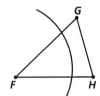 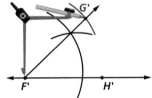

MORE HELP
See 350

5. Copy side $\overline{GH}$. Set your compass to the length of $\overline{GH}$. Place the compass point at G'. If your new arc doesn't intersect $\overline{F'H'}$ at H', something is off and you should retrace your steps. Use your straightedge to draw $\overline{H'G'}$.

 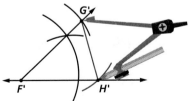

You know that only one triangle can be drawn with three specific side-lengths. You copied all the sides of $\triangle FGH$ to create $\triangle F'G'H'$. So, the two triangles are congruent.

Constructing a Rhombus

You can use what you know about copying line segments to construct a rhombus. Since all four sides of a rhombus are congruent, your goal is to construct a quadrilateral with four congruent sides.

1. Use your straightedge to draw $\angle G$.

2. Mark a point on one ray of $\angle G$ and label it Q.

3. Set your compass to the length of $\overline{GQ}$. Copy $\overline{GQ}$ onto the other ray of $\angle G$. Label the point of intersection P.

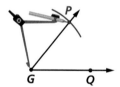

4. Keep your compass setting the same. Draw arcs from Q and P. Label the point of intersection J.

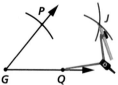

5. Use your straightedge to draw $\overline{PJ}$ and $\overline{QJ}$.

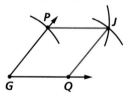

Since you used the same compass setting to draw them, all four of these line segments are congruent. The only way four congruent line segments can be put together in a quadrilateral is as a rhombus. So, $GQJP$ is a rhombus.

Constructing Parallel Lines

You know that opposite sides of a rhombus are parallel. So, if you construct a rhombus, you have also constructed two sets of parallel lines! There are several ways to construct parallel lines. Here's one of them.

1. Use your straightedge to draw ∠G.

2. Mark a point on one ray of ∠G and label it Q.

3. Set your compass to the length of $\overline{GQ}$. Copy $\overline{GQ}$ onto the other ray of ∠G. Label the point of intersection P.

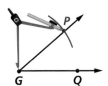

4. Keep your compass setting the same. Draw arcs from Q and P. Label the point of intersection J.

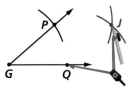

5. Use your straightedge to draw $\overleftrightarrow{PJ}$. You do not need to draw $\overline{JQ}$.

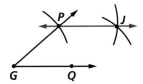

GQJP is a rhombus because all of its sides are congruent. Since the opposite sides of a rhombus are parallel, $\overleftrightarrow{GQ}$ and $\overleftrightarrow{PJ}$ are parallel. $\overleftrightarrow{GP}$ and $\overline{QJ}$ would also be parallel.

Constructing an Angle Bisector

To construct an angle bisector, you need to remember that the diagonals of a rhombus bisect their angles.

1. To bisect ∠G, start to construct a rhombus with ∠G as one of its angles. Place the point of your compass on G and draw an arc. Label the points of intersection with the rays Q and P.

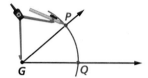

2. Use the same compass setting and draw intersecting arcs from Q and P. Label the point of intersection U.

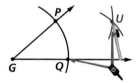

3. You don't need to draw the sides of the rhombus. Just use your straightedge to draw the diagonal $\overline{GU}$.

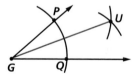

Since the diagonals of a rhombus bisect its angles, $\overline{GU}$ bisects ∠G.

Constructing a Perpendicular Bisector

To construct a perpendicular that bisects a segment, remember that the diagonals of a rhombus are perpendicular and bisect each other.

1. To construct a perpendicular bisector of $\overline{PQ}$, start to construct a rhombus with $\overline{PQ}$ as one diagonal. Set your compass to a little more than half the length of $\overline{PQ}$. Use this setting to draw two arcs from P and two arcs from Q. Label the points of intersection G and U.

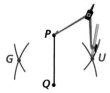

2. The sides of the rhombus are $\overline{PG}$, $\overline{PU}$, $\overline{UQ}$, and $\overline{QG}$. (You know they're all the same length because you used the same compass setting to draw all the intersecting arcs.) Use your straightedge to draw the second diagonal, $\overline{GU}$. Label the point of intersection T.

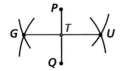

The diagonals of a rhombus are perpendicular to each other and bisect each other. So, $\overline{GU}$ is perpendicular to $\overline{PQ}$ and point T bisects $\overline{PQ}$.

Constructing a Square

523

If you can construct two perpendicular lines, you can construct a square.

1. Construct a line perpendicular to $\overline{GH}$. Label the point I where the perpendicular line intersects $\overline{GH}$.

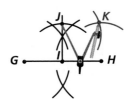

2. Set your compass to the length of $\overline{IH}$. Copy $\overline{IH}$ onto the perpendicular. Label the new segment $\overline{IJ}$.

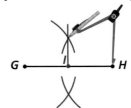

3. Keep the same compass setting and draw arcs from J and H. Label the point of intersection K.

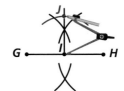

4. Use your straightedge to draw $\overline{JK}$ and $\overline{HK}$.

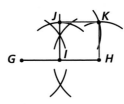

You constructed a rhombus around a right angle. Since a rhombus with right angles is a square, you have constructed a square.

Test-Taking Skills

Success in school depends on you! Be prepared and be involved, especially before a test. Studying for a test should be more than last-minute review.

525 Organizing and Preparing Test Material

- **What will be on the test?** Ask the teacher to be as specific as possible.

- **When is the test?** If you think it is about time for a test, ask your teacher if one is planned soon.

- **What will the test questions be like?** Will they be open-ended essays, multiple-choice or true/false questions, or a combination of these?

- **Review your notes carefully.** Compare class notes with notes from your assigned reading. Also go over previous homework.

- **Get any notes or assignments that you may have missed.** Your teacher or classmates will help if you ask ahead of time.

- **Make a list of questions.** If you are uncertain about anything, talk to your teacher well before the exam.

■ **Make an outline of topics.** Find an example for each topic that will be on the exam.

■ **Talk about the topics with other students.** By talking about how to work through problems, you will test your own understanding of the process.

Reviewing Test Material 526

■ **Start reviewing early.** Don't wait until the night before the test to study. You will remember more by studying a little over several days rather than cramming the night before the exam.

■ **Find a good place to study.** Make sure there's room to spread out your notes without losing them. Find a quiet place.

■ **Make sure you get enough rest.** If you get tired, take a break or get some sleep. If you're tired on test day, you'll have trouble concentrating and that could hurt your grade.

■ **Remember to eat well.** If you're hungry, it's hard to concentrate.

■ **Set up a specific time to study.** Keep to your schedule. Use the time to review your notes, re-read your textbook and appropriate handbook sections, and try sample problems.

■ **Practice, practice, practice.** Redo old homework problems or quiz problems. The more examples that you try, the better prepared you will be for the exam.

■ **Use study aids.** Silly sayings, called mnemonic devices, can help you remember complicated rules or procedures. Use the ones in this handbook or make them up yourself.

■ **Concentrate on how things fit together.** The more you understand, the less you'll have to memorize. A good example is using the area of a parallelogram to find the area of a triangle. You can make any triangle into a parallelogram by doubling it, so the area of a triangle is half the area of the parallelogram: $\frac{1}{2}bh$.

■ **Use flash cards.** Review important facts as often as you can.

■ **Study with other students.** As often as possible, talk out loud about how to work through a problem.

■ **Study by yourself.** You will be taking the exam alone, so you need to be able to do the problems on your own.

■ **Go over your material at least once right before the exam.**

■ **Try to unwind before the test.** Breathe deeply and try to relax.

■ **Check that you have all the materials you need for the test.** You may need a calculator, sharp pencils, eraser, paper, and so on.

■ **Know the rules of the test.**

> How much time do I have to complete the test?
> Do all the questions count equally?
> Can I use a calculator?
> Can I use my textbook or notes?
> Do I need any tables from my textbook?
> Does the teacher want explanations for short-answer
>   test items? Or am I supposed to explain my
>   thinking only when it is stated in the problem?

■ **Look over the entire test quickly.** Estimate the time each section should take. Then begin the test. Check the time occasionally.

■ **Read the directions carefully.** If something is unclear, ask your teacher. Follow all instructions.

■ **Answer the questions you are sure of first.** If you are stuck, move on to the next question. If questions are scored unevenly, make sure that you spend more of your time on the questions worth more points.

■ **If time is running out, try not to panic.** Do what you can do. Panicking will only waste time that you could be using to finish a problem or move on to another problem.

■ **Double-check.** Make sure that you have answered all the questions that you can. Check your work if you have time.

■ **Check that all your answers are readable.**

■ **If you have no idea how to solve a problem, move on.** Try your best and then check other problems for careless mistakes.

■ **Only change your answers if you are sure they are wrong.** Do not rush through a problem a second time and rashly change your answer. You are very often right the first time!

Tips for Taking Multiple-Choice Tests   528

In a multiple-choice problem, usually only one answer is correct. So, you can often eliminate at least one or two of the choices immediately. Read the problem carefully, think logically, and use your math sense.

If you get stuck on a multiple-choice problem and you have some extra time, you can always try each of the choices to find the correct answer. Go back to these problems after you have completed the problems that you know how to answer.

1. Use number sense to save time and work.

Compute $57.69 + (19.21 \times 2) \times 0$.

In this problem, notice that the product is zero. So the sum is the first addend. The answer is D.

A. 153.8   B. 115.39

C. 96.11   D. 57.69

2. Estimate when you can. Check for reasonableness.

Find the area of a circle with radius 40 cm. Use 3.14 for π.

You can use estimation in this problem. The area is approximately equal to $3 \times 40 \times 40 = 3 \times 1600 = 4800$. The only reasonable answer is D.

A. 125.6 cm²   B. 502.4 cm²

C. 1256 cm²   D. 5024 cm²

3. Eliminate obviously wrong choices.

Solve for the variable $\frac{3}{5}b + \frac{1}{5}b = {}^{-}8$.

Because $\frac{4}{5}b = {}^{-}8$, the answer must be negative. So, you need to decide between C and D. You can substitute each value in the equation and find which one works.

A. 10   B. $6\frac{2}{5}$

C. $^{-}6\frac{2}{5}$ D. $^{-}10$

$$\frac{4}{5} \times \left({}^{-}6\frac{2}{5}\right) = \frac{4}{5} \times \left({}^{-}\frac{32}{5}\right) = {}^{-}\frac{128}{25} \neq {}^{-}8$$
$$\frac{4}{5} \times \left({}^{-}10\right) = {}^{-}\frac{40}{5} = {}^{-}8.$$

So, the solution is D.

4. Try the easier choices first.

Solve for the variable 54 is $g\%$ of 90.

54 is more than half of 90. So, A cannot be the answer. 54 is less than 90 and D is more than 100%, so D cannot be the answer. So the answer is either B or C. Since B is an easy number, try it first. If it works, great. If it doesn't work, the answer is C. (The answer is B.)

A. $g = 36$ B. $g = 60$

C. $g = 66$ D. $g = 144$

529 **Problem Solving on Multiple-Choice Tests**

- **Read the problem carefully.** Underline or circle words in the problem that help you understand what you are asked to do.

- **Decide how hard the problem will be to solve.** If it looks easy, do it now; if not, come back to it later.

- **Look over the answers to see if you can eliminate any choices.** Use clues to help you solve the problem. Consider

  - the size of the units—should the answer be in the same units, square units, cubic units? Is a conversion necessary (such as from feet to inches or inches to feet)?

  - decimal places—if you must find a product, quotient, sum, or difference of decimals, estimating the correct number of decimal places may help to indicate the answer.

  - clues to signs—should an answer be negative or positive? This may help you eliminate one or two choices.

530 **When to Use a Calculator on a Test**

- Sometimes, calculators are allowed to be used during exams. In general, remember that your calculator is a tool but you are the problem solver.

- On a test, always ask yourself first: "Can I do it in my head?" If you can, it's usually faster to do so. Looking at the numbers can help you decide. Are they compatible numbers? Are they benchmark fractions $(0, \frac{1}{2}, 1)$ or benchmark percents (25%, 50%, 75%)?

- Whenever you have to compute with decimals, it may be a good idea to use your calculator. Be careful and check those decimal points.

- Use your calculator for percent problems that do not include benchmark percents or multiples of 10%.

- With fractions, the choice is yours. Remember, you need common denominators to add and subtract, so you might like to use your calculator. Since multiplying fractions is straightforward, consider just multiplying the fractions without your calculator.

- In statistics questions, your calculator may be able to calculate the mean of a set of numbers, but it probably will not be able to determine the range, median, or mode.

Tips for "Explain-Your-Thinking" Tests 531

As you work through a problem that asks you to explain your answer, include all the details you think are necessary for the teacher to understand your thinking process. Scoring is often based on how you do and explain each step of the problem.

> **SAMPLE PROBLEM:** Think of a whole number greater than 1. If you multiply this number by a number between zero and 1, will the product be greater than or less than your original number? Will this be true for the product of any whole number greater than 1 and any fraction between zero and 1? Explain your thinking.

1. The first step in solving this problem involves picking a whole number and some fractions. Since you can pick any whole number greater than 1, pick one that will be easy to multiply by several fractions.

$$8 \times \frac{1}{2} = 4$$

$$8 \times \frac{1}{4} = 2$$

$$8 \times \frac{3}{4} = 6$$

All of these products are less than 8 and more than zero.

2. If you stop the solution at this point, you will only receive partial credit. You may be tempted to generalize and say that this pattern will continue with other whole numbers and fractions. But you need to show other examples and explain why this must be the case.

Here are some other products:

$$9 \times \frac{1}{90} = \frac{1}{10} \qquad 10 \times \frac{1}{100} = \frac{1}{10}$$

$$9 \times \frac{1}{3} = 3 \qquad 10 \times \frac{1}{5} = 2$$

$$9 \times \frac{2}{9} = 2 \qquad 10 \times \frac{2}{5} = 4$$

$$9 \times \frac{4}{9} = 4 \qquad 10 \times \frac{3}{5} = 6$$

$$9 \times \frac{7}{9} = 7 \qquad 10 \times \frac{4}{5} = 8$$

$$9 \times \frac{8}{9} = 8$$

3. Continue to investigate the problem. But don't stop here. Look at the patterns and try to make a generalization about what you see.

4. Remember that you are asked to "Explain your thinking." That is exactly what you must do to receive full credit for this problem. Use your examples to make a generalization about the problem and explain how you reached your conclusion.

As the fractions get closer and closer to 1, the product gets closer and closer to the whole number. The product cannot equal the whole number unless the fraction is equal to 1. As the fraction gets closer and closer to zero, the product gets smaller but it never gets to zero. So the product of a number greater than 1 and a fraction between zero and 1 will always be less than the whole number and greater than zero.

532) Tips for Short-Answer or Fill-In Problems

- Do exactly what the directions tell you to do.

- These questions are often either right or wrong. So you want to be very careful with your computation.

- You will probably have to find exact answers. So, use a calculator if you can.

- Know and use the order of operations.

- If the directions ask for a fraction in simplest form, make sure that the answer really is in simplest form.

- If you are asked for a diagram, make sure to draw and clearly label the diagram.

533) After a Test

- Keep a record in your math journal of your test preparation and its results. Use it to help you plan for future tests.

- Describe how you studied for the test. Talk about how you could improve your study habits and how you study for an exam as well as how you could improve your test-taking skills.

- Talk about the test and how you did on it.

- Did you understand the problems?

- Were your mistakes computational or conceptual?

- Did you use a calculator, mental math, or estimation when each was appropriate in the test?

- Did you know when to use math sense or logical reasoning to help solve problems on the multiple-choice items?

- On the long-answer items, were you able to express your thought processes clearly? How can you improve this?

Handy Tables

The Metric System

LINEAR MEASURE

1 centimeter	0.01 meter	0.3937 inch
1 decimeter	0.1 meter	3.937 inches
1 meter		39.37 inches
1 dekameter	10 meters	32.8 feet
1 hectometer	100 meters	328 feet
1 kilometer	1000 meters	0.621 mile
1 myriameter	10,000 meters	6.21 miles

CAPACITY MEASURE

1 centiliter	0.01 liter	0.338 fluid ounce
1 deciliter	0.1 liter	3.38 fluid ounces
1 liter		1.0567 liquid quarts or 0.9081 dry quart
1 dekaliter	10 liters	2.642 gallons or 0.284 bushel
1 hectoliter	100 liters	26.42 gallons or 2.84 bushels
1 kiloliter	1000 liters	264.2 gallons or 35.315 cubic feet

VOLUME MEASURE

1 cubic centimeter	1000 cubic millimeters	0.06102 cubic inch
1 cubic decimeter	1000 cubic centimeters	61.02 cubic inches
1 cubic meter	1000 cubic decimeters	35.314 cubic feet

MORE ▶

MASS

1 centigram	0.01 gram	0.0003527 ounce
1 decigram	0.1 gram	0.003527 ounce
1 gram	10 decigrams	0.03527 ounce
1 dekagram	10 grams	0.3527 ounce
1 hectogram	100 grams	3.5274 ounces
1 kilogram	1000 grams	2.2046 pounds
1 myriagram	10,000 grams	22.046 pounds
1 quintal	100,000 grams	220.46 pounds
1 metric ton	1,000,000 grams	2204.6 pounds

LAND MEASURE

1 centare	1 square meter	1.196 square yards
1 acre	100 square meters	119.6 square yards
1 hectare	10,000 square meters	2.471 acres
1 square kilometer	1,000,000 square meters	0.386 square mile

536 The Customary System

LINEAR MEASURE

1 inch		2.54 centimeters
1 foot	12 inches	0.3048 meter
1 yard	3 feet	0.9144 meter
1 rod (or pole or perch)	$16\frac{1}{2}$ feet	5.029 meters
1 (statute) mile	5280 feet	1609.3 meters
1 (land) league	15,840 feet	4.83 kilometers

SQUARE MEASURE

1 square foot	144 square inches	929.0304 square centimeters
1 square yard	9 square feet	0.83761 square meter
1 acre	43,560 square feet	4051.08 square meters

CUBIC MEASURE

1 cord foot	16 cubic feet	0.453069 cubic meter
1 cord	128 cubic feet	3.625 cubic meters

DRY MEASURE

1 pint		33.60 cubic inches	0.5505 liter
1 quart	2 pints	67.20 cubic inches	1.1012 liters
1 peck	16 pints	537.61 cubic inches	8.8096 liters
1 bushel	64 pints	2150.42 cubic inches	35.2383 liters

LIQUID MEASURE

1 fluid ounce	0.25 gill	1.8047 cubic inches	0.0296 liter
1 gill	4 fluid ounces	7.219 cubic inches	0.1183 liter
1 cup	8 fluid ounces	14.438 cubic inches	0.2366 liter
1 pint	16 fluid ounces	28.875 cubic inches	0.4732 liter
1 quart	32 fluid ounces	57.75 cubic inches	0.9463 liter
1 gallon	128 fluid ounces	231 cubic inches	3.7853 liters

CIRCULAR (OR ANGULAR) MEASURE

60 seconds	1 minute	90 degrees	1 quadrant or 1 right angle
60 minutes	1 degree	4 quadrants or 360 degrees	1 circle

WEIGHT (AVOIRDUPOIS)

1 grain	0.0001426 pound	0.0648 gram
1 dram	0.00390 pound	1.772 grams
1 ounce	0.0625 pound	28.3495 grams
1 pound	16 ounces	453.59 grams
1 hundredweight	100 pounds	45.36 kilograms
1 ton	2000 pounds	907.18 kilograms

TIME

60 seconds	1 minute	7 days	1 week
60 minutes	1 hour	168 hours	1 week
3600 seconds	1 hour	12 months	1 year
24 hours	1 day	52 weeks	1 year
1440 minutes	1 day	365.25 days	1 year

General Measurement

537

BENCHMARK MEASURES

1 inch	≈	tip of your thumb
1 centimeter	≈	width of the tip of your index finger
1 foot	≈	length of your notebook
1 kilogram	≈	mass of your math textbook
1 minute	≈	time it takes to count to 60 saying "one thousand" between each number
1 pound	≈	weight of a loaf of bread
1 ounce	≈	weight of a slice of bread
1 gram	≈	mass of a shoelace

MORE ▶

ADDITIONAL UNITS OF MEASURE

Astronomical Unit (A.U.) . . . . . 93,000,000 miles: the average distance of the Earth from the sun; used in astronomy

Bible Cubit . . . . 21.8 inches

Board Foot (bd. ft.) . . . . 144 cubic inches (12 in. × 12 in. × 1 in.); used for lumber

Bolt . . . . 40 yards; used for measuring cloth

Btu (British thermal unit) . . . . Amount of heat needed to increase the temperature of one pound of water by one degree Fahrenheit

Calorie . . . . 0.00399 Btu

Cubit . . . . 18 inches

1° of Great Circle (Equator) . . . 60 nautical miles

Furlong . . . . 220 yards

Gross . . . . 12 dozen or 144

Hand . . . . 4 inches

Knot . . . . Rate of speed of one nautical mile per hour

Light, Speed of . . . . 186,281.7 miles per second

Light-year . . . . 5,880,000,000,000 miles: the distance light travels in a year at the rate of 186,281.7 miles per second

Military Pace . . . . $2\frac{1}{2}$ feet

Nautical Mile . . . . 6076.10333 feet by international agreement in 1954

Palm . . . . 3 inches

Pi (π) . . . . 3.14159265358979323846 . . . ; the ratio of the circumference of a circle to its diameter

Roentgen . . . . Dosage unit of radiation exposure produced by X rays

Score . . . . 20 units

Sound, Speed of . . . . About 1088 feet per second at 32°F at sea level

Span . . . . 6 inches

Short Ton . . . . 2000 pounds

Long Ton . . . . 2240 pounds

COMMON ABBREVIATIONS

c	cup	mg	milligram
cm	centimeter	mi	mile
cos	cosine	min	minute
d	day	mL	milliliter
dm	decimeter	mm	millimeter
fl oz	fluid ounce	mo	month
ft	foot	pt	pint
gal	gallon	qt	quart
g	gram	s	second
h	hour	sin	sine
in.	inch	t	ton
kg	kilogram	tan	tangent
km	kilometer	trig	trigonometry
L	liter	wk	week
lb	pound	yd	yard
m	meter	y	year

CONVERSION FACTORS

To change	to	multiply by	To change	to	multiply by
acres	hectares	0.4047	meters	feet	3.2808
acres	square feet	43,560	meters	miles	0.0006214
acres	square miles	0.001563	meters	yards	1.0936
centimeters	inches	0.3937	metric tons	tons (long)	0.9842
centimeters	feet	0.03281	metric tons	tons (short)	1.1023
cubic meters	cubic feet	35.3147	miles	kilometers	1.6093
cubic meters	cubic yards	1.30795	miles	feet	5280
cubic yards	cubic meters	0.7646	miles (nautical)	miles (statute)	1.1516
feet	meters	0.3048	miles (statute)	miles (nautical)	0.8684
feet	miles (nautical)	0.0001645	miles/hour	feet/minute	88
feet	miles (statute)	0.0001894	millimeters	inches	0.0394
feet/second	miles/hour	0.6818	ounces	grams	28.3495
furlongs	feet	660	ounces	pounds	0.0625
furlongs	miles	0.125	pecks	liters	8.8096
gallons (U.S.)	liters	3.7853	pints (dry)	liters	0.5506
grains	grams	0.0648	pints (liquid)	liters	0.4732
grams	grains	15.432	pounds	kilograms	0.4536
grams	ounces	0.0353	pounds	ounces	16
grams	pounds	0.002205	quarts (dry)	liters	1.1012
hectares	acres	2.471	quarts (liquid)	liters	0.9463
horsepower	watts	745.7	square feet	square meters	0.0929
hours	days	0.04167	square kilometers	square miles	0.3861
inches	millimeters	25.4	square meters	square feet	10.7639
inches	centimeters	2.54	square meters	square yards	1.196
kilograms	pounds	2.2046	square miles	square kilometers	2.59
kilometers	miles	0.6214	square yards	square meters	0.8361
kilowatts	horsepower	1.341	tons (long)	metric tons	1.016
knots	nautical mi/hour	1.0	tons (short)	metric tons	0.9072
knots	statute mi/hour	1.151	tons (long)	pounds	2240
liters	gallons (U.S.)	0.2642	tons (short)	pounds	2000
liters	pecks	0.1135	watts	Btu/hour	3.4121
liters	pints (dry)	1.8162	watts	horsepower	0.001341
liters	pints (liquid)	2.1134	yards	meters	0.9144
liters	quarts (dry)	0.9081	yards	miles	0.0005682
liters	quarts (liquid)	1.0567			

Fraction/Decimal Equivalents

$\frac{1}{2}$	0.5	$\frac{1}{8}$	0.125	$\frac{1}{11}$	$0.\overline{09}$	$\frac{1}{16}$	0.0625
$\frac{1}{3}$	$0.\overline{3}$	$\frac{2}{8}$	0.25	$\frac{2}{11}$	$0.\overline{18}$	$\frac{2}{16}$	0.125
$\frac{2}{3}$	$0.\overline{6}$	$\frac{3}{8}$	0.375	$\frac{3}{11}$	$0.\overline{27}$	$\frac{3}{16}$	0.1875
$\frac{1}{4}$	0.25	$\frac{4}{8}$	0.5	$\frac{4}{11}$	$0.\overline{36}$	$\frac{4}{16}$	0.25
$\frac{2}{4}$	0.5	$\frac{5}{8}$	0.625	$\frac{5}{11}$	$0.\overline{45}$	$\frac{5}{16}$	0.3125
$\frac{3}{4}$	0.75	$\frac{6}{8}$	0.75	$\frac{6}{11}$	$0.\overline{54}$	$\frac{6}{16}$	0.375
$\frac{1}{5}$	0.2	$\frac{7}{8}$	0.875	$\frac{7}{11}$	$0.\overline{63}$	$\frac{7}{16}$	0.4375
$\frac{2}{5}$	0.4	$\frac{1}{9}$	$0.\overline{1}$	$\frac{8}{11}$	$0.\overline{72}$	$\frac{8}{16}$	0.5
$\frac{3}{5}$	0.6	$\frac{2}{9}$	$0.\overline{2}$	$\frac{9}{11}$	$0.\overline{81}$	$\frac{9}{16}$	0.5625
$\frac{4}{5}$	0.8	$\frac{3}{9}$	$0.\overline{3}$	$\frac{10}{11}$	$0.\overline{90}$	$\frac{10}{16}$	0.625
$\frac{1}{6}$	$0.1\overline{6}$	$\frac{4}{9}$	$0.\overline{4}$	$\frac{1}{12}$	$0.08\overline{3}$	$\frac{11}{16}$	0.6875
$\frac{2}{6}$	$0.\overline{3}$	$\frac{5}{9}$	$0.\overline{5}$	$\frac{2}{12}$	$0.1\overline{6}$	$\frac{12}{16}$	0.75
$\frac{3}{6}$	0.5	$\frac{6}{9}$	$0.\overline{6}$	$\frac{3}{12}$	0.25	$\frac{13}{16}$	0.8125
$\frac{4}{6}$	$0.\overline{6}$	$\frac{7}{9}$	$0.\overline{7}$	$\frac{4}{12}$	$0.\overline{3}$	$\frac{14}{16}$	0.875
$\frac{5}{6}$	$0.8\overline{3}$	$\frac{8}{9}$	$0.\overline{8}$	$\frac{5}{12}$	$0.41\overline{6}$	$\frac{15}{16}$	0.9375
$\frac{1}{7}$	$0.\overline{142857}$	$\frac{1}{10}$	0.1	$\frac{6}{12}$	0.5		
$\frac{2}{7}$	$0.\overline{285714}$	$\frac{2}{10}$	0.2	$\frac{7}{12}$	$0.58\overline{3}$		
$\frac{3}{7}$	$0.\overline{428571}$	$\frac{3}{10}$	0.3	$\frac{8}{12}$	$0.\overline{6}$		
$\frac{4}{7}$	$0.\overline{571428}$	$\frac{4}{10}$	0.4	$\frac{9}{12}$	0.75		
$\frac{5}{7}$	$0.\overline{714285}$	$\frac{5}{10}$	0.5	$\frac{10}{12}$	$0.8\overline{3}$		
$\frac{6}{7}$	$0.\overline{857142}$	$\frac{6}{10}$	0.6	$\frac{11}{12}$	$0.91\overline{6}$		
		$\frac{7}{10}$	0.7				
		$\frac{8}{10}$	0.8				
		$\frac{9}{10}$	0.9				

Multiplication Table

×	1	2	3	4	5	6	7	8	9	10
1	1	2	3	4	5	6	7	8	9	10
2	2	4	6	8	10	12	14	16	18	20
3	3	6	9	12	15	18	21	24	27	30
4	4	8	12	16	20	24	28	32	36	40
5	5	10	15	20	25	30	35	40	45	50
6	6	12	18	24	30	36	42	48	54	60
7	7	14	21	28	35	42	49	56	63	70
8	8	16	24	32	40	48	56	64	72	80
9	9	18	27	36	45	54	63	72	81	90
10	10	20	30	40	50	60	70	80	90	100

n	n^2	$\sqrt{n}$	n^3	$\sqrt[3]{n}$	n	n^2	$\sqrt{n}$	n^3	$\sqrt[3]{n}$
1	1	1.000	1	1.000	51	2601	7.141	132,651	3.708
2	4	1.414	8	1.260	52	2704	7.211	140,608	3.733
3	9	1.732	27	1.442	53	2809	7.280	148,877	3.756
4	16	2.000	64	1.587	54	2916	7.348	157,464	3.780
5	25	2.236	125	1.710	55	3025	7.416	166,375	3.803
6	36	2.449	216	1.817	56	3136	7.483	175,616	3.826
7	49	2.646	343	1.913	57	3249	7.550	185,193	3.849
8	64	2.828	512	2.000	58	3364	7.616	195,112	3.871
9	81	3.000	729	2.080	59	3481	7.681	205,379	3.893
10	100	3.162	1000	2.154	60	3600	7.746	216,000	3.915
11	121	3.317	1331	2.224	61	3721	7.810	226,981	3.936
12	144	3.464	1728	2.289	62	3844	7.874	238,328	3.958
13	169	3.606	2197	2.351	63	3969	7.937	250,047	3.979
14	196	3.742	2744	2.410	64	4096	8.000	262,144	4.000
15	225	3.873	3375	2.466	65	4225	8.062	274,625	4.021
16	256	4.000	4096	2.520	66	4356	8.124	287,496	4.041
17	289	4.123	4913	2.571	67	4489	8.185	300,763	4.062
18	324	4.243	5832	2.621	68	4624	8.246	314,432	4.082
19	361	4.359	6859	2.668	69	4761	8.307	328,509	4.102
20	400	4.472	8000	2.714	70	4900	8.367	343,000	4.121
21	441	4.583	9261	2.759	71	5041	8.426	357,911	4.141
22	484	4.690	10,648	2.802	72	5184	8.485	373,248	4.160
23	529	4.796	12,167	2.844	73	5329	8.544	389,017	4.179
24	576	4.899	13,824	2.884	74	5476	8.602	405,224	4.198
25	625	5.000	15,625	2.924	75	5625	8.660	421,875	4.217
26	676	5.099	17,576	2.962	76	5776	8.718	438,976	4.236
27	729	5.196	19,683	3.000	77	5929	8.775	456,533	4.254
28	784	5.292	21,952	3.037	78	6084	8.832	474,552	4.273
29	841	5.385	24,389	3.072	79	6241	8.888	493,039	4.291
30	900	5.477	27,000	3.107	80	6400	8.944	512,000	4.309
31	961	5.568	29,791	3.141	81	6561	9.000	531,441	4.327
32	1024	5.657	32,768	3.175	82	6724	9.055	551,368	4.344
33	1089	5.745	35,937	3.208	83	6889	9.110	571,787	4.362
34	1156	5.831	39,304	3.240	84	7056	9.165	592,704	4.380
35	1225	5.916	42,875	3.271	85	7225	9.220	614,125	4.397
36	1296	6.000	46,656	3.302	86	7396	9.274	636,056	4.414
37	1369	6.083	50,653	3.332	87	7569	9.327	658,503	4.431
38	1444	6.164	54,872	3.362	88	7744	9.381	681,472	4.448
39	1521	6.245	59,319	3.391	89	7921	9.434	704,969	4.465
40	1600	6.325	64,000	3.420	90	8100	9.487	729,000	4.481
41	1681	6.403	68,921	3.448	91	8281	9.539	753,571	4.498
42	1764	6.481	74,088	3.476	92	8464	9.592	778,688	4.514
43	1849	6.557	79,507	3.503	93	8649	9.644	804,357	4.531
44	1936	6.633	85,184	3.530	94	8836	9.695	830,584	4.547
45	2025	6.708	91,125	3.557	95	9025	9.747	857,375	4.563
46	2116	6.782	97,336	3.583	96	9216	9.798	884,736	4.579
47	2209	6.856	103,823	3.609	97	9409	9.849	912,673	4.595
48	2304	6.928	110,592	3.634	98	9604	9.899	941,192	4.610
49	2401	7.000	117,649	3.659	99	9801	9.950	970,299	4.626
50	2500	7.071	125,000	3.684	100	10,000	10.000	1,000,000	4.642

(Roots are rounded to the nearest thousandth.)

Right-Triangle Ratios

Angle	Sine	Cosine	Tangent	Angle	Sine	Cosine	Tangent
0°	0.000	1.000	0.000	50°	0.766	0.643	1.192
5°	0.087	0.996	0.087	55°	0.819	0.574	1.428
10°	0.174	0.985	0.176	60°	0.866	0.500	1.732
15°	0.259	0.966	0.268	65°	0.906	0.423	2.145
20°	0.342	0.940	0.364	70°	0.940	0.342	2.747
25°	0.423	0.906	0.466	75°	0.966	0.259	3.732
30°	0.500	0.866	0.577	80°	0.985	0.174	5.671
35°	0.574	0.819	0.700	85°	0.996	0.087	11.430
40°	0.643	0.766	0.839	90°	1.000	0.000	——
45°	0.707	0.707	1.000				

(Ratios are rounded to the nearest thousandth.)

Prime Numbers Less Than 500

2	3	5	7	11	13	17	19	23	29
31	37	41	43	47	53	59	61	67	71
73	79	83	89	97	101	103	107	109	113
127	131	137	139	149	151	157	163	167	173
179	181	191	193	197	199	211	223	227	229
233	239	241	251	257	263	269	271	277	281
283	293	307	311	313	317	331	337	347	349
353	359	367	373	379	383	389	397	401	409
419	421	431	433	439	443	449	457	461	463
467	479	487	491	499					

Symbol	Meaning	Example
+	plus (addition)	$6 + 7 = 13$
$^{+}$	positive	$^{+}3$: the integer 3 units to the right of zero on a number line
−	minus (subtraction)	$15 - 7 = 8$
$^{-}$	negative	$^{-}6$: the integer 6 units to the left of zero on a number line
$\times$, $\cdot$, $a(b)$	multiplied by or times	$4 \times 5 = 20$; $8 \cdot 3 = 24$; $3(4) = 12$
$\div$ or $\overline{)}$	divided by	$4 \div 2 = 2$ $2\overline{)4}^{\,2}$
− as in $\frac{a}{b}$	divided by	$\frac{6}{3} = 2$
=	is equal to	$3 + 2 = 5$
$\neq$	is not equal to	$8 - 5 \neq 8$
$\cong$	is congruent to	In an equilateral triangle all of the sides are congruent: side $AB \cong$ side $BC \cong$ side CA
$\sim$	is similar to	$\triangle ABC \sim \triangle DEF$
$\approx$	is approximately equal to	$\pi \approx 3.14$
$<$	is less than	$7 + 6 < 15$
$\leq$	is less than or equal to	$3 \leq 4$
$>$	is greater than	$8 > 2$
$\geq$	is greater than or equal to	$6 \geq 3$
$\pm$	plus or minus	$3 \pm 2 = 5$ or 1
( )	parentheses: used as grouping symbols	$(3 + 4) - (3 - 1) = 7 - 2 = 5$
[ ]	brackets: used as grouping symbols	$[3(2 + 6) - 5] = [3(8) - 5] = 24 - 5 = 19$
{ }	braces: used as grouping symbols	$3\{7[(3 + 4) - 6]\} = 3\{7[7 - 6]\} = 21$
%	percent	50%: 50 percent
¢	cents	35¢: 35 cents
$	dollars	$5.25; say: *5 dollars and 25 cents*
°	degree	$360°$ is the total number of degrees in a circle

Symbol	Meaning	Example
°F	degrees Fahrenheit	60°F
°C	degrees Celsius	36°C
'	minute	4': 4 minutes
'	foot (or feet)	8': 8 feet
"	second	35": 35 seconds
"	inch	9": 9 inches
:	is to (ratio)	4:3; say: *4 is to 3*
π	the irrational number pi; approximation for $\pi = 3.14159265358979323846\ldots$	usually use $\pi \approx 3.14$ or $\frac{22}{7}$
| |	absolute value	$\lvert {}^{-}5 \rvert = 5$ and $\lvert 5 \rvert = 5$
√	square root	$\sqrt{16} = 4$
∛	cube root	$\sqrt[3]{8} = 2$
$\overline{3}$	repeating decimal symbol	$2.\overline{3} = 2.333333\ldots$
{ }	set	$\{A\}$: the set containing the letter A
∩	intersection	If $A = \{a, e, i, o, u\}$ and $B = \{h, i\}$, then $A \cap B = \{i\}$.
∪	union	If $A = \{a, e, i, o, u\}$ and $B = \{h, i\}$, then $A \cup B = \{a, e, h, i, o, u\}$.
⊂	is a subset of	If $A = \{a, e, i, o, u\}$ and $C = \{a, e\}$, then $C \subset A$, or C is a subset of A.
⊄	is not a subset of	If $A = \{a, e, i, o, u\}$ and $D = \{b, c, d\}$, then $D \not\subset A$, or D is not a subset of A.
∈	is an element of	If $P = \{3, 4, 5\}$, then $3 \in P$, or 3 is an element of the set P.
∉	is not an element of	If $Q = \{2, 4, 6\}$, then $8 \notin Q$, or 8 is not an element of the set Q.
∅	the empty set	If $R = \{a, b, c\}$ and $T = \{1, 2, 3\}$, then $R \cap T = \varnothing$, or the intersection of R and T is the empty set.
∠	angle	$\angle S$
Δ	triangle	ΔQRS

Symbol	Meaning	Example
$\overleftrightarrow{AB}$	line AB	
$\overline{JK}$	line segment JK	
$\overrightarrow{LM}$	ray LM	
$\overparen{QR}$	arc QR	
⌐	right angle	$\angle ABC$ is a right angle.
$\perp$	is perpendicular to	$\overline{AB} \perp \overline{CD}$
$\parallel$	is parallel to	$\overline{AB} \parallel \overline{DC}$
$\therefore$	therefore	$m\angle ABC$ is 90°, $\therefore \angle ABC$ is a right angle.
∞	infinity	
!	factorial	$5! = 5 \times 4 \times 3 \times 2 \times 1 = 120$
a^0	1	$3^0 = 17^0 = 1$
a^n	multiply the number a by itself n times	$3^4 = 3 \times 3 \times 3 \times 3 = 81$
a^{-n}	$\frac{1}{a^n}$, or multiply $\frac{1}{a}$ by itself n times	$2^{-3} = \frac{1}{2^3} = \frac{1}{8}$
$a^{\frac{b}{n}}$	$\sqrt[n]{a}$, or the nth root of a	$64^{\frac{1}{3}} = \sqrt[3]{64} = 4$ since $4 \times 4 \times 4 = 64$
$y = \log_a x$	y equals the logarithm to the base a of the number x	$3 = \log_2 8$ is equivalent to $8 = 2^3$

Number Patterns

Pascal's Triangle

Blaise Pascal was a French mathematician, philosopher, and scientist who lived from 1623 to 1662. Pascal, together with another French mathematician, Pierre de Fermat (1601–1665), studied the theory of probability and explored its applications.

This pattern is called **Pascal's Triangle** because he studied it. It may have been invented at least 500 years before that by a Chinese mathematician and by Omar Khay Yám.

MORE HELP
See 461

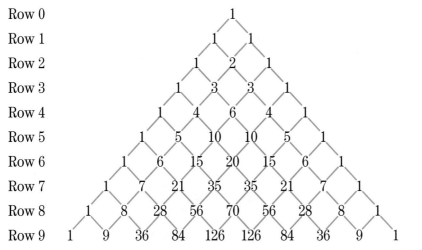

Row 0	1
Row 1	1 1
Row 2	1 2 1
Row 3	1 3 3 1
Row 4	1 4 6 4 1
Row 5	1 5 10 10 5 1
Row 6	1 6 15 20 15 6 1
Row 7	1 7 21 35 35 21 7 1
Row 8	1 8 28 56 70 56 28 8 1
Row 9	1 9 36 84 126 126 84 36 9 1

MORE ▶

Notice that the sum of the numbers in each row is 2 times the sum of the numbers in the previous row. The sum of the numbers in Row n is 2^n.

Row	Sum	2^n
0	1	2^0
1	$1 + 1 = 2$	2^1
2	$1 + 2 + 1 = 4$	2^2
3	$1 + 3 + 3 + 1 = 8$	2^3
4	16	2^4
5	32	2^5
6	64	2^6
7	128	2^7
8	256	2^8
9	512	2^9

546) Fibonacci Sequence

Leonardo Fibonacci, an Italian mathematician who lived from about 1180 to about 1250, found this pattern, and mathematicians are still finding interesting ways this series of numbers describes nature.

0, 1, 1, 2, 3, 5, 8, 13, 21, 34, 55, 89, 144, 233, 377, 610, 987, 1597, . . .

Each member in the series is the sum of the two numbers before it.

Pineapples, pinecones, and sunflowers all show two spiral patterns—one a clockwise spiral, the other a counterclockwise spiral. The number of spirals in each pattern is always one number in the **Fibonacci sequence**. Natural patterns often exhibit the Fibonacci sequence.

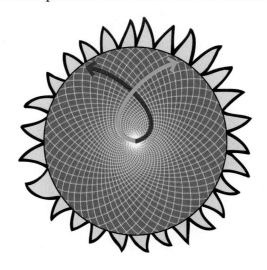

Golden Ratio

Artists often use the **golden ratio** because it produces shapes that are pleasing to the eye. One of the most famous buildings of Greek antiquity, the Parthenon, was designed using the golden ratio. An average person's total height compared to waist height is the golden ratio.

Golden ratio (ϕ) = $\frac{\text{length}}{\text{width}}$ = $\frac{(1 + \sqrt{5})}{2}$ ≈ 1.618

The golden ratio, ϕ, also appears in connection with the Fibonacci sequence. As each number in the Fibonacci sequence is divided by the number that precedes it, the quotient gets closer and closer to ϕ.

Exponential Growth

Exponential growth is an exponential function, in the form $y = Ca^x$, where $C > 0$ and $a > 1$.

The process of cell duplication, mitosis, in which one cell divides into two is an example of exponential growth.

An escherichia coli cell (*e. coli*) is one of the fastest–reproducing bacteria cells. It can reproduce itself in 15 minutes. If you begin with one cell, how many will there be in one hour? Think: In

15-Minute Intervals	Total Number of Cells	Pattern
0	1	2^0
1	2	2^1
2	4	2^2
3	8	2^3
4	16	2^4
…	…	…
…	…	…
…	…	…
…	…	…
x	y	2^x

one hour there are four 15-minute intervals. In the first 15-minute interval, the cell will divide and form 2 cells. In the second interval, each of the two cells will divide to form a total of 4 cells. The table summarizes this growth pattern.

MORE ▶

So, if the beginning number of cells is y and the number of 15-minute intervals is x, you can use the equation $y = 2^x$ to find the number of cells after y intervals.

Notice that the graph of an exponential equation curves, while the graph of a linear equation is a straight line.

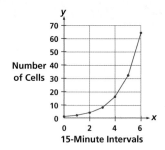

549 Sums of Numbers in Sequence

The formula for sums of numbers in sequence was discovered by Carl Friedrich Gauss when he was 5 years old! Gauss was a German mathematician who made wide-ranging contributions to mathematics and mathematical physics. One of his most interesting formulas is:

The sum of the first n counting numbers:

$$1 + 2 + 3 + 4 + 5 + \ldots + (n-1) + n = \frac{n(n+1)}{2}$$

This formula tells us that if you add the first and last numbers, $(1 + n)$, they will have the same sum as the second and second-to-last numbers $[2 + (n-1)]$ and the third and third-to-last $[3 + (n-2)]$, and so on. If you add all these sums, it would be the same as multiplying $(n + 1)$ by half of n (since there are half as many sums as numbers).

EXAMPLE: $1 + 2 + 3 + 4 + \ldots + 98 + 99 + 100 = \frac{100(101)}{2} = \frac{10,100}{2} = 5050$

550 Richter Scale

The **Richter scale** is named after the American seismologist Charles Francis Richter. Richter's scale measures the energy of an earthquake at its center. The scale runs from 1 to 9 and increases exponentially from one number to the next: a magnitude-7 quake is 10 times more powerful than a magnitude-6 quake, 100 times more powerful than a magnitude-5 quake, and so on.

RICHTER SCALE	EFFECTS
2.5	Generally not felt, but recorded on seismometers
3.5	Felt by many people
4.5	Some local damage may occur
6.0	A destructive earthquake
7.0	A major earthquake
8.0 and up	Great earthquake

Number Systems

Egyptian Numerals

In ancient Egypt, over 5000 years ago, the Egyptians used these numerals:

I **1**	IIII **4**	IIIIIII **7**	III III III **9**	∩I **11**	⌐ **10,000**
II **2**	III II **5**			૭ **100**	
III **3**	III III **6**	IIIII IIIII **8**	∩ **10**	𐊔 **1000**	

The Egyptians did not have place value. So, the number we write as 1998 would have been written like this:

𐊔 ૭૭૭ ૭૭૭ ૭૭૭ ∩∩∩ ∩∩∩ ∩∩∩ IIII IIII

553 Babylonian Numerals

At about the same time as the ancient Egyptians, the ancient peoples of Babylonia used different numerals.

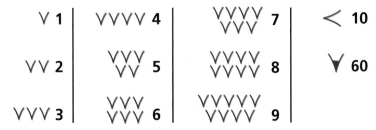

So, the number we write as 75 would have been written like this:

554 Roman Numerals

The Romans used numerals that are still used today. You can find them listed in movie credits, on clocks, and on buildings. They are not difficult to use but they are a little awkward.

I	1	IX	9	XL	40	D	500
II	2	X	10	XLV	45	M	1,000
III	3	XI	11	L	50	$\overline{V}$	5,000
IV	4	XII	12	LX	60	$\overline{X}$	10,000
V	5	XIX	19	LXX	70	$\overline{L}$	50,000
VI	6	XX	20	LXXX	80	$\overline{C}$	100,000
VII	7	XXV	25	XC	90	$\overline{D}$	500,000
VIII	8	XXX	30	C	100	$\overline{M}$	1,000,000

The Romans didn't have place value. One very interesting thing about Roman numerals is that the symbols don't always represent sums! When a symbol for a smaller number is to the left of another symbol, it represents a difference. So, IV = 5 − 1 = 4.

Our number 1999 would be written like this:

MCMXCIX

Mayan Numerals

The Maya Indians of Central America had a number system based on 20. They had concepts of place value and of zero.

○ 0   •••• 4   ⚬⚬/═ 7   ═══ 10

• 1   ═ 5   ••• /═ 8

•• 2   • /═ 6   •••• /═ 9   • /═══ 11

•••3

So, the number we write as 19 would look like this:

•••• ═══

Indian Numerals

Before the Romans used letters for numerals, the Hindus in India used nine number symbols with which they could write any number. These numerals have a place value like our numerals.

9 1   ŏ 4   ᴐ 7

ᴢ 2   ⅄ 5   Z 8

ʒ 3   ꙅ 6   ε 9

So, the number we write as 783 would look like this:

ᴐZʒ

Early in their history the Hindus would write for 303.

Later, they invented a zero and wrote ʒ • ʒ.

Arabic Numerals

The Arabs adapted the ideas of the Hindus and made some changes. Although they have changed several times, the numerals we use today are based on these.

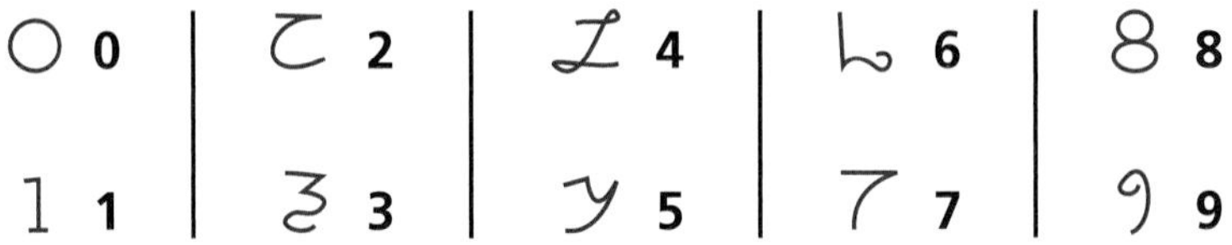

○ 0	ح 2	ﺡ 4	و 6	8 8
1 1	ﻜ 3	ﻯ 5	٧ 7	٩ 9

Binary Numerals

Computers are electronic devices and so they can only read whether a switch is ON or OFF. The ON switch can be represented by the digit 1 and the OFF switch by 0. This is a **binary**, or **base-two**, number system.

Decimal	Binary
1	1
2	10
3	11
4	100
5	101
6	110
7	111
8	1000
9	1001
10	1010

In the binary system, each place value is twice the following one.

128	64	32	16	8	4	2	1
2^7	2^6	2^5	2^4	2^3	2^2	2^1	2^0

So: $20_{ten} = 10100_{two}$

$40_{ten} = 101000_{two}$

$75_{ten} = 1001011_{two}$

$100_{ten} = 1100100_{two}$

The "$_{two}$" means the number is written in the binary system (base two). The "$_{ten}$" means the number is in base ten. If you see a number with no base listed, assume it's base ten.

Yellow Pages

The numbers in black at the end of many entries refer you back to topic numbers, not page numbers. You will find topic numbers at the top of each page and next to each new piece of information in *Math on Call*.

Glossary of Mathematical Formulas

Perimeter: The distance around a plane figure.

Figure	Formula	Variables	Example
Quadrilateral	$P = s_1 + s_2 + s_3 + s_4$	P: Perimeter s: side	3 cm 6 cm 3 cm 5 cm $P = 5 + 3 + 3 + 6$ $P = 17$ cm
Parallelogram	$P = 2l + 2w$	P: Perimeter l: length w: width	6 cm 3 cm $P = 2(3) + 2(6)$ $P = 18$ cm
Rectangle	$P = 2l + 2w$	P: Perimeter l: length w: width	3 ft 5 ft $P = 2(5) + 2(3)$ $P = 16$ ft
Rhombus	$P = 4s$	P: Perimeter s: side	2.1 cm $P = 4(2.1)$ $P = 8.4$ cm

Perimeter (continued)

Figure	Formula	Variables	Example
Square	$P = 4s$	P: Perimeter s: side	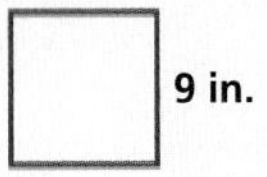 9 in. $P = 4(9)$ $P = 36$ in.
Circle	$C = \pi d$ or $C = 2\pi r$	C: circumference π: pi (about 3.14 or $\frac{22}{7}$) d: diameter r: radius	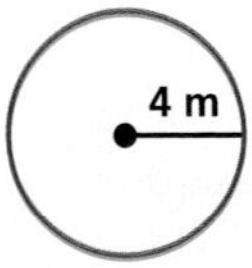 4 m $C \approx 2(3.14)(4)$ $C \approx 25.12$ m

Area: The number of square units a figure contains.

Figure	Formula	Variables	Example
Triangle	$A = \frac{1}{2}bh$	A: Area b: base h: height **The height is a perpendicular from the base to the opposite vertex. So, you can choose any side as the base as long as the height is perpendicular to that side.**	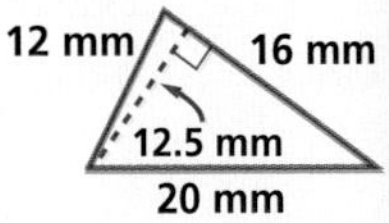 Case 1: 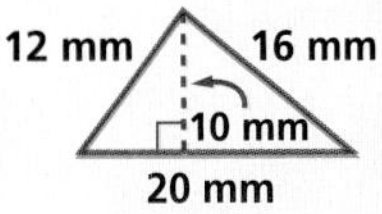 12 mm 16 mm 10 mm 20 mm $A = \frac{1}{2}(20)(10)$ $A = 100$ mm² Case 2: 12 mm 16 mm 12.5 mm 20 mm $A = \frac{1}{2}(16)(12.5)$ $A = 100$ mm²

MORE ▶

Area (continued)

Figure	Formula	Variables	Example
Parallelogram	$A = bh$	A: Area b: base h: height	
		You can choose any side as the base, as long as the height is perpendicular to that side.	$A = 11(4)$ $A = 44 \text{ cm}^2$
Rectangle	$A = lw$	A: Area l: length w: width	 $A = (5.2)(3.5)$ $A = 18.2 \text{ m}^2$
Square	$A = s^2$	A: Area s: side	 $A = (3.1)(3.1)$ $A = 9.61 \text{ m}^2$
Trapezoid	$A = \frac{1}{2}h(b_1 + b_2)$	A: Area h: height b_1: one base b_2: other base	
		The bases are the 2 parallel sides and the height is perpendicular to both.	$A = \frac{1}{2}(6)(8 + 16)$ $A = 72 \text{ ft}^2$
Circle	$A = \pi r^2$	A: Area π: pi (about 3.14 or $\frac{22}{7}$) r: radius	 $A \approx \left(\frac{22}{7}\right)\left(\frac{7}{2}\right)^2$ $A \approx 38\frac{1}{2} \text{ in.}^2$

Surface Area: The total area of the faces (including the bases) of a solid figure.

Figure	Formula	Variables	Example
Rectangular prism	$SA = 2lw + 2lh + 2wh$ or $2(lw + lh + wh)$	SA: Surface Area l: length w: width h: height	3 cm, 8 cm, 12 cm $SA = 2(12)(8) +$ $2(12)(3) +$ $2(8)(3)$ $SA = 192 + 72 + 48$ $SA = 312 \text{ cm}^2$
Cube	$SA = 6s^2$	SA: Surface Area s: side	2.5 m, 2.5 m, 2.5 m $SA = 6(2.5^2)$ $SA = 37.5 \text{ m}^2$
Square pyramid	$SA = b^2 + 2bh$ **This makes sense because there are 4 identical triangular faces and** $4(\frac{1}{2}bh) = 2bh.$	SA: Surface Area b: base h: height **Remember this *h* is the height of a *face*, not the height of the pyramid.**	11 cm, 4 cm, 4 cm $SA = 4^2 +$ $2(4)(11)$ $SA = 16 + 88$ $SA = 104 \text{ cm}^2$

MORE ▶

Surface Area (continued)

Figure	Formula	Variables	Example
Cylinder	$SA = 2\pi r^2 + 2\pi rh$ **$2\pi r^2$ is the area of the 2 circular bases. $2\pi r$ is the circumference of the circular base.**	SA: Surface Area π: pi (about 3.14 or $\frac{22}{7}$) r: radius h: height	3 cm / 8 cm $SA \approx 2(3.14)(3^2) +$ $2(3.14)(3)(8)$ $SA \approx 56.52 +$ 150.72 $SA \approx 207.24$ cm^2
Right circular cone	$SA = \pi r\sqrt{(r^2 + h^2)} + \pi r^2$ or $\pi r^2 + \pi rs$	SA: Surface Area π: pi (about 3.14 or $\frac{22}{7}$) r: radius h: height s: slant height	3 in. / 4 in. $SA \approx$ $(3.14)(3)\sqrt{(3^2 + 4^2)}$ $+ (3.14)(3^2)$ $SA \approx 47.1 + 28.26$ $SA \approx 75.36$ in.^{2}
Sphere	$SA = 4\pi r^2$	SA: Surface Area π: pi (about 3.14 or $\frac{22}{7}$) r: radius	5 ft $SA \approx 4(3.14)(5^2)$ $SA \approx 314$ ft^2

Volume: The number of cubic units a figure contains.

Figure	Formula	Variables	Example
Rectangular prism	$V = lwh$	V: Volume l: length w: width h: height	 $V = 8(3)(4)$ $V = 96$ cm³
Cube	$V = s^3$	V: Volume s: side	 $V = 5^3$ $V = 125$ m³
Prism	$V = Bh$	V: Volume B: area of base h: height **The base must have a parallel congruent face. The height is perpendicular to both.**	 $B = \frac{1}{2}(10)(5)$ So, $V = \frac{1}{2}(10)(5)(10)$ $V = 250$ cm³
Pyramid	$V = \frac{1}{3}Bh$	V: Volume B: area of base h: height **The faces of a pyramid are triangles. If any side of a pyramid is *not* a triangle, that's the base. The height is a perpendicular from the base to the vertex.**	 $V = \frac{1}{3}(3)(4)(8)$ $V = \frac{96}{3} = 32\frac{1}{3}$ in.³

MORE ▶

Volume (continued)

Figure	Formula	Variables	Example
Cylinder	$V = \pi r^2 h$ **πr^2 represents the area of the circular base.**	V: Volume π: pi (about 3.14 or $\frac{22}{7}$) r: radius h: height	 3 ft 4 ft $V \approx 3.14(3^2)(4)$ $V \approx 113.04$ ft^3
Cone	$V = \frac{1}{3}Bh$ or $V = \frac{1}{3}\pi r^2 h$ **πr^2 represents the area of the circular base.**	V: Volume π: pi (about 3.14 or $\frac{22}{7}$) r: radius h: height B: area of base	 7 m 3 m $V \approx \frac{1}{3}(\frac{22}{7})(3^2)(7)$ $V \approx 66$ m^3
Sphere	$V = \frac{4}{3}\pi r^3$	V: Volume π: pi (about 3.14 or $\frac{22}{7}$) r: radius	 2 m $V \approx \frac{4}{3}(\frac{22}{7})(2^3)$ $V \approx 33\frac{11}{21}$ m^3

Euler's Formula: Relationship among the number of faces, vertices, and edges of solids.

Euler's Formula	Variables	Example
$F + V = E + 2$	F = faces V = vertices E = edges	 $F = 6, V = 8, E = 12$ $6 + 8 = 12 + 2 = 14$

Economics Formulas

Type of Interest	Formula	Variables	Example
Simple Interest **Interest on the principal amount only**	$I = prt$	I: interest p: principal (investment) r: annual rate of interest (per year) t: time (in years)	How much interest will be accumulated if $1200 is invested at 6% for each of 4 years? $I = 1200(0.06)(4)$ $I = \$288$
Compound Interest **Interest on the principal plus any accumulated interest**	$A = P(1 + \frac{r}{n})^{nt}$	A: amount of money after t years P: principal r: interest compounded annually t: time (in years) n: number of yearly compounds	How much money would a person have if $1200 is invested at 6% interest compounded every year for 4 years? $A = 1200(1 + 0.06)^4$ $A = 1200(1.06^4)$ $A \approx 1200(1.26)$ $A \approx \$1512$

Temperature

Formula	Variables	Example
$C = \frac{5}{9}(F - 32)$	C: degrees Celsius F: degrees Fahrenheit	$F = 50°$ $C = \frac{5}{9}(50 - 32)$ $C = \frac{5}{9}(18) = 10°$
$F = \frac{9}{5}C + 32$	C: degrees Celsius F: degrees Fahrenheit	$C = 25°$ $F = \frac{9}{5}(25) + 32$ $F = 45 + 32 = 77°$

Probability

Type of Probability	Formula	Example
Probability of an event	Probability (event) = $\frac{\text{number of outcomes}}{\text{number of possible outcomes}}$	A bag is filled with 2 red balls and 4 blue balls. Pick a blue ball at random. $P(\text{Blue}) = \frac{4}{6} = \frac{2}{3}$
Probability of A and B, if A and B are independent	$P(A \text{ and } B) = P(A) \times P(B)$	Throw two 1–6 number cubes. $P(2 \text{ and } 3) = P(2)P(3)$ $P(2 \text{ and } 3) = (\frac{1}{6})(\frac{1}{6}) = \frac{1}{36}$
Probability of A or B **Probability Event A occurs or Event B occurs or they both occur**	$P(A \text{ or } B) = P(A) + P(B) - P(A \text{ and } B)$ **Note: P(A and B) = 0 if Events A and B are mutually exclusive**	Probability of selecting a King or a Heart at random from a deck of cards: $P(\text{King}) = \frac{4}{52}$ $P(\text{Heart}) = \frac{13}{52}$ $P(\text{King and Heart}) = \frac{1}{52}$ $P(\text{King or Heart}) =$ $\quad P(\text{King}) + P(\text{Heart}) -$ $\quad P(\text{King and Heart}) =$ $\quad \frac{4}{52} + \frac{13}{52} - \frac{1}{52} = \frac{16}{52} = \frac{4}{13}$
Probability of not A	$P(\text{not } A) = 1 - P(A)$	Select any card but a Queen from a deck of cards $P(\text{Queen}) = \frac{4}{52} = \frac{1}{13}$ $P(\text{not Queen}) = 1 - P(\text{Queen})$ $\quad = 1 - \frac{1}{13} = \frac{12}{13}$
Odds of A occurring	Odds = $\frac{\text{number of favorable outcomes}}{\text{number of unfavorable outcomes}}$	A bag is filled with balls numbered from 1 to 5. The odds of choosing the "3" ball are $\frac{1}{4}$, 1:4, or 1 to 4.
Different permutations of n things	$n! = n(n-1)(n-2)(n-3)\ldots$ (say: n factorial)	$3! = 3 \cdot 2 \cdot 1 = 6$ $4! = 4 \cdot 3 \cdot 2 \cdot 1 = 24$ $5! = 5 \cdot 4 \cdot 3 \cdot 2 \cdot 1 = 120$

Statistics

Measure of Central Tendency	Formula	Example
Mean	$\frac{\text{sum of numbers}}{\text{number of numbers}}$	Find the mean daily low temperature: $^-6°C$, $4°C$, $7°C$, $0°C$, $5°C$, $^-1°C$ Mean = $\frac{(^-6 + 4 + 7 + 0 + 5 + ^-1)}{6}$ Mean = $\frac{9}{6}$ = 1.5°C
Median	(a) middle number of a set of numbers when numbers are arranged from least to greatest, OR (b) average of two middle numbers when set has two middle numbers	Find the median daily high temperature: (a) 38°C, 24°C, 34°C, 29°C, 26°C Order numbers: 24, 26, <u>29</u>, 34, 38 Median is the middle number: 29°C (b) 41°C, 35°C, 46°C, 41°C, 38°C, 39°C Order numbers: 35, 38, <u>39</u>, <u>41</u>, 41, 46 Median is the average of the middle two numbers: Median = $\frac{(39 + 41)}{2}$ Median = $\frac{80}{2}$ = 40°C
Mode	number that appears most frequently in a set of numbers	Find the mode of the temperatures: (a) 56°F, 64°F, 48°F, 56°F, 63°F Mode: 56°F (b) 72°F, 68°F, 80°F, 68°F, 75°F, 80°F Mode: 68°F and 80°F (called bimodal) (c) 92°F, 89°F, 85°F, 94°F Mode: none
Range	greatest number − least number in a set of numbers	Find the range of the temperatures: 86°F, 72°F, 88°F, 80°F Range = high − low Range = 88 − 72 = 16°F

Triangle Relationship	Formula	Variables	Example
Pythagorean theorem	$a^2 + b^2 = c^2$	a = length of one leg of right triangle b = length of other leg of right triangle c = length of hypotenuse of right triangle	Find the length of the hypotenuse if the legs are 3 feet and 4 feet long. $3^2 + 4^2 = c^2$ $9 + 16 = c^2$ $25 = c^2$ $c = \sqrt{25} = 5$ ft
sine ratio	$\sin \theta =$ $\dfrac{\text{length of opposite leg}}{\text{length of hypotenuse}}$	θ: theta, Greek letter indicating angle measure	$\sin \theta = \frac{3}{5} = 0.6$
cosine ratio	$\cos \theta =$ $\dfrac{\text{length of adjacent leg}}{\text{length of hypotenuse}}$	θ: theta, Greek letter indicating angle measure	$\cos \theta = \frac{4}{5} = 0.8$
tangent ratio	$\tan \theta =$ $\dfrac{\text{length of opposite leg}}{\text{length of adjacent leg}}$	θ: theta, Greek letter indicating angle measure	$\tan \theta = \frac{3}{4} = 0.75$

Formulas Used in Graphing

Geometric Concept	Formula	Variables	Example
Slope	$m = \dfrac{(y_2 - y_1)}{(x_2 - x_1)}$ or $m = \dfrac{\text{change in } y}{\text{change in } x}$	m: slope (x_1, y_1) and (x_2, y_2): coordinates of 2 points on a line.	Slope of line connecting $(2, 3)$ and $(4, 6)$: $m = \dfrac{(y_2 - y_1)}{(x_2 - x_1)}$ $m = \dfrac{(6 - 3)}{(4 - 2)}$ $m = \dfrac{3}{2}$
Straight line	$y = mx + b$	m: slope b: y-intercept	$y = 2x + 1$ **The slope of the line is 2. The line crosses the y-axis at 1.**

Glossary of Mathematical Terms

A

abacus: A device used to keep track of computation, usually a frame that allows beads to slide along rods that represent place value.

abscissa: *See x-coordinate*

absolute value (| |): The distance of a number from zero on the number line. Always positive. $\lceil 4 \rceil = 4$; $|4| = 4$ **(050)**

abundant number: A number whose factors (except for the number itself) have a sum greater than the number. 20 is an abundant number because $1 + 2 + 4 + 5 + 10 > 20$. **(063)**

accurate: An approximate number is accurate (correct) to the last decimal place shown if all its digits are significant and if the true value is within $\frac{1}{2}$ the value of the last place. You could say that 3.14 is pi, accurate to the hundredths place because pi is between 3.14 and 3.15, closer to 3.14.

acute angle: An angle with a measure less than 90°. **(331)**

acute triangle: A triangle with no angle measuring 90° or more. **(351)**

add (+): Combine. **(087)**

addend: Any number being added. **(094)**

$$32 + 0.3 + 4 = 36.3$$
addends

adjacent: Next to. **(337)**

algebra: A branch of mathematics that includes the use of variables to express general rules about numbers, number relationships, and operations. **(201)**

algebraic expression: A group of numbers, symbols, and variables that express an operation or a series of operations. $3x$ is an expression for three times some number. **(203)**

algorithm: A step-by-step method for computing.

alternate angles: When a line (called a transversal) intersects two other lines, it forms 8 angles. Angles 1 and 7 are alternate exterior angles (so are angles 2 and 8). Angles 3 and 5 are alternate interior angles (so are angles 4 and 6). **(338)**

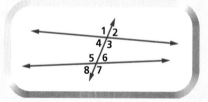

altitude: *See height*

angle (∠): Two rays that share an endpoint. **(328)**

angle of depression or elevation: The angle between a horizontal line and the line of sight. If you're looking down, it's an angle of depression. If you're looking up, the angle is an angle of elevation.

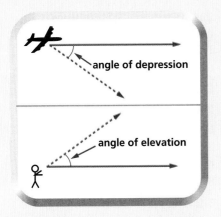

angle of depression

angle of elevation

apex: The point on a geometric figure farthest from the base line or base plane. The apex of a pyramid is its vertex.

apothem: The perpendicular line segment from a side of a regular polygon to its center.

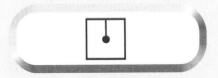

approximate number (≈): A number that describes another number without specifying it exactly. 3.14 is an approximation for pi. **(035)**

approximation: A method for obtaining an approximate number. **(035)**

Arabic numerals: The digits used in our base ten (decimal) number system: 0, 1, 2, 3, 4, 5, 6, 7, 8, 9. **(557)**

arc (⌒): The part of a curve between any two of its points. **(374)**

area (A): The measure, in square units, of the interior region of a 2-dimensional figure or the surface of a 3-dimensional figure. **(347)**

arithmetic: Calculation using addition, subtraction, multiplication, and division.

arithmetic mean: *See mean*

arithmetic progression: A set of numbers in which the difference between any two numbers in sequence is the same. 2, 4, 6, 8, . . . is an arithmetic progression because the difference between any two numbers in sequence is 2.

arithmetic series: The sum of the numbers in an arithmetic progression. $2 + 4 + 6 + 8 + . . .$

arm: (1) One of the legs or sides of a right triangle, not the hypotenuse. (2) One of the rays forming an angle. **(358)**

Associative Law: *See Associative Property of Addition/Multiplication*

Associative Property of Addition: The sum stays the same when the grouping of addends is changed. $(a + b) + c = a + (b + c)$, where a, b, and c stand for any real numbers. $(6 + 4) + 2 = 6 + (4 + 2)$ **(217)**

Associative Property of Multiplication: The product stays the same when the grouping of factors is changed. $(a \cdot b) \cdot c = a \cdot (b \cdot c)$, where a, b, and c stand for any real numbers. $(6 \cdot 4) \cdot 2 = 6 \cdot (4 \cdot 2)$ **(218)**

average: A single number that describes all the numbers in a set. Usually, this is the mean, but sometimes it is the median or the mode. **(273)**

average deviation: The mean of the absolute values of all the deviations in a set of data. The average deviation tells by how much each data point differs from the mean. **(281)**

axes: Plural of *axis*.

axis: A reference line from which distances or angles are measured on a coordinate grid. **(318)**

 B

base of an exponent: The number used as the factor in exponential form. In 3^4, the base is 3 and the exponent is 4. **(074)**

base of a percent: The number for which the percent is found. In 10% of 50, the base is 50.

base of a solid figure (B): A plane figure. If the solid is a cylinder or prism, there are two bases that are parallel and congruent.

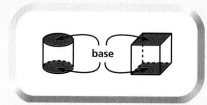

base

base ten: A number system in which each digit has ten times the value of the same digit one place to its right. $77 = 70 + 7$ **(002)**

base of a triangle (b): The side of a triangle that contains one end of the altitude. **(368)**

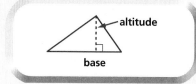

altitude

base

binary number system: A number system with place values that are powers of 2. The only digits used in

this system, which is the basis of computer code, are zero and 1. 110 in binary is 6 (one 4, one 2, and no 1s) in base ten. **(558)**

bisect: To cut or divide into two equal parts. **(326)**

bisecting: Finding the midpoint of a line segment, or finding the ray that divides an angle into two congruent angles. **(326)**

bit: Abbreviation for binary digit—a zero or a 1 in the binary number system. 110 in binary contains three bits (two 1s and a zero).

borrow: Regroup from one place value to a lower place value in order to subtract. *See regroup* **(127)**

box plot: *See box-and-whisker plot*

box-and-whisker plot: A graph that uses a rectangle to represent the middle 50% of a set of data and "whiskers" at both ends to represent the remainder of the data. **(302)**

 C

cancel: To remove equal factors from both sides of an equation or from the numerator and denominator of a fraction. $\frac{6}{8} = \frac{2 \times 3}{2 \times 4}$. Since both numerator and denominator have 2 as a factor, the 2s can be canceled to simplify the fraction to $\frac{3}{4}$. $4x = 12y$ is the same as $(2 \cdot 2)x = (2 \cdot 2 \cdot 3)y$. Since both sides of the equation have two 2s as factors, they can be canceled to simplify the equation to $x = 3y$. **(037)**

capacity: The maximum amount that can be contained by an object. Often refers to measurement of liquid. **(535)**

cardinal number: A whole number that names how many objects are in a group.

carry: Place an extra digit—from adding or multiplying the digits in a place value—in its proper place value until it can be included in the computation. *See regroup*

Cartesian coordinate system: *See coordinate grid*

Celsius (C): The metric-system scale for measuring temperature. 0°C is the freezing point of water at sea level. 100°C is the boiling point of water at sea level.

center: (1) A point that is the same distance from all points on the circumference of a circle or the surface of a sphere. (2) A point that is the same distance from the vertices of a regular polygon. (3) Occupying a middle position. **(370)**

centigrade: *See Celsius*

central angle: An angle that has the center of a circle as its vertex. **(340)**

certain event: An event that will definitely happen. A certain event has a probability of 1. **(462)**

characteristic: The integer part of a common logarithm. $\log 12 \approx 1.0792$. The characteristic of this logarithm is 1. *See also mantissa*

circle: A closed curve with all its points in one plane and the same distance from a fixed point (the center). **(370)**

circulating decimal: *See repeating decimal*

circumference (C): (1) The boundary line, or perimeter, of a circle. (2) The length of the perimeter of a circle. **(372)**

circumscribed: A plane figure whose sides are tangent to a circle is circumscribed *about* the circle. A circle containing a plane figure whose vertices are on the circle is circumscribed *about* the figure. Solid figures may be circumscribed about other solid figures. Not all figures can be circumscribed.

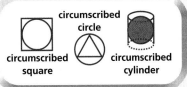

circumscribed circle

circumscribed square

circumscribed cylinder

clearing fractions: When working with an equation that contains fractions, multiplying both sides of the equation by some number that will eliminate any denominators.

$$\frac{1}{2}x + \frac{3}{4}y = 2$$
$$4(\frac{1}{2}x + \frac{3}{4}y) = 4(2)$$
$$2x + 3y = 8$$

collecting terms: *See combining like terms*

collinear: On the same line. **(256)**

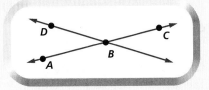

Points A, B, and C are collinear. Points A, B, and D are *not* collinear.

combination: A group of items or events. Placing these items or events in a different order does *not* create a new combination. A nickel, a dime, and a penny are a combination of coins. A dime, a nickel, and a penny are the same combination. **(460)**

combining like terms: When working with an expression, combining terms that have the same variable in the same form.
$4x + 3y + 8x^2 - x - \frac{1}{2}y$ is the same as $8x^2 + 3x + 2\frac{1}{2}y$ **(239)**

common: Shared.

common divisor: *See common factor*

common factor: A number that is a factor of two or more numbers. The numbers 1, 2, 3, and 6 are the common factors of 18 and 24. **(065)**

common fraction: Any fraction whose numerator and denominator are whole numbers.
$\frac{4}{5}$ and $\frac{8}{3}$ are both common fractions. $\frac{4\frac{1}{2}}{5}$ is not a common fraction.

common logarithm (log): An exponent showing the number of times 10 is used as a factor to find another number.
$\log 100 = 2$ means $10^2 = 100$ **(085)**

common multiple: A number that is a multiple of two or more numbers. The numbers 6, 12, 24, and 30 are some of the common multiples of 2 and 3. **(068)**

commutativity: *See Commutative Property of Addition/Multiplication*

Commutative Property of Addition: The sum stays the same when the order of the addends is changed.
$a + b = b + a$, where a and b are any real numbers. $6 + 4 = 4 + 6$ **(213)**

Commutative Property of Multiplication: The product stays the same when the order of the factors is changed.
$a \cdot b = b \cdot a$, where a and b are any real numbers. $6 \cdot 4 = 4 \cdot 6$ **(218)**

compatible numbers: Numbers that are easy to work with mentally. The numbers 240 and 60 are compatible numbers for estimating $257 \div 56$.

complementary angles: Two angles that have measures with a sum of $90°$. **(335)**

complementary events: Two or more mutually exclusive events that together cover all possible outcomes. The sum of the probabilities of complementary events is 1. The results of a coin toss are complementary events because the coin can only land heads-up or tails-up. **(470)**

complex fraction: A fraction with a fraction in the numerator and/or denominator. $\frac{4\frac{1}{2}}{5}$ and $\frac{\frac{1}{3}}{\frac{3}{5}}$ are complex fractions. $\frac{4}{5}$ is not a complex fraction. **(042)**

composite: Made up of several different things.

composite figure: A figure made up of several different shapes.

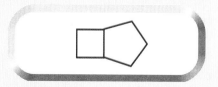

composite number: A number that has more than two factors. 8 is a composite number because it has four factors: 1, 2, 4, and 8. **(060)**

composite solid: A combination of several solids.

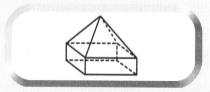

compound event: A combination of simple events. If you roll a 1–6 number cube, the probability of rolling a 2 *or* a 3 is a compound event. **(468)**

compute: To find a numerical result, usually by adding, subtracting, multiplying, dividing, or finding roots. **(086)**

concave polygon: A polygon with one or more diagonals that have points outside the polygon. **(345)**

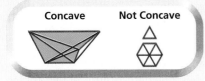

concurrent: With a common point.

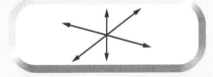

cone: A 3-dimensional figure with one curved surface, one flat surface (usually circular), one curved edge, and one vertex. **(414)**

congruent (≅): Having exactly the same size and shape. **(381)**

conjugate angles: Two angles with a sum of 360°.

consecutive: In order. 8, 9, 10 are consecutive whole numbers. 2, 4, 6 are consecutive even numbers.

convex polygon: A polygon with all interior angles measuring less than 180°. **(345)**

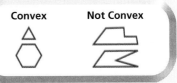

coordinate grid: A 2-dimensional system in which the coordinates of a point are its distances from two intersecting, usually perpendicular, straight lines called axes. **(318)**

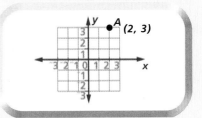

coordinate plane: *See coordinate grid*

coordinate system: *See coordinate grid*

coordinates: An ordered pair of numbers that identify a point on a coordinate plane. **(318)**

coplanar: In the same plane.

correlation: An association between two variables used in statistics. *See also positive correlation, negative correlation* **(308)**

cosine ratio (cos): In a right triangle, the cosine of an angle is the ratio of the leg adjacent to that angle to the length of the hypotenuse.

MORE ▶

The value of the cosine of an angle depends upon the measure of the angle. **(427)**

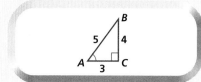

$\cos A = \frac{3}{5} = 0.6$

counting principle: If one event can happen in a ways and a second event can happen in b ways, the two can occur together in $a \cdot b$ ways. **(459)**

cross multiplication: A method for finding a missing numerator or denominator in equivalent fractions or ratios by making the cross products equal. **(434)**

cross product: The product of one numerator and the opposite denominator in a pair of equivalent fractions. The cross products of equivalent fractions are equal. **(434)**

cross section: A shape formed when a plane cuts through a 3-dimensional figure.

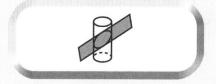

cube: (1) A regular solid having six congruent square faces. (2) The third power of a number.
$4^3 = 4 \times 4 \times 4 = 64$ **(399)**

cube root: A number whose cube is equal to a given number.
$\sqrt[3]{8} = 2$. So, 2 is the cube root of 8. **(080)**

cubic measure: *See cubic unit*

cubic unit: A unit such as a cubic meter used to measure volume or capacity. **(397)**

cuboid: A prism with six rectangular faces.

curve: (1) A line that smoothly and continuously deviates from straightness. (2) A line representing data on a graph. **(327)**

customary system: A system of measurement used in the U.S. The system includes units for measuring length, capacity, and weight. **(536)**

cylinder: A 3-dimensional figure with two parallel and congruent circles as bases, one curved surface, two curved edges, and no vertices. **(409)**

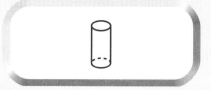

D

data: Information, especially numerical information. Usually organized for analysis. **(270)**

decimal (decimal number): (1) A number written using base ten. (2) A number containing a decimal point. **(011)**

decimal point: A dot separating the ones and tenths places in a decimal number. **(011)**

degree (angle measure): A unit of angle measure. $1°$ equals the central angle of a circle formed by rays that cut $\frac{1}{360}$ of its circumference. **(330)**

degree Celsius (°C): The metric unit of measurement for temperature. *See also Celsius*

degree Centigrade: *See degree Celsius*

degree Fahrenheit (°F): The customary unit of measurement for temperature. *See also Fahrenheit*

denominate number: A number used with a unit. 24 inches or 95°.

denominator: The quantity below the line in a fraction. It tells the number of equal parts into which a whole is divided. **(028)**

dependent events: Two events in which the outcome of the first event affects the outcome of the second event. **(469)**

deviation: The difference between a number in a set of data and the mean of all the numbers in the set. **(281)**

diagonal: A line segment that joins two vertices of a polygon but is not a side of the polygon.
AC, AD, and *AE* are some of the diagonals of this hexagon. **(345)**

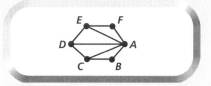

diagram: A drawing that represents a mathematical situation. **(483)**

difference: The amount that remains after one quantity is subtracted from another. **(120)**

digit: Any one of the ten symbols: 0, 1, 2, 3, 4, 5, 6, 7, 8, or 9. **(004)**

dilation: A proportional shrinking or enlargement of a figure. **(390)**

dimensions: (1) The lengths of sides of a geometric figure. (2) The number of coordinates needed to locate a point in space. A 2-dimensional figure is located in a plane and is named by two coordinates.

directed number: A number with a positive or negative sign to show its direction from zero. Temperatures and altitudes are directed numbers. Area and volume are always positive so they are not directed numbers.

disprove (a statement): Give an example or conclusive reason to show that a statement is not true for all numbers.

Distributive Property: $a \cdot (b + c) = (a \cdot b) + (a \cdot c)$ and $a \cdot (b - c) = (a \cdot b) - (a \cdot c)$, where a, b, and c stand for any real numbers.
$6 \cdot (4 + 3) = (6 \cdot 4) + (6 \cdot 3)$ **(220)**

divide (÷): (1) To separate into equal groups. (2) To be an exact divisor of. **(171)**

dividend: A quantity to be divided.
dividend ÷ divisor = quotient
$$\text{divisor } \overline{)\text{dividend}}^{\text{quotient}}$$
(171)

divisible: One number is divisible by another if their quotient is an integer. 16 is divisible by 2 but is not divisible by 3.

division: The operation of making equal groups. There are 7.5 groups of 6 in 45. **(171)**

divisor: The quantity by which another quantity is to be divided.
dividend ÷ divisor = quotient
$$\text{divisor } \overline{)\text{dividend}}^{\text{quotient}}$$
(171)

domain: In a function, the possible values for x in the given situation.

E

edge: The line segment where two faces of a solid figure meet.

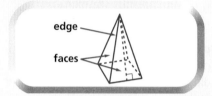

endpoint: Either of two points marking the end of a line segment. **(323)**

equal (=): Having the same value.

equal ratios: *See proportion*

equally likely: Two or more possible outcomes of a given situation that have the same probability. If you flip a coin, the two outcomes—the coin lands heads-up and the coin lands tails-up—are equally likely to occur. **(465)**

equation: A statement that two mathematical expressions are equal. $n + 50 = 75$ means that $n + 50$ must have the same value as 75.

equidistant: Equally distant. All points on a circle are equidistant from its center.

equilateral triangle: A triangle whose sides are all the same length. **(352)**

equivalent: Naming the same number. 4.6 and 4.60 are equivalent decimals. $\frac{2}{3}$ and $\frac{4}{6}$ are equivalent fractions. 2:6 and 1:3 are equivalent ratios.

estimate (es' ti mate): To find a number close to an exact amount. **(094)**

estimate (es' ti met): A number close to an exact amount; an estimate tells *about* how much. **(094)**

evaluate: To find the value of a mathematical expression.

even number: A whole number that is divisible by 2. **(055)**

event: A possible result or outcome in probability. **(462)**

expanded form: A way to write numbers that shows the place value of each digit. $789 = (7 \times 100) + (8 \times 10) + (9 \times 1)$ **(005)**

experimental probability: A statement of probability based on the results of a series of trials. **(466)**

exponent: The number that tells how many equal factors there are. $3 \times 3 \times 3 \times 3 = 3^4$; the exponent is 4. **(005)**

exponential form: A way of writing a number using exponents. $425 = (4 \times 10^2) + (2 \times 10^1) + (5 \times 10^0)$ **(005)**

expression: A variable or combination of variables, numbers, and symbols that represents a mathematical relationship. $4r^2; 3x + 2y; \sqrt{25}$ **(203)**

extremes: The first and last terms in the ratios of a proportion. $\frac{2}{3} = \frac{10}{15}$, or 2:3 = 10:15. The extremes are 2 and 15. *See also means* **(433)**

F

face: A plane figure that serves as one side of a solid figure. **(393)**

factor: (1) An integer that divides evenly into another. $2 \times 6 = 12$; 2 and 6 are factors of 12. (2) *See factorize* **(056)**

factorial (!): The product of a whole number and every positive whole number less than itself. Abbreviate as *n!* and say: *n factorial.*
$$4! = 4 \times 3 \times 2 \times 1 = 24 \qquad \textbf{(057)}$$

factorize: (1) To find the factors of a number or expression. (2) To write a number or expression as a product of its factors.

Fahrenheit (F): Temperature scale. 32°F is the freezing point of water at sea level. 212°F is the boiling point of water at sea level.

favorable outcome: In probability, the outcome you are interested in measuring. The possible outcomes of picking a marble out of a bag are red, blue, and yellow. If you want to know the probability of picking blue, then blue is the favorable outcome. **(465)**

Fibonacci sequence: A special series of numbers in which each number is the sum of the two preceding numbers. 1, 1, 2, 3, 5, 8, 13, . . . **(546)**

figure: A closed shape in 2 or 3 dimensions. **(393)**

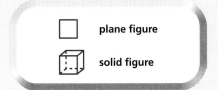
plane figure
solid figure

finite: Having bounds; limited.

flat angle: *See straight angle*

flip: *See reflection*

formula: A general mathematical statement or rule. **(560)**

fraction: A way of representing part of a whole or part of a group by telling the number of equal parts in the whole and the number of those parts you are describing.
$\frac{4}{5}$ ← numerator (4 parts)
← denominator (5 equal parts) **(028)**

frequency: The number of times something occurs in an interval.

function: A relation in which every value of x has a unique value of y. **(231)**

geometric: Having to do with geometry.

geometric progression: A sequence of terms in which each term is a constant multiple of the preceding term. 1, 4, 16, 64, . . . In this sequence, each term is four times the previous term.

geometry: The mathematics of the properties and relationships of points, lines, angles, surfaces, and solids. **(314)**

graph: A pictorial device used to show a numerical relationship. **(245)**

greatest common factor (GCF): The largest factor of two or more numbers. The greatest common factor of 12, 18, and 30 is 6. **(066)**

greatest possible error (GPE): Half the unit of measure used in making a measurement. If you use an inch ruler marked in fourths to find that a board is $8\frac{1}{4}$ inches long, the GPE is $\frac{1}{8}$ inch. So, the board is between $8\frac{1}{8}$ and $8\frac{3}{8}$ inches long.

grid: A pattern of horizontal and vertical lines, usually forming squares. **(245)**

H

half line: *See ray*

half turn: A rotation of 180° (or half of one revolution) about a point.

height (altitude, *h*): (1) The perpendicular distance from a vertex to the opposite side of a plane figure. (2) The perpendicular distance from the vertex to the base of a pyramid or cone. (3) The perpendicular distance between the bases of a prism or cylinder. If there is more than one side or edge that can be used as a base in a figure, then the figure has more than one possible height. **(349)**

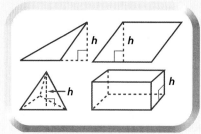

hexagon: A polygon with six sides. **(394)**

hexagonal prism: A prism with six-sided bases.

highest common factor: *See greatest common factor*

histogram: A graph in which the labels for the bars are numerical intervals. **(295)**

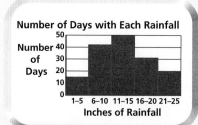

Number of Days with Each Rainfall

Number of Days

50
40
30
20
10
0

1–5   6–10   11–15   16–20   21–25

Inches of Rainfall

horizontal: Parallel to or in the plane of the horizon. In a coordinate grid, the *x*-axis is a horizontal line.

hypotenuse: The longest side of a right triangle. **(358)**

I

Identity Property of Addition: Adding zero to a number gives a sum identical to the given number. $8 + 0 = 8$ and $0 + 8 = 8$ **(222)**

Identity Property of Multiplication: Multiplying a number by 1 gives a product identical to the given number. $8 \times 1 = 8$ and $1 \times 8 = 8$ **(222)**

impossible event: An event with a probability of zero. If you roll a 1–6 number cube, rolling a 7 is an impossible event. **(462)**

independent events: Two events in which the outcome of the first event does not affect the outcome of the second event. **(469)**

index: An exponent or the number indicating what root you are looking for. In 4^5, the index is 5; in $\sqrt[3]{4}$, the index is 3.

indirect measurement: Finding a measurement by measuring something else and then using relationships to find the measurement you need. **(379)**

inequality: A mathematical sentence that compares two unequal expressions using one of the symbols $<, >, \leq, \geq$, or $\neq$. **(258)**

infinite: Having no boundaries or limits.

inscribed: An angle or polygon whose vertices are part of another figure is inscribed in that figure. A circle or other curved figure tangent to all surfaces of another figure is inscribed in that figure.

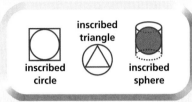

inscribed triangle

inscribed circle

inscribed sphere

integers: The set of whole numbers and their opposites.
... ‾2, ‾1, 0, 1, 2, ... **(047)**

integral: Refers to an integer. An integral solution to a problem cannot be a decimal or fractional solution.

interquartile range: The difference between the upper quartile and the lower quartile.

intersect: To meet or cross. **(324)**

irrational numbers: Numbers that cannot be written as a ratio of two integers. The decimal extensions of irrational numbers never terminate and never repeat. $0.10110111011110...$ or $3.14159...$ **(052)**

irregular polygon: A polygon whose sides are not all the same length.

isosceles triangle: A triangle that has at least two congruent sides. **(352)**

 L

latitude: Distance north and south of the Equator. Measured in degrees from 0° at the Equator to 90° at each pole.

least common denominator (LCD): The smallest common multiple of the denominators of two or more fractions. The LCD of $\frac{1}{4}$ and $\frac{5}{6}$ is 12. **(038)**

least common multiple (LCM): The smallest common multiple of a set of two or more numbers. The LCM of 4 and 6 is 12. **(068)**

leg: In a right triangle, one of the two sides that form the right angle. **(358)**

length (*l*): (1) The distance along a line or figure from one point to another. (2) One dimension of a 2- or 3-dimensional figure. **(352)**

like terms: Terms that have the same variables and the same corresponding exponents. In $3x^2 + 2x^2 + 5x + 6$, $3x^2$ and $2x^2$ are like terms. **(239)**

line (⟷): An infinite set of points forming a straight path extending in two directions. **(321)**

line of best fit: A line drawn on a scatter plot to estimate the relationship between two sets of data. **(306)**

line plot: A diagram showing frequency of data on a number line. **(301)**

line segment: A part of a line defined by two endpoints. **(323)**

line symmetry: A figure that can be folded along a line so that the two halves match exactly. **(389)**

line of symmetry: A line that divides a figure into two congruent halves that are mirror images of each other. **(389)**

linear equation: An equation whose graph in a coordinate grid is a straight line.

logarithm (log): The number of times a factor is used to produce another number. The logarithm to the base 5 of 125 is 3 ($\log_5 125 = 3$) means $5^3 = 125$. 5 is the factor and 3 is the log. *See also common logarithm* **(085)**

logic: Formal structure for reasoning. Also, the mathematical study of ways to reason through problems.

longitude: Distance around the earth from a line running north and south through Greenwich, England. Measured in degrees from 0° at Greenwich east and west to 180°.

lower quartile: The median of the lower half of an ordered set of data. **(278)**

lowest terms: *See simplest form*

mantissa: The positive decimal part of a common logarithm. $\log 12 \approx 1.0792$. The mantissa of this logarithm is .0792. *See also characteristic*

mass: The amount of matter in an object. Measured by balancing against an object of known mass. While gravity influences weight, it does *not* affect mass.

mean: The sum of a set of numbers divided by the number of elements in the set. **(274)**

means: The two middle terms in the ratios of a proportion. $2{:}3 = 10{:}15$. The means are 3 and 10. *See also extremes* **(433)**

measure: (1) The dimensions, quantity, length, or capacity of something. (2) To find the dimensions of something.

median: The middle number of a set of numbers when the numbers are arranged from least to greatest, or the mean of two middle numbers when the set has two middle numbers. **(275)**

mental math: Computing an exact answer without using paper and pencil or other physical aids. **(088)**

metric system: A system of measurement based on tens. The basic unit of capacity is the liter. The basic unit of length is the meter. The basic unit of mass is the gram. **(535)**

midpoint: The point on a line segment that divides it into two congruent segments. **(474)**

minuend: In subtraction, the minuend is the number you subtract from.

```
  1496  ←— minuend
−  647  ←— subtrahend
   849  ←— difference
```

minute ('): (1) One-sixtieth of an hour. (2) One-sixtieth of a degree of angle measure.

mirror image (flip): *See reflection*

mixed decimal: A decimal number with an integer part and a decimal part.

mixed fraction: A number with an integer part and a fraction part.

mixed number: *See mixed decimal and mixed fraction*

mode: The number that appears most frequently in a set of numbers. There may be one, more than one, or no mode. **(276)**

monomial: The product of numbers and variables is a monomial. A monomial may be a term in a longer algebraic expression. $14y^2$ is a monomial.

multinomial: *See polynomial*

multiple: The product of a whole number and any other whole number. A multiple of 4 is 8. **(067)**

multiplicand: In multiplication, the multiplicand is the factor being multiplied.

4.6 ←—multiplicand
× 0.2 ←—multiplier
0.92 ←—product

multiplication: The operation of repeated addition. 4×3 is the same as $4 + 4 + 4$. Four is used as an addend three times in 4×3. **(142)**

multiplication principle: *See counting principle*

multiplier: In multiplication, the multiplier is the factor being multiplied by.

4.6 ←—multiplicand
× 0.2 ←—multiplier
0.92 ←—product

multiply (× or ·): *See multiplication*

mutually exclusive events: Two events that cannot occur at the same time. **(468)**

natural numbers: The counting numbers: 1, 2, 3, 4, 5, . . .

negative correlation: A relationship between two sets of numerical data in which one set generally increases as the other decreases. **(308)**

negative numbers: Numbers less than zero. **(046)**

negative slope: A line that slants downward from left to right has a negative slope.

net: A 2-dimensional shape that can be folded into a 3-dimensional figure is a net of that figure. **(395)**

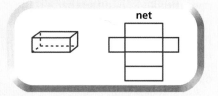

net

number line: A diagram that represents numbers as points on a line. **(007)**

number sentence: An equation or inequality with numbers. $6 + 3 = 9$

numeral: A symbol (not a variable) used to represent a number.

numerator: The number or expression written above the line in a fraction. **(028)**

oblique: A relationship between lines and/or plane figures that is not perpendicular or parallel. **(394)**

obtuse angle: An angle with a measure greater than 90° and less than 180°. **(331)**

obtuse triangle: A triangle whose largest angle measures greater than 90°. **(351)**

octagon: A polygon with 8 sides. **(404)**

odd number: A whole number that ends in 1, 3, 5, 7, or 9. **(055)**

odds: The ratio of favorable outcomes to unfavorable outcomes. There are 8 shirts in a dark closet and 2 of them are blue. The odds in favor of reaching in and grabbing a blue shirt are 2 to 6 because 2 outcomes (blue) are favorable and 6 outcomes (not blue) are unfavorable. **(471)**

operation: Addition, subtraction, multiplication, division, raising to a power, and taking a root are mathematical operations.

opposite: (1) Directly across from. ∠*B* is opposite side *AC*.

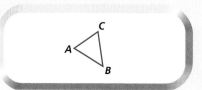

(2) Having a different sign but the same numeral. ⁻6 is the opposite of ⁺6. **(046)**

opposite angles: (1) Angles in a polygon that have no common sides. ∠*A* and ∠*C* are opposite angles.

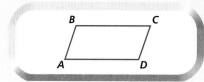

(2) *See also vertical angles*

order of operations: Rules describing what sequence to use in evaluating expressions:
(1) Evaluate within grouping symbols.
(2) Do powers or roots.
(3) Multiply or divide left to right.
(4) Add or subtract left to right. **(207)**

ordered pair: A pair of numbers that gives the coordinates of a point on a grid in this order (horizontal coordinate, vertical coordinate). Point *A* is at (3, 2). Point *B* is at (2, 3). **(232)**

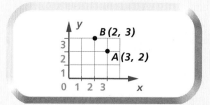

ordinal number: A whole number that names the position of an object in sequence. *First, second,* and *third* are ordinal numbers.

ordinate: *See y-coordinate*

origin: The intersection of the *x*- and *y*-axes in a coordinate plane, described by the ordered pair (0, 0). **(318)**

outcome: One of the possible events in a probability situation. **(465)**

outlier: A number in a set of data that is much larger or smaller than most of the other numbers in the set. **(283)**

overestimate: An estimate greater than the exact answer.

 P

parallel (∥): Always the same distance apart. **(324)**

parallelepiped: A prism whose bases and faces are all parallelograms.

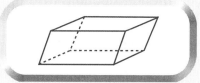

parallelogram: A quadrilateral with two pairs of parallel and congruent sides. **(363)**

pentagon: A polygon that has five sides. **(383)**

pentomino: A plane figure made up of five congruent squares, with each square having at least one side shared with another square.

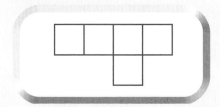

per: For each.

percent (%): A special ratio that compares a number to 100 using the symbol %. 40% of 100 is 40, 40% of 200 is 80. **(441)**

percentage: A number that is a given percent of another number. 25% of 60 is 15. The percentage is 15.

percentiles: The numbers that divide a set of data into 100 equal parts. **(279)**

perfect number: A whole number equal to the sum of its factors (excluding the number itself). 6 is a perfect number because $1 + 2 + 3 = 6$. **(062)**

perfect square: The product of an integer multiplied by itself. 36 is a perfect square because $6 \times 6 = 36$ and $^-6 \times {}^-6 = 36$. **(083)**

perimeter (P): The distance around a figure. **(346)**

periodic decimal: *See repeating decimal*

permutations: Possible orders or arrangements of a set of events or items. If you put the items or events into a different order, you have a different permutation. RAT and TAR and ART are three of the possible permutations of the letters A, R, and T. **(457)**

perpendicular (⊥): Forming right angles. **(325)**

perpendicular bisector: A line that divides a line segment in half and meets the segment at right angles. **(326)**

perpendicular distance: (1) The length of a segment from a point to a line, perpendicular to the line. (2) The length of a segment between two lines, perpendicular to both.

pi (π): The ratio of the circumference of any circle to its diameter, approximately equal to 3.14, or $\frac{22}{7}$. **(373)**

place value: The value of the position of a digit in a number. In the number 7863, the 8 is in the hundreds place and its value is 800. **(004)**

plane: A flat surface that extends infinitely in all directions. **(317)**

plane figure: Any 2-dimensional figure. circle, polygon, angle **(344)**

point: An exact position in space. **(316)**

point symmetry: A figure that can be turned exactly 180° about a point and fit exactly on itself has point symmetry. **(387)**

polygon: A closed figure formed from line segments that meet only at their endpoints. **(345)**

polyhedron: A 3-dimensional figure in which all the surfaces are polygons. **(394)**

polynomial: Having a sum of monomials (terms). $14y^2 + 25y - 6$ is a multinomial algebraic expression. Note that $- 6$ looks like a difference, not a sum, but since $- 6 = + {}^-6$, it fits the definition.

population: A group of people (or objects or events) that fit a particular description. **(265)**

positive correlation: Two sets of data are positively correlated if, as the numbers in one set tend to increase, the numbers in the other set also tend to increase. **(308)**

positive numbers: Numbers that are greater than zero. **(046)**

positive slope: A line that slants upward from left to right has a positive slope. **(248)**

power: An exponent. **(070)**

precision: An indication of how finely a measurement was made. When you calculate with measured values, you may need to round to the smallest unit in the actual measurement. You run a marathon in 6.5 hours. To find your hourly rate, you divide 26.2 miles by 6.5 hours and your calculator display shows 4.0307692. Since the original measurements were in tenths, the hourly rate is precise only to the tenths place: 4.0 mph.

prime factorization: The expression of a number as the product of prime factors. The prime factorization of 12 is $2 \times 2 \times 3$. **(061)**

prime number: A number that has exactly two positive factors, itself and 1. **(058)**

prism: A 3-dimensional figure that has two congruent and parallel faces that are polygons. The remaining faces are parallelograms. **(394)**

probability: The chance of an event occurring. The probability of an event is equal to the number of favorable outcomes divided by the number of possible outcomes:

$$P(\text{event}) = \frac{\text{number of favorable outcomes}}{\text{number of possible outcomes}}$$

(456)

product: The result of multiplication. **(056)**

proper fraction: A fraction whose numerator is an integer smaller than its integer denominator. $\frac{3}{4}$

proportion: An equation showing that two ratios are equivalent. $\frac{1}{2} = \frac{2}{4}$ **(428)**

proportional: Having equivalent ratios.

pyramid: A polyhedron whose base is a polygon and whose other faces are triangles that share a common vertex. **(403)**

Pythagorean theorem: The sum of the squares of the lengths of the two legs of a right triangle is equal to the square of the length of the hypotenuse. $a^2 + b^2 = c^2$ **(359)**

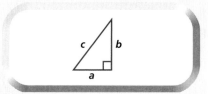

Pythagorean triples: A set of three positive integers that name the sides of a right triangle. 3, 4, and 5 are a Pythagorean triple because $3^2 + 4^2 = 5^2$.

quadrants: The four sections of a coordinate grid that are separated by the axes. **(318)**

```
            y
Quadrant  |  Quadrant
   II     |    I
----------+---------- x
Quadrant  |  Quadrant
  III     |   IV
```

quadrilateral: A four-sided polygon. **(362)**

quantity: An amount.

quarter turn: One-fourth of a revolution (90°) about a given point (turn center).

quartiles: Along with the median, the quartiles divide an ordered set of data into four groups of about the same size. **(278)**

quotient: The result of the division of one quantity by another.

dividend ÷ divisor = quotient

$$\frac{\text{quotient}}{\text{divisor })\overline{\text{dividend}}}$$ **(171)**

R

radical ($\sqrt{}$): A symbol that indicates the root to be taken.

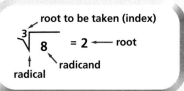

The symbol $\sqrt{}$ with no index indicates the square root.

radicand: The number or expression under a radical.

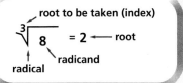

radii: Plural of *radius*.

radius (r): The segment, or the length of the segment, from the center of a circle to a point on the circle. **(370)**

random: By chance, with no outcome any more likely than another.

random sample: A sample in which every person, object, or event in the population has an equal chance of being selected for the sample. **(267)**

range: (1) The difference between the greatest number and the least number in a set of numbers. (2) The possible values for a variable in a given situation. In the area formula $A = lw$, the variables must be positive numbers, so the range for the variables is all positive numbers. (3) The possible values for y in a function. **(272)**

rate: A ratio comparing two different units. Miles per hour and heartbeats per minute are rates. **(435)**

ratio: A comparison of two numbers using division. **(029)**

rational number: A number that can be expressed as a ratio of two integers. **(027)**

ray ($\longrightarrow$): A part of a line that has one endpoint and extends indefinitely in one direction. **(322)**

real numbers: The combined set of the rational and irrational numbers.

reciprocals: Two numbers that have a product of 1. $\frac{3}{4}$ and $\frac{4}{3}$ are reciprocals because $\frac{3}{4} \cdot \frac{4}{3} = 1$. **(188)**

rectangle: A quadrilateral with two pairs of congruent, parallel sides and four right angles. **(363)**

rectangular prism: A prism with six rectangular faces. **(394)**

recurring decimal: *See repeating decimal*

reduce: Put a fraction into simplest form. $\frac{4}{8} = \frac{1}{2}$

redundant number: *See abundant number*

reflection (flip): A transformation creating a mirror image of a figure on the opposite side of a line. **(388)**

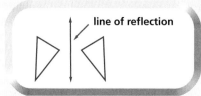

line of reflection

reflex angle: An angle that measures more than 180°. **(331)**

region: A part of a plane.

regroup: In place value, to use part of the value from one place in another place to make addition and subtraction easier. You can think of

$$
\begin{array}{r}
43 \quad \text{as} \quad (30 + 13) \\
-27 \quad -(20 + \ 7)
\end{array}
$$

Either way, the difference is 16. **(099)**

regular polygon: A polygon with all sides the same length and all angles the same measure.

regular polyhedron: A solid figure with congruent regular polygons for all faces. **(394)**

regular solid: *See regular polyhedron*

relation: A set of ordered pairs. **(318)**

relatively prime: Two numbers are relatively prime if they have no common factors other than 1.

remainder: In whole-number division, when you have divided as far as you can without using decimals, what has not been divided yet is the remainder.

$$
20\overline{)43} \quad \text{(2 R3)}
$$
(182)

repeating decimal: A decimal that has an infinitely repeating sequence of digits. $5.2424\ldots = 5.\overline{24}$ **(023)**

revolution: One turn of 360° about a point.

rhombus: A parallelogram with all four sides equal in length. **(363)**

right: Having to do with right angles. In a right circular cone, the height meets the circular base in a right angle at its center.

right angle (∟): An angle that measures exactly 90°. **(331)**

right triangle: A triangle that has one 90° angle. **(351)**

rise: The change in y-value between two points in the graph of a line.

Roman numerals: The symbols used in the ancient Roman number system:

I	1	C	100
V	5	D	500
X	10	M	1000
L	50		

(554)

root: In an equation in the form $a^x = b$ or $\sqrt[x]{b} = a$, a is the xth root of b. **(076)**

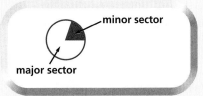

rotation (turn): A transformation in which a figure is turned a given angle and direction around a point. **(386)**

round: To drop or zero-out digits in a number and change the digit in a specified place using these rules:
- If the digit in the first place after the specified place is 5 or more, add 1 to the digit in the specified place. This is rounding up.
- If the digit in the first place after the specified place is less than 5, do not change the digit in the specified place. This is rounding down. **(010)**

Rule of Three: From ancient Hindu mathematics: In a proportion, the product of the means equals the product of the extremes.

$$25{:}75 = 1{:}3$$
$$\boxed{75 \times 1 = 75}$$
$$25 \times 3 = 75$$

run: The change in x-value between two points in the graph of a line.

sample: A number of people, objects, or events chosen from a given population to represent the entire group. **(264)**

scale: A ratio between two sets of measurements. **(377)**

scale factor: The ratio between the lengths of corresponding sides of two similar figures.

scalene triangle: A triangle that has no congruent sides. **(352)**

scatter plot: A graph consisting of points, one for each item being measured. The two coordinates of a point represent the measures of two attributes of each item. **(305)**

scientific notation: A form of writing numbers as the product of a power of 10 and a decimal number greater than or equal to 1 and less than 10. 2600 is written as 2.6×10^3 in scientific notation. **(016)**

second ("): (1) One-sixtieth of an angle minute (one thirty-six hundredth of a degree). (2) One sixtieth of a minute of time (one thirty-six-hundredth of an hour). (3) The number two position in a line.

sector: A part of a circle bounded by two radii and the arc they create.

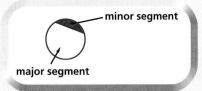

minor sector

major sector

segment: (1) *See line segment* (2) A part of a circle bounded by a chord and the arc it creates.

minor segment

major segment

semicircle: An arc that is exactly half of a circle. A diameter intersects a circle at the endpoints of two semicircles. **(374)**

sequence: A set of numbers arranged in a special order or pattern.

set: A collection of distinct elements or items.

short radius: *See apothem*

side: (1) A line segment connected to other segments to form a polygon. (2) An edge of a polyhedron. **(345)**

Sieve of Eratosthenes: A way of finding prime numbers in a sequential list of whole numbers.

sign: *See signed number*

signed number: Positive or negative number. $^+25$ and $^-30$ are signed numbers. **(046)**

significant digit: In measurement, the significant digits tell how much of a measured value can be used with confidence. The most significant digit is the first non-zero digit in the number. The least significant digit may be a rounded digit. In 6.0024, the most significant digit is 6. If the least significant digit is 4, you know the true value is between 6.00235 and 6.00245. *See also precision*

significant figure: *See significant digit*

similar figures (∼): Figures that have the same shape, but not necessarily the same size. Corresponding sides of similar figures are proportional. **(376)**

similar terms: *See like terms*

simplest form: A fraction whose numerator and denominator have no common factor greater than 1. The simplest form of $\frac{4}{8}$ is $\frac{1}{2}$. **(037)**

simplify: Combine like terms and apply properties to an expression to make computation easier. **(037)**

sine ratio (sin): In a right triangle, the ratio of the length of the opposite leg to the length of the hypotenuse. The value of the sine of the angle depends upon the measure of the angle. **(427)**

slant height: (1) The perpendicular distance from the vertex of a pyramid to one edge of its base. (2) The shortest distance from the vertex of a right circular cone to the edge of its base. **(414)**

slide: *See translation*

slope: The slant of a line as you look at it from left to right. A line that slants upward from left to right has a positive slope. A line that slants downward from left to right has a negative slope. A numerical value for slope is found using two points on the line. Find the change in y-value and divide by the change in x-value. **(248)**

solid: *See solid figure*

solid figure: A geometric figure with 3 dimensions. **(393)**

solution: Any value for a variable that makes an equation true. A solution of $2x = 24$ is $x = 12$.

space figure: A 3-dimensional figure.

sphere: A 3-dimensional figure made up of all points that are equally distant from a point called the center. **(419)**

square: A parallelogram with four congruent sides and four right angles. **(363)**

square measure: A unit, such as a square meter, or a system of units used to measure area.

square number: The number of dots in a square array.

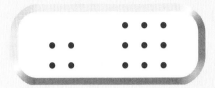

The first two square numbers are 4 and 9. *See also perfect square*

square root ($\sqrt{\ }$): *See root*

square unit: *See square measure*

standard form: A number written with one digit for each place value. The standard form for the number three thousand three is 3003. **(005)**

stem-and-leaf plot: A method of organizing data from least to greatest using the digits of the greatest place value to group data. **(303)**

straight angle: An angle with a measure of 180°. **(331)**

subtract ($-$): *See subtraction*

subtraction: An operation that gives the difference between two numbers. The difference between 15 and 6, $15 - 6$, is 9. **(115)**

subtrahend: In subtraction, the subtrahend is the number being subtracted.

$$\begin{array}{r} 1496 \quad \longleftarrow \text{minuend} \\ -\ 647 \quad \longleftarrow \text{subtrahend} \\ \hline 849 \quad \longleftarrow \text{difference} \end{array}$$

sum: The result of addition. **(092)**

supplementary angles: Two angles that have measures whose sum is 180°. **(334)**

surface: The boundary of a 3-dimensional figure.

surface area: The total area of the faces (including the bases) and curved surfaces of a solid figure. **(396)**

symbol: A sign that represents something. $+$ means "add," $-$ means "subtract," and $<$ means "less than."

symmetry: *See line symmetry, point symmetry, and turn symmetry*

 ─────────────────

tangent: (1) Touching at exactly one point. (2) In a right triangle, the ratio of the length of the leg opposite an angle to the length of the adjacent leg. **(371)**

tangent line: A line that touches a circle at just one point. **(371)**

tangent ratio (tan): *See tangent*

term: A number, variable, product, or quotient in an expression. A term is *not* a sum or difference. In $6x^2 + 5x + 3$, there are three terms, $6x^2$, $5x$, and 3. **(204)**

terminating decimal: A decimal that contains a finite number of digits. 0.408 **(025)**

terms of a fraction: Each element of a fraction is a term. In $\frac{4}{5}$, 4 and 5 are both terms.

terms of a proportion: Each element of a proportion is a term. In $1:2 = 3:6$, 1, 2, 3, and 6 are all terms. **(433)**

tessellation: A covering of a plane without overlaps or gaps using combinations of congruent figures. **(391)**

theorem: A proved mathematical generalization.

theoretical probability: *See probability*

3-dimensional: Existing in 3 dimensions; having length, width, and height.

topologically equivalent: Figures that can be made into one another by stretching, bending, and shrinking without cutting. **(392)**

topology: The study of those properties of figures that remain unchanged when the figure is distorted. **(392)**

transformation: A rule for moving every point in a plane figure to a new location. *See also dilation, reflection, rotation, and translation* **(384)**

translation (slide): A transformation that slides a figure a given distance in a given direction. **(385)**

transpose: Appear to change the sign and move a number from one side of an equation to the other. In the equation $x + 3 = 25$, subtracting 3 from both sides looks like changing $^+3$ to $^-3$ and moving it to the other side: $x = 25 - 3$.

transversal: A line that intersects two or more other lines. **(338)**

trapezium: A quadrilateral with no parallel sides.

trapezoid: A quadrilateral with exactly one pair of parallel sides. **(363)**

triangle: A three-sided polygon. **(348)**

Triangle Inequality: In any triangle, no side can be longer than the sum of the lengths of the other two sides. **(350)**

triangular number: The number of dots in a triangular array.

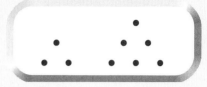

The first two triangular numbers are 3 and 6.

triangular pyramid: A pyramid with a triangular base. **(404)**

trigonometric ratios: Sine, cosine, and tangent are ratios among the sides of right triangles. **(358)**

trigonometry: The branch of mathematics that uses similar right triangles to find measurements indirectly.

truncate: (1) To make numbers with many digits easier to read and use by ignoring all digits to the right of a chosen place. (2) To cut off part of a geometric figure. This is a truncated pyramid.

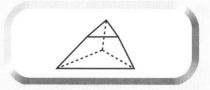

turn: *See rotation*

turn center: The point around which a figure is rotated. **(386)**

turn symmetry: A figure that can be rotated less than 360° about a point and fit exactly on itself has turn symmetry. **(387)**

twin primes: Two prime numbers that are also consecutive odd numbers. 3 and 5 are twin primes but 2 and 3 are not, nor are 7 and 11.

2-dimensional: Existing in 2 dimensions; having length and width.

underestimate: An estimate less than the actual answer.

unit: A precisely fixed quantity used to measure.

unit fraction: A fraction with a numerator of 1.

unit rate: A rate with a denominator of 1.

upper quartile: The median of the numbers greater than the median in an ordered set of numbers. **(278)**

variable: (1) A quantity that changes or that can have different values. (2) A symbol, usually a letter, that can stand for a variable quantity. In $5n$, the variable is n. **(202)**

variable expression: An expression that represents an amount that can have different values. $8r + 2s + 6$ has a different value for every value assigned to r and s.

Venn diagram: A drawing that shows relationships among sets of objects. The diagram shows that two students have both dogs and cats, three students have only cats, and four students have only dogs. **(364)**

STUDENTS WITH DOGS · STUDENTS WITH CATS

Chris Dana Cricket Sean Belana Alf · Juan Aly Robin

vertex: The point at which two line segments, lines, or rays meet to form an angle. **(329)**

vertical: At right angles to the horizon. A vertical line is straight up and down.

vertical angles: The opposite angles formed when two lines intersect. Vertical angles are congruent. Angles 1 and 3 are vertical angles. So are angles 2 and 4. **(337)**

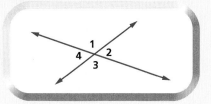

vertices: Plural of *vertex*.

volume (V): The number of cubic units it takes to fill a figure. **(398)**

vulgar fraction: *See common fraction*

weight: Heaviness. Determined by the mass of an object and the effect of gravity on that object.

whole number: Any of the numbers 0, 1, 2, 3, 4, 5, and so on. **(003)**

width (w): One dimension of a 2-dimensional or 3-dimensional figure.

x-axis: In a Cartesian grid, the horizontal axis. **(318)**

x-coordinate (abscissa): In an ordered pair, the value that is always written first. In $(2, 3)$, 2 is the x-coordinate. **(318)**

y-axis: In a Cartesian grid, the vertical axis. **(318)**

y-coordinate (ordinate): In an ordered pair, the value that is always written second. In (2, 3), 3 is the *y*-coordinate. **(318)**

Zero Property: The product of any number and zero is zero.
$8 \times 0 = 0$ and $0 \times 8 = 0$ **(225)**

Index

This index contains topic numbers, not page numbers. You will find topic numbers at the top of each page and next to each new piece of information in the book.

Illustration Credits
David Bamundo: 006, 014, 017, 019, 024, 028(b), 029, 033, 036, 041, 060, 062, 064(a), 069, 076, 077, 092, 099, 101, 106, 108, 116, 128, 143, 149, 153, 159, 185, 228, 229, 248, 251, 260, 267, 268, 280, 284, 289, 294, 305, 306, 316(a), 318, 324, 327, 346, 350, 360, 364, 366, 379, 380, 384, 388, 391, 394, 401(b), 403, 414, 417, 421, 422, 428, 438, 444, 458(b, c), 460, 468, 503, 510, 546, 547, 558

Inkwell Studios: 009, 012, 013, 021, 028(a), 032, 035, 044, 049, 055, 058, 063, 064(b), 071, 089, 090, 092, 093, 123, 126, 144, 146, 151, 161, 176, 214, 236, 255, 257, 274, 275, 279, 285, 286, 309, 316(b), 317, 322, 323, 338, 340, 354, 359, 361, 365, 372, 376, 377, 387, 389, 392, 400, 401(a), 405, 409, 410, 411, 412, 413, 420, 424, 436, 442, 453, 458(a), 459, 460, 463, 465, 469, 480, 489, 490, 496, 498, 499, 531, 533

Joe Spooner: 001, 053, 086, 200, 262, 314, 423, 456

Robot Characters: Inkwell Studios

Technical Art: Kane Publishing Services, Inc.

Map Art: The Write Source development group

Cover Illustration: Bill SMITH STUDIO